Praise for aol.com

"A fascinating and instructive story . . . a detailed, warts-and-all history of one of the great capitalist success stories of all time . . . well researched and comprehensive."

— Richard Bernstein, *The New York Times*

"Maybe Swisher has a knack for bringing personalities to life on the page, or maybe there just aren't any boring people at AOL; either way, the result is a story inhabited by brash, bold characters. . . . In many ways, aol.com reads like a corporate disaster movie; it depicts entrepreneurial bodies falling everywhere, a hero whose sole desire is survival and experiences we'd much rather read about than live through."

— David Pogue, *The New York Times Book Review*

"Swisher makes excellent use of her resources to show how Steve Case and his hand-picked management team met these challenges, rebuilding their rocket not once but several times."

— *Washington Post Book World*

"The adventures of AOL contain the raw material for a riveting tale . . . Swisher excels in relating the chronology of AOL's endless perils and occasional triumphs . . . aol.com is a faithful chronicle of the considerable surface drama of a surprising victor that continues to face down challenges. . . ."

— *Business Week*

"The best tech-scene book of the year."

— Jim Coates, *The Chicago Tribune*

"Excellent . . . Swisher vividly recreates AOL's roller-coaster ride to the top, and her lucid book will surely entertain Netheads and novices alike."

— Fred Hamerman, *The Chicago Tribune*

"Swisher's book is a meticulous, step-by-step tracing of the birth, growth, and evolution of America Online. The personalities of the players—many of whom make the term 'eccentric' seem like oatmeal—crackle with clarity. . . . One of the more impressive efforts I have found in the last several years."

— Michael Pakenham, *The Baltimore Sun*

"Surprisingly gripping . . . this is very much a book about a company, and a pretty peculiar one, too."

— *The Economist*

"The almost surreal inside story of the world's biggest online company is told with a ripped-from-the-headlines energy that matches the intense drama of market-share maneuvering, delicate negotiating, and disastrous errors in this high-tech, high stakes world."

— *Modern Maturity*

"Swisher trenchantly documents the company's quixotic journey from a ragtag collection of cybervisionaries to a corporate powerhouse . . . Swisher's breezy read is brimming with colorful quotes and anecdotes on how AOL withstood the catcalls of Wall Street and the digerati to become the Internet equivalent of Coca-Cola."

— *San Francisco Chronicle*

aol.com

HOW STEVE CASE BEAT BILL GATES, NAILED THE NETHEADS, AND MADE MILLIONS IN THE WAR FOR THE WEB

kara swisher

TIMES BUSINESS

RANDOM HOUSE

Swisher, Kara:
    AOL.COM : how Steve Case beat Bill Gates, nailed the netheads, and
made millions in the war for the Web / Kara Swisher.
        p.   cm.
    ISBN 0-8129-3191-2
    1. American Online, Inc.—History. 2. Online information services
industry—United States—History. 3. Internet service providers—
United States—History. 4. Case, Stephen McConnell. 5. Gates,
Bill, 1955– . 6. Von Meister, William F., 1942–1996.
7. Businesspeople—United States—Biography. I. Title.
HE7583.U6S85   1998
338.7′61004696′0873—dc21   97-44127

Random House website address: www.atrandom.com

9 8 7 6 5 4 3 2

First Edition

For my father and my grandmother—
who had to go, but who have never left me

We are here and it is now.
Further than that all human knowledge is moonshine.

—H. L. Mencken

from the author

Almost since it emerged from nowhere in the early 1990s to become the best-known brand in cyberspace, AOL (America Online) has been the subject of intense debate by those who abhor it and those who adore it. Like any two sides of an impossible-to-settle argument, I expect they will bicker until the end of time about the merits and vices of AOL.

This book is for everyone else.

When I began this project in the fall of 1996, AOL was considered a goner. Today, it straddles the online world like the giant it has become. And tomorrow—who can really say?

So what I set out to do is tell you where AOL has come from— a remarkable story of entrepreneurship, of hard-won victories and flat-footed stumbles, of unusual and complex people who have worked to create a part of the incredible new communications medium that is called the Internet. I hope that an understanding of how one of the most important companies in this industry was formed will begin to point the way to the uncertain future. The story of AOL—a company with plenty of promise and plenty of problems—can perhaps shed some light on that journey.

A huge amount of credit for the effort represented here also belongs to Lisa Dickey. As my researcher and critical sounding board,

Lisa has lived, breathed, and slept AOL. Her unflinching support, incisive insights, important criticism, and unfailing good humor have been invaluable to me, and I could not have done this book without her.

The final product also benefited from the willingness of AOL and its employees to continue to give interviews to me through what turned out to be a very tumultuous year. From the nineteen-hour outage in August 1996 to the company's access debacle in 1997, and during wild swings in its stock and massive changes in its management, AOL honored its promise of talking to me until this lengthy project was completed. I give special credit to Steve Case, Jean Villanueva, Jim Kimsey, Ken Novack, Ted Leonsis, Bob Pittman, and others at AOL too numerous to mention. Lisa McCabe was also a trouper, working to get me access to the people I needed to talk to at AOL. Melissa Andrews made a long and difficult process flow much more smoothly with professionalism.

And for their help throughout this endeavor, I want to particularly thank: Bernadette Flagler, Laura Einstein, Joe Brown, Kristin Rechberger, Nancy Andrews, Robert Seidman, Karen Friedman, Kate Fleming, Bo, and Cosmo, all of whom had to put up with the varying degrees of mild panic and dementia that accompany a first book. Much gratitude too goes to my family, especially my mother, for their support. My journey toward publication was made much easier by the place where I worked on the manuscript—the heavenly hamlet of Bluemont, Virginia. In addition, Walt Mossberg, the real and true guru of cyberspace, provided me with invaluable mentoring and guidance that have been much appreciated. My agent Flip Brophy deserves special kudos for working hard to give this book life.

I also extend a great deal of recognition to all my former colleagues at *The Washington Post*—an extraordinary newspaper—especially David Ignatius, who has pushed me far in the never-ending process of becoming a better journalist. I give special thanks to John Burgess, Vicki Shannon, Elizabeth Corcoran, Laura Blumenfeld, Tony Faiola, Bob McCartney, Tom Wilkinson, Mary Hadar, Leslie Walker and Mike Abramowitz. And I also thank my new colleagues at *The Wall Street Journal*—especially Greg Hill—for giving me the extra time I needed to complete the book.

Finally, I owe thanks to my editor, Jon Karp, whose humor, support, and patience made reporting and writing this book seem almost easy.

Almost.

KARA SWISHER
San Francisco, California
January 1998

contents

contents

meet mr. bill

Was it over?

Perhaps so, if what the most powerful man in the technology industry was telling Steve Case on May 11, 1993, was true.

"I can buy 20 percent of you or I can buy all of you," began Bill Gates in a most reasonable and even tone, a tone that was flatly matter-of-fact, neither angry nor blustery. The legendary co-founder of the software giant Microsoft Corporation rocked back and forth as he spoke; his hands touched lightly, forming a ten-fingered globe. The pose—which would become much more famous over the next few years—struck one person in the small, stuffy room as vaguely comforting, as if Gates were a learned sage about to impart the ultimate wisdom to the thick-headed masses gathered before him.

And the truth was?

"I can buy 20 percent of you or I can buy all of you," said Gates. "Or I can go into this business myself and bury you."

Steve Case, his round and boyish features fixated on the speaker, knew that this was the belly-up decree many small, struggling technology start-ups like his had received after being noticed by the cash-rich Microsoft.

How many dozens of hopeful entrepreneurs had been invited here to Microsoft's lush suburban campus in Redmond,

Washington, thirty minutes east of Seattle, and had heard the same thing? They had probably sat in this same windowless gray conference room just outside of Gates's office and had all received this same cold-water splash of reality as a warning that would quickly bring them to their senses. Usually, a lower-level princeling of Microsoft delivered the bad news. Instead, the emperor himself—the human quintessence of the digital era—was lowering the boom.

Case respected Gates, and he knew that—in his nerdy but logical manner—Gates was not delivering an explicit threat. He was making an educated, almost philosophical guess as to the fate of the underfunded, understaffed, still-underwhelming business Case and others had been trying to build for almost a decade. Those years had brought a never-ending series of financial close calls, dysfunctional business plans, and too many moments of doubt as to the point of continuing the venture.

That his efforts had gotten this far was itself a minor miracle, Case knew. He headed a business that had been near death so many times that intensive-care crisis management had become a part of the company culture. Besides the typical scrounging for money from quick-profit-seeking venture capitalists, there were face-offs with legions of creditors wanting their bills paid. An endless series of hopeful, sky-high ideas had been ground down by the realities of the marketplace. And, always, exhausting chameleon changes had to be made, to figure out exactly what the consumers wanted in an industry that was still largely undefined.

Plagued by constant uncertainty and little rational hope for success, Case's journey was like jumping from one unstable ice floe to the next in a frantic attempt to prevent the whole enterprise from sinking into the icy depths of capitalism's ever-churning sea.

Yet, Case's company was afloat. The year before, it had raised about $10 million in a public offering—which had valued his company at the improbable worth of $70 million—and the money was being used to grow its puny market share. But his company was still stuck in a distant third place in a business dominated by deep-pocketed competitors, and other more powerful start-ups were poised on the near horizon.

Still, Case and his crew had created something at least tasty enough to whet Gates's appetite. Was another good idea on the verge of getting sucked into the hungry maw of Microsoft, which some in the computer industry, and even Case's employees, had taken to calling "The Death Star," after the ultimate weapon of the Evil Empire in *Star Wars?* In the entire universe, to be sure, there was no one who would bet on one tiny company when the opponent was Microsoft.

Would anyone really care if they quit now, took the pile of money that Microsoft would doubtless offer them, and declared a different kind of victory? They could conduct a jolly cash-out triumphal parade all the way back to their humble northern Virginia headquarters. If they went home richer than they ever thought they could be, what would be the shame in that? Case could say comfortably that they had taken it as far as they could and now it was time for the big boys to take over, as they always did. And the small business he and others had built would become only a trifling footnote in the very early history of a new medium.

Anyway, would anyone really miss a speck of a company called America Online?

"I can buy 20 percent of you or I can buy all of you," said Bill Gates to Steve Case on May 11, 1993. "Or I can go into this business myself and bury you."

Was it over?

the canary in the coal mine

The truth is: nobody knows.

And, because most often they do not know that they do not know, no one will ever tell you that truth.

Some people don't know because they are too hopeful and sometimes because they are very greedy. Some are profoundly stupid or are a little too smart.

But in the spanking new world of the Internet, *nobody knows* because everyone and everything has just been born.

Which is why Steve Case found himself on May 8, 1997 cruising on the calm waters of Lake Washington in Seattle on a boat carrying him and more than 100 other chief executives toward the 20,000-square-foot, $40 million home of Bill Gates.

Case was definitely not supposed to be there—if you had paid heed over the years to a variety of learned Wall Street pundits, savvy journalists, pontificating technology consultants, and waspish naysayers in Silicon Valley. And the computer online service, America Online Inc., which he had built into the world's largest, was just one tiny step away from falling right over the precipice.

The dirge had been endless: AOL was nothing. AOL was history. AOL was dead.

Yet there Case stood—perhaps the liveliest corporate corpse one might ever meet—chatting with American Airlines head Robert Crandall, kibitzing with a cadre of Microsoft's top executives, and joking with Vice President Al Gore.

In the near distance, in Bellevue, Case could just make out the outlines of Gates's glass-and-wood palace, still being built on the lakeshore, where an elaborate dinner awaited them. Getting to see the famed technological Xanadu that Gates was constructing for himself was the highlight of a flashy, two-day CEO "technology summit" Microsoft had organized. There had been speeches all day. Now a dinner of spring salmon, fiddlehead fern bisque, and tortes with Rainier huckleberries awaited them.

As the boat wended its way from its launching point on Lake Union, surrounded by a flotilla of security boats to protect this small ship carrying very powerful people, to the place Case jokingly was calling "Bill's San Simeon" (after William Randolph Hearst's egotistical monument to himself), the man from AOL thought it was all just a little too bizarre.

He was happy to have been invited, of course, but felt decidedly out of place. He had quipped to Microsoft finance chief Greg Maffei and other executives from the company that he felt like a spy deep in enemy territory. He ribbed them, asking playfully if he should be taking notes on any stray Microsoft secrets he could glean, and sending them off in a bottle over the side of the ship. But inside his head, he wondered seriously: Should he even be here at all, still standing? Had it only been four years ago that Case had been told by Gates that it was probably the end for AOL?

Gates—whose leadership of Microsoft and ensuing vast wealth had made him into an American business icon on the level of John D. Rockefeller—had been spectacularly wrong.

After the talks between them in 1993 had led nowhere, Gates had created his own online service as he had promised. But, in two years of trying and after hundreds of millions of dollars were spent, Gates's Microsoft Network had not bested AOL. With AOL now four times as large, it had not even come close.

No one had—yet.

This much was true: in the last decade of the twentieth century, an entirely new medium—online communications via the personal computer—had been born. It was being hailed as the next great technological innovation, in the same league as the telephone, the radio, and television.

Few times in American business history has an entire industry been created from almost nothing and captured the attention and imagination of millions of consumers, setting off a titanic clash for money, power, and dominance among some of America's greatest businesses. But such has been the case with the Internet and the online services industry since its mainstream emergence at the start of the 1990s. And of the many companies vying to create empires in cyberspace, there was now none better known than AOL.

In much the same way that Coca-Cola had become the name most people associated with sugared soda, the brand of this emerging new medium had turned out to be AOL. Since its founding only ten years before, the company had grown from a dinky computer games service aimed at teenage boys into a huge business with more than $1 billion in revenue. It had become, in the process, the way most Americans reached the Internet. With nearly ten million subscribers worldwide, its "circulation" was much larger than that of any of the major newspapers in the United States.

Yet it was also a company in constant danger. Innumerable challenges had given AOL a heart-rending roller coaster ride all along the way, and many observers had long predicted AOL's imminent demise. In 1993, they claimed that AOL was too small to compete with CompuServe and Prodigy (online services backed by big bucks from major U.S. corporations). AOL was too glitchy and simplistic to catch on with consumers, they opined in 1994. AOL was vulnerable to a withering frontal attack from Microsoft, they declared in 1995. AOL was going to really get knocked flat by the growing popularity of the Internet's World Wide Web, they announced in 1996. And finally, in 1997, they could say with absolute assurance, AOL was going to be its own executioner, shooting itself dead with a dizzying series of corporate missteps.

And there were so many other AOL killers: the telephone companies, with their advantage in all things wired; the media conglomerates, with their abundant content; the scrappier Internet service providers, with their low prices.

Beginning in the spring of 1996, the punches came hard: a precipitous stock drop that had cut AOL's market value by two-thirds; the increase of an online trend called "churn" that signaled dangerously restless customers; the embarrassing departure, after only four months, of a top executive brought in to discipline AOL's freewheeling culture; another drastic restructuring of the corporate body and business plan; a restating of financial results that wiped out all the profits AOL had ever claimed it made; a shift in pricing that caused subscriptions to surge, but resulted in seriously blocked access for users; and one lawsuit after another over pricing, access, and stock value.

Case, who had come to personify the company, had been called sleazy, a soap salesman, a liar, a fool.

But he was still there. Case, in fact, had turned out to be the Rasputin of the Internet, with no one able to deliver the long-expected deathblow. All the nicknames AOL had acquired over the years had the exact same theme: the cockroach of cyberspace, the digital Dracula, the Lazarus of the online world.

"Someday, the history of cyberspace will be written as a chronicle of the predictions of AOL's demise," *Wired* Magazine had written once. "From claims that America Online would fail because it wasn't 'open' to charges that it was inherently unreliable, the service has been a canary in the coal mine of cyberspace."

By the spring of 1997, AOL's stock was up again to double its price during the summer and fall doldrums. Member numbers were moving slowly toward the golden 10 million mark, and the company had reported a small profit—a development that had taken off some of the pressure from Wall Street.

But, as always, new rumblings were beginning to surface. With a new flat-rate pricing offering, AOL would not be able to attract advertisers who would yield the sustained profits needed to pay for its burgeoning costs. AOL would not be able to grow as fast as it needed to, because new consumers were becoming harder to find. AOL's proprietary design language would hinder its ability to attract much needed popular content that was flocking to the Web.

And even this: AOL's new service head, MTV founder Bob Pittman, whom Case had recruited, was going to stage a corporate coup and displace Case at the top.

AOL was nothing. AOL was history. AOL was dead.

At the CEO conference that day, Bill Gates had talked of the importance of ensuring the excellence of a corporation's "digital nervous system."

"The meetings, the paperwork, the way information workers are organized, the way information is stored—it's my thesis that, with the incredible advances in technology, it's now possible to have a dramatically more responsive nervous system," Gates had opined.

If that was true, if you listened to all the noise, AOL's nervous system was suffering from an acute case of hypertension. But you couldn't tell that from Steve Case, a man whom his employees had taken to calling "The Wall" because of his ability to exude an otherworldly calm and have virtually no reaction to a wide variety of pressures. He was, in fact, a deeply shy man, not given to small talk and schmoozing—unusual traits, given that he was squarely at the forefront of the newest communications revolution. But his nonchalant style had given Case a reputation of aloofness and of haughty arrogance in the online world.

But in Case's own head, another mantra had been playing for more than a decade, masking out all the cacophony of complaints.

Over and over again; it said: AOL would be everywhere.

Someday, somehow, Case dreamed, his service would be in America's dens, living rooms, kitchens, offices, and malls. And the elitists who ran most Internet companies—the doubters of this singular vision, the ones who told him he was going down so many times—they always had been wrong and they would be wrong once again.

How did Case know all this?

He didn't.

Nobody did.

But as he floated along on that sunny Pacific Northwest evening, the imperturbable Steve Case knew one thing for certain.

The ride had just begun.

they came from nowhere

death and birth

Bill Von Meister's mourners had no idea what Steve Case was talking about.

Case had come to Great Falls, Virginia, on May 20, 1995, to pay his respects at an informal memorial service for Von Meister, who had died just six months after being diagnosed with a swift and vicious melanoma that had finally managed to bridle his unruly spirit.

Von Meister's friends and family had invited anyone with a memory of him to speak. There were many memories to choose from because, in his half-century of hard living, Bill Von Meister had cut a capacious and kaleidoscopic swath through the world.

Some talked of Von Meister's fondness for fast cars, fine wines, pretty women, and good times.

Some recalled how his jovial personality never seemed to wane even as the cancer sucked the life out of his beefy frame.

Some recalled his fervent zeal for starting new businesses, and the way his mind percolated with ideas for new technology and communications companies.

And others could not help but refer to the darker side of Von Meister—the relentless drinking problem that had forced him into a rehab program years earlier and had never really been cured; the nagging restlessness of his life as he jumped from one project to the next; his inability to follow through in both his business and personal life.

"He was the most human of human beings I ever knew," said Stu Segal, one of his business associates. "His flaws were never disguised—it was all there in full glory for everyone to see."

The small crowd in the backyard of Von Meister's elaborate home nodded in agreement. That was the Bill they remembered and would probably never forget.

Then Steve Case began to speak, stating something that few gathered there seemed to know. Without Bill Von Meister, there would have been no America Online.

America Online? The very idea seemed bizarre to Von Meister's family, who thought that most of Bill's many business forays had ended in utter failure. Wasn't AOL now the world's biggest consumer online service, worth billions of dollars?

But Bill Von Meister had died broke, with huge debts, including hefty medical bills and burgeoning mortgage demands, and very little to show for his itinerant journey from one hopeful start-up venture to the next.

Indeed, his obituary that very day in *The Washington Post,* the local newspaper, had placed his notice fourth—buried on page four of the Metro section—behind death notices for a prominent doctor, a gallery owner, and a church leader.

"William F. Von Meister, 53, a local communications entrepreneur, who had been founder and chief executive officer of a number of high-tech and consulting firms, died of cancer on May 18th at his home in Great Falls," it read in part.

But not anywhere was there a mention of AOL.

And so, Bill Von Meister was passing unnoticed into obscurity, except for the words of those gathered in a large circle in the garden on this sunny Saturday afternoon.

The idea of it made Marc Seriff sad. He had also come to the service because, like Case, Seriff's life was inexorably changed because of Von Meister. He had brought them both to a company called Control Video Corporation (CVC) in the early 1980s. And

CVC was the initial spark—after many iterations, a series of near-deaths, and more close calls than Seriff could count—from which AOL was ignited.

But Seriff—who had become AOL's chief technologist—hadn't seen Bill for a long time. He lost touch after his mentor was forced out of CVC by its investors, whose fortunes had turned sour. Major market changes were surely to blame, but Von Meister shared the blame for nearly scuttling the whole enterprise with his pie-in-the-sky dreams, profligate spending, and characteristic disregard for the detail work that is the foundation of any long-lasting business.

Von Meister had moved onto new projects—as usual, optimistic as ever. And, though both Seriff and Case became multimillionaires many times over from the company that had sprung out of the ashes of CVC, Von Meister had never said anything negative about not benefiting from the riches AOL threw off to his protégés in time. Von Meister had always played the start-up game for the sake of the fun, and CVC was just another stop on his trip.

Seriff had heard that Von Meister was sick several months before, but he thought it was just another obstacle that Bill was likely to overcome with a smile. There would be another idea, another fast car, and another long laugh. So, the swiftness of Bill's demise surprised Seriff.

While others memorialized Von Meister's effects on their lives, Seriff found himself deeply upset because the service made him realize the debt of gratitude he owed the man. Von Meister had saved him from losing himself inside a big company and had taught him that he didn't have to choose between enjoying what he did for a living and being successful.

Although Von Meister had left long before AOL grew large, Seriff saw that the path to glory—not just the technical evolution, but the core team that had managed AOL for so many years—led directly from companies started by Von Meister.

Did anyone assembled here, aside from himself and Steve Case, realize that?

Not far away, even as the memorial service was taking place, AOL was holding an annual picnic for its 1,800 employees, who were now working for a company with almost three million customers across the United States. And Seriff—who had stopped going to the gatherings because the company had grown so large—knew that few there even knew the name of the person he considered the "spiritual father" of AOL.

He declared this at the memorial service, echoing Case's sentiments. But Seriff expected that if he were to say Von Meister's name to the average AOL employee now attending the picnic, he would be greeted mostly with blank and uncomprehending stares.

Indeed, Bill Von Meister was almost like a *doppelgänger*—the ghostly double of all those who were now living and breathing AOL, the invisible spirit who could never be seen.

This much was certain: it was in a tiny ember of the soul of Bill Von Meister that AOL was born.

billy's beginnings

His father, F. W. Von Meister, was the godson of Kaiser Wilhelm II, and his mother, Eleanora Colloredo-Mannsfeld, was a countess. And—in a delicious irony for some, since Bill Von Meister later presided over a lot of business disasters—one of his father's first jobs in the United States was as a representative of the German company that built the ill-fated *Hindenburg* zeppelin.

"Billy," the eldest of his family, was born in New York on February 21, 1942. His father became an entrepreneur of sorts; when his job with the zeppelin company literally blew up with the crash of the *Hindenburg* in the late 1930s, F. W. Von Meister moved from project to project and finally founded a chemicals company.

The business proved a success and allowed F. W. to raise his growing family in modest wealth in the leafy suburbs of New Jersey. Billy was an indulged child who displayed an early interest in tinkering. In high school, he formulated the name for a company he would continue to operate throughout his life: Creative Associates.

And Billy seemed to be very creative.

One Christmas, for example, he devised a complex system of strings and pulleys that would result in the opening of his bedroom door if triggered by the arrival of Santa Claus through the front door.

Another electronic device, called "Papa's Tea Tutor," sat atop the refrigerator in the Von Meisters' kitchen. A signaling unit placed in F. W. Von Meister's car would set off a red light and a bell as he neared home, giving the household a warning to prepare the tea service in time for the patriarch's arrival.

In contrast to his father's stiffer European demeanor, Billy was known as the family's Peter Pan—a boy who delighted in toys and gadgets and fun. Early on, he got hooked on racecars and adventure sports. But tragedy came during the early teens of Billy's life, with the death of his mother from breast cancer. "It hit Billy harder than he let on," recalled his sister Nora. "I think sometimes his very upbeat personality was a reaction to the pain—acting like nothing was ever wrong and everything was great—in order to mask a lot of hurt caused by mother's death."

After high school at Middlesex Academy in Massachusetts and a post-boarding-school stint at a finishing school in Switzerland, where he spent much of his time racing cars and skiing, Von Meister attended Georgetown University in Washington, DC. Once again known for his pranks and party image, he didn't ever finish at Georgetown, though he persuaded nearby American University to enroll him in its master's program for business. He told his younger brother Peter that he was onto big things.

"I'm going to make a mark," said Billy Von Meister. "Just you watch."

von meister shyster

After completing his master's degree, Von Meister set in motion his peripatetic lifestyle; woven through it was a decided interest in emerging telecommunications applications. With the explosion of a variety of technologies on the horizon—from computers to faxes to wireless—Von Meister obsessively began to formulate a vision for finding new, better, and cheaper ways of delivering information.

One of his first jobs was as a consultant with Western Union, where he developed an early application called "Telemail"—an unusual message delivery method of faxing and delivering mail to users—which supplemented the large company's more traditional offerings.

At age 27, Von Meister continued to fiddle. He started a company called Advanced Research Corporation in 1969. Its products included "Light-Alert," a photoelectric aid that allowed night watchmen to shine a light through a window and cause lights to turn on in a store; and "Ray-Alert," a detector parents attached to their televisions to monitor radiation levels thrown off at their children.

Such imaginative fare—a combination of the useful and silly, but always captivating—was pure Von Meister. He had begun to acquire a reputation as a pied piper among the denizens of the small world of emerging communications technologies.

He was a large man with a ruddy face and dark hair that was always falling into his eyes. Not much to look at, he would often say, but Von Meister was possessed of a mesmerizing charisma that drew people to him. A gifted conversationalist, he seemed to know something about everything—whether the topic was movies or wines or exotic places to visit. Partial to gold jewelry, loudly striped shirts, and shaded aviator glasses, Bill Von Meister had vast appetites.

He'd puff continually on cigarettes as he played set after set of tennis with potential investors, wearing them out physically right before beginning negotiations. Or he'd grab a venture capitalist and take him for a 140-mph drive late at night around Washington's Beltway in his latest Ferrari or Porsche, pitching his new inspiration for a business until the passenger gave in and invested. He'd eat big slabs of beef and down two bottles of his favorite Chianti Classico Reserva Ducale at a sitting, often picking up the tab for his many associates. Or he'd throw lavish parties in the variety of increasingly larger houses he acquired.

When times were flush, he'd blossom. When money dried up, Von Meister would hunker down and begin his tireless quest for the next big score.

"Super!" he'd typically exclaim after hearing about new technologies from the variety of techies whom he began to collect along the way or whom he'd contact almost immediately after reading about them in the technical journals he consumed voraciously. Gary Arlen, a Washington-based technology consultant and writer who got to know Von Meister in these early days, dubbed him "Von Meister Shyster"—an affectionate jibe at the buoyant entrepreneur. "He would bob to the top, always with a new idea, a new fist of money, a new way of doing something, no one had thought of," remembered Arlen. "He was like a colorful moving circus in a world that was not very interesting by its nature."

Not all of Von Meister's ideas were far-fetched. After searching around for a variety of technologies to support an idea he had for least-cost routing of long-distance telephone lines, he came across a technologist named Alan Peyser, who was working on such devices at a Washington-area company.

Von Meister's idea was simple: use specialized switches controlled by a central computer to better manage a company's long-distance calls. The guaranteed savings: 20 percent. It was one of the moments of far-reaching vision often displayed by Von Meister, who presaged what would later become business as usual in the hypercompetitive telecommunications market.

With the idea of helping companies to have better control of their communications costs, Von Meister and Peyser started TDX Systems Inc. in 1975, with clients such the Montgomery Ward retail chain and the Marriott hotel company. Their idea attracted the London-based Cable & Wireless PLC, which invested more than $500,000 in the venture.

But Von Meister quickly ran through his investor's money and was not adept at the day-to-day management of TDX. When more funding was required, Cable & Wireless gained control with more investments and later forced Von Meister into a buyout of almost $700,000 for his 24 percent stake. Peyser stayed on and rose to the chief executive's position. He later built the U.S. business—now called Cable & Wireless Inc.—to revenues of $1 billion.

But Von Meister had no patience for waiting. By 1978, he was onto several other ideas, such as delivering information for companies—for example, price changes between grocery stores or bank check data—using a subcarrier technology in the FM broadcast band. That too went bust, but it got Von Meister interested in the transmission of information, and he soon changed his tack. Surveying the scene, he noticed the work being pioneered by a computer time-sharing company called Compu-Serv (later to be called CompuServe and owned by H&R Block Inc.), which had begun in 1969.

At the same time, worried about declining readership and interested in new technological advances, major newspaper companies nationwide had begun experiments with a new product they dubbed "videotex"—information that would be electronically delivered over a variety of still-undetermined devices. Most prominent of the new ventures was "Viewtron," used by the Knight-Ridder newspaper chain.

Other major players were emerging, including the nation's cable companies, which were testing a variety of offerings that provided customers with interactive television. Perhaps most important of all, telephone companies eager for new revenue streams were also ready to enter the interactive arena.

"We'll be aiming to service a global information market that simply did not exist even a few short years ago," said AT&T Corporation president William Ellinghaus at the time. "Not just the telephone or even the telecommunications business but rather the business of moving information—whether voice, data, graphics or pictures—from just about any place in this nation to any other or throughout the world."

Most of the many efforts underway focused on business customers. But Von Meister decided that the technology he was developing would be used for a service he described as a "home information utility." Combining least-cost telephone routing technology he had worked on at TDX, cheap computer time, and many databases waiting to be plumbed, Von Meister thought he could send airline reservations, restaurant reviews, banking information, and just about anything else to people in their homes.

Von Meister gave it a simple name: The Source—which implied the origins of things, the beginnings of a new medium, the place of creation. It was, for all intents and purposes, a forerunner of what would later become AOL, and it was the first online service that was aimed at the average consumer.

With the information he began to collect, Von Meister was in business. With few American homes owning computers at the time, Von Meister even sketched out ideas for a small, low-cost terminal he would sell to allow people access to the Source.

"I'll give away the razors, to sell the razor blades," he confidently told Clay Durrett, one of his engineers. "And we'll all get rich on razor blades."

It was an unfortunate metaphor, because Von Meister's cutting edge quickly turned very sharp. Searching about for money, once again, to make his dream a reality, he hooked up with Jack Taub, a Washington investor, who managed to get a multimillion-dollar loan for the company. But Von Meister's partnership turned sour quickly. By October 1979, Taub had ousted him, claiming that Von Meister had run up huge debts and that there was little cash left. Taub also sued Von Meister for mismanagement.

"Money was spent like water. The company had so many problems when I took over, it was an assault to my system," Taub said to a reporter from *The Washington Post* at the time. "Bill Von Meister is a terrific entrepreneur but he didn't know how to stop entrepreneuring." There were too-plush offices, too many employees, and too much spent on research and development of any idea that popped into Von Meister's fertile mind.

At first, Von Meister left without a fight because there was little to fight over.

But within a year, Taub managed to attract the interest of Reader's Digest Inc., which agreed to pay him $3 million for a 51 percent stake in the Source. "The baby's finally out of the incubator and crawling," said Taub on September 23, 1980.

Not exactly. Two days later, Von Meister resurfaced and obtained a court order barring the sale pending a resolution of his claim that he held a 32 percent interest in the company. A U.S. district court judge in Richmond agreed with him in December, and, in the end, Reader's Digest ended up paying Von Meister close to $1 million for control of the service. Von Meister needed that money. He was already onto another project that had captivated him: sending studio-quality music via satellites and cable lines to users in the home. He called it the "Home Music Store."

The technology for such an ambitious effort was worked on by a trio of techies Von Meister had managed to persuade to come on board: Clay Durrett, Ray Heinrich, and a young programmer named Marc Seriff.

Seriff, only 33 years old, was already an experienced technologist, having worked on the ARPANET, the government-funded network that was the precursor to the Internet. He had then moved over to another start-up with ARPANET "father" Larry Roberts, who headed an effort to commercialize the data network called Telenet. Telenet went public and was later bought by GTE Corporation, a major telecommunications company. Von Meister had known Roberts through the Source, which had bought up surplus data networking time from Telenet. It was there Seriff had met Von Meister, who was consulting for Roberts at Telenet in 1980.

Von Meister had immediately intrigued Seriff, so when he was assigned to a dull staff job at GTE, he jumped at an offer made to him by Von Meister to help design the technology for the Home Music Store.

"You'll never get anywhere sitting behind a desk," beckoned the enticing Von Meister.

"He's wild-eyed," Seriff told his friends at the time. "And I need something wild."

The Home Music Store was indeed wild—a huge and complex challenge in every aspect of its operation. To launch it, Von Meister needed to get record companies to agree to give him the master recordings of popular music. He would then mix them into different offerings, encode the sound digitally by computer, then bounce it to a satellite. Cable stations nationwide would pick it up from the satellite and target it to individual subscribers. In their homes, users would need a decoding and reassembling device to play the music on analog stereos.

Von Meister planned five stations for listening, two for recording, and one that would allow customers to preview music. The monthly fee would range from $6.95 to $9.95. If customers wanted to buy the recordings, Von Meister would sell them at 20 to 60 percent off.

In an era when compact disks were not widespread enough to provide a better quality of sound than tapes and records, such an idea was groundbreaking, compelling, and even a little sexy. And the dreamy scope of the complex idea made it seem almost impossible to pull off.

"We thought Bill was just crazy," said Durrett. "But we just followed him anyway because it seemed like it was going to be a lot of fun."

For a while, it seemed that Von Meister might pull off the complicated arrangement. He immediately began to attempt to get letters of intent from major record companies. He also proved adept at getting help from a range of investors, including an unusual deal with the 1970s singing icons, the Osmond family, to use their state-of-the-art recording studio in Orem, Utah, to establish the uplink facilities to the satellites.

For Seriff, it was all a wild trip, whether it involved visiting the Osmonds' compound in a pristine setting of snow-capped mountains, or being part of the Wall Street press conference that Von Meister had called to flack the upcoming service.

But the flashy announcement, so very Von Meister, proved to be a grave miscalculation: it tipped off music distributors and retailers to the impending service. Within weeks, there was a full-page letter in the recording business's bible, *Billboard,* from the Waxie Maxie chain, claiming Von Meister's scheme would destroy the industry.

Behind the scenes, more complaints were sent to the record companies by retailers and other music industry middlemen who would be frozen out if such a distribution scheme worked. Quickly enough, the Home Music Store was dealt a deathblow when one of the major label owners, Warner Brothers, decided to forgo participation. With no hit music, there was no business.

Clay Durrett was distraught over having nothing to show after creating an innovative new electronic product. "It was cutting-edge technology with no place to go," he said.

"The whole thing was ghostlike and it scared them," said Stu Segal, who had worked in the music industry before joining Von

Meister at the Home Music Store. "It was a concept well before its time." Indeed, today, the record industry is working hard to figure out how to do via the Internet much the same thing Von Meister had once proposed.

But, as usual, Bill Von Meister was a day early and many dollars short.

another run around the rose bush

Von Meister was still not discouraged. As his deflated troops met for a wrap-up dinner at Joe & Mo's restaurant in downtown Washington, Bill was ready for another deal.

"Let's take another run around the rose bush," he said, raising his glass of Chivas Regal. "How can we use what we have already learned and use what we've got to make something new?"

And so, he began to sketch out on the back of a napkin another use for the technology they had created, using bits and pieces of ideas along the way and combining them with new trends.

"Video games are hot," a Warner executive had mentioned offhandedly, in the meeting at which the company broke off its agreement with Von Meister. Feeling badly about how things had turned out, he promised to hook up Von Meister with executives at a Warner subsidiary, Atari. "Why not use your technology to send video games instead of music?"

Why not, indeed? The video game business, spurred by the sales of millions of units of the Atari 2600 game console, was sizzling in 1981 and 1982. And it looked like it was only getting hotter; every young boy in America seemed to be suddenly deciding that he needed a game console and a lot of cartridges to play. The underlying consumer need, thought Von Meister, was access to a variety of selections in a quicker time than traditional retail channels could provide.

After being rebuffed by Atari—which was working on its own new delivery system, called Ataritel, under the code name Project Falcon—Von Meister still thought he could ride along in its swiftly moving stream of success, building a games delivery system to work with the Atari console and using existing telephone lines.

He didn't need Atari's permission to sell such a service, so Von Meister decided to turn to others in the industry for help. He went to the Consumer Electronics Show (CES), in January 1982, to search for likely prospects. Held in Las Vegas, the exhibition was the place where all of the action in the industry took place; major deals were done, and major new products made their debut.

Wandering the floor, Von Meister ran into a booth for a new video game start-up called Imagic, founded by an ex-Atari marketing vice president named Bill Grubb. He struck up a conversation with Grubb, who seemed mildly interested, and Grubb told Von Meister to call him after the show.

The Saratoga, California-based Imagic was the hot company of the CES that year, backed by such prominent Silicon Valley venture capital firms as Kleiner, Perkins, Caufield & Byers. The company was founded in 1981, and sales had shot up to $83 million in its first full year of shipping. Imagic's "Demon Attack" game was the toast of the CES.

Von Meister was persistent, calling Imagic relentlessly. Grubb finally sent his 23-year-old vice president of engineering, Brian Dougherty, to a dinner meeting in Los Gatos, California, in the spring. Not expecting much, Dougherty found himself enthralled by the ideas Von Meister began to spin. He felt he had met the perfect combination of "P. T. Barnum and a technologist in the same body."

Video games were the initial product to send, but by the end of dinner, Von Meister was talking about much more—software, news, e-mail, chat, tickets, reservations, almost any kind of information a person wanted. The Source had only been the beginning, Von Meister told the young man. Now we add the graphics being developed by video games, and the excitement too. Video games were, he said, the "Trojan horse" to get interactive services into the homes of the average American.

"This is inevitable," insisted Von Meister. "It could be one of the greatest business stories of all time."

Dougherty was hooked. "We gotta do this," he urged Grubb. "There is no downside." Grubb agreed: Imagic would have a new distribution channel and be an investor on the ground floor of a new medium.

"It was a strategic investment, since games had only a two-month retail life cycle at best," Grubb surmised. But this scheme by Von Meister had prospects of residuals, a channel for games and a way to test market and whet the appetites of players. He contacted two of his own investors: Kleiner veteran Frank Caufield, and the San Francisco-based investment firm, Hambrecht & Quist, which was represented by an aggressive young banker named Daniel Case III.

Dan Case was a star from early on. After earning A's and being class president in high school, he earned Phi Beta Kappa membership when he graduated from Princeton University and then was awarded a prestigious Rhodes scholarship. He was a glib and handsome man who looked impossibly young and fresh-faced. With his whippet-thin build and quick smile, the energetic Dan Case made a fast jump to the job at Hambrecht, where he was rising quickly as a protégé of founder Bill Hambrecht.

But he was still typically the lowest-ranking guy in the deals he had done so far, and what Von Meister was offering might be an opportunity to be in the driver's seat. For the ambitious Dan Case, hungry for a splashy score, this deal could be good for a lot of reasons.

Both he and Caufield considered the investment decision a no-brainer, said Dan Case. "Atari had the biggest installed base in homes," he said. "The notion was that we could use the installed base to fund a business concept that would trail those gains."

Case, Caufield, and Grubb agreed to invest $100,000 each. Von Meister had also persuaded Citicorp's venture capital arm, represented by George Middlemas, to invest another $100,000. By the fall of 1982, Control Video Corporation (CVC) had set up shop in a set of small offices behind a car dealership in Vienna, Virginia.

They all knew of Von Meister's less-than-steady reputation. "Bill was a brilliant technologist and visionary with a record of less business and financial execution," said Case. "We had concerns about him managing milestones and budgets and he had to prove he could do it."

But Von Meister captivated Dan Case, as he had many others. For an impressionable young banker, here was a classic entrepreneurial personality, full of ideas, charming, and well meaning. More importantly, Case and the others thought Von Meister was onto something. Paranoia, as much as good business instinct, was the fuel for a lot of the venture capital decisions, and they did not want to be left out if the ebullient Von Meister had finally found the big payoff.

"It was the golden age of video games, and even though here was clearly a wild and woolly guy, a big kid who should probably be locked in a room and told to just send out ideas, Von Meister was also one of those guys you are always rooting for," said Middlemas. "We went in with our eyes open."

When Middlemas mentioned to a mutual friend that he was going to invest with Von Meister, the man jokingly gave him one piece of advice: "Keep him out of the first-class airport lounges and you should be OK."

Frank Caufield heard the same thing from his colleagues. "I was told that every new generation of venture capitalists had to be hoodwinked by Von Meister," he said. "He was like that cartoon character in *Who Framed Roger Rabbit?*—he wasn't bad, he was just drawn that way."

The venture capitalists were pleasantly surprised to discover that Von Meister made good use of the seed money over the next several months, pulling in talented marketing, sales, and engineering types to begin CVC.

"It turned out to be one of the more efficient uses of $400,000 I had ever seen," said Dan Case. To his surprise, Von Meister met every one of the investors' concerns, so a decision was made to step up the financial commitment.

What was needed was a kind of beauty pageant that would attract some buzz at the 1983 CES show in Las Vegas. Von Meister and his team—which included Durrett, Segal, and another long-time collaborator, a marketing man named John Kerr—had worked up a prototype of a "GameLine Master Module," a device that would attach to the Atari 2600 console. Proprietary software would then allow a user to download a video game, pay for it with a credit card, and then play it for a set number of times until it erased when the machine was turned off.

To flack the unit, Von Meister rented a room at the famed Tropicana Hotel, hired sexy showgirls, and ran a raffle to win a small gold bar. In the room, a zippy commercial played in a loop for a product that did not even exist yet, and a character called "Commander GameLine" urged a bored American family to get online and have fun.

Von Meister—inspired by Malcolm Forbes—had even used marketing dollars to buy a hot air balloon. He slapped the Game-Line name on it and tethered it in front of the Trop.

Von Meister's traveling circus was a hit with the crowds who gathered in his suite, and orders for GameLine began to pour in. Sensing a hot product about to be born, the venture capitalists also began to circle, attracted by the excitement Von Meister's idea had generated.

"The money guys just sat in the back and practically salivated," said John Kerr. "Bill was going to be the next big thing."

viva las vegas

One of the curious onlookers in the back of the room was a pacific 24-year-old who had more than a passing interest in the work Von Meister was up to. He had been an eager user of Von Meister's Source and had also become a fan of futurist Alvin Toffler, author of *The Third Wave,* who wrote about an emerging electronically linked community that would change the world.

The young man had never worked in the consumer electronics industry before, but its glamour intrigued him, perhaps because he was becoming increasingly bored with his job as a mid-level marketing drone at a major corporation, located in one of the dullest heartland cities of the nation: Wichita, Kansas. When asked much later about what one should do when headed to the Wichita area, his acerbic response was: "Step on the accelerator and never look back."

In the Las Vegas hotel room—looking on as Von Meister, with his typically ebullient zest, spun his tales of the new interactive worlds—Stephen McConnell Case did just that.

This world was downright intoxicating, he thought.

Case—a deliberate and quiet person given to saying little and observing a lot—needed a little light-headedness. He had grown tall and solid, had a mop of dark hair, boyish features, and a decidedly preppy demeanor. He looked like a cardboard cutout of a typical eager young executive on the rise. He had begun to sense career atrophy after only a few years as a middle manager at Pepsi-Co's Pizza Hut subsidiary and before that as an assistant brands manager at the nation's premier consumer products company, Procter & Gamble.

His resume thus far was typical of many earnest college graduates from suburban families, except perhaps that he had grown up in the more exotic locale of Honolulu, Hawaii. His family had settled there generations before. On one side, he descended from a Midwesterner who settled in a tropical climate and went into retail, and, on the other, from a German-born sugar entrepreneur.

Case's parents were born in Hawaii. They met after both had gone to school in California. His father, Dan, became a lawyer for a top island firm representing big sugar and pineapple interests. His mother, Carol, was an elementary teacher at the Punahoe School, the tony private school where the couple sent their four children—an adopted older sister named Carin, and three boys: Dan, Steve, and Jeff.

Life in the Case family was full of white-bread activities such as Cub Scouts, Little League, and stamp collecting. "Steve was always an easy child, very self-sufficient in everything he did," said Carol. "He would quietly watch everyone. . . . I guess you could say that still waters run deep."

His serene nature contrasted with that of his more outgoing older brother, Dan. Only thirteen months apart in age, Dan and Steve formed an unusually close bond from their early years. The chatty and skinny Dan took the lead, and the methodical and sturdier Steve was always close behind.

As teenagers, under the moniker Case Enterprises, the pair started a variety of businesses ranging from a limeade stand to a small operation that distributed and sold magazines. Dan—glib, and a born salesman—would be the front person; Steve would quietly handle the back end of their various schemes. They took to calling their bedrooms "offices," and Carol would often find Steve pecking away on a typewriter until late into the night.

Later, onlookers would wonder whether the overachieving brothers had been fueled by sibling rivalry; if so, it was without much rancor. The pair have long aided each other in their efforts. "Growing up, we were both close and also competitive, I guess," said Dan. "But Steve always tried to avoid any overt rivalry."

Rather than trying to be better at tennis than Dan, for example, Steve picked his own activities. They included photography, journalism, and the music business. In high school, he was the editor of the school newspaper, called *Ka Punahou.* By age 17 years, he was also writing music reviews and features for *Youth Unlimited,* a publication with a large circulation among teens in Hawaii.

The subdued Case brother was attracted to the glitz of the music business. He enjoyed the thrill of being at concerts and getting to interview rock stars. When he began to think about college, his first impulse was to attend Occidental College in Los Angeles, where he would be near the action. His parents, who considered the music business "flaky," opposed the choice. Case ultimately decided on his father's alma mater, Williams College, tucked in the northwest corner of Massachusetts.

At Williams, he continued his pursuit of the music business. He chaired the school's entertainment committee and served as music director and a disc jockey at the student-run radio station. In a departure from his usually shy behavior, he also fronted for his own bands: The Vans—a name inspired by The Cars—and The The, which mimicked The Knack.

He was a B-minus student, taking mostly political science courses, but also dabbling in others. His least favorite course was computer programming. Case hated the punch cards and the confusing techspeak. Only one feature intrigued him: the ability of the college's computers to talk to others located elsewhere. "The faraway connections seemed magical," Case remembers. "It struck me as the most completely obvious use for them, and the rest was just for computer wonks."

Case's growing interest in the use of technology for human interaction showed up in an application for an advertising job at the New York-based J. Walter Thompson Company in the spring of 1980. "I firmly believe that technological advances in communications are on the verge of significantly altering our way of life," wrote the 21-year-old Case. "Innovations in telecommunications (especially two-way cable systems) will result in our television sets (big-screen, of course!) becoming an information line, newspaper, school, computer, referendum machine, and catalog."

He didn't get the ad job and was also rejected at first as a marketing trainee at Procter & Gamble's elite program in Cincinnati, where consumer products such as Tide detergent and Crest toothpaste were created and packaged. After the college recruiter turned him down, Case flew out to P&G headquarters at his own expense for another interview. He was hired as an assistant brand manager.

Soon, Case was heading down a well-beaten path for marketing managers at P&G, the company regarded as the epicenter of brand management. He toiled to develop and sell a variety of products, including a wipe-on hair conditioner called "Abound!" which had the deeply unappealing slogan of "Towelette, you bet!" After that, he was part of a team that attempted to revive the moribund Lilt home permanent.

Case admired P&G's relentless drive to build brand loyalty and marveled at its ability to develop personal relationships with consumers by persuading them, through a clever combination of marketing and advertising, to become loyal users of a product. Crest toothpaste users insisted on using Crest and would not switch even if presented with the same formula in different packaging. Managing brands properly offered an opportunity to own a category, even in the face of intense competition.

But Case also found himself increasingly frustrated by the inertia that can afflict any big company—the methodical moves, endless memos, repetitive planning meetings, and insular thinking. Nothing could happen quickly; no reaction could be instant, and there was little room for flexibility.

When a job offer came from Pizza Hut, with the heady title of "manager of new development," it seemed to offer Case the opportunity to get a bit more creative. What the title meant was a bit less fancy—Case was in charge of thinking up new toppings and other changes that would sell more pizzas to the masses. The task was not easy: all the changes had to be simple enough to be repeated by inexperienced staff in exactly the same way at thousands of Pizza Hut locations. Case took the opportunity to travel widely to small pizza shops nationwide, taste-testing what small operators were doing.

It was a lonely life for the young bachelor, especially when he was located in Wichita while his friends nabbed more exciting jobs in New York and San Francisco. On one of the many nights empty of activity, Case decided to try to make a Kaypro computer, which he had bought months before, finally work with the Source, the only online service he had heard of.

Configuring it properly and attempting to find a working telephone node he could access took weeks. "It was like climbing Mount Everest, and I think my first thought was to wonder why it had to be so hard to work it," said Case. "But when I finally logged in and found myself linked to people all over the country from this sorry little apartment in Wichita, it was just exhilarating."

Case had the same kind of feeling as he stood in the back of the Tropicana hotel room in 1983, listening to Von Meister—the man, Case quickly realized, who had thought up the Source—talk about his dreams of an online empire.

Steve was at the trade show at the invitation of his older brother Dan, who sensed that his younger sibling needed a bit of a change. Perhaps, suggested Dan, you'll get some leads at the show for the Marketing Group, a marketing consulting company that Steve had recently started with a friend from P&G. Case worked on the consulting business in his spare time from Pizza Hut and was trying to land some clients who would lend much-needed credibility. A Wichita address wasn't exactly impressive, so Case created a letterhead with a fancier San Francisco address. His mail went to a California post office, which sent it back to his home in Kansas.

But business was not booming, so Dan got Steve and his P&G friend a couple of free passes to the convention floor and let them bunk in with him at an inexpensive hotel room off the Strip. He also told his kid brother that he could tag along at a dinner that Von Meister was throwing, on one of the nights of the show.

At that dinner, Steve Case and Bill Von Meister met and hit it off immediately. They began to argue over theories of how to sell the GameLine unit and what had to happen in the consumer market to spur the uses of interactive services. But both agreed that the new medium would surely emerge to change the world.

In the bathroom, about halfway through the meal, Von Meister turned to Dan Case.

"Would you mind if I hired Steve as a consultant?" he asked.

Dan Case thought the slightly drunk Von Meister was kidding, perhaps just kissing up to a major investor. But Von Meister needed help in consumer marketing, so he thought it might work.

"Go ahead," said Dan Case. "But since I'm his brother, just leave me out of it."

Instantly, Steve acquired the nickname "Lower Case," with Dan being "Upper Case."

swan dive to belly flop

After the show, Von Meister's team was fueled by the renewed excitement of the investors. That is, except for Imagic, which was having problems of its own.

The month before the CES, within days of an overbooked public offering when the video game company was set to raise almost $50 million by selling 2.7 million shares of stock for $18 each, the deal was temporarily tabled by its lead investment bankers. The reason: Warner's announcement of huge losses at its Atari subsidiary, which signaled trouble for video game developers.

Such news, though, did not dissuade the venture capitalists now engaged in CVC. The impressive group that began to step forward to join Kleiner, Hambrecht, and Citicorp included top investors nationwide, such as the venture arms of Allstate Insurance Company, International Nickel Company (called Inco Securities Corporation), Union Venture Corporation, and Merrill, Pickard, Anderson & Eyre. The group began to funnel, in several financing rounds, millions of dollars to be used to build and market the GameLine service, which planned to begin shipping in July 1983.

Bill Von Meister was ecstatic; it seemed as if his many years of struggle had finally paid off. He now was heading a great team that was creating a sizzling product, and he was backed by an impressive board of financiers and premier technologists such as Larry Roberts and networking pioneer Len Kleinrock.

With the new funds, CVC began to bring GameLine to life, inking a deal with St. Louis-based LaBarge Inc. to make the downloading units at plants in the South. LaBarge, which was looking to expand its business away from military contracts, agreed to finance the manufacture with components bought by CVC and even opened a new plant for the project in Marshall, Arkansas. Expectations began to ramp up when CVC ordered 125,000 GameLine units in anticipation of huge sales by the fall and winter of 1983.

Von Meister, on a high, was spending money to give his Game-Line a huge splash. He decided to launch the product nationally without conducting focus groups or testing it in various cities, as is usually the practice. Case thought this wasn't the best idea, but, in his role as a consultant, he worked up the kind of marketing plans Von Meister had requested.

As he was doling out cash, Von Meister chose to ignore the stiff wind of resistance that was beginning to build in the video game industry in the middle of 1983. As dozens of new game makers entered the market, a danger of oversupply threatened.

Every little boy in America would be clamoring for a Game-Line under the Christmas tree, Von Meister insisted. It was a great idea, so how could sales not soar?

"He kept telling us that everything was going to be OK," said Doug Peabody, the venture capitalist representing Inco. "He was presumptuous about inevitable success, and when things began to change he suffered from a reality distortion."

The warning signs became completely clear when Atari announced even larger losses over the summer, and when other major names—including Coleco and Mattel—began to struggle. The video game business was clearly in distress. "It was a bloodbath," said Brian Dougherty, whose Imagic never went public after the meltdown began. "There were enough video game cartridges floating around to give a dozen to every person in the U.S."

Von Meister ignored the trends and kept touting the service at the June CES show in Chicago. He brought along his hot air balloon to promote the service that he officially launched there. With much fanfare, CVC said GameLine would cost $59.95 for the terminal, plus a $15 registration fee and $1 per session. Preparing to ship the 75,000 GameLines on July 4, as he had dreamed, Von Meister also promised he would later introduce SportsLine, Info-Line, StockLine, MailLine, and a range of other services. "We could be the most successful product of the year," predicted Von Meister.

In reality, he was draining cash at an alarming rate as prospects of revenues dwindled. In a report after the disaster that would follow, CVC named four major problems that scuttled its high-flying business: (1) retail orders evaporated overnight; (2) costs to compete rose; (3) it was difficult to acquire hit games to offer; and (4) the up-front purchase of the module was too costly for consumers.

It was no surprise, then, when the venture capitalists began to panic. Dan Case was even more distraught; his brother Steve had accepted a full-time job with CVC, offered by Von Meister that fall.

"Steve wanted to go there full-time, but I said, 'No, don't go in the middle of a meltdown,'" said Dan Case. "He took the information and did his own thing. But I felt badly since when I introduced Steve to the company it was hardly a favor at the time."

Case's parents were also concerned. "Job hoppers don't wind up anywhere," Case's father advised his son. "And this new job seems a little crazy."

Nonetheless, after working as a consultant with CVC for several months, Steve had ignored his parents' warnings and accepted a job at the lowest level in the marketing department during the summer. Before he began, Case had decided to travel to Europe for a vacation.

Now 25 years old, Case figured he could afford a disaster as long as he was at the center of the action, rather than a small cog inside of a huge conglomerate. There might be a few bumps, but that was the price of being an entrepreneur. "I don't know if it's going to work or not," Case told his worried parents. "But I could learn a lot even if it doesn't survive."

After he arrived for work in late summer, Case soon found out exactly how high the cost would be for this education. A low-grade nervousness was apparent throughout the company, a kind of fear that Case had never experienced inside the comfort of the large corporate businesses of which he had always been a part.

On his very first day, Case accompanied Von Meister to a presentation at a local hotel where, in a speech, Von Meister predicted that CVC's business would be one of the biggest splashes ever. It turned out to be more of a belly flop. The nervous venture capitalists soon decided to ride in and take over from Von Meister, who was resisting their suggestions for change and continued to spend as if he had a hit product on his hands.

"We warned Bill, who did some superficial things," said Dan Case. "He knew there was a problem, but he did not know how to fix it. He had no coherent business plan for fixing things."

On one of Dan Case's trips into Washington to deal with the troubles at CVC, the problem became exemplified for him in one moment. As he arrived via coach at the local airport, Dan Case ran into Von Meister—who had flown to the same airport first-class and had a limousine waiting for him. Case, who had dubbed himself the "chief burn-rate worrywart," joked dryly: "Now I know where the money is going."

The money was mostly gone, in fact, as Dan Case and George Middlemas soon found out. In September, they arrived and began interviewing employees. Shuttling CVC workers into the conference room all day, and poring over financial statements, with Caufield on the phone from California, the investors decided they could only hold on if there were major cutbacks in costs.

There would be layoffs, of course; ultimately, the staff was cut to a dozen people. With Dan abstaining from voting, Steve was spared, despite some calls for his job because he had been part of the disastrous marketing effort.

In addition, the offices in Vienna would be pared down to a single floor of the building. Efforts would go into a small city-by-city rollout of GameLine, rather than the national one envisioned by

Von Meister, while the investors decided what to do next with the modem technology that had been developed by Seriff and his team.

The investors then voted that Von Meister could remain chairman and chief executive officer but insisted that James Kimsey be installed as chief operating officer and de facto head of the company until a new manager could be appointed. Kimsey was one of the many small investors in CVC; he had been brought into the deal through purchase of the rights to run the Washington-area computer hubs for CVC. A successful Washington bar owner, Kimsey was an old friend of Frank Caufield—they had gone to the U.S. Military Academy at West Point together. When he first decided to invest in CVC, Caufield had told Kimsey about the company while on a rafting trip to the Grand Canyon with their sons. (An adventure trip was an annual tradition with the pair.) Caufield had hoped that Kimsey, who lived in the area, could be his eyes at CVC.

Until then, Kimsey had only helped at the company part-time—hooking CVC up with LaBarge and monitoring manufacturing. He knew little about manufacturing and even less about online technology. Now the company was in extremis and he happened to be walking by. "Kimsey was a shadowy figure, since he wasn't around much at first, so the question was: Did he know a computer chip from the end of a shot glass?" said Len Batterson. "All we knew was that he knew how to make money and we were desperate."

Von Meister tried to talk them out of taking away his power. "You don't have anyone else," he told Middlemas. "The company will go down without me because you don't know what you are doing."

Von Meister loyalists, such as John Kerr, thought Von Meister had gotten the blame unnecessarily. "It was not Bill Von Meister's fault that the video game market died," said Kerr. "They needed a scapegoat and they never remembered him as anything except the guy who spent the money."

Exactly *how much* money became frighteningly clear, by the time a board meeting rolled around. At Rickey's Hyatt House in Palo Alto, a favored hangout of Silicon Valley types, the investors found out that, in the Christmas selling season, the company had sold only 2,400 GameLine modules and spent almost $9 million doing so.

"You think they'd have shoplifted more," remarked Caufield sarcastically. "We could have sold more off the back of a truck on Route 1."

They wished they had. Along with the venture investments, there was $7 million in bills outstanding. With the phone lines of CVC's headquarters ablaze with calls from more than 100 creditors, Middlemas redubbed the conference room "Process Serving Central." The threat of a forced bankruptcy loomed, and Allstate's rep, Len Batterson, suggested bringing in turnaround executive Bob Cross, who had worked with several other distressed businesses, to settle things down until a path became clear about what to do next.

Cross quickly decided that CVC should have been called "Out of Control Video." He had seen this scene many times before—frustrated investors, an entrepreneur who did not know when an idea had stopped working, and an entire company devoted to selling something no one wanted to buy.

Scraping together enough of the leftover working capital, Cross paid off the small creditors and began to go to work on the large ones, hoping to convince them not to panic and to give CVC enough breathing room to find a way out of its troubles.

Cross was not helped by Von Meister, who was still saying that GameLine just needed a little more time to catch on. Soon, they would be able to extend the service to other areas he had envisioned. Von Meister did not seem even slightly bothered by the clamors of the creditors, because there was a bigger idea at stake.

"He thought he could just get more investors and spend our way out of it," said Cross, who was managing a dwindling bank account with revenues only dribbling in. "That was one way of looking at what I considered the Olympics of bad business."

Von Meister's delusions reached their apogee one day as Cross and others were waiting for a group of the large creditors to arrive at the Vienna offices for another round of brutal negotiations. Glancing out the window, the group watched a new Mercedes sedan being driven into the parking lot. "My new baby," declared Von Meister with glee, when he saw it.

"What do you think the creditors are going to think when they see that?" sputtered Cross, who was incredulous that Von Meister didn't see the problem.

"Don't the creditors know that I have a personal life?" Von Meister asked, as he trundled out to admire his latest automotive prize with a huge, boyish smile spread across his face.

goodbye to all that

It was over for Von Meister at CVC that day—it would be a company that would survive him, even if he would not survive with it.

Nonetheless, Von Meister remained at the troubled company for a while. The investors decided to keep him around because he still had a lot of contacts in the industry and it was easier to have him inside the tent than out of it.

But with his dream being taken into others' care, he drifted slowly away from the business and, as always, onto others. By September, he had cooked up a telephone product called Prize-Line, a service that allowed users to call into computers via the phone number, 1-800-CASHPOT. They could play trivia games and win prizes and then pay for the session with a credit card. He got the inspiration for the service from the popularity of the game Trivial Pursuit and the huge business that 976-number sex lines were doing. There would be $17 million in revenues in the first year, Von Meister bragged, from 136,000 users. Soon, he was certain, there would be a lucrative public offering.

But the business quickly failed and so did many others to come, all based on some combination of telephones, computers, and interactive services. Because of CVC, Von Meister had poisoned his reputation in the venture community, so he would never get the sizable investments he needed for new projects. His stock in CVC would soon become worthless, and he was unable to take advantage of an offer to investors to transfer their stakes into a new business that would emerge from CVC's ashes.

But Von Meister stayed sunny throughout. Said John Kerr: "He left behind a series of miserable SOBs who benefited from his ideas. And yet he was always looking forward to tomorrow's sunshine in the middle of a monsoon."

Perhaps so, but Von Meister soon faced a torrent of storms, including mounting debts and growing problems with his drinking. His family and friends intervened in 1991, and Von Meister entered a rehab program in a small town near his home in northern Virginia.

One holiday, soon after he was on the wagon, his grown children kidded him about all his many ups and downs, teasing him for all they had endured because of the way he had conducted his life.

The usually jovial Von Meister became serious for a moment. "Would you rather I was a postman?" he asked his family. "I am what I am."

When he found out he was sick with a fast-growing cancer, Von Meister was still thinking up new entrepreneurial schemes, even suggesting to his doctors that they should computerize the way medicine was delivered through his intravenous needle. And after he received the diagnosis that he had only months to live, he even began another business—using a combination of fax machines and computers to deliver government documents.

He went out a number of times with Kerr to reminisce about the old days—proud that he had been at the start of the company that later evolved into AOL. "We really did something," he told Kerr, as if that was enough for him. "What do you say we take another run around the rosebush?"

But, by the spring of 1995, he became too sick and found himself in more pain. After being hospitalized until it was clear there was nothing more to do, Von Meister moved home and died on May 18th.

Von Meister's son Rick was surprised when he heard what Steve Case—who had also lost touch with Von Meister—and Marc Seriff had said about his father at the memorial service. The relationship between the father and son had been strained, especially after his parents had divorced early in the son's life. After that, his father had been absent a lot, off chasing one new idea after another. But Rick, who later became a police officer in the Washington area, never really understood the restless quest his father was on. All Rick saw at the end was a man who died too early, in pain, broke, and without the kind of legacy he had always wanted to leave.

Because Bill Von Meister had said nothing to his son about being part of the beginnings of a company like America Online, Rick had listened carefully when Case and Seriff had said that Bill Von Meister was one of the fathers of the online industry.

That was something, thought Rick.

After everyone had spoken, Bill's brother, Peter Von Meister, stood and read "Autumn Song," which Bill Von Meister had penned years before, at age 16.

The last words of his poem about dying leaves hung in the soft spring air:

And so they sing their song to all,
As from their cold high thrones they fall,
Red and green and brown and gold,
They die in peace, their story told.

reports of our death aren't greatly exaggerated

plan b (ell south)

"There must be a pony somewhere in this shit," was the piquant expression Jim Kimsey found himself using over and over again.

It was the punch line from a joke he'd borrowed from his pal Frank Caufield. A boy was digging in a huge pile of horse manure like some happy fool. Someone asked him why he expended so much effort only to find himself knee-deep in crap, and the boy responded. . . .

That's exactly how Kimsey felt as he surveyed the disaster that was Control Video Corporation in the spring of 1984. "My job was to make chicken salad out of chicken shit," said Kimsey, whose conversation at the time seemed prone to the scatological. Such pronouncements were classic Kimsey, for he was not inclined to move delicately through life. Von Meister was merrily irresponsible; Kimsey played the role of a straight-shooting tough guy in the Robert Mitchum mode. In the course of the years when AOL grew, Kimsey's brashly honest style was often a little hard-knuckled for many at the company.

Kimsey provided the important anchor needed after Von Meister's flights of fancy. His ability to keep the business from sinking in the early 1980s and to find much-needed cash was also undeniably the reason that the company survived its earliest years. More importantly, his decision to place an extraordinary amount of responsibility in the hands of a young executive named Steve Case—a move that at the time seemed a bit capricious—would later be recognized as a decision of great foresight.

And, however he expressed it, Kimsey was dead-on about CVC in 1984. It had no clear product, no apparent market, no real money. Creditors hovered, venture capitalists were ready to attack at any sign of weakness, and a dispirited group of employees was poised to bolt for the door.

This was definitely not the place this ex-Army airborne ranger ever expected to find himself. Kimsey had started out with nothing and had managed to build a lucrative real estate and restaurant business. CVC was a genuine mess, which—in an odd way—appealed to Kimsey's gung-ho nature.

A contrarian spirit had lifted Kimsey from his modest upbringing. Born in 1939, he was the son of a career bureaucrat in post-World War II Washington. The eldest child in a large Irish Catholic family, Kimsey was lucky enough to get a scholarship to one of the city's leading Catholic private schools, Gonzaga. But he chafed under the strict regime, and his self-described "wise-ass" nature got him tossed out of the school in his senior year for being a disruptive influence. At the time, Kimsey didn't care whether he got a degree; but his mother did, and she managed to get him enrolled in another Catholic high school in the area. After graduation and a year at Georgetown, the city's major Catholic university, Kimsey became obsessed with getting into the nation's premier military academy—West Point.

"It was the macho idea of it, from a lot of images in John Wayne movies," Kimsey admitted. "To be a young guy and be part of it seemed like the right thing to do."

He thrived in the environment of controlled aggression, and the eight years in military service that followed were perhaps the most formative and eventful time for Kimsey. His photos from that era show a young man with a wolfish and lean look.

One of his earliest stints in the U.S. Army was as commander of one of the first companies to land in the Dominican Republic in

1965. Later that year, he began his first tour of duty in Vietnam. Kimsey took an assignment near Duc Pho, where the previous combat team had been killed in an attack. It was Kimsey's job to stabilize the area and to construct an orphanage to house hundreds of Vietnamese children. While there, he developed a working knowledge of the Vietnamese language and became interested in the martial arts.

After returning to the United States for a year spent at a base in Washington state, Kimsey went back to Vietnam in 1968 to work in special operations, which Kimsey called "Sneaky Pete stuff." During this second tour, he began to see that life in the military was perhaps not for him anymore. His tendency to mouth off to superiors was becoming a liability. And, as he looked around at the officers in charge, Kimsey began to realize he had no interest in rising in the ranks, the military equivalent of a slow-moving climb through a thicket of corporate bureaucracy.

Instead, he wanted to vault to the "head of the food chain," to become the guy whom the high-ranking brass and politicians worked for—a successful businessman. But when he left the military and returned to the Washington area to join his wife and children, Kimsey had only $2,000 in cash.

Walking in downtown Washington one day, he saw a "For Sale" sign on a building and called to inquire. The developer who met him in the street that day was also a young striver, and he convinced Kimsey that the deal could be done with no money down by renting out the building and borrowing money based on those leases. Kimsey snagged an investment brokerage to rent the top floor. And, when another group of brokers decided they wanted to open a bar downstairs, it seemed as if Kimsey was on his way.

That is, until the brokers ran out of the money needed to open the bar—a project Kimsey took over himself by borrowing even more money. He seemed to have a flair for the business. He created a buzz for the new bar, dubbed "The Exchange," by installing a working ticker tape machine.

His success at The Exchange allowed him to further leverage his business. Through the booming 1970s, Kimsey opened a series of trendy singles bars with names like Madhatter, Cousteau's, and

Bullfeathers. When he began selling out in the early 1980s, Kimsey was a wealthy man.

Kimsey continued to putter around in banking and real estate investments, but was looking for another challenge when his close pal from West Point, Frank Caufield, asked him to become involved in CVC. Now a favor for a friend had turned into a full-scale disaster.

"I kept thinking of the personal implications, of how I could get out of this clean," said Kimsey, who had by now taken to a life of limousines and front-row seats. "I definitely did not want to be associated with a bankrupt organization."

His financial status was important because Kimsey was involved at the time in creating a bank holding company. On the forms from the Securities and Exchange Commission was a scary question: "Have you ever been involved in a bankruptcy?"

CVC was, as Kimsey often described it, "like Br'er Rabbit and the Tar Baby"—the more he tried to shake it off, the more stuck he became. Kimsey, a stubborn man, was not interested in presiding over a failure. No matter what, CVC was not going to go down on his watch.

But how to salvage something from the meltdown of Game-Line? The team—Kimsey, Case, Seriff, and the others who were left—quickly ticked through the options:

Television ads to sell the service? Too expensive.

Direct marketing? Too expensive.

Deals with national chains? No one wanted to buy the video game modules CVC was selling.

"A lot of companies are born from disaster," joked Citicorp's George Middlemas to Kimsey. "And since this is a first-class fiasco, maybe it'll work out."

Help came at first from an unlikely source—the announcement, in February 1984, of an unusual joint venture among three of the nation's largest corporations: CBS Inc., Sears Roebuck & Company, and International Business Machines Corporation. Their aim: to create a popular consumer online service for users of personal computers. The interests of the trio would drive the effort: CBS was looking for more outlets to distribute its information; Sears wanted to find new ways of retailing; and IBM simply wanted to sell more computers. By April, Ted Papes—a longtime IBM vice president of a division that developed medium and large systems and semiconductor components—was named president and chief executive officer. Top brass from each company had also committed large sums of money to the effort, which was tentatively called Trintex.

With major companies willing to get involved in the medium for the home market—rather than the more business-oriented market that was CompuServe's focus—a lot of media and communications companies grew nervous that they would be left out. They decided they needed a foothold in the home market. One of those companies was Bell South.

After being approached by cash-desperate CVC, the aggressive regional phone company decided to lend CVC $5 million to test-market an at-home subscription service called "MasterLine," for use on Apple II and Commodore 64 machines, which were then the only personal computers with mass penetration in the home market.

The deal would give CVC a breather until the company could decide what to do next; meanwhile, it could rejigger the defunct GameLine modules and convert them for another purpose. Instead of video games, CVC would send customers educational and entertainment software by phone. A subscription would cost the user $20 a month for use of twenty different programs.

CVC had an ambitious plan; it would either sell its modems directly to consumers or would rent them out for $5 to $8 a month. Customers would save money by using the superior CVC modems to make a request for software off-line, automatically dial it in, download the material and then cut off.

"A missing link has existed: no company has developed a low-cost home terminal that accesses desirable home information services," said CVC in a corporate outline in the summer of 1984. "A chicken-and-egg problem exists: The mass consumer market is unwilling to purchase modems until they are able to access

high-quality, desirable services, and services have been seemingly
unable to provide this quality without large subscriber bases."

The answer, according to the plan, was to let major companies
such as Bell South distribute the module—rather than CVC,
which could not create a new market on its own. The service
would have 1.5 million users by the end of 1989, the business plan
projected, and would realize $110 million in revenues and $23.5
million in net income.

The test was a lot less successful than planned—not a disaster,
but not the home run expected by Bell South. It quickly became
apparent that few customers were willing to buy or rent a specialized modem to attach to their computers. The problem? CVC had
not—as Von Meister said—been willing to give away the razors in
order to sell the razor blades. Instead, it was trying to get customers
to buy a whole new way of shaving by requiring them to own a
proprietary device.

When results continued to drag, Bell South's enthusiasm pe-
tered out, and the company decided to cut its ties with CVC.
Worse still, Bell South wanted its money back. But the money was
long gone and Bell South joined the long line of creditors, each
wanting a piece of the tattered business.

"The market was not there yet and we were," said Kimsey.
"This incredible modem, which we thought of as our only asset,
was yet another liability, so we had gambled and lost."

In other words, craps.

plan c (ommodore)

Then, Clive Smith had another idea.

In his job as vice president of corporate planning and new business development at Commodore International Ltd., the 34-year-
old knew that the market for the company's flagship Commodore
64 computer was fast maturing and would soon head downward.

Though the company was preparing another product—the
Amiga computer, to be marketed in the winter of 1985—that
would soon hopefully take over the growth at the West Chester,

Pennsylvania, company, the Commodore 64 was its mainstay. Many millions of units had been sold to average consumers. The significance of the Commodore was profound—it was the first popular introduction for most average consumers to the world of computing. But even as it seemed at the top of its game, Commodore needed a way to reignite consumers' interest. And the Amiga needed a new hook to pull users into taking full advantage of its groundbreaking multimedia capabilities.

Computers needed to be more than devices for word processing, figuring out household budgets, and playing games, Smith thought. It was not a new idea, but he was in a unique position to do something about it.

As head of consumer research at the respected Boston-based Yankee Group, Smith had watched with fascination the experiments that newspapers and other media were undertaking with videotex services. Some had tried to focus on delivering news; others had found a way to goose banking; and still others had aimed at the computer hobbyist. Trintex—the Sears/CBS/IBM venture—was obviously drilling in on shopping.

But Smith had disagreed with all these efforts. To him, the best use for computers was as a new form of communication. All the other uses were definitely good for interactive devices, but Smith felt that the ability to form communities electronically would bind a user to a company in ways that had never been possible before.

With new graphic and audio abilities soon to be available on the Commodore—and later, on the Amiga—such a service could be dazzling: visual in a way the telephone was not, and interactive in a way that television was not.

Commodore needed a way to unite its users in a large electronic world of their own, where they could trade information about computing and anything else they wanted to do. Equally important was an ability to store information locally rather than at some distant mainframe computer, making such an online world a truly dynamic organism.

Commodore's founder, Irving Gould, had promised Smith when he came on board that he could initiate one project of his own. This was it—Smith wanted to create a private-label online service for Commodore's computers.

When Smith went looking for a company to help him, he found a small start-up called PlayNet, in upstate New York, begun by a small coterie of techies. With its lively graphical user interface and innovative "lobbies" where users could move to different "rooms," the game service was a delight. It was precisely the kind of design Smith was looking for. But Smith was also worried that the small company could not scale the kind of service Commodore needed; its management was too inexperienced in the business of keeping a service running properly. PlayNet also resisted turning over too much control to Commodore.

Enter Jim Kimsey, Steve Case, and Marc Seriff.

Smith had heard of CVC through various encounters with Bill Von Meister over the years and in some short discussions with Kimsey.

Case had also run into Smith at the CES in January 1985, and had heard that Commodore was thinking about doing a deal with PlayNet. Why couldn't CVC do the same thing instead?

With Kimsey and Seriff, CVC could argue that its stronger management team might be more appealing to the Commodore executives. During 1984, an unusual triumvirate had been developed at CVC: Kimsey was the finance guy, Case would figure out what could sell, and Seriff would build it. PlayNet might have better software, but CVC had the battlefield experience to run it properly. More to the point, CVC officials were also willing to sell a huge chunk of the flagging company, while PlayNet was not.

The trio knew the kind of business Commodore was looking for, and they decided that CVC would be a perfect match. They could junk the specialized CVC modem altogether. Instead, they could hopscotch from one emerging computer platform to the next, building a patchwork business of private online services. The pitch to computer makers was obvious: We'll give you another feature to distinguish your product—a service that will focus specifically on you.

Smith liked the team at CVC, as did his boss, Marshall Smith (no relation), whom Gould had brought in to run the company. But

Commodore management had reservations about whether the burdens of the recent failure of the video game strategy would bleed into a new service, perhaps involving Commodore in lawsuits brought by creditors from CVC's previous disaster. The computer company, about to add a lot of graphical elements to its machines, also liked the PlayNet software a lot better than the package CVC had to offer. And, finally, CVC would need to be recapitalized.

Clean up your business, license the rights to PlayNet's software, and find some money, Clive Smith told CVC. "I only want to do this our way," he declared.

After Kimsey struck a deal to license PlayNet's software for $50,000, he handed it over to Seriff to tinker with; it would form the skeleton of the new system.

Bob Cross managed to rid CVC of a wad of its bills by transferring as much money as he could and settling the claims of the legions of small creditors. When only large creditors were left, Kimsey offered warrants to purchase stock later—in Quantum Computer Services, a separate new company that would be born out of the old.

CVC, instead of going bankrupt, would simply wither as the employees moved to the new company. Kimsey thought of it as putting the company in a drawer and leaving it there until it stopped making noise.

These moves provided a clean slate for new investors; their support was critical because the new company needed money. Commodore had agreed to distribute the service—saving Quantum huge outlays of marketing money—and to lend the new company $1 million, executing three promissory notes. Another investor was Alan Patricof, whose venture capital firm had also invested in PlayNet.

Kimsey still needed another $5 million—a dicey proposition because he was going hat in hand to venture capitalists that had been burned in the CVC deal.

The first backer to bolt was Kimsey's old pal, Frank Caufield, the venture capitalist who had brought Kimsey to CVC. Caufield had taken a leave of absence from Kleiner, Perkins and was trekking in Nepal in the spring of 1985, so he was not available to help. "You'll have to sell it to my partners by yourself," Caufield told Kimsey, who then traveled with Middlemas to San Francisco to meet with the Kleiner, Perkins partners, all of whom are given a voice in all investments decisions for the firm.

Good luck, Caufield told his buddy.

Kimsey needed a lot more than luck. Kleiner's Tom Perkins and others at the firm were less than thrilled with their losses from CVC and were not eager for another run around the rose bush, even with Von Meister gone. Kimsey also knew that the venture firm regarded him only as Caufield's old military chum.

"It's a dog," said the venture capitalists flatly to Kimsey and Middlemas. "You should take it out in back and shoot it."

Kleiner, Perkins took a pass on investing.

But, hoping somehow to recoup their losses, Citicorp, Inco, Allstate and most of the other original investors agreed to pony up more cash. By selling shares for $10 each, Kimsey managed to scrape together enough money to go forward.

On May 24, 1985, Quantum Computer Services Inc. was officially incorporated. The name meant nothing—it had been selected at the last minute because it sounded credible and had vague technology associations. But the moniker represented a quantum leap from near-death. At the new company's inception, employees presented Kimsey with a cartoon of a cockroach wearing boxing gloves, a nod to a newspaper article that had declared CVC a bug you couldn't kill no matter how hard you tried.

Seriff spent the summer trying to leverage the PlayNet technology to scale it for more users. He also made a deal with Telenet for cheap nighttime connections. Case drove weekly to Commodore's Pennsylvania headquarters to formulate marketing plans. And Kimsey reassured investors. "I think we've finally made it," he said.

After being tested all through the summer, the "Q-Link" service debuted on November 1, 1985, at 6 P.M. To save on telecommunications costs, Q-Link ran through the night but signed off at 10 A.M., allowing its programmers and content producers the whole day to fiddle with the system and iron out problems. The system was also up all day on weekends and on a half-dozen holidays.

The basic service—at a cost of $9.95 a month plus 6 cents a minute for online time in "premium areas"—included access to news, soap opera updates, and a variety of games. Chat, which was called "People Connection" and borrowed nearly directly from PlayNet, was a focal point and would turn out to be of critical importance later.

Seriff and others watched with glee as the first paying users of the service began dribbling through the electronic door of the online community that they had created. A technician ran to a liquor store near Q-Link's Vienna office and brought back cheap champagne. The small group toasted their first venture. That night, they had managed to attract twenty-four people to their computer community.

That is, until the system crashed. One night, when more than sixty users were logged in simultaneously, Q-Link froze. Outages were a constant problem back then—foreshadowing major technological problems later—as Seriff's team continued to search for ways to scale the system for the expected flow of more and more Commodore users. Soon after the launch, when the service was up for two weeks in a row without a total collapse, Seriff wrote a congratulatory memo to his staff.

Q-Link's debut came just as another round of worries enveloped the entire online industry. Indications pointed to little chance of developing a mass consumer interest in the medium. Times Mirror Company pulled the plug on its efforts in the spring of 1986. The media giant's videotex services president, James Holly, declared that online consumers were odd. "They're different, they're weird," said Holly. "There's no reasonable profit in the future." Knight-Ridder executives agreed and junked their costly Viewtron effort soon after.

Such defections by big names were hard on a small company like Quantum; their participation had brought much needed attention to the fledgling industry, and their departure tarnished its prospects. With—as Kimsey quipped—"cash tight and resources light," Quantum had to try a variety of methods to get Commodore users to sign up—including contests and treasure hunts on the service. It even attempted to make a splash with a multiplayer game called "Habitat," designed in conjunction with *Star Wars* impresario George Lucas's film company.

These efforts were the best a small company with few resources could do. Besides, Quantum was banking on the big marketing guns of Commodore for the bulk of its sign-ups. "We thought they were going to turn on their fireplugs and marketing would cost us zero and we were home free," Case said. "Then we could just sit back and take in customers."

Not so. The Q-Link service was not a major priority at Commodore, which was becoming increasingly embroiled in internal problems as its core businesses began to encounter troubles. Quantum suffered especially when Commodore did not focus on its need for more modems to be shipped with computers. Case and Kimsey made frequent trips to Commodore headquarters, begging for more modems and marketing.

They made an unlikely pair—the blustery Kimsey and the aloof Case. But they shared one intention: to goose Commodore into paying attention to them so that they could deliver modems as promised to consumers.

By January 1986, the Q-Link service had only 10,000 users, and growth through that year was slower than expected, considering the clout of Commodore marketing. By mid-1987, annual revenues were about $8.6 million, with a small net income of $238,000. But the future was uncertain, especially as the Commodore 64 began to lose market share. And there were no signs that Quantum would ever be close to paying back all the equity that had been pumped in.

"Our fate is inextricably linked with Commodore," said Kimsey to Case and Seriff. "We have to take control of our destiny." A new deal was needed, they all knew, as cash began to run out again.

Kimsey put it as delicately as he could: "If we stay on this course, we'll have to eventually shoot the company."

plan a (pple)

If only Quantum had the resources of Trintex, whose owners were pumping money into their upcoming project. Having already spent $18.8 million each, the Trintex trio was committed to investing $250 million each overall.

But such spending was increasingly worrisome to CBS shareholders, and—after denials that it would leave—the television network pulled out of the project in October 1986. Sears and IBM moved forward with plans for a national service that was dubbed Prodigy in mid-1987. Its logo had white serif letters and a stylized five-pointed star.

Such rich options were not available to Quantum, which plodded along on the edges of obscurity. While Prodigy plowed the mainstream and prepared the average consumer to accept online services as a given, the question for Quantum was: how do we stay alive today so that we can flourish when the clouds open up tomorrow?

When Commodore proved to be an ineffective rainmaker, Quantum needed another platform to latch onto. The only one with any consumer penetration was the quirkily popular Apple II series, from the creative denizens of Apple Computer Inc. in Cupertino, California.

Apple was not an easy target. Its culture was tight and insular. Its ride on a wave of popularity and success gave it a superior attitude that veered dangerously toward extreme arrogance. In addition, the company had always been disdainful of third-party partnerships.

But after the success of the Apple II series, introduced in the 1970s, the company was focused intensely on its latest computer offering—the Macintosh. That focus created an opportunity for Quantum to aim at the already mature Apple II market and to propose a private online service for its huge pool of users. If Quantum could convince Apple to let them design such a service, the company would immediately get a huge halo of credibility in the computer community that could lead to other deals.

Quantum also had an ulterior motive—to have enough success with the Apple II product for Quantum to then create the official online service for the Macintosh.

At the time, though, Apple already was using General Electric Information Services (GEIS) for a private online service—called AppleLink—that traded information between the company and its dealers. There were also large Apple II areas on CompuServe.

If Apple was in the market to build a service, the question was: Who would build it? CompuServe and GEIS were more obvious choices because of their existing business relationships with Apple. In addition, GEIS had started a consumer online service called GEnie, in 1985.

But they didn't have Steve Case camping out in Cupertino. After Kimsey made the initial contacts with Apple to get him in the door, Case moved to California for three months in late 1986 to convince Apple to give the account to Quantum. Case's strategy was to take advantage of Apple's decentralized management by working on several different departments where such a service might reside.

Case positioned himself as the "internal evangelist" for the service and went back again and again, trying to iron out problems among the prickly Apple managers. He even finagled a small desk at Apple, where he put up a whimsical sign that read "Steve Held Hostage" and showed the number of days he had been there.

Case's quiet persistence and his savvy at taking advantage of Apple's disorganization worked. In early 1987, the customer service department gave him the go-ahead. Case had struck the deal of his young life.

Quantum would create and run Apple's private online service for Apple II, and later for the Mac and would be able to use the magical Apple logo to sell them, as long as they incorporated the strict design standards of Apple to make it look like an Apple product. Apple would help market the product and receive a 10 percent royalty from all users. Quantum would make its money from running the services.

Case went home to Vienna a hero. Soon after, on a trip to Texas, he cited the Commodore and Apple deals to persuade executives at Tandy Corporation to let Quantum create an online service for its DeskMate computer. (DeskMate was expected to be the computer that would be bought by the masses.) The DeskMate service would be called PC-Link.

The Tandy deal proved to be a portent of tribulations ahead. It irritated Apple's managers, who had expected that all of Quantum's resources would be devoted to them. But Quantum—especially after the Commodore experience—was determined to be linked with as many platforms as possible.

In February 1987, because of the broader range of online services that Quantum would be offering, Kimsey was able to get a $5 million investment from Berkeley Development Capital Ltd., a venture capital firm, in another $10-a-share round. Six months later, Kleiner, Perkins returned to the fold, getting 125,000 shares at the cheap price of $2 per share, and allowing Kimsey to begin diluting Commodore's huge stake in the company.

To build the services it had promised, Quantum needed all the cash it could find. Neither the Apple nor the Tandy deal came with financial infusions from those companies. In essence, Steve Case had wagered his company's survival on these pacts, hoping that they would bring huge revenues in the future.

The arrangement seemed like a good bet. In September, Case was promoted to executive vice president for his work.

But before long, the clash of Apple's massive ego and Quantum's inexperience and lack of resources brought trouble.

The venture began well enough. Case hired Tom Morgan, a close colleague, to open a five-person office near Apple and to handle the relationship with them. He loaded up staff in Vienna again and began to invest the new money in bringing to life the deals he had made. Apple created a team and organization that mirrored those formed by Quantum to work on the project.

But as the meetings between the two sides proceeded, differences surfaced immediately. In time, they turned into a major power struggle.

Apple was—justifiably—fiercely protective of its brand logo. It had no intention of allowing a dinky little company from Virginia to wreck its carefully cultivated image by supplying any service that was less than perfect. After all, its carefully constructed brand name was out front, Apple told Quantum.

Quantum welcomed some of Apple's requests, especially in the design of the interface, because they forced the young company to improve its own operations. But, as the list of Apple's demands grew long and expensive, and as Quantum's cash dwindled, tensions rose. Apple insisted that Quantum had to create a huge customer service department well before the service was operational. Every time the logo appeared, it had to be printed in a certain manner, in specific colors and sizes, and with exacting placement. A pricey manual would also be needed for the service, at a cost of $250,000.

Some of Apple's requirements seemed ridiculous to Quantum. A rugby shirt was designed for the service and carried the ad-line: "Once you're linked, you're hooked." Apple said it sounded drug-related, and the shirt was subsequently junked. Apple managers sniffed at ads Quantum wanted to run in computer magazines, and called them "tacky" because they listed a toll-free telephone number for sign-up. Apple proposed using only the service's name and logo, with a lot of white space.

"Apple wanted to keep up quality to incredibly high standards, and Quantum wanted to cut corners as much as possible to get it up and running," said Morgan, who found himself catching most of the fire between Vienna and Cupertino. "Steve had risked the company for a reward further down a road that turned out to be incredibly bumpy."

As the service moved to launch, the differences got worse and more serious for Quantum. Apple wanted the service to be sold in retail stores like regular software; Case wanted it to be given out free and via bundling into Apple computers or direct marketing channels. The idea of free software was anathema to Apple—indeed, to many others in the computer industry—but Case saw it as a way to get customers to taste products without spending a lot of resources.

"We want to be able to attract customers and you won't let us," complained Case to Apple executives. But Case could only push so far; the holy grail for Quantum was to launch the service for the Macintosh later.

The wrangling continued, even as the AppleLink Personal Edition made its official debut in the summer of 1988 at the Apple Fest conference in Boston. In addition to a $35 annual fee, the metered service would cost $6 an hour at night and $15 by day. The first online forum featured legendary Apple founder Stephen Wozniak. The service's come-on declared: "Break into Apple's corporate headquarters."

Soon, though, Quantum was trying to figure out a way to break out. The service attracted tens of thousands of customers, but the continuing expensive restrictions that Apple had placed on the company yielded limited benefits. Quantum knew there was interest—a blind item it had run in a computer magazine in the spring of 1988, as a test of the service, had yielded tens of thousands of inquiries.

But Apple still held the reins tight on marketing, even as Quantum's prospects for being on the Mac bandwagon were shriveling. While Quantum toiled in the less sexy Apple II arena, other departments at the company paid little attention to its efforts. But everyone at Apple was interested in every aspect of the Mac and, soon enough, Quantum had a lot of competitors, both internally and externally, for control over the service.

"We ran into a political buzzsaw that we were simply not going to emerge from," said Morgan. "And after our back-and-forth over AppleLink Personal Edition, we had few friends inside."

Case was facing his own tribulations inside Quantum. Workers were laid off as the 1988 holidays approached. The company had already spent a large chunk of its operating budget, the problems running the Apple II service did not let up, and new investors at Berkeley were threatening to sue because the promised results turned out to be less than spectacular. Some board members demanded that Kimsey—who had largely left all day-to-day decisions up to his protégé—fire Case. If Case had screwed up, he now had to suffer.

But Kimsey resisted. A strong relationship had developed over the years between the two men, who had vastly different temperaments. Kimsey was a backslapping businessman, comfortable in the role of an elder statesman; Case, a shy person, hovered in the back rooms and ran the show. Kimsey had always liked the fact that Case would take care of all the details, and Case had appreciated the huge amount of leeway Kimsey had given him. Later, they would clash more directly over issues of credit and control. But as the company's powerful outside counsel, Ken Novack, said later, "It was no accident that they created this business together." At the time, there was no choice—the fates of Kimsey and Case were tethered together, swim or sink.

And so, Kimsey made an important call. "Consider it on-the-job training," he told the angry investors. "You don't take a 25-pound turkey out of the oven and throw it out before it's done." Besides, Case had not been wrong about the direction the company should go in—he had just been body-slammed by Apple.

Instead of dumping Case, Quantum would dump Apple, which was also mulling divorce options. But even with mutual agreement that they did not agree, the break-up wasn't easy. Kimsey threatened to make the flap public. Apple refused to pay Quantum the millions of dollars it had laid out to create the service. What could a small company do anyway?

A lot, it turned out, especially because of Apple's insistence on such close ties between the companies in the first place. The agreement crafted by Case in 1987, which had given Apple control of so much of the development of the service, also gave Quantum the rights to use of the Apple logo for online services. Even if Apple stymied Quantum, Quantum could stop Apple from officially marketing any other online service that displayed the Apple logo.

If you want the logo back, said Kimsey, pay up.

In June 1989, Apple forked over $2.5 million for Quantum to relinquish its rights. The money was sorely needed. In the fiscal year that ended on June 30, 1989, Quantum posted a net loss of $5.7 million. It had burned through millions of dollars on the Apple and Tandy deals and had less than $1 million in cash in the bank.

"We knew we needed to be free," said Case. "But free to do what?"

plan a (ol)

Its freedom brought yet another moment of reckoning for the online cockroach.

On the positive side, revenue from the services was still bringing cash in, the software and customers from the Apple service were Quantum's and, most of all, the company had a lot of hardwon experience in the online business.

But the minus column was a bit longer. So far, the company—in its many incarnations—had misjudged the video game market, failed as a software downloading service, and done only a middling job as a creator of private online services. And customers for Commodore's Q-Link, Apple's AppleLink, and the PC-Link for Tandy (launched by Quantum in 1988 with minimal fuss) totaled 75,000. In addition, the link to Apple was about to be severed, leaving Quantum on its own without the strong brand name that it had hoped would lead to quick growth. Strapping itself to the sides of major companies—Bell South, Commodore, and Apple—as they sailed along had allowed Quantum to float. But the company had swallowed a lot of water along the way.

Analysts and investors were still unsure whether there was indeed a market for online services. Much money had been invested and much lost in a wide range of attempts at interactive communications—from interactive television to videotex. Few experts were predicting big things in 1989.

And yet, if such services were to take off, it was important to be ready to take the lead. Although Quantum still wanted to pursue creating private online services, was it time to strike out with a service of its own, ultimately consolidating all its products under one name? Could the company thrive without the benefit of having a well-known name closely attached? Could it distinguish itself in the still-new market where potential competitors such as Prodigy were swinging multimillion-dollar ad campaigns?

And, anyway, what would they call it?

With the cutoff date for using the AppleLink name set for October 2, 1989, Case decided to hold a company contest for a name for the service after the separation from Apple.

The suggestions were plentiful—and mostly bad. "Quantum 2000" sounded like an electric shaver, and "Crossroads" suggested a rehab clinic. "Explore" and "Infinity" were simply too vague.

Case himself had toyed with the idea of "Online America," perhaps suggested by "California Online," a service that Quantum had explored doing with Pacific Bell. When he flipped it around and added it to the pile, many of the young employees derided it jokingly as too patriotically red, white, and blue.

"It was thought of as kind of too much," said Marc Seriff. "And a bit hokey." But if the service was going to appeal to a wide range of people, it had to be a bit corny. Case voted himself the winner, and America Online was born.

Quantum—which remained the parent name because the America Online product would be only one of many services—hired a local ad firm in Washington. Artists there came up with a blue triangular logo with two clasped hands that were reaching for each other. Marketing Vice President Jean Villanueva, who had come to Quantum in late 1988 and had developed a list of objectives for the design, believed it was most important to reflect the person-to-person communication element. The hands were developed to do that, but when they ended up looking like snakes' heads, she dropped them. Instead, the center held an indistinguishable swirl reminiscent of the Nike swoosh.

Debate also surrounded choice of the best abbreviation for the service. Some sided with AO and others with AOL. Again, Case prevailed. Many great and well-known companies had a trio of letters—CBS, IBM, AT&T, ITT. And, anyway, joked one internal newsletter: "AO sounds too much like BO, as in body odor."

The service that began in October, basically replacing Apple-Link Personal Edition, included games, e-mail, chat, news, forums, travel, and other information. It cost $5.95 for one hour of access, after which it cost $10 an hour on weekdays and $5 an hour on weeknights and weekends. The first 25,000 charter members were offered one month free and a 20 percent lifetime discount.

With AOL not linked to bigger partners, Case and his team could experiment with their new theories of marketing an online service. They decided to give away the service free at first, to entice customers. They would insert free software for AOL in unlikely sources, such as magazines. They would use direct mail rather than rely on being bundled into computer boxes.

Continuing to hedge its bets, Quantum agreed to create a service for the upcoming IBM PS/1 computer—a minor coup because IBM co-owned Prodigy. By this time, Quantum had learned a thing or two. IBM committed to spending $1 million on advertising and to shipping AOL with its computers. It also agreed to pay Quantum $1.7 million up front to develop a service called Promenade. It debuted in 1990.

"IBM had to use a proctoscope on us before putting us in its box," declared the always quotable Kimsey to newspapers at the time.

Case had seemed to pass the test too, by making a smooth transition from the Apple service to AOL and by acquiring IBM as a customer. He was—at the tender age of 32—for all intents and purposes, running the company. He was promoted to president in January 1991.

In an issue of an satiric internal newsletter called the *Quantum Quick*, AOL employees were happy enough now to joke about their many setbacks. A list of "Business Plan Highlights and Company Objectives for 1991" included these goals:

> Attempt to keep strategic partners over eighteen weeks.
>
> Prove once and for all that we can spend money much faster than we can ever dream of making it.
>
> Become a meaningless subsidiary of a huge conglomerate.

That joke was a bit prophetic. Kimsey began talks that winter to sell the company to CompuServe. Other majors, such as Prodigy and AT&T Corporation, had expressed interest in acquiring Quantum before, but no earlier bid was as serious as this one.

CompuServe was in a buying mood. Only eighteen months before, in an acquisition also considered by Quantum, CompuServe had bought the Source and its 53,000 members for $3.1 million from Welsh, Carson, Anderson & Stowe, a New York-based venture capital firm. The reasons for the purchase were simple: To prevent companies such as AT&T—one of many that were mulling online alternatives—from buying it, and to clear out another competitor. Those were also the reasons CompuServe began talking to Quantum, which had grown to about 110,000 customers by then.

For some principals on Quantum's side, such a deal made sense. It provided its itchy venture investors with an exit strategy, now that the company was on more solid footing and moving forward. There was no question that, at some point in the near future, the investors would want some payoff for their many years of patience.

Without a sale, there were few ways of achieving that level of income. The company had stabilized, but there was little cash for the true expansion that could make Quantum leap ahead, and plodding along and only growing slowly left it in a vulnerable position. In addition, Commodore, which still owned a chunk of the company, was calling in its loan, which now totaled $1.5 million. Commodore had frozen Quantum's bank accounts to retrieve the debt.

Quantum had only two real choices: get big or get bought.

Kimsey had already had a number of discussions with Henry Bloch and his executives at H&R Block, which owned CompuServe and was well aware of Quantum's credentials. The aggressive team from Quantum would be the perfect way that stolid CompuServe could goose its consumer business.

Talks went on unofficially for months. CompuServe executives, including its CEO, Maurice Cox, came to Washington in the winter of 1991 and met with Kimsey at the Pisces Club. CNN's coverage of the Gulf War flashed on TV screens in the background. "You've gone about as far as you can go," the CompuServe executives noted. "We can take over from here."

Kimsey did not disagree. It had been an exhausting trek that he had never meant to stay with this long. "Why not," he thought, "just give up the struggle and give in to these guys?" Was Quantum ever going to be able to scare up another offer?

Case and others on the staff had an opposite opinion. Quantum was about to launch a version of America Online for PC platforms, and the Apple service was building nicely.

"We had a high degree of confidence, but no proof it would work," recalled Case, who told Kimsey he would not stay if Quantum was sold to CompuServe.

With the support of many of the investors, Kimsey accepted Bloch's invitation to come to Florida, where the company was holding a board meeting and where a more serious discussion of options could be conducted.

CompuServe's offer was $50 million. Executives considered the figure generous, considering Quantum's rocky history and dicey future. It was also a huge valuation over the Source, so if the Quantum people turned it down, they were just too dumb to see a good deal.

Kimsey was disappointed with the figure; he very much wanted out—a desire that would surface with each new bid for the company. If CompuServe had offered even $60 million, he knew, Quantum would have been sold. But at $50 million, the investors would get back little of the money they had sunk in already.

Also, the young staff—led by Case—did not want to sell and were not likely to remain in the event of a CompuServe takeover. Losing them might scotch the deal.

"We stayed open for business this long," shrugged Kimsey in disappointment. "So, why not just go a little further?"

plan w (all street)

When the CompuServe deal did not happen, Quantum clearly needed a little bit of help to get anywhere.

It came first, in the summer of 1991, from the Chicago-based Tribune Company, which had been scouting around for any deals it could make in the emerging new media market. The company's head, Charles Brumbach, had used a number of the early online services, including the Source, CompuServe, and Prodigy.

He had had problems with all of them—Prodigy, for example, was too clunky—but Brumbach knew that the medium was promising and that the Tribune Company needed to add technological capabilities to its business. The company had dabbled in the trendy CD-ROM market—it bought the digital version of Compton's Encyclopedia—but it was only a bridge to more strategic investments. The potential growth of online services presented a challenge to all newspaper interests. If information became widely distributed electronically, the underpinnings of the traditional media business might face a difficult challenge.

Unless a media company owned a piece of it, that is. Brumbach sent out executives in search of companies that could help to design an online service for the flagship *Chicago Tribune*. They came back—not surprisingly—with the name of Quantum.

For the Tribune, the small business was perfect—it was independent, not linked with other major companies, young and innovative and in need of cash. For Quantum, the investment with the Tribune provided a potential windfall. With Tribune Company publications located all over the country, AOL could use the trove of content and marketing might they represented to create locally based online services. Such a deal could be just the springboard AOL needed.

Brumbach wanted to get a look at the Quantum team, so he invited Case and Kimsey to a Canadian fishing camp owned by the Tribune. As they angled, Case spun his nonstop spiel about his visions of the emerging market for interactive services—his grand dreams of the huge force the tiny Quantum would become.

Brumbach was hooked. In August, Quantum agreed to produce local versions of AOL for the Tribune Company. In September, the Tribune Company invested $5 million for a nine percent stake of 255,964 shares.

The Tribune deal marked a major shift for Quantum on the definitive road to consolidating all its online services under the AOL banner. When Quantum managers went to industry conferences, they began noticing that few people knew them until they mentioned that they were also AOL.

As the AOL service grew, the corporate name that now meant nothing disappeared. In October, Quantum officially became America Online Inc. It was now a brand, even if the brand recognition was low. At the time, AOL still had under 150,000 users, revenues of about $20 million and only a modest profit. And, despite Prodigy and CompuServe, a lot of people did not understand what the company did.

Could that be remedied, perhaps, by going public?

This move by AOL had three major objectives: (1) fresh capital for taking the technological steps that would build the infrastructure and create a major corporation; (2) the publicity that such an offering brings, including more opportunities to partner with businesses more likely to work with publicly traded companies; and (3) a way to finally cash out its private investors. As a public company, AOL could move away from its start-up roots and join the larger world of commerce.

But, as difficult as it is to imagine, as late as 1992, there was no commercial Internet, no World Wide Web; little was known about the "new media" market. And few businesspeople—especially in investment houses—believed that consumer networking was anything more than a fad, much like CB radios.

It came as no surprise that AOL had trouble attracting firms to take the company public. When first approached, for example, Baltimore-based Alex. Brown & Sons Inc.—which eventually became AOL's lead investment banker—took a pass.

Later, along with San Francisco's Robertson, Stephens & Co., Alex. Brown agreed to take on the small company and prepared an offering to raise $10 million for the company and $11 million for selling shareholders. As is typical in all public offerings, investors would be able to cash out if they chose to do so.

AOL prepared a video to take on its road show. Prominent supporters of the service were featured—including, somewhat ironically, Apple's John Sculley. With the video in hand and their narrative about an independent company that was the only "pure" player in online services, Kimsey and Case criss-crossed the country to sell AOL to a new passel of investors.

But, before they went, the board decided that the gray-haired and more statesmanlike Kimsey made a better-looking chief executive officer, a title that the too-baby-faced Case had also acquired in late 1991. The impetus came from others on the board, but Kimsey got the task of telling Case—during lunch at a restaurant called Clyde's, near the AOL office.

Kimsey recalls that, as he delivered the bad news, "Steve had an Elmer Fudd expression on his face. He could have quit over it, but he handled it perfectly."

Case was incredibly calm, in spite of the ego-slapping snub. He was certainly upset by the move; he had been running the company on a day-to-day basis. But the public offering was more important, so he decided to keep quiet. The troops under him—all of whom had become intensely loyal to their quiet young leader—were devastated that the company's board could treat him that way. "If they could do that to him," said Jean Villanueva, "what could they do to us?"

In time, the successful public offering made most of the 116 employees very rich. Case's own shares were worth more than $2 million on the day of the offering. That was a switch; early AOL employees, such as Seriff, still had their worthless CVC shares in their possession and few had thought that similar "founders'" shares in Quantum, given to them in 1985, would ever have any value.

Despite the uncertainty, on March 19, 1992, AOL went public on NASDAQ, offering two million shares for $11.50 each. In Vienna, Case stood on a chair in the cafeteria at 8619 Westwood Center Drive and thanked all the employees for their fortitude through the years of ceaseless turmoil. Champagne corks popped all over the room. "This a great day," said the normally taciturn Case. "One of many to come, I hope."

At one of the more formal celebrative dinners, at Washington's swank River Club, Kimsey was ecstatic. He had joked many years before, with Commodore's Clive Smith and many others—even as he trudged along looking for money to keep the company alive—that he couldn't quite understand why people would want to spend their Saturday nights online in front of a computer unless they had failed social lives.

"C'mon," the former bar owner would tease the tech-obsessed all around him. "Do you think it's all bullshit?"

Luckily for Kimsey, Wall Street didn't. On the day of the public offering, he sold some of his shares for $243,708 and was holding other shares valued at $3.2 million. He'd be worth many dozens of times that amount within a few years.

Jim Kimsey had found the pony after all.

► chapter.four

david versus goliaths

new kid on the block

Walt Mossberg, a former Pentagon reporter, squeezed off a definitive warning shot in the very first "Personal Technology" column that appeared in *The Wall Street Journal* in October 1991.

"Personal computers are just too hard to use, and it isn't your fault," began Mossberg. He envisioned the column as a journalistic lifeline to average people who were flummoxed by the complexities of ever-changing technologies that were becoming indispensable to their lives.

And who was to blame? Naturally, the techno-elites—also called the "digerati"—who ran the computer industry and were not thinking nearly enough about their terminally confused customers. That idea had become a kind of personal jihad for the avuncular Mossberg, who railed weekly against perplexing software, glitchy hardware, and any kind of convoluted and costly technology that required an advanced degree in computer science to operate.

If computers were supposedly designed to make our lives easier, posed Mossberg, why was there so much stuff out there that caused nothing but frustration?

There were indeed a lot of tech targets to aim at. But Mossberg was soon inundated by calls from technology company flacks—all of whom were willing to put their products in the cross-hairs to get a little bit of ink in his increasingly influential take on the state of the industry.

One of the many who contacted him soon after the column debuted was Jean Villanueva of AOL, which had just gone public and happened to be located in the northern Virginia suburbs, not far from the *Journal*'s downtown Washington bureau where Mossberg was based. Even though AOL was now a public company and its executives had gotten rich in the public offering, it was hardly well-known, still very small, and underfunded. And, there was always the question of whether it would survive, given that its competitors included the massive CompuServe and Prodigy.

"You should come out," urged Villanueva, who was running AOL's marketing and public relations and was trying to get the company some attention. "I think you'll be amazed at what we're doing here."

Mossberg had, in fact, been aware of AOL for a while, having used the AppleLink Personal Edition service designed for Apple and later introduced as America Online for the Macintosh. He liked it a lot, especially because the attractive and simple graphical user interface meshed so well with the computer. And upcoming AOL software for Microsoft's newest version of its Windows operating system looked promising.

But with only a couple hundred thousand users, AOL was still a niche product, so Mossberg was not expecting much as he made his way west on Virginia's Route 66 to meet with the AOL executives. In all likelihood, AOL would prove to be just another small technology company.

That notion was reinforced when Mossberg saw the firm's modest and nondescript digs: a dull-looking brick building behind a car dealership, up the road from a suburban mall. This seemed about as far as one could get from the revolution in Silicon Valley.

The office of the man in charge—Steve Case—was located only ten feet from the drab little lobby. Through the glass, you could actually see him tapping away on a computer. "It probably made a favorable impression, because it said he was not egotistical," said

Mossberg. "But it also said this was no major corporation that was going to blow anyone away."

Instead, within minutes, the columnist found himself listening to Case—who, in a baggy Hawaiian shirt, looked more like a college student than an executive. Case immediately told the incredulous Mossberg that AOL would soon be the biggest online service in the world and, later, would become a huge multimedia empire.

While AOL was small enough in those days that a visit from a reporter from *The Wall Street Journal* was a pretty big deal, Case kept up his cocky banter with Mossberg, played on a Macintosh on his desk, and detailed his ambitious plans to beat competitors who had millions of users. Unlike the ad-laden and shopping-oriented Prodigy, AOL would focus on chat and community. Unlike the information-rich but staid CompuServe, AOL would be simple and sexy-looking.

"Without blinking, he said he was going to blow away all the other competitors," said Mossberg. "He was almost morally certain."

Mossberg only shook his head and laughed at the audaciousness of Case's plans for AOL. It was an interesting little company, to be sure, with much more of a free-wheeling feel than the government-oriented companies he had encountered in northern Virginia's sprawling suburbs. And it was definitely much more entrepreneurial than CompuServe and Prodigy. AOL was most certainly a scrapper, thought Mossberg, but he wasn't sure that it was equipped to blow away anything more than its funding.

But over the next several months, Mossberg began to explore the service in depth as he prepared a pair of columns on the nascent consumer online industry. In one, he planned to compare the text-based services like CompuServe and his own company's Dow Jones News/Retrieval service; in another, he would compare the graphically oriented services, Prodigy and AOL.

As he researched the columns, testing each service in depth, he began to replay his conversation with Case. Though it had only 200,000 members compared to the 1.75 million claimed by Prodigy, AOL was in the first rough stages of creating just what Mossberg had been preaching about: a simple and lively service with an easy-to-use point-and-click interface anyone's grand-mother could install on personal computers. With an unfussy clarity in price and design, snazzy graphics, a focus on community and communication, a nimble entrepreneurial company culture that could change quickly and executives who ate, slept, and breathed the online business, Mossberg thought Case could pos-sibly be on the right path.

And on October 8, 1992, Mossberg said so in no uncertain terms:

"At present, I regard Prodigy as seriously flawed," wrote Mossberg, describing the joint venture by IBM and Sears as clunky and confusing. "In contrast, I see America Online as the sophisticated wave of the future among such services."

Prodigy executives, furious at the snub, complained to Moss-berg's bosses at the *Journal*. AOL was thrilled, of course. This vali-dation would turn out to be the first critical push of an upward climb.

And Mossberg wasn't the only one who was paying attention to the small company. Even though it had barely begun to define itself or figure out a way to catch up to its competitors, across the coun-try, a pair of billionaires—each with a lot of money to spend and new worlds to conquer—would soon notice AOL too.

a - p a u l e d

Paul G. Allen had been interested in AOL from the very beginning.

The shy mogul—cofounder of Microsoft Corporation, who had long dwelled in the shadow of his better-known partner and longtime friend Bill Gates—was eagerly looking for breakthrough technology companies in which he could invest his vast wealth.

With Gates, he had founded the software giant in the Seattle area in 1975. He left the company in 1983 when he was diagnosed as terminally ill with Hodgkin's disease. The disease went into re-mission, and the secretive Allen began to use his billions of dollars to make a crazy quilt of investments in the interactive arena.

Allen—a large man with an unruly, bushy beard—was one of the richest men in America. He fancied himself as a new-media mogul, a Johnny Appleseed of the emerging technologies who could make a series of critical strategic investments that would jump-start the industry. His main interest as the 1990s dawned was to find ways to use computers to create a new communications paradigm.

"When the microprocessor was first invented, no one called the computer a communications device," said Bill Savoy, who served as Allen's financial right hand in his investment company. "But at the start of the 1990s, Paul saw communications via computers as a long-term opportunity that was about to be realized, and he wanted to have investments all over the map in the area."

A longtime online dabbler, Allen had noticed AOL in the late 1980s. Later, he discussed its prospects with David Liddle, who had headed up a group at the Xerox Palo Alto Research Center and now headed Allen's $100 million think tank, Interval Research Corporation. Interval had been conducting early research into on-line usage, and—coincidentally—Liddle's wife, Ruthann Quindlen, had worked on the AOL account at Alex. Brown, which had taken AOL public in 1992. Intrigued, Allen grabbed a block of 50,000 shares at AOL's initial offering.

To him, an investment in a small and feisty company like AOL seemed natural. It had all the elements he was looking for—it was independent, small, on the cutting edge, and, most importantly, in need of money to get bigger. As subsidiaries of much larger companies, CompuServe and Prodigy were not the kind of "pure" online player that AOL represented. AOL seemed to be at the start of a growth curve that could make it a major company, and Allen wanted to get in on the ground floor of its development.

"Paul thought these guys were onto something," said Savoy. "It was the early stages of a hockey-stick kind of growth—it seemed as if they might be headed upward fast." Allen thought he could shoot them skyward even faster. He was especially intrigued with AOL's focus on community and chat, and was eager to help it port its proprietary online service to the wider world. His idea: Take AOL's service and begin to render it in a more "open" architecture.

Allen was convinced that the future of computers and of the interactive industry lay in rapid development of "broadband" technologies. High-bandwidth data distribution would allow an enormous stream of multimedia offerings to flow to consumers in a way that telephone-anchored online services could not. Access to the worldwide network of computers now known as the Internet had not yet taken place, and the industry's focus was on the best way to develop interactive television—a marriage of computer technology with one of the most important consumer devices ever invented.

To take advantage of the coming communications revolution, Allen began to spend money. In 1992, he had founded, in the Seattle area, a company called Starwave Corporation, to create innovative interactive content in several forms. He also owned a company called Asymetrix Corporation, which made multimedia software tools. Allen envisioned a synergistic melding of all these companies. Combining their efforts with AOL's consumer distribution would give birth to a new communications medium on the scale of television.

"We wanted to be a big shareholder, so we could get the company to see the sea change that was about to take place, and take advantage of it," said Savoy. "We said we were committed to spending a lot of money on taking AOL to the top."

AOL was thrilled with Allen's attentions at first, so when Savoy started buying more stock over the end of 1992 and early 1993, the company was not alarmed. The attention of a high-profile investor was not necessarily a bad thing—in fact, it attracted others who might not have looked twice, and it provided more credibility. The quirky Allen was known to be reclusive in his personal life, but most participants in the nascent interactive area knew exactly who he was and what his enormous pool of cash could do for them. "At first, I saw him as a potentially important ally, and I thought there might be some structure where he could vault the company to the next level," said Case. "If I had to make a list of investors I would have loved to have at the time, Paul Allen would have had to be right near the top."

But AOL's executives did not want any one investor to own too much of the company. Among other reasons, they wanted freedom to do deals with a wide range of businesses without conflicts of interest. The company had no problem, however, with someone's holding a 5 percent or 10 percent stake. If Allen proved to be an investor on a par with the Tribune Company, he might prove a great boon for AOL. To sound Allen out, Case had dinner with him at PC Forum in the early spring. They discussed the future of the fledgling medium.

Later, Allen and Savoy traveled to Vienna to meet with AOL's executives and explore Allen's ideas about using AOL to develop the broadband offering he wanted to create. In a small conference room, Allen and Savoy outlined their vision of an online service, which would entail a dramatic change in AOL's route.

"They thought that we were going in the wrong direction and claimed we were too wedded to narrowband communications delivery over the telephone, when broadband was the bridge to the future," said AOL board member Bill Melton, who was brought in to meet with Allen's group because of his technology background. "The pitch to AOL was simple: you have large residential usage at low bandwidth, and maybe I can bring high bandwidth to you and we can own the future together."

For AOL, however, the future was now. It had to use existing technologies to grab as much market share as possible from CompuServe and Prodigy, which were huge by comparison. AOL had just announced its compatibility with Microsoft's latest version of its Windows operating system, and company officials expected an increase in subscriptions as the linkage became known. AOL had also recently tried the tactic of cutting prices to spur users to leave other services.

To further solidify the business, Case hoped to license the AOL technology to be the backbone for as many services as possible. He would help rivals to get into the business, as long as AOL controlled the software. Case had even struck a deal, in December 1992, to license operating software for its planned service to its old partner Apple, which had bought warrants in AOL for a stake of almost 9 percent.

Allen's dream of a broadband "wired world" wasn't a bad idea, thought Case, but it was still too far off and it risked missing the many opportunities that lay before AOL now. Allen—dubbed "Clueless in Seattle" by some detractors, for what they considered a haphazard style of investing—was dreaming of a far-off time; his billions of dollars afforded him that luxury. Case felt that AOL's efforts needed to focus on creating a solid consumer brand name that would dominate his competitors. The industry still had not reached the mainstream. Reveries about things to come were unaffordable.

AOL officials were also worried about Allen's close relationship with Microsoft. Although retired from the company, he was still its second biggest stockholder after Gates, and he served on the board. Everyone knew Microsoft was eyeing the online business; a purchase of AOL would allow Microsoft a quick leap into the consumer online industry. Was Allen a stalking horse from Seattle?

As part of its overall strategy—born of the failure with Atari, Commodore, and Apple—AOL wanted to be fully catholic in its alliances; AOL would be universally usable on any operating system that existed. Too close a relationship with Allen might cause problems and limit AOL's market.

"I told him it was impossible for us to consider any scenario if he was on the Microsoft board, because it was rife with conflict," said Case. "If we had said, 'Paul, we'd love you to buy us, but you must quit Microsoft,' I think he would have done it."

But Allen had no intention of leaving the Microsoft board. Talks continued all spring, without a resolution. Allen continued to be interested in having a major influence at AOL, but AOL wanted him to be only one of its many passive strategic investors.

Case had suggested a "standstill" agreement, ensuring that Allen would not increase his stake to more than 20 percent. Savoy refused. The Allen group was getting annoyed at Case's attempts to slow them down in bringing AOL into the tight configuration of other Allen companies.

"We wanted AOL to play, and we were perplexed as to why we were not welcomed with open arms," said Savoy. "Paul considered it personally rude to him—Steve Case was paying lip service to our ideas and then doing nothing—so we just thought, 'Let's just go and buy the company.'"

Which is just what Savoy—then only 28 years old—began to do with Allen's money. Soon, the Allen stake rose to 10 percent, then 12 percent, and then 13.5 percent.

Case was not immediately aware of Allen's pique. He spoke frequently with Savoy, who continued to assure him that Allen was only interested in AOL as an investment and was not trying to take over. Case persuaded the AOL board not to put in a "poison pill" takeover defense at 15 percent—a move that would have flooded the market with new shares and made it prohibitively expensive for Allen to take over the company. Case worried that such a move would offend Allen.

"It seems naive now, because I was arguing with the board not to build a wall, to let him in the whole time," said Case. "But every time I got a fax listing new holdings, it was clear to me that what they were saying and what they were doing were not in lockstep."

As Allen's stake began to rise quickly in mid-April, Case knew the slow dance was over. "It suddenly took on the tone of the Cuban Missile Crisis, and it was clear we had to be mobilized for anything," said Case. "As he bought more, I had to presume that they were out to acquire the company in a hostile fashion."

Case felt duped by Allen, though he blamed Savoy, whom he began to distrust and even to dislike. "I think I was misled and it was embarrassing," said Case. "I argued against a containment strategy and it blew up in my face. I was frustrated by that."

Savoy thought Case was being willfully naïve. "He knew what we were doing and tried to pacify us rather than engage in serious discussions," he said. "Case had no one to blame for our actions than himself."

With Savoy buying up as much of AOL as he could, AOL held a board meeting, in the late afternoon of Friday, April 22, to institute a shareholder-rights plan. The board quickly decided to adopt a protective plan: a 20 percent holding threshold would be the trigger for the issuance of rights. At the same meeting, the board elected Case to the job of chief executive officer, finally giving back the title that had been taken away from him the year before.

Those moves, reasoned the AOL board members, would show Allen that AOL wanted to stay independent and that further stock purchases were futile. "I thought of Allen as a sociopath—he was insecure and had a lot of money, which was a dangerous combination," said AOL chairman Kimsey. "He was going to Pac Man us and we had just been sitting there with a big red target on our butts. So we stopped him."

Or so they thought.

Kimsey and Frank Caufield—old partying buddies—took off for a raucous weekend trip to a music festival in New Orleans, unaware that Savoy had blown past the 20 percent mark before AOL had put its plan into place. The Allen stake was raised to 1.45 million shares and was now headed for the 25 percent mark—an overwhelming ownership stake that would have made it nearly impossible for AOL to say no to Allen's plans.

The situation was dire, but AOL had a little luck on its side. The markets were closed for the weekend, making it harder for Savoy to get his hands on outstanding AOL shares that could allow him to reach 25 percent or higher before AOL could stop him.

But an emergency meeting would have to be called immediately, and Kimsey—who was needed to preside as AOL board chairman—was hard to track down in New Orleans. When he was finally found on Saturday morning, on the city's fairgrounds, and told that Allen had broken the pill, Kimsey tried to get cellular phones on which to hold a telephonic board meeting to set a new pill in place at an unprecedented 25 percent.

But the cell phones did not work. Kimsey and Caufield began driving frantically around the poor and largely African-American neighborhood, looking for a pay phone to use to conduct the meeting. They soon found a pair of phones outside a liquor store and commandeered both of them. "There was a line of Black people . . . behind us, saying, 'I've got to call my mother and here are these two White boys talking about money,'" recounted Kimsey. "Frank was saying only, 'Yes . . . yea . . . nay,' so people were trying to figure out what the hell we were doing."

This time, the emergency efforts worked. The board, citing the shares purchased by Paul Allen during the previous day, voted to redeem rights that had been issued the day before and to raise the threshold to 25 percent. Now, if Allen acquired more than 25 percent of the company, AOL would be allowed to issue stock that would make it prohibitively expensive for Allen to take over the company.

It was a close call. Within hours of the pill placement, Savoy announced that he had managed to acquire just over 25 percent of the company. Because he got there a bit later than AOL's countermeasure and did not want to trigger the poison pill, Savoy was then forced to sell down to just below 25 percent (24.9 percent). That sale triggered a short-profit rule of the SEC, and Allen's investment group was forced to pay AOL $115,000, to avoid violating the rules of the poison–pill defense.

It was a minor victory because the word was now out that AOL and Allen were at odds. Although Savoy told *The Wall Street Journal* the following week that Allen had no plans to seek a seat on AOL's board and called the huge stock purchase only a "market opportunity," a potentially acrimonious battle was clearly brewing between AOL and its biggest shareholder.

And, no surprise, a week later, in a filing on April 30, Allen publicly stated his intentions to the SEC, declaring that he might seek to "acquire AOL in a tender offer, asset acquisition, merger or other business combination."

It was, said Savoy, "about time that AOL paid attention to us." Irked that AOL would not give Allen a copy of the shareholder-rights plan, Savoy began to prepare for a hostile takeover scenario, a rare event in the high–technology industry.

The AOL board was also livid. The fracas put the company into play and would surely attract others to the table. What should they do now? "If Paul Allen didn't have $3 billion," said an angry Kimsey to the other board members, in a meeting in early May to discuss the crisis, "you wouldn't cross the street to say hello to him."

"Well, he *does* have $3 billion," countered Alexander M. Haig Jr., the hard–charging retired general who had served as Secretary of State in the Reagan Administration and as Nixon's chief of staff. Haig had come to the AOL board in 1989 through his affiliation with Commodore.

"So I think," continued the gravelly-voiced Haig, "we had better cross the street."

The board decided that Case—accompanied by Kimsey and AOL's outside counsel, Ken Novack, of Boston-based Mintz, Levin, Cohn, Ferris and Popeo—should travel to the Pacific Northwest to face Allen in person and perhaps defuse the situation. Also along was a rising investment banking star, Steve Rattner of Lazard Freres & Company, whom Case had called in when the relationship with Allen had changed.

The meeting was set for the morning of Tuesday, May 11, at the Bellevue office of Allen's lawyer, Allen Israel, of Foster, Pepper & Shefelman. Allen's investment bankers from Bear Stearns & Company Inc., were also asked to attend. With tensions running high, Case had asked that Savoy not be present in the meeting room. It was unusual for Case to get this angry, but he felt that Savoy, by not being forthright with him about Allen's plans, had made a difficult situation worse.

To tamp down the obvious tensions, Allen and Savoy agreed to Case's unusual request. Savoy stayed in a nearby office at the law firm and got updates of the meeting in progress from an associate who shuttled back and forth.

Though they began by discussing possible joint development ventures in the multimedia arena, an underlying question lurked beneath the surface: Would a war break out between them?

Allen's advisers were perplexed as to why this small company was treating their boss like a pariah and did not want their help. Didn't AOL see that big things were coming down the pike and it needed all the assistance it could get? Allen was personally chagrined: who did these guys from this tiny company think they were, telling him to buzz off?

"This is America and I should be able to invest in AOL if I want to," said Allen, in one of his few utterances during the meeting. "What is wrong with that?"

But the message AOL wanted to deliver that day was clear—it was not going to enter into any business relationship with a gun to its head. There would be no board seat, no change of strategic direction, no giving up independence to be part of Allen's group of companies.

"He just did not understand that we didn't want him," recalled Novack. "We would not give him anything, even if he did own a lot of the company, because we simply did not want to follow his particular vision."

In other words: Paul, go away!

out of the frying pan

While the AOL delegation talked with Allen, they were unable to put aside their awareness of an afternoon meeting that would take place only a dozen miles away. Bill Gates, Paul Allen's former partner and close friend—and, more importantly, the master of Microsoft—was scheduled to talk to them.

The appointment had been put together by an aggressive, 30-year-old Microsoft executive named Russell Siegelman. In 1992, Siegelman—who had worked on several high-profile projects within Microsoft, including Windows for Workgroups—had been casting about for another challenge at the company.

"I was kind of like a free agent and, near the end of the Windows for Workgroups stage, people suggested that I try for a technical adviser job to Gates that was open," said Siegelman. "Since I knew him, they suggested I tell Bill what I wanted to do."

Instead, Gates proposed another idea for his restless employee.

"I've been thinking about online services. It's a big thing. It's happening," said Gates to Siegelman. "What should we do about it?"

Gates said he wanted Siegelman to go and find out what was available; a purchase of an online company would be the easiest path. Over the next six months, Siegelman scoured the online world. His first stop, naturally, was at CompuServe. Microsoft had a long-standing relationship with the online service through its extensive series of Microsoft-oriented bulletin boards and consumer help areas.

"I met the chief financial officer of CompuServe and asked, 'Would you want to sell? Spin off?,'" said Siegelman. "But they did not seem interested." There were other complications too, including the worry that CompuServe's owner—H&R Block—would want to continue to share a stake in the company.

Next, Siegelman went to look at Prodigy. But because of its ownership by IBM and his perception that the technology did not mesh well with Microsoft's, Siegelman quickly scratched it off his list. "They had lost so much money, and had tons of these mainframes that were not what we were interested in, that it seemed not for us at all," said Siegelman. "Even though they claimed that they had millions of members, it seemed as if it might already be a mess that we did not want to even deal with."

Soon enough, he honed in on AOL and traveled to northern Virginia to meet with Audrey Weil, who was AOL's vice president of corporate development. Weil, a soft-spoken woman who had come to AOL in 1988 from marketing and product management jobs at Ralston Purina, had been charged by Case to talk with Microsoft's reps. Case's message was firm—there had to be a pretty good reason if AOL and Microsoft were to consider marrying.

For its part, Microsoft had a lot of reasons. From the start, Siegelman and Greg Maffei—a consultant who would soon join Microsoft and would later become its powerful, deal-making financial executive—liked what they saw.

The pair didn't raise the possibility of a purchase at the time, but AOL seemed perfect as a Microsoft acquisition if it was available. First, it was full of bright and aggressive people who would mix well Microsoft's go-go culture. Second, it was independent of any major corporate owner that might muck up the deal, and small enough that integration of its operations would be easy and smooth. Third, it could put Microsoft ahead quickly in the online arena, saving it several years of work and expense to create its own service from scratch.

"They were already Windows-centric and seemed to understand best where this was all going," said Siegelman. "It seemed a good fit and there was real interest on our part to buy the company."

And Steve Case, thought Siegelman and Maffei, would make a great Microsoft executive.

Allen's involvement complicated matters for Microsoft. Gates, said both Siegelman and Maffei, was loath to cross his old business partner and friend. "It's Paul's thing, so maybe we should back off," said Gates.

"Paul's involvement drove us crazy since it made AOL paranoid and therefore more resistant that there was some deal between Allen and Gates to divvy up the company," said Maffei. "Without him there, I think we might have been able to do the deal."

Perhaps the proposal might be finessed, they thought, if Gates met with AOL executives while they were in town to talk with Allen in May. Gates knew of AOL's reluctance to be part of Allen's "wired world" dreams. A Microsoft bid might solve the problems for everyone.

There would be no specific agenda. The session would be exploratory, to see where each side was coming from and to get a better idea of where some alternatives could lead. An afternoon meeting was scheduled at Microsoft's lush "campus" in the Seattle suburb of Redmond, just east of the city. Soon after the AOL group was ushered into a windowless conference room near his office, Gates arrived dressed in a T-shirt and casual slacks. He was wearing his trademark thick glasses, and his unruly bangs flopped over his forehead.

From the start, the meeting did not go well.

The first statement the AOL group remembers Gates making was an apparent threat from one of the world's richest men: "I can buy 20 percent of you or I can buy all of you. Or I can go into this business myself and bury you."

This group had been battered for weeks by another mogul closely linked to Microsoft, so the effect was strong. *Uh-oh,* thought Rattner, who had been in enough deal meetings to know that AOL perhaps had a problem. *He's got to be kidding,* thought Kimsey, who had been in enough battles to be worried.

Case—who did not want to give any message that AOL was eager to be taken over, despite the presence of his chairman and a high-powered investment banker—blurted out quickly, "The company's not for sale."

The remark threw Gates, said Siegelman, because Gates was talking philosophically, reviewing the variety of options in front of Microsoft in the online arena, and not delivering an ultimatum that he planned to carry out or else.

"Gates wasn't obnoxious or combative," insisted Siegelman. "He didn't mean, 'I'm gonna crush you.' He meant that he was interested in this area and wanted to find the right way to leverage the technology for Microsoft and figure out the best direction to go in."

It was a point lost, considering Microsoft's growing reputation for highly aggressive business tactics, and the tone was immediately set for what Siegelman would later characterize as "not a very juicy conversation."

Instead, Case launched into his notion of the best relationship for the two companies—AOL could build and manage a private-label service for Microsoft. AOL's aim was to persuade Gates to let AOL run an online service for Microsoft, as it was doing for Apple, so that it would profit even if another competitor entered the market. The agenda was simple: to find a way to work with Microsoft, without becoming eaten by them.

"Their view, I think, was that we were serious and that they would rather co-opt us than compete with us," said Siegelman. "They wanted to glue themselves to us, so they could see what we were doing and perhaps delay us from starting anything interesting."

Actually, that was precisely the main fear of Case and the rest of AOL's management: that Microsoft was talking to AOL only to learn as much as it could about the online market. Was this a fishing expedition before Microsoft began an all-out assault on the online world? Was it dangerous to be this close to the company that was viewed with such fear by much of the technology industry and within AOL?

"We didn't trust Microsoft's motives, because we knew they could emerge as a major competitor," said Case. "At one point in the meeting, Siegelman proposed a 50–50 joint venture, but from our point of view, it was 'OK, we'll help build it, teach you all about it, then just when it gets interesting, you'll shoot us.'"

The group went round and round for more than an hour without coming to any conclusion about the best path for future discussions. As the meeting with Gates ended, Siegelman suggested the groups think about more concrete proposals that would benefit them both. "We're interesting, you're interesting," he said to the AOL group. "Let's try to find a way to work together."

Or not, thought Case, who was thrown by Gates' earlier "bury you" declaration. And when Gates later noted that success in the online business was simply a "software problem" that needed to be solved, the suggestion shocked Case. If Microsoft's vision of the online world's future was only about bits and bytes, there was little to talk about.

yea or nay

AOL was now at a critical inflection point. A question had been stirred up by Allen's interest and made unmistakable by the fact that AOL would be facing Microsoft either across a bargaining table or across the online battlefield: Would AOL remain independent and take on all comers or would it ultimately have to sell out before it got too competitive? Case's suggestion to create an online service for Microsoft was only a tactic to postpone the inevitability of a choice.

AOL had managed to avoid the coils of CompuServe many years before by teaming up with the Tribune Company and later going public. It was again time to wonder exactly how big it could hope to get without help. Even if the online industry was poised for takeoff, AOL was really small, had little money, and was still stuck in third place.

Both Allen and Gates were clearly interested in buying or at least controlling AOL. Others—big multimedia companies and telephone behemoths—would surely be interested too. Two of the richest men in the world had turned their sights to AOL and said, "I want your market." Gates and Allen were offering two different graceful exits that no one would criticize AOL for taking.

Was it time for a sanity check?

When the little group returned, the company—its employees and board members—began to engage in debate about what to do. Should they encourage potential buyers with word that the company was for sale, or should they resist? It was another defining moment for a company that seemed to have them on a monthly basis.

The debate was made urgent when Siegelman called Weil the following Friday. As she tried to widen the scope of the talks, Siegelman made Microsoft's position clear. "We want to buy you in some form," said Siegelman. "Otherwise, we are wasting our time." The price that Microsoft would likely pay for AOL—whose stock was hovering in the mid-20s—would be around $40 a share. If Microsoft bought the company whole, the selling price would be around $268 million—or more, if there was a premium.

This was the real thing: Bill Gates was determined to enter the business one way or another, and AOL needed to decide whether to enter into discussions with him or go it alone. It was a stark choice because AOL had only 250,000 subscribers, and pushing past CompuServe and Prodigy was going to take all the resources that the company could muster. Even with strong buzz about the potential for AOL, growth remained sluggish and there was no guarantee that the company could prevail.

And yet, wasn't it remarkable that the big boys wanted to come into the market? If they thought the potential for the company was so great, that it could be worth billions of dollars some day, should AOL sell itself right when it seemed as if the whole industry was just starting to take off? If so, $40 a share was cheap—quite a tiny price to pay for a piece of the future.

Those were the lines drawn clearly for AOL in June 1993, when its board gathered to figure out what to do, in consultation with its investment bankers, Lazard Freres and Alex. Brown. The situation was made more difficult by the fact that no official offer was on the table—only an oral expression of interest by Siegelman and some signals delivered through other sources at Microsoft. The next move was AOL's, and the board was split into two factions: those who wanted to go ahead with discussions with Microsoft—led by AOL chairman Jim Kimsey—and the group that included Case and many employees, who did not want to encourage Gates that the company was for sale.

The meeting began with a presentation by AOL's investment bankers on what the company was worth. Their outlook was optimistic. The company was likely to be worth much more than the $40 to $50 a share that Microsoft might be willing to pay now. But, said the bankers, if the per-share price got near $60 or above, for a total of about $402 million, it might be a good bet to sell.

After the presentation was over, the discussions began. Kimsey was firm from the get-go—he had long thought AOL should ultimately be sold, an attitude that had not endeared him to many at the company. "We never knew when the bubble was going to burst and I thought we had to consider what's the best thing for the stockholders," he said. "This was a good end game."

He was joined firmly in this camp by Kleiner's Frank Caufield and by Al Haig, both of whom doubted AOL could best Compu-Serve and Prodigy, let alone Microsoft. "We could get vaporized," said Haig. It was a strong argument. Few of those present doubted the marketing heft that a company like Microsoft could summon at will.

On the other hand, many large companies had already tried to make it in the online world and had fallen by the wayside. Who was to say that Microsoft would succeed any better than the major newspapers and telecommunications companies that had already failed? The upshot of the anti-sell contingent was: Maybe AOL could actually win.

Case was a great admirer of cable titan John Malone of Tele-Communications Inc., and hoped to make AOL equally large and powerful. But he also knew he had to be careful in promoting this perspective. Some powerful board members favored beginning serious negotiations with Microsoft. Though he had been running the company from an operational standpoint, Kimsey still held the power in the boardroom. Case, in fact, had only joined the board in September 1992.

"Steve was not in a position to stand up to Jim and say, 'Absolutely not,' although that is what I think he felt," said board member Bill Melton. "I remember that he was careful to present both sides to the board, just in case it went either way."

Case felt that an evenhanded approach was the best tack, given that so many on the board wanted to talk about a sale. If he opposed the sale too strongly and openly, the board would have only one question: was it an ego thing? If he appeared too recalcitrant to talk to Microsoft, it might be precisely what the board would decide to do.

"I recognized that if we sold, everyone would make a bunch of money and we could all just go off," said Case. "It wasn't without its possibilities. I could see that. At the time, we were a distant third to Prodigy and CompuServe, so the question was: did we want to be an also-ran?"

Inside his head, though, Case was certain that if the board voted to talk about selling the company to Microsoft, or to any of the other big companies that would surely be interested, they would make a mistake that they would regret for the rest of their lives. AOL was not even into Act I yet, thought Case.

That point was most strongly underscored by board member Doug Peabody, who thought Case was being too ambivalent. "Do we want to be a footnote on Bill Gates's resume, or do we want to be the king of the online industry?" said Peabody. "We have constantly undervalued ourselves and we have gotten this far—now it's too late to turn back."

The point was well taken by those in the room who had struggled for years to keep AOL going. But it also emphasized the fact that the struggle had been costly so far and would continue that way in the even scarier future.

Frank Caufield was of this mindset. He worried about the great challenges going forward, and he recognized that an attractive offer by Microsoft—especially when valuable Microsoft stock was being tendered—would be hard for the board to ignore. "It was our fiduciary duty to look out for the best interests of the shareholders," he said. "And we were also worried what would happen to AOL shares after Gates and Allen had left the room."

Kimsey called for a vote—the first time the board had ever needed one. There had always been consensus. But now the choice was too stark.

Around the table, they spoke in order: Scott Smith of the Tribune Company voted to begin talks; Haig voted the same;

venture capitalist Steve Sherrill voted the same. This was bad for Case; only six votes were needed to begin discussions leading to a possible sale, and Kimsey was known to be pro-sale. That made four certain votes to begin talks.

But the slate was quickly evened out. Time Inc. executive Chris Meigher voted to stay independent and not talk to Microsoft. So did Case and Peabody and Melton. The vote was tied.

And it remained so when Commodore-installed board member Harry Copperman voted not to enter sale discussions, and Caufield voted to do so. The only vote left was Kimsey's friend Jim Andress, who had been on the board only since the fall of 1992. He had flown in on the Concorde from Paris to attend the meeting and was not expecting to be the director who would determine the fate of the company.

Andress, who ran an information services company called Information Resources Inc., had been a classmate of Kimsey at West Point and was not the most active board member. "He was kind of a gadfly and had a poor record of attendance—plus, we all thought of him as Jim's guy," said one anti-sale board member. "So we all thought there was no question that he would sell us out."

So did Kimsey, who thought he had won.

But Andress would surprise the entire room. "I just thought that if these really rich guys wanted to buy us," said Andress simply, "then we must be worth something."

And so it was done. AOL would not enter into any discussions with Microsoft or anyone else.

It was a bit of a moot point because, out in Redmond, Washington, plans were changing quickly. After the meeting with Case, it seemed that AOL was not going to sell itself for a price that Gates would even begin to entertain. It was time for Microsoft to act. While still talking to AOL about an acquisition, on May 11, Gates had officially approved a plan by Siegelman to create a new rival online service (code name: Marvel) that would be included in another project called Chicago—the newest version of its operating system, Windows 95.

"We're not buying AOL, CompuServe is not available, Prodigy we don't want," said Gates. "The bottom line is: we've got to get going."

the plains are covered with the bodies of pioneers

alone at last?

AOL
12-2-93
500 K CUSTOMERS
8,000 PEAK USERS
$67 ¾/SHARE
BEST OPERATIONS ANYWHERE

They had etched it sloppily in the newly poured concrete of the subfloor of the new computer room in Vienna as 1993 drew to a close. Below the inscription, the two dozen or so techies of AOL had scratched their initials. It was, said operations director Matt Korn—who had joined the company in March—a way of staking their claim.

"One day, we thought, someone would find it and would either say: one, 'I remember those guys, they burnt through a ton of venture capital and then went bankrupt,'" said Korn. "Or, two, 'Can you remember back when AOL was really small?'"

Neither Korn nor anyone else at AOL knew which way the future would go. After ridding itself of Allen and Microsoft in the summer of 1993, AOL had firmly put itself on a risky path. In the immediate present, the company was still stuck squarely in last place in the online industry, far from striking distance of the leaders, CompuServe and Prodigy. And in the not-too-distant future lay the real threat—the looming promise made by Gates that he'd be back.

AOL needed a bold strategy that would place it in a position of strength before Gates arrived. But because it was the smallest and least-endowed company, AOL could not win by just doing a good job. It would have to risk everything in an almost reckless, go-for-broke rush to win. Considering the later stumbles that came with the hyper-growth, and the hundreds of millions of dollars AOL would ultimately lay out for marketing and acquisition costs, "reckless, go-for-broke" is perhaps the most apt description for the course AOL chose.

The core of the business strategy was formed in the process of deciding what to do about Gates and Allen—in a way, it was inspired by them. A possibility of a sale was negated, so the company had to start thinking of the massive investments needed to build an industry that would have its true value only far in the future. Garnering a mass-market share had to become the holy grail. AOL would write its own "growth story," in the parlance of Wall Street, dedicating itself to a "March to a Million" subscribers and initiating a new thrust to gain the most market penetration possible in the shortest amount of time.

"It is a land grab," said Case to his executives, using a phrase that would become a mantra for AOL. "And it is never going to be cheaper or easier to own that territory."

To get to terra firma, AOL would employ a series of key strategies that ultimately set it apart from CompuServe, Prodigy and all others: a loose-limbed management—personified by Case, whose single-minded devotion to the medium set him apart; a relentless focus on communications and community—taking the best advantage of the growing popularity of Microsoft's Windows operating system, and employing a simple, easy-to-use interface; and, most importantly, an inspired but risky disk-marketing initiative—making AOL the best-known brand name in cyberspace.

Would it work? No one knew. But only a company that had the least to lose would be able to step up to the table and gamble it all. And that is precisely what AOL decided to do in 1993.

first but worst

CompuServe had always had a different scenario in mind—
slow and steady growth over time. The strategy worked well for
years. The service became the stalwart and commanding leader of
the industry and had a reputation for rock-solid reliability.

Such bedrock sensibility was embedded in the service's genes
from its beginnings in 1969 as the "Compu-Serv" network in
Columbus, Ohio. Then owned by the ILEX Corporation, it was
designed to run the internal computer networks of Golden
United Life Insurance Company, a subsidiary. It was thought that
if the idea proved successful, the service, which had only five employees, could be sold to other national companies that needed
the use of a time-sharing computer network and had not built one
of their own. By 1972, as the network expanded and added local
phone access, the company had hundreds of business accounts
across the country.

Business was good and lucrative. Most firms did not want the
complications of running their own networks and were willing to
pay large sums for computing time. After acquiring a similar time-
sharing company, Alpha Systems Inc., based in Dallas, in 1973, the
combined entity was spun off in 1975 to ILEX shareholders in a
stock deal that left it a publicly held business. Business grew
strongly in the mid-1970s; annual revenues rose to more than $16
million. After some image testing, the name of the company officially became CompuServe Inc. in 1977.

The business computing market was solid and steady, but companies were using the service only on weekdays, leaving a vast
amount of computing time underutilized at night and on weekends.
Why not use the excess capacity for something other than corporate
network services?

In 1979, CompuServe opened a consumer online service
called MicroNet—at the same time, coincidentally, that Bill Von
Meister was founding the Source. MicroNet was aimed at the
growing body of hobbyist computer users interested in trading
information and, because of its business orientation, its focus was

on financial and computer data. This information resided mostly in CompuServe's famed "forums"—interactive computer bulletin boards that grew to more than 1,000 special-interest sites packed full of information from its members and bolstered by periodic live conferences. It proved a good idea. Within a year, 28,000 people—mostly men between the ages of 30 and 49—were signed up for the proprietary service.

The varied offerings drew the attention of H&R Block—the giant tax-preparation company based in Kansas City, Missouri—which was looking to diversify. It bought CompuServe, in May 1980, for $523 million and allowed it to continue to run as an independent company. Block officials were attracted by the financial solidity of the network and felt that its appeal to consumers could be easily integrated into Block's national tax-preparation business. But, because the MicroNet name seemed too nerdy, Block redubbed it the CompuServe Information Service (CIS).

During the early 1980s, many features were added, including electronic mail, the first-ever online shopping service (the Electronic Mall), a groundbreaking chat service called CB Simulator, and news from a vast array of sources. CIS then quickly moved internationally. In a joint venture with Nissho Iwai and Fujitsu Ltd., it started a service called NIFTY-Serve in Japan. Later, another deal linked it with the Swiss company Radio-Schweiz to develop CompuServe in Europe.

By the end of the 1980s, CompuServe held a definitive lead in the fledgling consumer market, which had long been abandoned by the videotex experimenters. The company signed up its 500,000th member for the largely text-based service.

Most analysts agree that its early success was the result of a slow and steady rise to the top, born of and nurtured by a corporate culture characterized by stolid Midwestern deliberateness. The service aimed at mature and sophisticated users. Its motto told the story best: "The information service you won't outgrow."

CompuServe's conservatism was also in evidence in its ads, which presented the service as a productivity tool rather than a fun place to be. Trendy, losing products were pictured—an eight-track tape with the title "Greatest Hits of Disco"; an Edsel sedan; a Betamax tape—and the tag line was stern: "When picking a computer information service, CompuServe urges you to choose wisely."

Its conservative corporate attitude was pure H&R Block. The parent company was thrilled by revenues that grew at a robust 30 to 40 percent a year. When low-budget promotions produced such solid profits, Block had no interest in spending more to goose the business.

CompuServe chief executive and president Maurice Cox said as much, when quoted in a 1993 report on the company by Jupiter Communications Company, a New York-based research and consulting firm:

> In an interview for this report, [Cox] admitted that the company tends to be pragmatic and that management takes small steps toward a larger goal. Consequently, the current management is unlikely to make revolutionary upgrades in systems or marketing but will make competent incremental upgrades as time goes by.

This was an astonishing admission in a business that would soon require constant and continual change and massive shifting of resources and strategy. CompuServe management viewed the industry as being mature rather than newborn.

Executive vice president Herb Kahn has said that Block felt its growth had been so strong that no more was expected, and the company saw no need to spend much money chasing business that would arrive without effort through the door. "To them, it was this cash cow that they thought would never end," he said later. "Our users seemed to be happy with what we delivered, so there was no reason to change our tactics."

If CompuServe avoided risk, its newest competitor—Prodigy, which finally burst onto the national scene as the 1990s dawned—did not. In contrast to the buttoned-down image of CompuServe, Prodigy was aiming for one of fun and entertainment. After Prodigy's tumultuous delivery by Trintex, Sears and IBM had gone forward in the mid-1980s without CBS. Their ambitious agenda outlined active and aggressive plans to make Prodigy the nation's number one consumer online service.

Sears chairman Edward Brennan was so confident of Prodigy's success that he bragged to *Forbes* magazine in 1989: "We're not going to fail. It's really a question of how big we're going to be." One statistic was certainly big—the pair spent an incredible $500 million to launch the service, and then hundreds of millions of dollars more to popularize it over the next several years.

The colorful and heavily graphical "interactive personal service" was named, said its creators, to convey a product that was knowledgeable, friendly, and always willing to help people learn and find answers. What wasn't mentioned at the time was the unfortunate connotation that its title had—a know-it-all child with airs of nerdiness.

Prodigy planned to dispel that image with a service aimed at the mainstream. A celebrity-studded "family of experts" was created to aid users: Howard Cosell on sports, Liz Smith on Broadway, Rowland Evans and Robert Novak on politics. Also important were colorful "Naplips" graphics, which aimed to make the service seem as nontechnical as possible.

Prodigy's main focus, though, would be shopping—the ability to buy records, clothing, or plane tickets online. Over time, management hoped, the service would be free—paid for via transactional fees.

Prodigy's Ross Glatzer, who would take over from Ted Papes in 1992, noted that the retail orientation was seeded into the service from the start and was one of its main goals. Extensive focus groups, conducted by the company, indicated that people were eager to buy things via computers.

"We had a belief that goods will be sold electronically, so why not establish dominance in the marketplace?" he said. "You could make the case that there eventually would be no need for malls."

Advertising would ultimately be the real engine for profits. That notion was so ingrained that, from the late 1980s until AOL became an obvious threat in 1994, Prodigy actually allowed AOL to advertise on Prodigy to attract new members. It was, in the beginning, one of the cheapest ways for the barebones AOL to attract prospects.

Prodigy didn't think much of AOL because the IBM–Sears service was supposedly headed for bigger things. Instead of the slow-growth mode of CompuServe, Prodigy aimed at a 0-to-60-in-seconds start. Whether hiring hundred of employees, nabbing fancy celebrity endorsements, creating its own editorial service, or rolling out a service mascot called "Iggy," the message from Prodigy was aimed at the dead center of the mass market. Rather than CompuServe's techie focus, Prodigy wanted women, children, and noncomputer types to be able to sign up. "Finally, what the PC was invented for," one company ad declared in 1989.

To get its software out, Prodigy planned to distribute it via retail channels nationwide and to launch a $20 million advertising campaign with a variety of tag lines, such as "Anything you can do, you can do better."

After testing in a variety of major markets across the United States, Prodigy debuted nationally in the fall of 1990 with retail distribution of its $39.95 software at 11,000 stores, offering a mix of features such as travel guides, restaurant reviews, horoscopes, and more, for a $9.95 flat rate.

With another new motto, "You gotta get this thing," Prodigy was off and running. In less than three weeks after the nationwide rollout, the service claimed an incredible 500,000 members.

"There was no sense of competition from the beginning, which bred a lot of blindness," said Scott Kurnit, a cable industry executive who was brought in to help run the service under Glatzer in mid-1993. "AOL was just a little thing off to the side."

the king of the little thing

It was indeed a little thing. In mid-1993, AOL had only several hundred employees, 300,000 subscribers, and $40 million in revenues. But those statistics began to change when Case finally implemented AOL's go-go growth plans.

After the board had rejected the Microsoft bid, Case finally came out of the shadows and truly began to lead the company. He had been running the day-to-day operations for a long time, but always deferred to the various caveats from the venture capitalists, the major investors, and Kimsey.

Now, AOL was his show.

Case was unusually remote for a head of a communications company. The placid and quietly observant child had turned into a placid and quietly observant adult. At an off-site management meeting in the late 1980s, the AOL executives had all taken the Myers–Briggs Type Indicator (MBTI), a personality test based on the teachings of Carl Gustav Jung. The test results classify individuals' behavior via a series of letters that signify traits.

Case came up as INTP—introverted, intuitive, thinking, and perceptual. That combination describes a person who handles thoughts and emotions internally, makes decisions on a logical and intellectual basis, is flexible and adaptable, but is also quiet and detached. That description fit the management style that Case began to execute at AOL. Few knew what he thought about a variety of issues. One joke among the executives was that you were doing well if he did not say anything to you.

His typical pattern was to allow and observe a long series of meetings or group e-mailings in which the entire staff debated aspects of decisions. Finally, like a sponge (one of many nicknames he would acquire), Case would absorb all the opinions and contentions, weigh them carefully, and then decide, on his own, what he thought was best for the company. He was enamored of leaders who held power as singular figures—Malone, at TCI; Jobs, at Apple; Gates, at Microsoft—and he knew that employees, investors, and the press were more motivated if a single leader personified an enterprise and took responsibility for its decisions.

And yet, Case seemed to be most comfortable when hidden behind his computer or hovering in the background of conferences. As he became better known, the need to cultivate a public persona was difficult for this man who largely kept his thoughts to himself. In private, Case had a dry and teasingly sarcastic personality; to the outside world, he often appeared a cipher.

Lise Buyer, an Internet analyst for T. Rowe Price Associates Inc., which has owned large chunks of AOL stock over the years, remembered being in an elevator with Case at a New York investors' conference. Given Buyer's strong influence over investment decisions as a major shareholder, most CEOs might take the time to chat up such an important figure.

"Usually, they are like: 'How are you? How are things going? What's new? Let me tell you about the six hundred amazing things we are doing,' heavy on the schmooze factor," said Buyer, a petite, energetic woman. Instead, Case said nothing over the long ride they shared, causing Buyer's fertile mind to race. *Is he angry with me? Did I say something stupid? Am I stupid?* And then another course of thought: *wait, since I'm the investor, what's wrong with him? Is he stupid for not kissing up?* "I think he almost didn't understand why that would be odd," laughed Buyer, "and I think it is because he is one of the most self-contained and focused executives I have ever known."

Later, his tendency to be non-communicative would create, among employees and investors, an irksome feeling that 180-degree shifts in direction had occurred. But his ability to change directions quickly was also a plus. Case was not beholden to corporate bosses above him. Most decisions, especially in the early days, could be finalized around a meeting room table. Marketing head Jean Villanueva, finance chief Len Leader, technologist Marc Seriff, vice president Audrey Weil and CEO Case were the usual attendees.

The freedom would enable Case, for example, to make lightning-fast price changes. In April 1993, Prodigy raised its original $9.95 flat rate when the commercial model lagged behind expectations and its owners began to pressure Glatzer to staunch the flow of losses. Instantly, Case responded by changing his prices. Instead of $7.95 for two hours, subscribers paid $9.95 for five hours. The outlay was higher, but AOL offered a better per-hour value. Prodigy waited a full year before lowering its prices again. Case met the new challenge within the same day.

Case's ability to be nimble, coupled with his calm and clear leadership, created a steady persona in an unsteady business. Employees began to relate to him almost as an older brother figure. "It's always had a bit of a cultish feel, but not in a negative way," said one employee. "Steve was our leader who always knew what to do."

The focus on Case, both in the service and the company, was a good strategy. AOL had a face where Prodigy and CompuServe had none. Case underscored this cult of personality by eschewing any trappings of his job title. A casual dresser by nature, he typically worked in khakis, sneakers, and polo shirts, hosted weekly beer bashes for employees, and was approachable to all employees.

Perhaps most important was his obsession with the medium. Using a variety of computers in his office, Case would spend hours a day on his own service and his competitors'. Sometimes he would hang around silently online, taking in the opinions of customers; at other times, he would engage in lively discussions with users who did not always believe they were communicating with Case himself.

At CompuServe, there was no such compelling leader. At Prodigy, Glatzer's outdated computer still operated on the old DOS operating system and did not even have a mouse.

"Steve Case became the heart and soul of the business," said Marc Seriff. "And that made all the difference."

communications, community, clarity

Case may have been the salesman, but Seriff and others had given him a product that would sell—the simplest and easiest-to-use online service available at the time. And Case sold it, whether he hovered behind a conference audience, waiting to buttonhole an executive at session's end, or stood at a podium, preaching the gospel of the consumer online services envisioned by AOL.

"If you let him, he would tell you, because he was this cheerleader, a kind of one-man show," remembered Silicon Valley consultant Tim Bajarin. "It was always this bunch of Cs that he kept hammering on, and he never shifted from it."

The Cs identified the necessary traits, the soul of a successful online service, and told why AOL felt it would prevail. While Prodigy might be selling stuff and CompuServe doling out useful information, the hallmark of AOL would be communications, community and clarity.

"From the early days, we recognized that communications—a combination of chat and e-mail—were critical building blocks," Case said. "So our bias was on creating tools, empowering people, and letting them use them in any way they thought appropriate—sort of 'Let a thousand flowers bloom.'"

Much of the chat was sex-oriented. AOL did not want to become known as a sex-chat service, but it also did not want to avoid what Case and others thought was an inevitable stage in the development of a new interactive medium. Online communication was a two-way medium that, instead of being stifled, ought to be promoted. Chat was a compelling form of content that the cash-poor AOL did not even have to pay for. With thousands of people chattering away nightly, AOL subscribers could entertain themselves.

CompuServe had strong forums and had invented one of the first chat vehicles, but community-oriented interactions were not heavily promoted. Preferring their own rich business content and similar offerings, CompuServe officials thought AOL had little to offer. Said CompuServe's Herb Kahn: "To us, AOL was junk food and CompuServe was nutritional." The key fact that was ignored: America loves junk food.

While CompuServe declined to encourage the creation of a community, Prodigy—owned by two major corporations concerned about their reputations—committed worse errors. It made great attempts to bottle up all kinds of information in an effort to sell a "family" service; chat was not initiated until mid-1994. Prodigy chose to cut off subscribers who complained of price increases; eliminate information areas that became too controversial; and charge customers for using more than 30 e-mails per month.

The tone was heavily paternalistic. In an effort to make the experience easy for new users it was looking to attract, Prodigy went too far the other way and forced a kindergarten service on consumers rather than relying on them to decide what they wanted. Prodigy represented—as one critic pointed out—everything Sears knew about computers and everything IBM knew about retailing.

"A corporate guy thought, 'Wow, someone could type the word *fuck*,'" said Kurnit. "That very idea was anathema to IBM and Sears."

The freedom of expression in the AOL service naturally brought it a strong word-of-mouth buzz that attracted subscribers. For those not interested in the serious discussions on CompuServe or in being subjected to the suffocating "family" atmosphere on Prodigy, AOL was one of few alternatives. There were hipper services—most notably, a California-based service called The Well— but AOL aimed to be right along the edge of the mainstream but not beyond the fine line that defined it.

A freewheeling community soon developed, as if a real city was being built. E-mail names were personally chosen and casual; bulletin boards were open to all; chat rooms were linked into every part of the service.

And there would always be a friendly voice.

Case wanted the service to have a personalized feel. One way that could be accomplished, he thought, was by attaching a voice file to the software—a voice that could welcome users logging on, or let them know they have mail. A voice would make them feel they were in a community, not in some computer netherworld.

"We wanted people to think they were members and not customers," said Case. "That was important, because we needed to be different than big, faceless services."

The idea was simple enough, but the trick was to attach a compatible sound file that wouldn't significantly slow down the software. It was not at all clear, in the pre-sound card days, that this could be done, so the idea would need to be tested.

One afternoon in 1989, as Case stood in a hallway discussing the voice file question with some employees, a customer service representative, Karen Edwards, happened to overhear the conversation.

"My husband's a professional broadcaster," she told Case. "If you need someone to do a voice-over, he can do it for you."

Elwood Edwards was a big man—6 feet, 6 inches tall—with a warm, hearty voice. A broadcaster since his high school days in New Bern, North Carolina, Edwards, at age 40, was the operations manager of WFTY-TV in Washington. Ironically, he and Karen had met online in 1987, while sending messages back and forth on Q-Link.

AOL quickly settled on four simple phrases, which were then typed out on a sheet of paper: "Welcome," "You've got mail," "File's done," and "Goodbye."

"I recorded them at home on a portable cassette recorder," said Edwards. "It took me about twenty minutes. Then I gave them the tape, and they digitized it." He was paid about $100 for his work and thought it would be used only temporarily as a test tape.

"My voice was added to the software in the infancy of when that kind of thing was being done. There were mostly programs that generated speech, but the addition of sounds like my voice, it moved you more to something like 'Hal' in '2001'" said Edwards.

Little did Edwards know that, in the decade to come, the sound of his voice, greeting millions of users every day, would become one of the most recognized facets of AOL. His cheery "Welcome!" would be mocked, imitated, and anticipated by users across the country.

"We've had quite a lot of people tell us that when they get snail mail and bring it in the house, they'll pass it out and say 'You've got mail,'" said Karen Edwards. "A lady we met here in Texas [where the couple now live] wanted a picture of El and wanted him to autograph it. She said she was going to frame it and give it as a birthday present to a female relative who is in love with El's voice."

Edwards, who still does voice-over work and is now general manager at KVVV-TV in Houston, Texas, had no idea the service—and his voice—would ever get so big. "I thought it was just a little job," he said. "It's gratifying [that I am the voice of AOL], but it can be quite odd. . . . I still get people who say when they meet me, 'I've heard your voice before somewhere.'"

There were other experiments with giving the service a human personality. One was a character called "Jenny C"—the fictional daughter of Betty Crocker, who answered customers' queries. But it soon became clear that the best way to engender community and personal connection was to position Case himself as a kind of mayor of AOL. From the start, he had sent out chatty letters to users, signing them "Steve," and had trolled through the chat rooms and bulletin boards on a regular basis.

Real-life member parties—which had been going on for years in the Washington area—were rolled out nationwide to link customers more closely to the service. In the fall of 1993, for example, Case went on a "Getting America Online" road tour with stops (in schools and local Hard Rock Cafés) in San Francisco, Los Angeles, Dallas, Chicago, Boston, New York, Orlando, and Washington.

"AOL wanted to make sure that the users felt as if they were not alone," said AOL's Randy Dean, an ex-bartender who, in 1988, began running an online hangout called "Tardino's Tavern." "We wanted them to have these little epiphanies, out there by themselves typing on their computer, that they were part of something bigger, that technology did not have to be a cold place, that there was comfort out there."

Ease of use had also been an aim from the start, a trait of AOL's heritage as a service designed for Apple computers. The graphical user interface was icon-based; simple point-and-click navigation led a user directly to an area of interest. A library would be depicted as a stack of disks; a text file, as a folder. If anyone felt lost, "keywords" gave a way to find things. The service also frequently provided users with information about events occurring on the system.

Important to this effort was a seamless integration with the two major operating systems—Apple and Microsoft Windows. Because AOL was designed for the Apple computer, it was easily compatible. But perhaps more importantly, it also worked closely with Windows, which was finally becoming a powerful force in personal computing. Users could easily move text and information or manipulate data between the service and the operating system.

"We quickly realized that Windows was going to win the war of the operating systems, and we made sure we had software that worked with it," said Seriff, still AOL's chief technologist. "It was never a matter of religion for us, as it was for others."

That response was unusual because both of AOL's newest technology hires—who would take Seriff's place when he wanted to devote himself to trouble-shooting projects at AOL—were ex-IBMers. Mike Connors, who arrived in the fall of 1992 as senior vice president of technology and operations, had spent twenty-five years with Big Blue, ending up as director of computing systems for its research division. Matt Korn, who was Connors's second-in-command as director of operations, had also been working for IBM.

But both newcomers understood the need to be on as many platforms as possible.

By contrast, CompuServe made only negligible attempts to work well with Windows. A Windows shell occupied the first several screens, but underneath remained the complex text-based service that had always existed.

Prodigy did not come out with a Windows version until December 1993. Many blamed the damaging delay on its ownership by IBM, which was firmly behind its own OS/2 operating system and competed with Windows. "The IBM side couldn't accept that Windows was it," said Prodigy's Kurnit. "So we dragged our feet, while the rest of the world, using Windows, went to AOL."

Perhaps the most important part of the AOL strategy was to make the service easy to install—a five-minute process—and as free from computer tinkering as possible. Case had long remembered his first, difficult experiences with the Source, an online service that seemed designed to make access hard for users. His aim was to "make it easy and make it fun" for the inexperienced users that AOL was trying to attract. Automatic updating of software and graphics allowed AOL to make small changes continually rather than having users wait for new software.

By contrast, to get new features, Prodigy customers had to wait until major changes were made in the service. The Naplips graphics were soon deemed clunky, slow, and archaic-looking. CompuServe users—no surprise—had to go through a complex process of downloading and installation to add the latest features.

Prodigy's Kurnit was so taken by the consumer-oriented system AOL had assembled that, on his first day at work, he introduced himself to his new employers as "kurnit@aol.com." He would be using AOL's simpler e-mail until Prodigy introduced a similar system.

"AOL made it a no-brainer," said Kurnit, "which in itself is a very hard thing to do."

marketing mania

In July 1993, Jan Brandt got on the phone and called her new boss.

"I'm going to do a direct mail campaign. It'll cost $250,000 and I don't know if it'll work," she said. "Do you have a problem with that?"

"It's not going to work, but go ahead," was Steve Case's joking response, according to Brandt.

Thus began what has become one of the riskiest and most innovative branding campaigns of the digital age—the carpet-bombing of America with free AOL disks. The marketing plan ultimately sent out more than 250 million disks bearing AOL software to the mass market and was the principal tool in making AOL one of the best known names in cyberspace.

The strategy was born of necessity. AOL might have had the right aim and the right product, but getting its complete package to the mass market was critical. AOL was not affiliated with a major company, so it had to do everything on its own. The situation called for a daring effort—a marketing ploy that would put an AOL disk in the hands of everyone who was even slightly interested in trying the service.

At first, AOL's marketing had followed more traditional methods, though each effort had a definite twist. For example, when AOL signed bundling deals with major computer makers to include AOL disks in their units, it offered a bounty fee to them for each new subscriber gained. The other services charged manufacturers for their software. When alliances were inked with major media companies—including Disney, Hachette Filipacchi, *The New York Times*, *TIME*, NBC, and ABC—AOL paid them for well-known content that raised AOL's visibility and gave AOL access to their audiences. Potential customers might never have heard of AOL, but they most certainly would be attracted to famous names. AOL gave away software and free hours whereas costly software packages were required to use Prodigy and CompuServe. AOL had been the first online service to get magazines to attach disks—called "onserts"—to their issues.

Riding the coattails of someone else's brand name was not enough. To truly succeed in the market, AOL had to become as well known to online customers as Coca-Cola was to soda drinkers or Kleenex was to snifflers. To prevail, AOL had to become ubiquitous.

While Case provided the vision of the mass-market reach AOL was aiming for, the nitty-gritty of carrying it out was the job of Jan Brandt, employee number 173.

A large woman with a tough persona, Brandt was born in the Williamsburg section of Brooklyn. After attending college at Boston University and graduate school, her first job was as a copywriter at an educational publishing division of Xerox. She moved into marketing after she got an MBA. At a large insurance company, she did direct marketing and developed new products, including some with specifically targeted markets. A series of jobs in California followed: circulation of another educational publication, launch of a newsletter, and marketing for a seminar division. She led a company that specialized in marketing a series of liberal nonprofits and Democratic political campaigns, and later founded her own direct marketing agency. In 1988, Brandt returned east to work as vice president of advertising for Newfield Publications.

In the course of her work, she had met Case and was later enticed to come to AOL, attracted by the idea of working for a small entrepreneurial company. "The ability to get things done quickly was very appealing," said Brandt. "I was very passionate about marketing and thrive on being accountable for my decisions, so the environment was very fertile to me."

She was certainly no techie. "I was afraid to touch a computer," said Brandt. "But I was fascinated by the social dynamics of people in the online culture and how democratic it was. . . . I immediately saw the service as something that could really change the shape of our everyday lives—the way people communicate with each other."

But only if it got to the mass market. Soon after Brandt arrived at AOL's Vienna headquarters in April of 1993, she received a phone message from an unfamiliar voice. It was Matt Korn, the man charged with ensuring AOL technology could handle customer access demand. "I heard we were getting this hotshot marketer and we'd be really busy here," he wheedled teasingly in the message. "But I'm bored. If I wanted a boring job, I'd have stayed at IBM."

Brandt borrowed an idea from her stint at Newfield, where she had sent out a children's book as a sample mailing to potential customers. AOL had been giving away free software and hours for many years. She expanded that idea on a huge scale.

She had first considered a cheaper mailing that would entail getting users to send in a postcard requesting a free disk, but Brandt decided she had to eliminate all barriers to consumers' using the service. They'd get the disk, free hours, and the first month's fee waived. There would be no reason for a customer not to at least try AOL.

"You have to conduct marketing from a position of strength, even if you don't have it," said Brandt. "We needed high visibility and what did that was the disks, because if you've got a great product, people need to see it, they need to use it."

Preferring to be careful, she was disdainful of Prodigy's efforts. By spending money on television ads, when the general public still had no clue as to what an online service was, Prodigy was putting the cart before the horse, she felt. "Four years ago, most people were like, 'Online service? What's that? Chat? Talking through computers? You're crazy,'" said Brandt. "We had to move from the early adopters to the less experienced rather than the other way around."

Disks first went out to names on lists bought from popular computer magazines. After the mailing, Brandt waited with apprehension. As much as she thought her strategy was right, she did not know whether the mailing would work.

It did. The effort garnered a 10 percent response rate—a high return for a direct marketing campaign. Brandt was off, moving from her tiny circle of experienced users to larger and larger pools of potential customers. Soon, disks were distributed on American Airlines (with the peanuts), in cereal boxes, with flash-frozen Omaha Steaks, on seats at football games, and, mostly, in multiple mailings to homes.

"I thought I was probably going to direct marketing hell," said Brandt. "But we needed to get to a critical mass in the fastest way we could, so no one could blow us over." She arrived at her office daily, expecting to find CompuServe and Prodigy disks on her desk. "It was like blessing from heaven every minute that went by and that didn't happen," she said.

Not that AOL's competitors didn't notice. At Prodigy, where some small disk giveaways had been tested, marketing executives told Kurnit and Glatzer that such efforts did not work. At CompuServe, executives concluded that such a huge direct marketing effort was only an indication that AOL had become desperate. Until 1994, neither competitor initiated the type of massive direct marketing programs Brandt was using.

By then, it was too late. The response to the disks mailing and the word of mouth that had been building combined to make AOL suddenly "hot," according to *Advertising Age* and other publications. In January 1994 alone, AOL gained 70,000 users.

The marketing had worked a little too well—a precursor of better-known troubles the company would have later. The system built thus far by Seriff was not capable of handling the increase in subscribers. Brandt's marketing was delivering thousands of additional users who all wanted access to the system at peak times.

By February 1994, the service's systems became badly clogged. Customers were greeted with busy signals, and AOL got a well-deserved nickname: America On Hold. At a press conference, a Prodigy spokesperson predicted that AOL would never be able to recover.

In a letter to subscribers on March 28, 1994, Case tried to cast the problem in the best light possible. "Interest in AOL continues to grow at a remarkable pace," he wrote. "Needless to say, keeping up with growth has been challenging."

Matt Korn, director of operations, had the most challenging problem—an architecture that could take a maximum of only 8,217 users simultaneously. "The clock caught us since there was more demand and the performance started to degrade," said Korn. "It was clear that we had to 'rearchitect' it."

But first, he called Brandt back with a one-word message: "Uncle." And, as a joke, he pretended to lock her for a while in a steel-walled secure room—a remnant from when the space had been occupied by a defense contractor. "Nothing could transmit outside," he said. "So we thought it might stop her."

Despite the trouble they encountered in signing on, AOL customers were surprisingly forgiving of the growing pain of the new medium, and, with Brandt's aggressive marketing, there were always more "newbies," as new users were called.

On August 16, 1994, AOL announced that it had 1 million members online. It had tripled in size in one year. Brandt bought a Jaguar in celebration, affixing license plates that read "2MILL"— her next goal.

"The challenge now for America Online is to move this medium into the mainstream by reaching out to the 97 million households [not online]," wrote Case in a letter to customers. "It's 1 million down, 97 to go."

closing the chapter

AOL had accomplished this incredible achievement in a short time and all by itself. Now it was alone—though one final brush with a big stakeholder was taking shape.

Throughout the hyper-growth, Paul Allen had continued to own his huge stake of nearly 1.5 million shares. By the fall of 1993, he wanted out. But because of his tense relationship with AOL, he had to seek its cooperation in selling the stake since no one was going to buy a huge piece of a company that was hostile to the purchase.

Among those coming to pay a visit to AOL offices in Vienna, in early 1994, were executives from ITT Corporation, which planned to diversify its hotel, gaming and information services company, and television programming star Barry Diller, who was running the home shopping network, QVC Inc., and was seeking a deal that would include one of QVC's major shareholders, Tele-Communications Inc. (TCI). Case was excited about Diller; he thought he "would add a lot of pizazz to the story." The shopping and marketing strength of QVC could give AOL another huge marketing and transactional boost. But, as 1993 ended, Diller was preoccupied with his bitter and bigger fight with Viacom Inc. over control of Paramount Communications Inc. With billions of dollars at stake, AOL was soon off his radar screen.

With such a large block of stock available, the chattering on Wall Street began, and AOL stock rocketed during the early winter of 1994. Bolstered by a variety of speculative takeover rumors, the share price moved from $75 to an incredible high of $91.50. Finally, on July 29, 1994, Allen's investment arm, Vulcan Ventures, unloaded 733,000 shares—representing 9 percent of AOL shares—to institutional investors for about $59 per share. His profit was $70 million.

Interest in the remaining block (about the same number) of shares came from a more intriguing media mogul, John Malone of TCI, one of Case's corporate heros. TCI, which had agreed with Comcast Corporation in February to acquire the rest of QVC, had not lost interest after its first look at AOL. A marriage of Malone's huge Denver-based cable empire—the world's largest—and AOL's service could dominate the delivery of online services to the home, as cable became a bigger player in interactive services. The combination would be powerful, and Case talked frequently with Malone about the variety of possibilities. When it seemed as if TCI was serious and Case was confident of a deal, he sent Malone a draft press release one weekend in September, and prepared for an announcement of a major investor.

But Malone unexpectedly broke off talks, more intrigued by an even bigger online prospect, Bill Gates. Soon, Malone secretly agreed with Gates to take a 20 percent stake in Microsoft's online project for $125 million. The intent was to deliver the online service via cable lines. The deal, which would not be announced until December 21, would give the online service an instant valuation of $625 million. (Two years later, Malone would end up pulling the entire investment in MSN to devote the cash to other Internet ventures.)

But, in 1994, Case was crestfallen and especially perturbed that the deal-breaker was Gates. Had Malone used AOL to scare Gates into offering him a piece of Microsoft's online service? "I had this vision of him sending off the rough draft of the press release to Gates the minute it came off the fax from me," said Case.

Allen sold off the rest of his stake to a group of big institutional shareholders. "A key criterion of Mr. Allen's investment strategy is to work with companies that can contribute [to] or benefit from the technology and strategy of other Paul Allen companies," said an Allen spokesperson at the time. "The desired synergy was not realized with AOL."

AOL agreed. "This is positive news," said a spokesperson. "We believe it closes the chapter on Paul Allen and AOL."

Positive news, yes; but CompuServe and Prodigy had only been a warm-up for the next, more intense battle that lay ahead. The chapter on Bill Gates and AOL was about to heat up again.

david versus godzilla

bill gates wants you!

"Someday," declared Ted Leonsis to the hundreds of AOL employees gathered at the Sheraton Premiere ballroom in Tysons Corner, Virginia, on November 11, 1994, "your children will ask you what you did in the war."

The crowd laughed at the martial declaration coming from the boisterously good-natured Leonsis. A rotund man with the ebullience of a magic carpet merchant, Leonsis had an infectious good cheer that was hard to resist. But he was dead serious, and he wanted the AOL troops to get the message. He had just come to this small company that had managed to: survive the turmoil of a start-up, thwart a takeover attempt by two of the world's richest men, and get the best of CompuServe and Prodigy with far fewer resources.

The AOL faithful were—no surprise—pretty damned pleased with themselves. Leonsis's job, as he saw it, was to scare them into unified action in response to probably the biggest challenge AOL would ever face. Bill Gates was back—armed with an online service named Marvel—and drastic measures were called for.

AOL needed an old-fashioned call-to-arms pep rally, but its employees were used to Case's understated style. To rouse them, a little showmanship was in order. And, thought Leonsis, paranoia as a management technique was vastly underrated. It was time for a little devil casting, and Big Bad Bill Gates was the perfect Beelzebub.

Leonsis stood on the stage, an immense screen behind him. He pressed a button and a slide flashed up on the screen, projecting the words of Winston Churchill: "Courage is the first of human qualities, because it is the quality which guarantees all of the others."

The pep rally had begun. Leonsis quickly moved to the message: Establish absolute market dominance in the online services industry, and pave the way for AOL to become the world's first $1 billion interactive new media company.

It wasn't going to be easy. Leonsis put up quotes from a variety of articles that denigrated AOL, including one in which *Wired* magazine declared that the online service was on the scrap heap of history. "They are a dinosaur, they are obsolete," the digerati magazine had said of AOL.

But, shouted Leonsis, roaming the stage now like a revival preacher, "We're not the dinosaur." At that moment, a *Jurassic Park*-style video he had concocted flickered on the big screen behind him. As the thumping of an approaching flesh-eating lizard echoed through the room, Leonsis declared: "It's Microsoft that is the real dinosaur."

And, unlike the sorry saps in the movie, AOL would electrify its defenses to keep from becoming the lunch of the T-Rex from the Pacific Northwest. Microsoft was now the official enemy.

Why? "Marvel is designed as an 'AOL Killer,'" warned Leonsis. "And the presumption of victory is to Microsoft." Leonsis painted an ugly scenario: Microsoft would ravage relationships with content providers, bundle its service with its ubiquitous operating system, deploy hundreds of people, and spend hundreds of millions of dollars to win. Microsoft wanted to drive AOL out of business, take jobs from AOL employees, and food from their children's plates. It was big, rich, powerful, aggressive, broad-based, ruthless, and well-funded—and easy to hate. The number one priority was to create a warlike atmosphere against Microsoft, while girding AOL in the process.

The choice Leonsis presented was stark: Would this be the interactive age or the Microsoft age? "If not us, who?" exhorted Leonsis dramatically. "If not now, when?"

With the crowd now cheering and whooping, bright lights spinning and the music of Irish rock band U2 blasting over the speakers, Leonsis wheeled out a huge wooden cutout of a dinosaur. "Come sign it," urged Leonsis. "Make your pledge that you will help destroy the beast." Hundreds of AOL employees converged on the stage, pens in hand. "Death to Marvel," one scrawled.

The moment was pure Leonsis—flash, splash, and more than a little balderdash—but it worked. "Maybe the dinosaur thing was a bit of hyperbole, but I also believed it," said Leonsis. "I was asking, 'Are you going to let Bill Gates do this?' I wanted people to feel like 'I personally stopped Bill Gates from dominating this industry.'"

Leonsis's timing was impeccable and purposeful. In three days' time, on November 14, at the Comdex computer trade show in Las Vegas, Bill Gates took to the stage and unveiled his online service (now dubbed the Microsoft Network or MSN), which would be bundled in with the millions of copies of the new version of Windows that would be marketed within a year.

"There is really an opportunity to come in and bring some innovation that will help this market grow," said Gates in introducing the service. "We don't think this is anti-competitive at all."

In his office in northern Virginia the next day, Leonsis scanned the piles of press clippings that predicted MSN would be a huge online juggernaut—a threat that, just days before, he had convinced his troops they could beat.

Only one thought crossed his mind: "God, I hope I'm right."

red ted

The possibility of making a meal of Microsoft was tasty for a man with the appetites for riches and fame that Leonsis had always had.

Born in Brooklyn and raised in Lowell, Massachusetts, Leonsis hailed from humble beginnings in a working-class Greek Orthodox family; his father was a waiter and his mother was a secretary. When he went to Georgetown University on a scholarship, he sold ladies' shoes to support himself.

During his college years, a rich friend invited Leonsis to his home—a capacious spread called Red Gate Farms because of its colorful welcoming portals. "As [the gate] opened to let us go up the drive," remembered Leonsis, "I thought that one day I was going to have something like that because it represented to me all that I wanted."

His first job after his graduation in 1977 was in advertising and public relations for Wang Laboratories Inc., not far from his home. He then moved over to a more intriguing project—working with an IBM contractor on the launch of the IBM PC.

Leonsis quickly realized that the personal computer would create a new industry, and a wide range of companies would be associated with its development. Especially of interest to him were all the software companies that emerged. He was not a programmer, but Leonsis saw an opportunity to provide people with information about the variety of products linked to the personal computer. He began his own company, called the *Leonsis Index of Software Technology* (LIST), which produced a guide of the same name listing the range of software then available. He soon sold LIST to International Thomson Ltd., but stayed on to run the company and created a series of custom magazines for the personal computer industry.

After writing *Blue Magic,* an insider's account of the IBM PC's development, Leonsis veered from dead-tree publishing to the more intriguing world of multimedia. In 1986, he founded Redgate Communications Corporation (named for his dream spread) in Vero Beach, Florida. The aims of the business were multifaceted—from putting databases and custom shopping catalogs on CD-ROMs, to advising major corporations how they should get involved in the new online world.

"I was trying to communicate to as many people as I could that everything was going to change and that the delivery of advertising, transactions, information would not be the same and that they had to be ready," said Leonsis. "It was as hot and hyped as it could be."

Although it was not profitable, his work attracted a lot of attention—if only because he was one of the few people doing such projects. Among those who noticed him was a young investment banker named Dan Case. In 1992, he not only helped Leonsis when several large companies expressed interest in buying Redgate but even discussed the possibility of a public offering.

"But what you should really do is talk to my brother first," said Case, "because you two are starting to sound exactly alike."

Leonsis's early impression had been that AOL was too slow for his broadband sensibilities. He was more interested in the day when interactive services over the computer would have lightning-fast video and sound—a new form of digital communication that married Hollywood and Silicon Valley.

After Steve Case called him several times, Leonsis agreed to a breakfast meeting, in October 1993, in Boston's Le Meridien Hotel. The topic would be: the possibility of doing some work together. But after only a short exchange of chitchat, Case made a proposal.

"I think we ought to merge our companies," he said.

Leonsis thought the suggestion was more than just a little premature. Case certainly had a lot of nerve, although there was something endearing about his bluntness. "Shouldn't we kiss first?" countered Leonsis. "Meet each other's parents? Date?"

They made an unlikely pair and would later acquire a variety of nicknames in the industry, including "The Prep and the Pep," "The Monk and the Clown," and "Mutt and Jeff."

But Steve Case knew he had found the person who could take AOL to the next level. Ted Leonsis, it turned out, was a classic extrovert on the Myers–Briggs scale—just what AOL and the cerebral Case needed at that moment.

"There was a need for a rallying cry, internally and externally, and it was based on a fear that the world was changing again, and so we had to," said Case. "And Ted was the chief evangelist."

girding for battle

It was time to remake AOL once again—using the oncoming threat of Microsoft as the chief motivator. Painted as an underdog—much as it had been when contending with CompuServe and Prodigy—AOL would emerge an even bigger winner.

"We had no idea what Microsoft would come out with, so we had to rethink and innovate based on what we had done," said Case. "We were a lot focused on Prodigy and CompuServe, but they were the interim battles for the real one that lay ahead."

The first tactic was to bulk itself up as an online company—add to its infrastructure and offerings, to make it as multifaceted as possible. Until then, online services as an industry had existed in what Morgan Stanley analyst Mary Meeker had called the "Iron Age." Its hallmarks—all of which AOL had excelled in—included member-generated community, branded but essentially repurposed content, reference database materials, icons for information, logos for ads, and only rudimentary transactions.

Now AOL had to enter the "Bronze Age," marked by multimedia shopping, interactive marketing areas, new content programming and organization, and a greater linkage with the fast-growing Internet.

The first new weapon—Ted Leonsis—was brought to the ramparts when AOL completed the acquisition of Redgate, on August 19, 1994. Redgate stockholders received shares of AOL representing approximately 5.8 percent of AOL's outstanding common stock, then worth $40 million. Redgate was purchased in an attempt to improve AOL's opportunities in electronic commerce. The grand plan was to combine online and CD-ROM technology to allow shoppers to make purchases easily via their computers.

AOL later abandoned the computer shopping business. In fact, several of the acquisitions AOL made during the next year turned out to be short-life companies that later disappeared for technological or balance-sheet reasons. But Microsoft's entry into the market spurred a kind of land-rush race to see who could claim the biggest territory in the shortest amount of time.

Such an effort cost money. Luckily for AOL, its share price was red hot, and most of its purchases could be made with its stock as currency. Over the next year, AOL would use the stock market to literally print money—in the form of AOL shares. This tactic allowed it to grow far larger than would have been possible without the stock.

Indeed, throughout its volatile history, one of AOL's greatest strengths—and also the subject of later criticism—has been its ability to fund itself through a variety of innovative and controversial methods. Whether through a well-timed sale of common stock, or critical cash infusions from investing partners, or clever and perfectly legal manipulation of its balance sheet, AOL was able to stave off the basic fact that its business operations never threw off enough cash to cover the costs of its growth.

In 1994, Case and his team pushed aside any remaining conservative financial considerations; they were intent on pulling to the front of the market before Microsoft's entry. To gird for the coming battle, AOL had gone to the financial markets in December 1993 and had sold four million more shares, garnering $62.7 million. Armed with its hot stock—which would split for the first time in November 1994—AOL was ready to play.

The game of the moment was rapidly shifting to the Internet (and its graphical subset, the World Wide Web), which was just beginning to develop, from its origins as a communications vehicle for scientists, into a medium that would be used commercially.

AOL had been a slow comer to the Internet, delayed in part by a focus on managing its phenomenal subscriber growth, and in part by disdain for the Net's complexity. "The reality of it was that it took off faster than any of us thought it would," said Marc Seriff. "And we were also skeptical of it at first, because it was not a consumer product like ours."

It was a calculation AOL knew it had to correct. By September 1994, AOL had restructured itself to include an Internet division with Steve Case at the helm. After Prodigy announced that it would provide access to the Web in the fall of 1994—one of the few moments when it beat AOL handily to the punch—getting into the game fast was critical. An aggressive and expensive strategy was applied. The aim was simple: to co-opt the Internet with a series of purchases that would put AOL ahead in access and software tools, and to attempt to create the standard for Web navigation browser software.

No surprise then that AOL's first buys in November 1994—BookLink Technologies Inc. and NaviSoft Inc.—were aimed at the Internet. BookLink made a then well-regarded browser software to navigate the Web, and NaviSoft made high-end Web publishing and development tools. David Cole of NaviSoft took over, from Case, the Internet services effort.

AOL had grabbed BookLink from the jaws of Microsoft, which was looking for similar Internet technology for MSN. Microsoft's Russ Siegelman had been in protracted negotiations with Book-Link through 1994, but had only offered a $2 million flat fee for the code for its browser. Case swooped in and agreed to pay the parent company, CMG Information Services, more than $30 million in AOL stock for the entire business. In a simultaneous but separate transaction, NaviSoft shareholders were also paid in AOL common stock, worth $3 million.

Case was willing to pay that much because he had come late to the party, delayed by another date: He had tried at first to buy a piece of the then-private Netscape Communications Corporation.

Netscape was the name for a company originally called Mosaic Communications Corporation, founded by Silicon Graphics Inc.'s founder Jim Clark and a young Internet wunderkind named Marc Andreessen. While working at the University of Illinois at Urbana–Champaign's Center for Supercomputing Applications, in late 1992, Andreessen and Eric Bina had created the original browser for the Web and had called it Mosaic. They posted it on the Internet for free and it became an instant success.

Clark had contacted Andreessen, who ended up at odds with university officials over the Mosaic browser, and the pair had started their own browser company, in April 1994, to take advantage of the market. By November of that year, their first test version of the "Navigator" browser was posted on their company's Web site and was soon another winner.

Case was interested in investing in the first round of financing of Netscape, in early 1994, through its venture capitalists—Kleiner, Perkins, AOL's original investor. Another familiar face was involved as one of the investment bankers for Netscape: Steve's brother, Dan.

Steve Case was keen on purchasing a substantial stake. But Netscape—wary, much like AOL had been, of becoming too cozy with any one company—wasn't interested in selling. Could it ever sell the Navigator browser to AT&T's Internet subsidiary, for example, if AOL was one of its big owners? Instead, Netscape was more intent on a lucrative initial public offering in the near future.

"At the final hour, Jim decided he didn't want us to invest, because he felt there would be a taint to it if Netscape was linked too closely with AOL," said Case. "I certainly understood that, though I was disappointed—it felt like they left us at the altar."

But Case kept up discussions for AOL to license Netscape's browser, which was clearly on its way to being the hit of the market. "They were very aggressive about selling the browser, but they wanted a very high per-copy fee," said Case. "The attitude was, 'We're so hot, we'll license to everyone, so you better take it.'"

Case decided he'd rather try to build his own—"so we went with BookLink." The imbedded BookLink browser was later much criticized as being substandard, but at the time it was considered a good one. Case even dreamed of perhaps setting the industry standard with it—with AOL completely in control.

The decision to build an AOL network was also the impetus for the purchase, in late November, of Advanced Network & Services Inc. (ANS) for $35 million—$20 million in cash and $15 million in stock. AOL sought to cut its own network costs and to gain an ability to give its members connections to the Internet through a dial-up network based on its protocols. The Elmsford, New York, company, one of the builders of the original Internet backbone, fit the bill.

Until then, AOL had relied on Sprint Corporation for 80 percent of its network access carriage. The arrangement had begun to limit AOL's ability to grow and had left a huge variable cost on its books. By building its own network through purchases, AOL would be able to determine its own needs as a user and could thwart any attempt by Microsoft to buy up capacity. Technologists Mike Connors and Matt Korn had formulated a "three-legged stool" strategy: AOL would use its own ANS network and would also buy access from Sprint and BBN Corporation to drive down costs.

Case had at first been interested in a neighboring Internet access company—UUNet Technologies Inc., of Fairfax, Virginia. Its chief executive, John Sidgmore, and Steve Case were members of a small cadre of online entrepreneurs in a region populated mostly by federal government contractors. Before UUNet, Sidgmore had worked as general manager at General Electric Information Services, where he had met Case and others at AOL.

When he got to UUNet, in June 1994, "The first thing I did was call Steve," said Sidgmore. He wanted to get out of the consumer business UUNet had developed, and focus exclusively on the business arena. But, as he grew that more lucrative market, he still had nighttime capacity to sell, and AOL seemed a perfect customer.

UUNet—which would later become part of the massive empire of a telecommunications upstart, WorldCom Inc.—was then much smaller than AOL, with only $11 million in annual sales. Sidgmore was actively interested in linking up with—or possibly being bought by—the fast-growing online service.

Through the summer, Case and Sidgmore often met at local hotels for breakfast, and talked of possibilities that could bring their companies together. In one scenario, AOL would pay cost plus a certain percent for an Internet dial-up network that UUNet would build and maintain.

But Sidgmore was also talking to Microsoft—which was in the market for access capacity for MSN. "While I wound up really committed emotionally to AOL, I also dreamed of having them both as customers," said Sidgmore. "And I tried to convince Steve and Siegelman that it would work."

But Case, already paranoid about Microsoft, would have none of it, especially since Microsoft was also interested in a large stake in UUNet. Over Thanksgiving weekend, using e-mail for several hours at a stretch, Case and Sidgmore wrangled over what kind of deal could be done if AOL were to buy UUNet.

"I was eager, to say the least, so we went round and round on how we could do a deal, but we could never come to terms," said Sidgmore.

In the end, Case found ANS had fewer complications. Soon after, Microsoft inked a deal with UUNet to buy an 18 percent stake and pay for building its huge Internet dial-up network.

Deal-making did not stop at the U.S. borders, especially since Microsoft had indicated that MSN intended to become a worldwide service. On March 1, 1995, AOL and Bertelsmann AG—the giant German media company—announced an agreement to create a European online service. In the deal—brokered by Jack Davies, a former recording industry executive who had come to AOL years before and would take over as head of AOL's international arm— Bertelsmann would invest $100 million in the venture and would also buy a 5-percent stake in AOL for $54 million. This propitious investment fattened AOL's diminishing cash coffers.

In May 1995, AOL announced a pair of purchases: (1) Medior Inc., a developer of interactive media properties, to improve AOL's look and feel, for 825,000 shares; and (2) Wide Area Information Servers Inc., maker of Internet tools, for 400,000 shares. Medior founder Barry Schuler then took over AOL's production arm.

In June, AOL bought the popular Web navigation site called the Global Network Navigator (GNN), a subsidiary of O'Reilly & Associates, Inc., for $9 million in stock and $2 million in cash. AOL also got GNN's WebCrawler search tool and Internet index as part of the deal.

It was a breathtaking series of deals in a very short time. By early 1996, some of the acquisitions would be called ill-conceived.

content is king?

Trouble loomed if AOL continued to rely on its increasingly moribund content offerings. Like much of the online industry, AOL had come to depend on major media brand names such as Time Warner, Disney, and others. Their parcels were heavy with regurgitated material from magazines and news services. The level of substance was low. For much of its life thus far, in fact, the most interesting content on AOL had been generated from its own customers.

Now, Microsoft was vowing to create content of its own or to steal away AOL's existing information providers by offering higher revenue-sharing deals. The growth of the Internet was also presenting the unwelcome possibility of draining other content into a much larger and more open world.

But Leonsis, the impresario, saw another possibility: AOL could become a producer or own stakes in a wide variety of companies creating interactive material. In addition, it would find the best of the Internet and point to it from AOL. By integrating Web sites into the content mix, AOL customers could hardly tell the difference, and AOL would get added content.

This blending of AOL and the Internet would take place in "channels," a new service configuration that Leonsis had decided on to mimic broadcast television. The channels would group topics of interest and provide even more order for users.

Leonsis hoped that having channels would help AOL begin to think like a media company rather than just an online service. His goal was to take Jan Brandt's mass marketing success and solidify it in the stone of brand marketing.

"We're a brand company," he continually repeated—using the ubiquitous Coca-Cola as the prime example—to his employees. "I took a trip to Florida," he would tell them, "and in the first day of any trip, I always have to go shopping. I went to Publix, Block-buster, CVS, the local pizza parlor, and in every place they were selling or advertising Coke. There is literally always a Coke wherever you are. It should be the same with AOL: you should always see us. Great marketers can do that."

New content creation was important to strengthening the AOL brand name. First, Leonsis bulked up AOL's own producing (under Schuler) by adding a San Francisco-based division. He also initiated the partners' conferences, where information providers could take a stronger hand in guiding their efforts.

Perhaps most importantly, in November 1994, he declared himself a new-age studio mogul and venture capitalist by creating Greenhouse, envisioned as an "in-house content studio," where AOL provided money and distribution for start-up sites. After soliciting applications from prospective content providers, Leonsis invited promising "infopreneurs" to make a presentation to him at AOL. Over 1,700 completed applications arrived, and dozens of hopefuls trudged through his offices over the next several months.

Like an online version of Hollywood's Louis B. Mayer, Leonsis saw five pitches a week for six months. He was partial to those that amused him, and had little patience for bland and ordinary presentations. Once, he sent home a group selling a surfing site. They had arrived in suits and ties, and he said he would only see them after they showed up wearing shorts and sporting zinc oxide on their noses.

By the spring of 1995, Leonsis had selected the first half-dozen stars to back: The eGG, Inc., a gourmet guide; InterZine Productions, Inc., creators of an area for golfers called iGOLF; Health ResponseAbility Systems, Inc., a health site; the Afrocentric cultural site called NetNoir, Inc.; World Pulse, Inc., a fitness area; and, perhaps most promisingly, The Motley Fool Inc., an irreverent financial site.

The "Fool" was already a grassroots phenomenon on AOL by 1995. Two irreverent brothers named David and Tom Gardner had created the site to offer the average investor a more humorous way to invest and, mostly, to tweak the "Wise" of Wall Street.

The Gardner brothers became interested in the stock market after graduating from high school, when their father, a banking lawyer, had given each of them a chunk of money to invest. After college, the brothers and a friend started a print newsletter called *The Motley Fool,* a name they found in Shakespeare's *As You Like It.* It was not a huge success—the subscriptions sold never numbered more than a few hundred. To goose circulation and attract buyers for the newsletter, they decided to open an online discussion on a variety of services.

As an April Fool's Day joke on Prodigy's Money Talk bulletin board, they posted information about a penny stock for a company called "Zeigletics" that they said traded on the "Halifax Canadian Exchange." Neither the company nor the exchange existed, but the Gardners made up reports about the company and even created a fictitious stock adviser, named "Joey Roman," who would post messages on the bulletin board hyping the stock. Incredibly, it became the focus of intense investor interest, and the stock's "value" climbed 3,000 percent in a week. No wonder that the brothers received threats online when people realized "Zeigletics" was a hoax.

But it put the Gardners on the map—and delivered their lesson: Small-time investors needed to learn more about their investments.

Prodigy officials were horrified, but AOL's Katherine Borsecnik quickly noticed the hive of activity around the message folders the Gardners had started on AOL. She offered them a chance to run their own site, and it was launched in August 1994.

"Our initial contract with AOL was that we would receive 8 percent of usage hours, which came out to about $25,000 a year," said David Gardner. "We figured we could work, make a little cash." A lot of cash, in fact. In September, the site logged 6,000 hours; in October, the log time shot up to 20,000 hours—about $60,000 a month.

The Motley Fool was just the kind of bubbling-up interactive content that Leonsis was looking for, even though the Gardners and Leonsis would wrangle before he made them a Greenhouse company. In the midst of testy negotiations over AOL's equity investment in the Fool, Leonsis penned a letter to the Gardners in February. "We believe that Motley Fool no longer fits the profile of our Greenhouse incubator program and that you will be better served developing your own stand-alone business," he wrote.

But the Fool was creating exactly the kind of material that Leonsis wanted, to set AOL apart from others. He knew he needed the brothers, and others like them, for the company to succeed.

Only two months later, after AOL had put in $500,000 for a 20 percent stake, he was touting them as the next big thing. "They will be the rock stars of cyberspace," enthused Leonsis, who grandly dubbed himself "Godfather of the Motley Fool." Such content success, he knew, was important for AOL's attempt to differentiate itself from Microsoft and others, giving it the sexy sheen of a happening.

When the Gardners teased him about taking credit where it perhaps wasn't due, Leonsis only winked at them.

"Boys," he said, "myth is reality."

fear and loathing

While AOL could improve its offerings and juice up its content, the real challenge was going to be about beating Microsoft with every bit of bull, braggadocio, and swagger it could muster.

The strategy was to turn MSN's frightening arrival into a positive force rather than a negative steamroller. If AOL could set the agenda, both internally and externally, it would be at the center of attention.

"The demonization of Microsoft was key, especially since Microsoft was saying 'We're going to dominate this market," said Leonsis. "So we had to act like D-Day was coming—that it was a doomsday scenario—to really motivate ourselves."

Within the company, Case and Leonsis needed to keep the message simple: Microsoft is trying to kill us, and Bill Gates embodies Microsoft. "It was a fear factor, driven mostly by respect," said Case. "Some felt it was a bit manufactured, but the time this company was most in sync was when Microsoft was coming at us."

Hence the dinosaur rally—and more. Leonsis set up an MSN war room, where all information on the enemy was collected. Employees were designated "Microsoft Watchers." Buttons showing a red slash through a dinosaur were printed up and distributed. Case flinched a bit at Leonsis's vivid characterization of the online battle as "Microsoft's Vietnam," but revving up the troops was paramount.

There were endless internal meetings—all focused on MSN. In one session, Audrey Weil pretended Microsoft had raided AOL's ranks and she was going to be the next president of MSN's online service. As she began to tick through the list of AOL weaknesses she would attack—from thin content to access troubles—Leonsis got so drawn into the playacting that he found himself becoming furious at her for leaving.

Ace marketer Jan Brandt perhaps got deepest into the act. Rather than replacing her "2MILL" license plate (AOL hit that subscriber figure on February 21, 1995) with "5MILL," as many expected, Brandt carried her message for Microsoft on her car in 1995:

"FG8S"—Fuck Gates.

To the outside world, that was precisely AOL's message about what Microsoft wanted to do to the online industry. Rather than minimize MSN's threat, thought Case and Leonsis, perhaps it was better to maximize it. Growing expectations would have two possible positive results for AOL. First, if MSN was made to seem enormous, then its actual performance could look like a failure if it did not excel from the start.

Second, and perhaps more importantly, if AOL could successfully communicate that Microsoft was taking advantage of its total dominance of computer operating systems to launch MSN, then the federal government's antitrust officials might be interested.

The Justice Department had long been focused on Microsoft and its troubling market power: Contention with the company dated back to a broader Federal Trade Commission investigation in August 1993. Justice had narrowed the focus to look at how the company licensed its operating system by charging a processor fee.

The investigation was settled when Gates and assistant attorney general Anne Bingaman, the chief of Justice's antitrust division, signed a consent decree, in July 1994, in which Microsoft neither denied nor admitted guilt. But it did agree to stop using per-processor licensing agreements and certain multiyear licensing agreements, and to maintain very restrictive confidentiality agreements with software developers.

Many observers thought the deal was lenient, considering Microsoft's control of the operating systems of most computers in use. Federal Judge Stanley Sporkin overturned the consent decree on February 14, 1995, after which Microsoft and the Justice Department—unusual allies—quickly appealed. Sporkin was soon removed from the case, and Judge Thomas Penfield Jackson finally approved the consent decree on August 21.

By then, the Department of Justice was already after Microsoft on another issue—its planned $2 billion merger, announced in October 1994, with the leading maker of financial software, Intuit Inc. The following April, Justice filed to stop the Intuit–Microsoft merger. Microsoft capitulated three weeks later and canceled the merger plans.

In the course of the Intuit investigation in 1994, Justice had contacted the top executives in the big three online services, including Case. He considered the Intuit action a "good first step" and took the opportunity to bring up another topic—his concerns about MSN's being bundled into Windows 95.

Case had actually launched the first sound bite of the struggle in an online conference in New York in November 1994, just days before Gates was to introduce MSN at Comdex. Calling the Windows operating system "what the dial tone is to the phone industry," Case argued that MSN must be sold as a stand-alone service and not linked seamlessly to Windows 95, so that all the services would compete on a level playing field.

CompuServe executive Herb Kahn, when he heard the phrase Case used, knew that AOL would win. "Case had defined the argument with one image—the dial tone that everyone has a right to," said Kahn. "It was brilliant."

To Case, the idea of a dial tone was the perfect way to attack Microsoft; he knew everyone understood how universal the phone sound was. Case had thought of the comparison while trying to figure out how to make Microsoft seem like a monopoly. With approval from AOL's board, he began an aggressive public policy campaign to thwart Microsoft by painting it as a danger.

"This was an AOL-organized skunkworks to create an anti-MSN atmosphere," said Jeff Richards, who worked on the initiative for telecommunications companies and who later would head the Interactive Services Association (ISA), the Washington-based industry trade group that represented online services. "Everyone—including Gates—had to think of Steve from then on."

(Case's visibility was further raised in an unlikely place—as an avatar of fashion by the Gap retail chain, which featured him in its ad campaign for khakis in spring of 1995. Wearing khakis and a typically straight-faced expression, Case had his picture snapped by the famed photographer Richard Avedon in New York. The tagline: "Do your best. Work in khakis. What's best is always a benchmark." Gap's focus was on business "visionaries," and Case was picked as someone who could make waves while dressing casually.)

Aside from the obvious business opportunities in leading such a fight, Case was genuinely concerned that Microsoft would be able to muster such a huge marketing advantage that he and others could not compete. MSN had a graphical icon on the Windows 95 desktop that would allow users to access the service with only one click.

Case had thought a lot about how to communicate the situation. "On a fundamental level, it did strike me as unfair what they were going to do," he said. "I'm not bothered by how they got there, but with more than 80 percent of the world's PCs having one operating system, that's a de facto monopoly."

He'd hoped the debate would cause Microsoft to tread more lightly. But there was a downside to sounding the alarm: If it was overdone, it might make AOL's internal paranoia too public.

"Wall Street would think: If the Justice Department doesn't stop Microsoft, nothing can," Case said. "But Microsoft was about to do something that was bad public policy and could kill AOL. Everything else is a sidebar."

So Case pressed forward—using Audrey Weil and Ted Leonsis to walk Justice lawyers through the online world. By the spring, although occupied with Intuit and the operating system investigations, Justice decided to add MSN's now-questionable bundling to the pile.

In June, it subpoenaed documents on the issue from Microsoft, which objected to the move, claiming it was being harassed by the government. More to the point, said Microsoft's lawyers, MSN had no subscribers, so how could it be that dangerous?

"MSN had no customers then, zero," said David Heiner, a senior Microsoft attorney who worked on the issue. "So it seemed rather far-fetched for AOL to claim that we were a threat to them or anyone else."

Along with its argument that it had no customers, Microsoft noted that MSN was not a separate product but a fundamental enhancement to Windows 95, and the very fact that AOL disks were so ubiquitous proved that no one player had an overwhelming distribution advantage.

But Case nudged further the idea that Microsoft's unfair advantage would produce frightening results. At a press conference, he and the chief executives of CompuServe and Prodigy released an open letter to Bill Gates, asking him to separate access to Microsoft's new online service from Windows 95.

Most effectively, he touted a poll by Luntz Research, commissioned by the Interactive Services Association (ISA). It predicted that between 11 million and 19 million people would sign up for MSN in its first year, based on sales projections of Windows 95. This was more than a bit of an overstatement, considering that there were fewer than 10 million online customers so far, including all of the AOL, CompuServe, and Prodigy subscribers.

But Case wanted to make a point: If Justice allowed Microsoft to do as it pleased, MSN could conceivably rocket to a near monopoly. And it would be too late to try to reverse it later.

His point was not convincing enough, it seemed, because the antitrust prosecutors were divided about what to do as the investigation progressed. Some were urging that action be taken, but senior attorney Joel Klein—who would later replace Bingaman as antitrust chief after she left Justice—thought caution was a better path. AOL might be a lot heartier, he surmised, and Microsoft's market power might not ensure its success in the online business.

On August 8, federal regulators issued the following statement: "The Department of Justice said today that its investigation into the Microsoft Network and other issues associated with possible anticompetitive practices relating to Windows 95 is ongoing. The Department does not expect to complete its investigation or reach a decision on possible enforcement action prior to August 24, 1995."

That is, the launch date for MSN.

meanwhile, back at the redmond ranch

Case's campaign did have a big effect back in Redmond, where the Justice scrutiny added a lot of stress. "The antitrust thing added a lot of pressure and a lot of extra work," said Siegelman. "It was complete bullshit."

To Siegelman, AOL went overboard with the myth of the monolithic MSN. Internally, MSN had been struggling—a lot more than many knew—from its very start.

After the rebuff from AOL, Siegelman was charged by Gates, in mid-1993, to build the online service in a new online services group under the direction of Microsoft's chief visionary, Nathan Myhrvold. The Marvel team soon had 100 people working away.

A lot of sweat was needed. The service had to be done completely from scratch in a short amount of time—content, huge e-mail and billing systems, software, and interface design—something its competitors had taken a decade to build.

The easiest and best move was accomplished first—naming the service. After a name consultant had come up with a variety of weird techie monikers—including the bizarre and meaningless ONVO—the group decided to stick with one of the best know brand names around. The Microsoft Network—or MSN—was born.

MSN was a good name, thought Siegelman. It benefited from Microsoft branding and, over time, it could be positioned more in the image of a broadcast network, such as NBC.

From the start, the marketing of the service would be tied closely to the new Windows 95 desktop. Gates had told Siegelman clearly at the start: "We want the registration built into Windows."

"We thought, this is a natural reason to do an online service," said Siegelman. "We have these users who need support."

Soon, a variety of problems began to surface—often tied to the fact that MSN was part of a bigger company.

Siegelman, for example, did not want to use Microsoft's mail program, called Exchange, for the service. He considered it too business-oriented and complex for the average consumer. He tried to create another mail client, but in the end was told to use Exchange.

The service interface was designed to resemble the Windows folder system—making it too computerish, dull, and confusing at the same time—in order to minimize problems for the more important Windows 95 team.

"They had one very clear concern; they didn't want us to mess up the Windows launch, to mess up the product," said Siegelman. "We were seen as a kind of pain, I think."

The ties to Windows 95—the driver of the entire company at the time—proved a constant challenge for MSN. "We went through so many different iterations and had to think small, because whenever Windows 95 would ship, we had to get something with online registration in there," said Siegelman. "And, at first, everyone thought Windows would ship in June of 1994."

But the Windows 95 launch kept slipping. "At every check-point, we thought Windows would ship the next quarter," said Siegelman. "It was a constant thing, so we did not think we could veer off course."

At the end of 1993, Siegelman himself was shoved off the road completely, a brain aneurysm that required surgery and kept him sidelined for two months.

When he returned, he began to try to strike deals with as many information providers as he could. The problem was that many of the best were already tied up with the big three services, and little other good material existed. In addition, MSN's set of proprietary publishing software tools—called Blackbird and de-signed to give MSN content developers better graphical and interactive capabilities—was not completely developed. He man-aged to nab only NBC from AOL, but at a hefty $4 million cost. AOL had been paying the network only $1 million. But Gates urged aggressive deals, knowing the service must be robust from day one. "You had better compete with AOL across the board with content providers," he told Siegelman.

Soon, an even bigger worry emerged—the Internet. What the MSN team had been building until then had no Internet orienta-tion at all, raising the possibility that they were building an infra-structure that could be practically obsolete by the time it came out. Some at the company, including Rob Glaser, had sounded a warn-ing early on. But once the MSN team had gone far enough down the road toward creating a proprietary service like AOL, Siegel-man worried that it was too difficult to switch midstream. The danger was that the online team wouldn't be able to get out any-thing at all if it changed tack.

But huge changes going on at the core of Microsoft were about to upend two years of work on MSN. In May 1995, Gates ad-dressed to his troops a watershed memo called "The Internet Tidal Wave." In it, he said explicitly: "Every online service has to simply be a place on the Internet with extra value added."

"It just unraveled all our plans, because we had all these other kinds of deals in place and had created this whole other paradigm," said Siegelman. "It was like whiplash—go this way, now go that way."

But Microsoft had to take that direction, because the Internet presented the greatest challenge ever to Microsoft's hegemony over the computer. The company had to move quickly to incorporate Internet-centric thinking into its entire DNA. Siegelman had tried to shift through the year—making a deal with UUNet for Internet dial-up carriage, and with Spyglass Inc. for a Web browser—but the MSN that he had created was simply a junior version of AOL. And because AOL had also improved its Internet capabilities, MSN was offering nothing new to the online market.

A week before the launch, in his column in the *Wall Street Journal,* Walt Mossberg made it plain. "All the talk about Microsoft's new online service, the Microsoft Network, is about how it's being distributed. Competitors and critics complain that by bundling the service in its new Windows 95 operating system, the software giant will gain unfair advantage over online rivals," he wrote. "Personally, I am not bothered by the bundling plan. To me, the only troubling thing about the Microsoft Network, or MSN, is just how underwhelming it is."

Mossberg ranked it "dead last" of the services.

Internally, Siegelman's reluctance to move fast by shifting MSN to the Internet immediately was seen as a problem—though he seemed to be mostly the ultimate victim of bad timing.

"I thought MSN 1.0 should be the bridge to the next version, and it came off that I was trying to hold back the inevitable Internet," he said. "So, I think, within Microsoft, it was open season on us."

You could not tell that by the Windows 95 launch, held at Microsoft's Redmond campus on August 24, 1995, with Jay Leno as the special guest. The MSN launch was only a short part of the program—a few minutes in the 80-minute presentation, which was followed by a carnival.

Siegelman put on his very best face, but subtly alluded to the struggle that had occurred to get MSN up. "Bill Gates is not often wrong, but one year ago he told us we'd never be ready in time," he said. "But we turned it on last night at midnight, and are getting four sign-ups per second."

It would be the fastest MSN would ever attract customers. More than 100,000 new users reportedly signed up for MSN on the first day, and 190,000 had signed up by the end of the first week. But after that, especially because MSN was available only on Windows 95, growth came a lot slower. It was further dragged down by lack of heavy-duty marketing at Microsoft—which was relying primarily on its desktop spot for MSN's success.

Partly, the ambivalence and lack of gusto sprang from the fact that Microsoft knew it would be changing MSN drastically in the coming months—part of a dramatic and wholesale shift to the Internet for the entire company.

Back in Virginia, AOL's brass was flabbergasted by this "soft launch."

Jean Villanueva had been using a beta test of MSN for months and was convinced that the weak offering was only a ruse—that Microsoft would unveil a terrific version at the last minute. "We kept thinking some secret switch would be flipped and the real service would come online," she said. "So we were pretty relieved by what we saw—or, really, didn't see."

The typically circumspect Steve Case was even optimistic. "I underestimated us and overestimated the competition," he said. But he also knew he needed to remain vigilant: A dictum in the computer business warned that although Microsoft's first and perhaps its second versions of its products were usually awful, the third always turned out to be a killer.

"I thought they eventually would have to get it right," said Case. "So I said to myself, 'Don't celebrate too soon.'"

But the irrepressible Ted Leonsis would have none of that kind of caution. In the spirit of Bill Von Meister—whom Leonsis did not know—he had rented a blimp and sent it floating over the festivities in Redmond to let MSN know that AOL would always be hovering over them. Plastered on the side was a sly greeting, well known to the more than three million AOL customers who heard it every time they signed in.

"WELCOME," it read.

the tangled web

if a bear falls in the woods

Mark Walsh was telling the old bear-in-the-woods joke to an audience at a Goldman Sachs Investment Conference in Phoenix, Arizona, on December 8, 1995.

"There's an old story about two campers who are walking through the woods and they come into a clearing. They look across two hundred yards of open meadow, and coming out of the woods is an eight-hundred-pound Kodiak bear, drooling and clearly hungry, just coming out of its long winter nap. The bear sniffs the air and catches the odor of these two campers. And he looks at them, and starts loping across the meadow toward them, obviously about to eat them. Both campers are incredibly shocked, but one of them drops his backpack quickly, and starts taking off his hiking boots and putting on his sneakers. And the other camper, sort of enraged so close to death, says, 'What are you doing? You can't outrun the bear.' And the other one says, 'I don't have to outrun the bear; I just have to outrun you.'"

The crowd laughed at Walsh's glib delivery. He then moved on to his real point.

"I bring that up as a kind of clear-eyed way of looking at the competition, which is: Don't necessarily worry about things you can't control. Try and find the ways and places you can control, and make yourselves competitively strong," advised the AOL vice president. "Some people think the Internet is the bear. We think it's not the bear. Or we think the Internet is *maybe* the bear. But we think there are lots of other campers."

One of those campers seemed to be MSN, which, by late November, had signed up only 375,000 users. By comparison, AOL was bringing in 250,000 new customers every month and would soon pass the four-million-members mark.

That had happened, in part, because AOL had continued to add to its offerings and had improved its running speed. In September, it announced the $14.5 million stock acquisition of Ubique Ltd., an Israeli company that offered real-time interaction and joint navigation for the Internet. With this technology, AOL developed "Virtual Places," a client-server software architecture that allowed real-time chat on the Internet. That was followed by the first "Digital City" offering, in AOL's home territory of Washington, DC. This new localized service, located on AOL and eventually on the Web, drew and maintained regional community audiences with city-specific information. Finally, in late October, AOL launched GNN, its stand-alone Internet access service, aimed at customers who preferred the wilds of the Web.

To help goose its image as the cool place to be in cyberspace, AOL had announced its first service branding advertising campaign in September. The result was a quirky series of 15-second TV commercials created by the trendy TBWA Chiat/Day of New York, directed by Ben Stiller, and starring oddly behaving celebrities such as former "Batman" Adam West.

Its cash flow continued to lag behind its expenses, so AOL initiated another public offering of 3.5 million shares—underwritten by Morgan Stanley, Goldman Sachs, Merrill Lynch, and Alex. Brown—for $58.38 a share. This netted the company $110.2 million (and, as a selling shareholder of 200,000 shares, yielded Jim Kimsey $11.2 million). In November, AOL had its third two-for-one stock split.

All the company's efforts to blunt—and harness—the growing force of the Internet seemed to be paying off as 1995 ended. Some statistics appeared to indicate that AOL was already a powerful force on the worldwide network of computers. In an Internet user survey by FIND/SVP, fielded in late 1995, AOL, with a 30 percent share of all Internet access, was found to be the leading national provider of Web connectivity.

Had AOL managed to outwit the bear by riding on its back?

dead men walking

Once again, Bill Gates would change the game. On December 7, 1995, in a major speech, he declared that his company was going to shift its entire business focus on the Internet. In addition, MSN would be porting its recently launched proprietary service to the Web, initiating a massive redesign and shift in its business.

"There was an image issue developing fast," said MSN's Russ Siegelman. "Online services were perceived to be anti-Internet, whereas the leading people were working on Internet technology."

The wholesale race to embrace the Internet broke into a sprint at the end of 1995. Following Microsoft's lead, Prodigy and eWorld (Apple's service, powered with AOL technology) announced their intention to make their offerings Web-based. AT&T had also abandoned its proprietary Interchange service and declared it would be back in the spring of 1996 with a major Internet-only offering.

The sum effect was dramatic, part of a mood that had been building for a long time. Among the elite of California's Silicon Valley, the Internet was becoming the new technological altar at which to pray. The Web was an open system; anyone could access an endless sprawl of every conceivable sort of information stashed on computers worldwide, mostly for free. The course of events was obvious: content providers would move there, as tools were developed to improve it dramatically. Naturally, users would soon migrate, and they would be serviced by the legions of streamlined Internet-only access providers that had sprung up like kudzu— from 1,800 in 1994 to 3,200 in 1995.

To the digerati, it was beginning to look as though AOL was the last maker of buggy whips in the dawning era of the automobile.

AOL was foolish to spend all sorts of money on building a brand, they declared with complete confidence, when the biggest brand of all was the Internet.

Anti-AOL sentiments had actually been voiced much earlier. In 1994, James Gleick, founder of an early Internet access provider called Pipeline, had noted: "The Internet is an ocean, and these online services are isolated ponds. Their days are numbered."

In mid-1995, the drumbeat continued: "They're doomed," predicted Michael Murphy, editor of the Overpriced Stock Service, to *Interactive Week*. "Are people really going to pay substantial hourly fees to chat with one another when they'll be able to do it for free?"

A *Newsweek* article by Steven Levy, in January 1996, particularly irked AOL's executive team. It read, in part:

> [The online services] want to reap the benefits of the Internet explosion, the boom that has everyone excited about doing business and seeking pleasure via computer. Yet their viability depends on not blending so thoroughly into the Internet that they lose their identities, and maybe their reason for existing. It won't be easy and may not be possible. The online services, despite signing up millions of new subscribers and establishing themselves as national brand names, are enjoying the most transitory of successes. Every day the Net gets closer to filling its ambitious promise, their clock ticks closer to midnight. They look a lot like dead men walking. If the Internet doesn't develop as anticipated, the dead men of the online services may keep walking for some time, especially if they are nimble enough to change direction. Still, I would hate to be the one who issued them life-insurance policies.

It was an utterly condescending take—and one that turned out to be spectacularly wrong—but it perfectly represented the attitudes of the Net nobility at the time.

"AOL was seen as the J.C. Penney of cyberspace," said Paul Saffo, director of Institute for the Future, a modish California think tank. "Silicon Valley was completely puzzled as to why anyone would still continue to go to AOL."

In California, early in 1996, Ted Leonsis found himself pummeled by Saffo and other Internet pundits at a newspaper conference that degenerated into an anti-AOL screed. "I could see we were winning the election, but losing the debate," said Leonsis. "They just hated us."

Case was getting weary of being cast in the unusual role of defending his company's future even as AOL continued its dizzying growth. By mid-February 1996, AOL had 5 million members—it had doubled in size in one year. In Case's view, the Internet's rapid growth gave AOL more to offer consumers and positioned AOL as the easy way for them to navigate. The Internet was a pipe, not a place; AOL was a place with a pipe.

"I think the conventional wisdom is dead wrong, because we deliver what consumers care about—community and information; and what they don't care about is the underlying system they get it on," said Case at the time. "The problem is that there is too much insular thinking by technological elites in the industry that say we are finished, when we are just getting started."

The attitude in Silicon Valley—among nerdy Netheads who could fix the insides of their own computers as easily as most people could open a can of tuna—was typical, thought Case. They did not understand that the online phenomenon was not about what software was the coolest or most elegant. People were responding to another, more ephemeral quality that was linked to the basic human need to communicate.

And yet, if he chose to ignore the voices of derision, they might easily grow into a chorus of naysaying that could ultimately influence the average consumer. So much of AOL's success had depended on word of mouth, and there was a danger in allowing an image to develop that AOL was behind the times. So if the computer industry's aristocracy wanted AOL to get with the Internet program even more, Case would show them just how Net-savvy AOL could be.

march madness

As 1996 began, no company represented the promise of the Internet more than Netscape Communications Corporation. After its hugely successful posting of the Navigator browser in the fall of

1994, the company's software claimed an incredible 80 percent of the market share. Netscape's prospects had improved even more with the hiring of James Barksdale as its chief executive officer in January 1995. Getting Barksdale, who had earned a sterling reputation with his stewardship of McCaw Cellular Communications, was considered another home run for Netscape.

With its initial public offering of 5 million shares at $28 each, on August 9, 1995, Netscape cemented its position. Its stock doubled by the day's end. With only negligible revenues, the company (taking all shares into account) was instantly worth $3 billion.

Despite the first rebuff in 1994, Case still desperately wanted to find a way to link Netscape with AOL. By the end of 1995, he was once again in discussions about licensing Netscape's browser technology.

A proposal made sense because Netscape was the creator of the hottest software of the Web. Case figured that AOL might throw out its BookLink browser and replace it with Navigator. This "best-of-breed" strategy was quickly creating a smarter path for AOL. Rather than trying to do everything by itself, AOL could be on the cutting edge of the Internet by incorporating its most popular tools within the service.

In addition, many AOL executives felt a kinship with the kind of company Netscape was—a feisty entrepreneurial culture that was now doing battle with Microsoft, the biggest software company in the world. After its December 1995 Internet conversion, Microsoft had committed itself to the browser market with a vengeance. Its Internet Explorer (IE) was offered free to all. Microsoft was determined to catch up fast, since the browser was becoming an essential piece of software for computers. Like a "car," it drove users all over the Web and tooled them through smaller, company-size "intranets." Whoever built the vehicle most used would gain a lot of power over the future of computing as the industry became more and more centered on the Internet.

Netscape, not AOL, was now in Gates's crosshairs. How far would Gates go for business?

Right to the doorstep of Steve Case's AOL—which Microsoft's MSN was designed to vanquish. Much to Case's surprise, Gates called Case before the Comdex trade show in November 1995, and invited him to come to the West and talk about AOL's using the Microsoft browser. The browser market was now more important to Gates than MSN.

To Microsoft, winning the browser war was critical. Netscape's browser had the potential to hurt Microsoft's flagship Windows product badly, if it could minimize the importance of the operating system. "To maintain our leadership, it was important that we build a better browser than Netscape, and get people to try it and hopefully use it regularly. AOL was the number one Internet service provider," said Brad Chase, the Microsoft executive charged by Gates to get AOL to use the Internet Explorer. "Clearly, then, the opportunity to promote IE to its six million users would be a big win for us."

At first, such an idea was anathema to AOL's executive team. "Everybody wanted Netscape," said Leonsis. "And, after what we had just been through with MSN, the idea of doing a deal with Microsoft was just out of the question."

Jean Villanueva was also an early Netscape backer. "The deal was Netscape's to lose. We had been talking with them forever. They were dominant. We needed to get what the market wanted, so we felt we had to go to Netscape," she noted. "Most importantly, we saw ourselves as smaller companies, fighting the same foe—Microsoft."

Case calculated that Netscape would be more than thrilled to do a deal with AOL. It would get its browser into the hands of AOL's millions of members on a daily basis, and would tweak Microsoft in the process. In January 1996, Case traveled to California for a dinner at Barksdale's house. He hoped to cut a deal that would link the two companies' fates.

Case's proposal was to replace BookLink with Navigator as AOL's principal browser. But he also felt that Netscape had not taken advantage of its Web site: Tens of millions of users crossed through daily, yet Netscape had put up only a few press releases and other dull business information. Why not have AOL—which knew content better than Netscape did—take over the programming and advertising sales for the Netscape home page? Finally, to underscore how important the relationship would be for the two companies, Case asked Barksdale for a Netscape board seat.

Two weeks later, Case had his answer: Netscape wasn't interested in Case's plan. Barksdale told Case that AOL could buy Netscape's browser, most certainly, but that was all.

"It was a period [when] the press was predicting AOL's doomsday and, I think, Netscape thought AOL would become irrelevant. They thought if they had MCI, AT&T, and Netcom using Netscape, they'd be fine in the consumer space," said Case. "They had no desire to treat us as a partner; they only wanted to treat us like a customer."

Case decided to conduct a "bake-off" between Netscape's Navigator and Microsoft's Explorer. David Cole, AOL's Internet head, led an effort in which the entire executive team looked at the two deals from a variety of perspectives—price, technology issues, and simple company rapport.

From the start, Case and most of the AOL executives were still predisposed to Netscape—and, more to the point, against Microsoft. When Brad Chase first visited AOL's Virginia offices to talk about Explorer, his chances were broadcast quickly to him.

"I went up to the receptionist and signed in and she looked at me and said, 'Microsoft, ooooooh,'" he recalled.

Luckily for Chase, neither Cole nor David Colburn—one of AOL's top deal-making executives, who was assigned to coordinate the browser project—was leaning toward anyone. Given to wearing cowboy boots and a few days' stubble, Colburn styled himself as a kind of maverick at AOL.

"I basically looked at what was the better deal for AOL, what would give us the most advantages," he said. "I didn't care about what the hell Silicon Valley thought, or that Microsoft was the anti-Christ, or that Netscape was so cool. I only thought, Who's got what we need?"

He quickly found that Netscape did not have what AOL needed, and Microsoft did. On almost every issue, he said, "It seemed like Netscape was taking things off the table, while Microsoft kept putting them on."

There was price: Netscape insisted that AOL pay millions of dollars for the browser—on a per-user basis, like all of its customers—because it was not in the business of giving its software away to big corporate users. Microsoft—looking to extend its browser market share quickly—was offering it to AOL for free, even though Microsoft had to pay Spyglass Inc. a fee for each copy shipped. And Microsoft had licensed the IE code from Spyglass for millions of dollars.

There was technology: Netscape did not want to change Navigator in any substantial way to accommodate AOL, and wanted Navigator to sit on top of AOL, directing users to the Netscape site as they entered the Web. But AOL wanted to deliver to the consumer a customized browser that was seamlessly integrated into the service in much the same way that BookLink was, with no barrier separating the service from the Internet. "With the Netscape browser, users would absolutely know they were leaving AOL to go to the Web, which meant we handed our members over to them," said Colburn. On the other hand, Microsoft was willing to change the browser in any way that was amenable to its service design, making it easier to customize.

And there was rapport: "Netscape thought we had nowhere else to go," said Colburn. "It was like, 'AOL *has* to do a deal with us, because (1) we're the leading browser, and (2) Microsoft is its archenemy.'" Microsoft, again, seemed to bend over backward to get the AOL business. There was even a full-scale press of Case by Gates himself. "I went after the AOL business," said Gates in a later interview.

Exactly how much he was willing to do became clear when Gates put on the table the ultimate deal-maker—an information folder on the Windows 95 desktop, with an AOL registration icon inside. Gates' move was bitterly opposed by MSN executives—for good reason. Although not displayed as prominently as the MSN logo, the AOL symbol was hard to pass up. This is precisely what Case had been seeking since MSN was announced in late 1994, and it effectively eroded the major marketing advantage MSN had over

AOL. (And, to Microsoft's advantage, it eliminated the Justice Department's main problem with its bundling practices.)

In weekly meetings through February and early March, AOL's executives went around and around about which company was better to do business with. Throughout 1995, they had charged up AOL by making Bill Gates the enemy. Could they really make a deal with Microsoft when part of it—MSN—was still dedicated to knocking AOL off?

And yet, if this deal was made, the software part of Microsoft was actually going to help AOL knock MSN off. The executives argued back and forth, but Case finally made the decision. It was time to change direction again.

The better deal would clearly be with Microsoft, Case told a gathering of his executives. The onetime online nemesis Ted Leonsis had created would become a major technology partner.

"There's good news and bad news," Case joked in his deadpan style. "The good news is, we'll get the deal. The bad news is, we'll have to kill Ted."

Case still hoped he could pull off a double deal involving both Netscape and Microsoft—or even a quadruple deal because AOL was also talking with AT&T about putting AOL's icon on its new WorldNet Internet service, and with Sun Microsystems Inc. about licensing its equally hot Java software technologies. Such a string of deals in a short time—labeled "March Madness" internally—would make AOL a definitive force on the Internet, thought Case.

On March 7, AOL began the fury with yet another deal. AOL was to take in the 147,000 subscribers to Apple's soon-to-be defunct eWorld online service, and Apple agreed to include AOL software on all Macintosh computers.

But the real action began on Monday, March 11, when AOL announced the Netscape alliance. Colburn and AOL executives had spent the weekend negotiating the deal. Under the agreement, AOL would license Netscape Navigator client software technology for all its services—most immediately, for GNN—and AOL would have a prominent presence on the Netscape Web site.

(On the same day, AOL inked the deal with AT&T without revealing the Netscape announcement. AT&T officials were irked because the same-day timing diminished the interest in their own AOL interconnection alliance.)

The browser pact was immediately seen as a big win for Netscape; its stock rose 16 percent to $46.25 that day. Netscape wasted no time in declaring victory, and began to spin the deal to the press—off the record—as a slap at Microsoft. On the record, the Netscape execs were more matter of fact. "This agreement enables Netscape to immediately extend its reach into the consumer market by providing AOL's five million customers with access to Netscape Navigator," said Jim Barksdale.

Case seemed equally thrilled. "As technologies are more fully leveraged to make the World Wide Web easier and more enjoyable to use for consumers, we will continue to see greater and greater numbers of consumers embrace this emerging medium," he said. "This announcement is as much about the future of our industry as it is about the vision of each of our companies."

But each company's vision was different, it was soon revealed. The Netscape officials did not seem to know, when they made the announcement, that they would not be AOL's primary browser partner. There was no exclusivity to the Netscape contract, and Colburn had immediately turned his attention to finishing up the even bigger deal with Microsoft. It took until 2 A.M. on March 12 to reach the agreement, but when it was signed, Microsoft's Internet Explorer would be AOL's principal browser.

Before the press announcements went out, Case called Barksdale to inform him of the deal. It was a short conversation. "I'm sorry, Jim," Case said.

"I understand," said the courtly Barksdale, though Netscape sources said he felt completely sandbagged by AOL. He had known that AOL and Microsoft were talking, but had no idea how serious the discussions had become.

Soon, Case was on a conference call with reporters and his new—and unlikely—confrere, Bill Gates. "Microsoft will become our primary technology partner in this Internet space," Case told the reporters, who were incredulous that a turnabout had brought the two bitter rivals into business together.

And, although he stressed that Microsoft was still "hard-core" about MSN, Gates also noted that AOL had "created the most successful consumer online experience and we are excited about making this available to the millions of people who use Windows." It was a statement few people ever expected him to make.

After the conference call, Case jetted off to meet his new partner at a Microsoft developer conference being held in San Francisco. As they waited backstage at the event the next day, Brad Chase joked to Case, "We don't want to be seen with you! There are MSN people over there!" In fact, Case was the surprise guest at the conference. He appeared with Gates on stage as part of an elaborate photo opportunity meant to signal how important the deal was to Microsoft.

It all put Case in a daze.

"I could never have imagined myself standing there with Gates because of our history with Microsoft, but I thought it was best for AOL, so we did it," recalled Case. "But it was definitely bizarre."

And more than a little odd to Netscape officials, too. Case's eagerness to improve AOL's Web image left a trail of bad feelings with the one company Case had long hoped would be AOL's closest comrade. To Netscape, Case turned out to be a double-talking opportunist for striking one deal right after the next.

Their pique was a bit disingenuous. Netscape had been well aware that Microsoft was in talks with AOL. An article in *The Wall Street Journal* on March 7 was titled: "Microsoft Seeking To Derail AOL Talks With Netscape." And, Colburn insisted, he had warned Netscape of the problems AOL had with its offer and had called his Netscape contact immediately after the deal was struck.

Yet, on the day the Microsoft deal was announced, Netscape officials insisted to the press that the Microsoft/AOL pact was not bigger than its own, though it clearly was. Later, when it became clear that Microsoft had outmaneuvered Netscape, its chairman, Jim Clark, noted politely to the media that Case was "like a chameleon—like any good businessman who will change to suit the needs of the market."

Privately, though, Netscape executives were livid and told anyone in the industry who would listen that Case had double-crossed them. To several financial analysts and industry players, Netscape's top officials characterized AOL as "sleazy" and "slimy" for its actions. They implied that AOL had not acted honorably.

Case found such comments, which quickly got back to him, specious and frustrating.

"It was not my fault that the press was reporting that AOL had gone with Netscape, then AOL was going with Microsoft," said Case. "But it made us look tricky, even though both companies knew there were discussions going on."

Case felt he had given Netscape as many chances as he could. "It always seemed to me like AOL should work with Netscape. But then the heart went one way and the mind another. The mind won, because the heart kept getting stabbed," he said. "I would characterize AOL's relationship with Netscape as multiple attempts to try and work together that haven't been successful, and the vast majority of responsibility falls on their shoulders."

Wall Street certainly seemed to approve of AOL's new spouse. On the day of the Microsoft Internet Explorer announcement, AOL stock rose 15 percent more and closed at $55.50.

adult supervision

To the outside world in the winter of 1996, Case may have appeared to be on top of his company and his life, but considerable turmoil inside of AOL centered on him—both professionally and personally.

AOL had grown like topsy over the previous two years. Absorbing all the new employees, and incorporating all the businesses that Case had bought, had proved troublesome. AOL began to acquire a reputation as one of the more chaotic companies in an already chaotic industry. Partners found AOL increasingly unresponsive. Customer service standards were slipping and costs were booming. During the rush to compete, the development of the company's infrastructure had atrophied. Its casual culture sometimes made AOL seem like a bunch of kids putting on a show rather than the major industry force it had become.

Leonsis and Connors each ran a major part of AOL—the service and the technical sides, respectively—but each reported only to Case for decision making. This became a problem: Case was the only one who could decide all the issues.

Case had proved he could create an online powerhouse. Could he now run it efficiently as a bottom-line manager, on a day-to-day basis? More to the point, was Case—who had styled himself a visionary builder—the right person to do the day-to-day job?

That question had been phrased in a more streetwise way by AOL chairman Jim Kimsey, in an article that appeared in *USA Today,* in November 1995. Talking off-the-cuff to a reporter in a Georgetown bar, Kimsey was quoted as saying that AOL would need "adult supervision" after he assumed the title and role of chairman emeritus and handed the chairmanship over to Case.

Kimsey's typically loose lips were not appreciated in Vienna, but, in essence, what he was saying was true. AOL had to bring in a more seasoned manager to maintain and expand what had been created by Case and his team.

So, as 1995 was ending, AOL initiated a search for a president who would take on the duties of operating the company. After a variety of major online managers had been considered, the focus moved outside the industry, to William Razzouk, executive vice president of the innovative overnight delivery service, Federal Express Corporation of Memphis, now FedEx.

At age 48, Razzouk had a long history of the kind of management experience AOL's board was looking for. He had grown up in Atlanta and attended the University of Georgia. After a short stint as a sportswriter, Razzouk moved to Xerox Corporation, where he became an account executive and sold copiers. Later, his career took him to Phillips Electronics NV, Rolm Corporation, and, in 1983, FedEx.

Like AOL, FedEx was small, growing fast, and very deep into computers, which were used to track millions of packages daily.

Razzouk was involved with the company's computer efforts and thought the entire industry had huge potential. When an AOL headhunter contacted him, he jumped at the chance to be involved with what he considered the next wave of technology. Case, noting that FedEx and AOL were both service businesses that required someone who could effectively marshal people and resources, thought Razzouk was a perfect fit.

More importantly, Razzouk was capable of taking over a lot of the operations duties that did not interest Case. On the day he arrived, in late February, for example, Razzouk was thrown into a decision on whether to spend $25 million on a building in Dulles, Virginia, for the increasingly cramped staff. The plan, which was approved, was to create a single "campus" for AOL's employees, à la West Coast high-tech companies, such as Microsoft.

And just days after Razzouk had started working for AOL, another job was more delicate. Case walked into his office and announced that he had separated from his wife, Joanne.

The couple had met at Williams College in 1977, during Case's sophomore year. They did not marry right away, dating others in the interim years, as Case shifted from job to job. They married in 1985, after Case had come to Vienna to work for Control Video. Case, typically tight-lipped, did not talk a lot about his home life in the office. Joanne had attended many AOL social functions over the years, but she had decidedly not been part of its relentless march to dominate the industry. Instead, she stayed at home to raise the couple's three small children. In retrospect, many observers attributed the problems in their marriage to the long hours and intense focus that were required of Case in his work life.

But there was a second, and much more problematic, situation— a personal relationship between Case and Jean Villanueva, AOL's communications chief and its highest-ranking female executive.

"Steve understood it would be controversial, and said he needed my help to deflect controversy internally," said Razzouk. "So I took on that role, dealing with a bunch of guys I didn't even know, trying to smooth things over."

There would be a lot to smooth over. Some members of the inner circle were aware of brewing tension in Case's marriage, but the marital breakup came as a surprise to most AOL employees. Their surprise soon turned to shock when they learned that Case and Villanueva, who was also in the midst of a marital separation, were an item. Steve and Jean had always been close, but this?

In the first week of March, Case and Villanueva told the board members and executive staff about their developing personal relationship.

"We realized that we're a public company, a large company, and there was the element of my working for Steve, of there being respect for the perception of the company," said Villanueva, a slim, dark-haired woman with an intense, expressive demeanor. "We didn't want whispering behind our backs. And we wanted [the relationship] to be aboveboard."

The situation had serious implications for AOL. Villanueva was one of its most powerful executives, and her long tenure and experience gave her strong influence well beyond her title. She was outspoken, known for a fiery commitment to AOL that rubbed some the wrong way. "Jean was like the conscience of AOL, its missionary," said one long-time executive. "Where Steve held back, Jean almost played the role of a lightning rod—she was unafraid to be either disliked or liked as long as AOL did the right thing."

A native of Florida, Villanueva had come to Washington in the early 1980s. After working for a Republican congressman, she became more interested in the power and possibilities of computing and online communications. Her first industry job was as a marketing manager for The Source. Later, she moved to General Electric Information Services.

Both jobs were located in the Washington area, as was AOL. Villanueva had heard of the feisty start-up, and, in 1988, when AOL was looking for a marketing director, she got an interview with Case. She was taken aback by his casualness. He was wearing old clothes; his feet were up on his desk, and his chair was tilted back as they talked about the job. His sphinxlike manner made Villanueva think Case would not even consider her for the job. Then, to her surprise, Case called and offered her the position of marketing director.

Villanueva soon learned to read Case; indeed, she became the person whom AOL staff went to if they wanted to know what Case was thinking. That strong working relationship was important; Villanueva got the company a lot of its first notice in the 1990s, and represented Case to the industry as a leader. She rose to vice president of marketing in 1989, and—after a maternity leave—became vice president of communications in 1993. Her influence was not fully described by her title. Villanueva, Leonsis, Connors, and financial officer Len Leader formed the coterie of Case's closest executives.

The deepening of the "personal relationship" raised questions among the executive ranks. Would Case be able to directly manage someone with whom he was romantically involved? Would the relationship damage Villanueva's ability to work with other executives who might feel that she had more clout with Case? Where would the couple's business relationship end and their personal one begin?

Within the company, gossip about both Case's and Villanueva's personal life was widespread, partly because the situation contrasted so strongly with Case's plain-vanilla, boy-next-door public persona.

"Steve was just flat-out untouchable because we looked up to him as a perfect big brother," said one executive. "So it just hit a little hard that maybe he was a lot more human than we thought."

One board member worried about the business implications. "It was a damn difficult issue that went right to the question of Steve's judgment," he said. "I thought I had walked into the middle of *Melrose Place,* and such gossip was not what we needed at all."

Case and Villanueva, expecting discretion in response, had quietly informed several reporters of their personal situation and had naively hoped that business journalists would not report it as a "story."

But AOL had become too important and Case had become too famous. Nestled among tidbits about director Martin Scorsese's new movie, Katharine Hepburn's bout with pneumonia, and the late François Mitterand's illegitimate daughter, the first short item appeared on the third page of *The Washington Post* Style section, on March 5, 1996. The regular celebrity-news column, called The Source, couldn't resist the coy headline: "AOL's Love Connection."

"America Online Chairman Steve Case, one of the best-known business personalities in cyberspace, and the highest ranking female executive at the Vienna-based company are divorcing their respective spouses and are involved in a 'personal relationship,'" the tidbit read, in part.

Complications from their relationship began almost immediately. The day the item appeared in the *Post,* Case was to deliver a major speech about AOL and the industry at the National Press Club in Washington. It was an important time for Case and the company. The general public and the press were just beginning to focus on AOL as the definitive winner of the online wars, having bested CompuServe, Prodigy, and, most impressively, Microsoft.

"We started our company over a decade ago, when there was not a lot of interest in online services," Case began his speech. "In fact, there was virtually no interest in the concept."

The interest that day, among many in the room, centered on how Case interacted with Villanueva, who had arranged the speech and had accompanied Case to the Press Club.

Case and Villanueva were mortified by the public attention that began to grow; they especially worried about the effects on their respective families. But, because mainstream interest in cyberspace and its leaders was growing fast, the revelation of their relationship was even featured in *People* Magazine, a development that shocked the pair. The relationship soon became an inevitable paragraph in articles written about AOL and Case in 1996.

A month later, Case scored a major coup by appearing on the cover of *Business Week*'s April 15 issue. He was pictured lying atop a huge pile of AOL disks. It was the press equivalent of a big wet kiss, the kind of cover corporate public relations officers laminate for posterity and send out in every press kit. Contrasted with the flack AOL had gotten from the digerati all winter, the cover story was a victory.

"Now, everyone wants to be on Case's planet," gushed the piece. "With more than 5 million customers and 75,000 more joining every week, AOL is the most potent force in cyberspace." The cover story even featured an adorable baby picture of Case, a photo from his boyhood, and another in which, as a way-cool teenager, he was posing with his garage band.

But this public relations homer got no cheers from Case, largely because of the article's blink-and-you'll-miss-it mention of his relationship with Villanueva. Though the one-sentence reference was deep within the story, Case felt *Business Week* had sandbagged him. The magazine had given him the impression that his personal situation would not be part of the story, he felt, although its editors did not think they had made that agreement with Case.

When he realized, late in the process and after he had given multiple interviews, that the item was going in, Case flipped, called *Business Week* editors, and even said that he was withdrawing permission for the magazine's use of the childhood photos.

"It was like a nuclear explosion . . . the vitriol and intensity were remarkable to everyone, since Steve is usually so calm," said another *Business Week* reporter, Mark Lewyn, who had known both Case and Villanueva for many years. "I think it was probably not a surprising time to be hypersensitive because of the enormous pressures he must have been under."

Indeed, his older brother Dan—with whom he shared much of his personal turmoil—had kidded him that the article's mention of his personal strife was the least of his worries.

"The joke is that once you're on the cover of *Business Week*," Dan had quipped to Steve, "that's just when your stock is about to drop."

Unfortunately for Case and AOL, that jest would turn out to be a little too accurate.

now is the summer of their discontent

sayonara

May 8, 1996, should have been a day of celebration for Steve Case.

AOL's stock had gone stratospheric. Taking several stock splits into consideration, it had hit an all-time high of $71 per share the day before, valuing the company at $6.5 billion. It was Wall Street's reward after a series of coups had landed AOL at the top of the industry.

AOL had certainly delivered for its investors.

Most impressively, it had bested Microsoft in the online wars of 1995 and had then struck a groundbreaking deal to have its logo displayed and software sitting on the desktop of the software giant's new operating system. Its other longtime competitors—CompuServe and Prodigy—were inexorably headed downward, in large part because of AOL's success. The company had pulled off a series of glittery pacts with a range of prominent companies, including AT&T and Sun Microsystems, further solidifying its grip on the fast-growing new medium.

Case, clad in a kimono, had spent the day in Tokyo drinking ceremonial sake, exchanging gifts, and celebrating the announcement of a joint venture (with Mitsui & Co. Ltd. and Nihon Keizai

Shimbun Inc.) to bring the service to Japan, a crucial step in AOL's strategy to expand the business globally.

But as he sat in a conference room in Tokyo's Imperial Hotel, his notes arrayed on the table in front of him, Case's face was tired and drawn. All day, in between the lavish, wordy toasts, he had periodically skittered from the room to take calls from Len Leader back in northern Virginia. Their conversations were tense and edgy, even as expectations for the company were soaring.

Case had good reason to worry. Below the seemingly calm and happy surface of AOL, serious problems were churning—quite literally.

The calamity they had hoped to fight off all spring had finally happened—AOL's growth was suddenly slowing at an alarming rate, because of a trend known as "churn." After years of pulling in scads of new customers with ease, the company was facing the prospect of losing members nearly as quickly as it could sign them up. AOL's story had always been about growth, growth, and more growth; any sign that the party was over was unthinkable. Would the company have to ratchet up its already hefty marketing budget even more, to keep the same flow of customers through the front door?

Buried in this volatile mix was an even more frightening development. While Case had been long trying to blunt the effect of the Internet on AOL's business by building a variety of Web-friendly features into the service, direct-to-the-Web providers' flat-rate pricing for unlimited use was catching on. The competitors had set off an alarm; consumers were becoming dissatisfied with hourly-fee plans that forced them to watch the clock. Worried about burgeoning bills, they were beginning to expect the unlimited-use price of $19.95, which was fast on its way to becoming the standard rate—a rate that AOL did not offer.

If longtime customers began to abandon the service and to move to cheaper pastures, the pressure would be on for AOL—long used to the succor of lucrative hourly subscriber fees—to adopt a pricing plan it couldn't realistically afford.

So far, there were only warning signs—harbingers that a difficult period might lie ahead. Any serious troubles seemed far enough away for optimism to safely rule the day. Everyone—Wall Street, the press, the AOL employees counting their stock options in their cozy cubicles at the company's headquarters—was riding the wave of good feeling that a soaring stock price always produces. Case was one of the sizzling stock's biggest beneficiaries: His stock and options in AOL were worth about $224.1 million at that moment.

Still, he fretted that expectations were running too high. During the thirteen-hour flight to Japan, Case had decided that AOL needed to tone down the feel-good frenzy surrounding the company. In the upcoming trans-Pacific conference call, financial analysts not only would discuss the third quarter results (AOL's fiscal year ended June 30) but also would express a measure of uneasiness about AOL's state of affairs.

The trick, however, was not to go too far in the other direction. By tempering good financial news with caution, Case hoped to avoid wild volatility in the company's stock at a later time, when problems might become big enough to engender real panic.

On the phone from Japan, he told Leader that they should deliberately inject a note of circumspection into the conference call. Err on the side of being forthcoming about the problems, he instructed his chief financial officer. He didn't anticipate that he and Leader would fulfill their mission a little too well.

Night was already falling in Tokyo when the call began. Case, his new president Bill Razzouk, and Jack Davies, head of international operations at AOL, were speaking from the Imperial Hotel, as was Haruo Hoshizaki of Mitsui. At AOL headquarters in Vienna, where it was 8 A.M., Leader, Vice President of Investor Relations Richard Hanlon, and Jean Villanueva joined in as well.

They all hoped for the best. The art of properly spinning Wall Street was a delicate matter and AOL's management needed to show they were in control of the upcoming churn problem. The numbers seemed good enough: AOL had beaten Wall Street's predictions for profits in the quarter; revenues were up 186 percent to $312.3 million compared to $109.1 million the year before; and marketing costs were down as a percentage of revenues.

There was also some proactive news: the company was introducing a competitive new pricing plan—20 hours for $19.95 per month—to help staunch the flow of customers to flat-rate offerings. And the new and improved 3.0 version of AOL software, due to be distributed widely in the fall, would be another tool to attract and retain customers.

And then, Steve Case started to drop the bomb as gently as possible.

"It has been quite clear that the market is changing and the environment in which our services are offered is growing more competitive than ever before," he said. "We plan to use this slightly slower seasonal period to become a bit more careful in managing the customer acquisition process . . . we'll be shifting our focus a little, from aggressive acquisition toward significant investments in quality."

Leader took over, and Case listened intently as his voice wafted out of the speakerphone.

"One of the costs of growing our business as aggressively as we have, by maximizing trials, is that we get less qualified prospects," said Leader. "So we are seeing a higher churn in the March and April periods, as a result of very aggressive acquisition marketing spending."

Instant computer messages filled with worry began to fly between the company executives in the United States and Japan. Did we go too far? Did it work? Did we seem too nervous?

Yes. No. And, definitely.

For an audience who had never heard "slower growth" and "AOL" used in the same sentence, AOL's pronouncements were alarming. Churn? Lower marketing spending? A defensive pricing change that seemed to suggest a more drastic one down the line?

Worse still, listeners to the call began to pick up on what Case later called the "body language." The high-flying AOL team sounded hesitant, uncertain. Things felt a little discombobulated, especially with half the AOL team in Japan, jetlagged and spent after the events of the day. It was as though Case was saying, "Yes, all is well," while being betrayed by a nervous, telltale twitch in his demeanor.

And that was all it took. AOL had enjoyed the rousing run-up. Wall Street decided, then and there, that it was time for a little correction.

Case himself was surprised at the selling frenzy that resulted (the stock fell 10 percent that day); he considered it an overreaction to what was said in the phone conference. But the slide was to get a lot worse over the long, hot summer; it would shear nearly 70 percent off the value of AOL's stock by mid-October, leading some observers to question whether AOL could survive the fall.

to everything, churn, churn, churn

On May 30, AOL broke the six-million-member mark worldwide, making it the largest online provider on the entire globe. From third position a mere two years before, Case and his company had vaulted into the undisputed top spot.

But AOL's longtime naysayers were just beginning to be heard.

"It is far too early to write off Case, 37, who in a decade has built AOL into a colossus despite having to change strategies more often than most chief executives change underwear," wrote columnist Allan Sloan in *Newsweek*'s May 27 issue. "[But] even Steve Case's best scrambling can't prop AOL's stock forever."

For the acerbic Sloan, a sharp-eyed reporter who specialized in clever eviscerations of corporate pooh-bahs, this was a second take on AOL. He had chided the company, during the previous fall, for using accounting methods that made its bottom line look better.

Few had paid attention then; the excitement that surrounded the company's blistering growth blocked out negative observations. But Sloan's new column proved a bellwether, setting the stage for a massive flood of attacks on the very structure of the company. The rest of 1996 would turn out to be "one of the more horrible times in the company's history," according to one major AOL executive.

The gripes were wide-ranging and serious: AOL had been conducting a risky expansion-at-all-costs strategy with little regard to the price; marketing costs to pay for attracting subscribers were growing at a dangerous pace and were yielding a rapidly diminishing return; cash flow was declining precipitously; more serious competitors were on the horizon; and new revenues were slow in coming.

The churn was the first warning signal for the trouble to come. The key question in the spring of 1996 was: If the growth AOL was gunning for had stalled, would the whole model collapse?

Growth had always been AOL's mantra—the justification for the huge marketing budget that had buried the nation in AOL disks. The strategy had ensured that virtually anyone who was even remotely curious about the online phenomenon would have an AOL diskette at hand to pop into the nearest computer. Millions had responded, taking up AOL on its numerous free offers.

But this strategy also created a high level of churn. Too often now, new members simply used up their free hours, then canceled at the end of the trial period, without ever paying a dime to AOL. AOL had then lost the cost of acquiring the new member— around $50, according to the company's estimates—and the expense of providing free hours of connect time. When a trial member quit without "converting" and without paying AOL anything, the company had absolutely nothing to show for all the money it had laid out.

AOL's free programs had another negative side. Some customers would sign up for AOL over and over again, using different diskettes and different screen names, just to get the free hours. When the free trial period was up, the customer would cancel the account and start the process over again, as many times as possible before getting caught.

In addition, there was credit card fraud. For a time, AOL was signing up customers and beginning their service without immediately checking the validity of their credit card numbers. By the time the fraud was detected, the customer had usually abandoned the account—most likely to start another, continuing a cycle of virtually unlimited free usage.

None of these practices caused great harm while AOL was experiencing its huge customer growth. AOL had always had churn, but the number of new customers had always overwhelmed the number of people who left the service.

Case had outlined his strategy clearly: there would never be a cheaper time to build market share. The goal was to reach "critical mass"—10 million members was the target in 1996. With that cushion of subscriptions, Case believed, AOL's dominance of the field would open up numerous other revenue streams, such as lucrative advertising earnings.

Case's management team had long dubbed their quest to make AOL the number one service a "land grab," and people at the company targeted sweeping expanses to conquer. But now the available territory seemed to be disappearing fast.

The daily updates of user numbers that arrived in the electronic mailboxes of AOL executives began to be frightening. Monthly churn—which had hovered at about 1 percent or less only a year before—was averaging 6 percent and more, one top executive said. That meant the annual turnover rate was 72 percent. As the spring progressed, the numbers worsened. Despite large gross gains of users, net gains were becoming increasingly marginal. If the trend continued, the graph lines of customers who came and customers who canceled would begin to cross.

For many quarters, the net number of newcomers had been about 700,000; an astonishing 905,000 subscribed during the quarter that ended in March 1996. But over the summer, there were signs that AOL would add only about half that number. The planned cut in marketing spending might reduce the number even more. The redesigned 3.0 software, already months late, was to be ready during the summer, so sending out old versions of AOL would be stupid. That hiatus also would cut into subscriber growth.

Jeff Goverman, one of the most bearish AOL analysts, articulated the situation publicly. Instead of his original estimate of 750,000 newcomers, he predicted that AOL's domestic growth for the quarter ending June 30 would not exceed 400,000.

Worse still, the customers who were beginning to leave were not trial members, but those on the "back end"—longtime and heavy users who were AOL's biggest spenders. The heavy users represented only one-third of the base of subscribers, but they accounted for 60 percent of the usage.

"The churn was accelerating beyond our wildest imaginings," said Bill Razzouk, who was shocked by the extent of the problem soon after he arrived at AOL in late February. "The company had gone through some difficult times before, but this was the first time in several years they were faced with, 'Oh, shit! What do we do now?'"

Razzouk compared the danger to "rockets and grenades going off." In one meeting on the issue, Ted Leonsis, had put it best: "We're skiing in front of the avalanche, so we had better move fast."

But AOL foundered, without answers. There was slowness in acknowledging the problem, and too many people had a vague hope that it would just go away. At twice-weekly meetings, the members of a churn task force that Leonsis had created in the spring were flummoxed. Why were so many AOL customers leaving?

In an attempt to find the problem's source, AOL created "loyalty labs" that summer. To understand why subscribers canceled, the executives reasoned, they needed to know who the AOL users were, and what they were looking for in an online experience. What omission by AOL was making subscribers leave? How could AOL encourage better account retention? When someone becomes interested in AOL, how can that interest be sustained?

The loyalty labs featured a variety of tests to determine what kept people interested in AOL. Special focus was given to subscribers who had been on the service less than thirty days, because—internal studies showed—subscribers crossed a psychological barrier very early in their usage of the service.

"Retaining new customers will become like a new religion," said Leonsis in a speech to employees over the summer. "We all have to try to think of a million little ideas to try to slow [churn] down."

Religion had nothing to do with one very controversial moneymaking idea that was floated during the summer of 1996: services devoted solely to "adult content."

"When we were evaluating the move to 20/20 pricing, we were looking at how we could shore up against lost revenues from the new pricing plan," said Lyn Chitow, who was the vice president of Internet and community services and a six-year veteran of AOL. "It was like, 'Here's an idea: let's run with it, and see if it will work.' "

The equation presented was simple. Adult material on the Web was hugely popular—many people were even willing to pay fees to Web sites to see it. AOL needed a way to boost revenues. And AOL had the largest collection of eyeballs in cyberspace—which in turn made it one of the biggest portals funneling users to Internet porn sites. Why couldn't AOL just provide what the users wanted on its own service, and then charge a fee for it?

Throughout the summer, midlevel managers researched the idea of creating a premium "Adult Only" channel directly on the service. The channel would differ from AOL's other channels in several ways: it would be optional; it would carry a surcharge; and rather than pointing to original AOL content, it would connect the user to an aggregation of "adult content" culled from the Internet.

Even to consider this move was hugely risky. Wouldn't designing a special area on AOL send a signal that AOL welcomed porn peddlers? And how could AOL ever again label itself a "family friendly" service if the plan were approved? But AOL seemed more concerned with how its image—and bottom line—would be affected than with any thorny ethical questions about pornography.

"We did a lot of research and brand analysis, and determined we could make a lot of money on it," said Chitow. "But the question was: How much would it damage the brand?" So AOL hired an outside company—Seidmon Associates—to hold focus groups with its members and find out how harmful running such a service might be.

In a confidential memorandum dated August 7, 1996, AOL got its answer from focus groups conducted during the week of July 11–17, 1996, in Bethesda, Maryland, and Charlotte, North Carolina. Eight groups, each comprised of three current AOL users, were asked for their reactions to the "Adult Only Channel" idea.

According to the memo, "adult oriented" was defined as material that is "generally considered to include 'pornography' (i.e., explicit nude photos and videos), uncensored sexual and fantasy chat and sexually derived text."

The AOL members in the focus groups, many of whom had young children, were "initially outraged, critical and disappointed," according to the memo. One participant was quoted as saying, "It's like going to Disneyland and finding an X-rated cinema there."

Nonetheless, the focus groups had not ruled out such a service completely: "After thought and discussion," according to the memo, "their position became 'resigned disappointment.'" AOL knew better than to expect everyone to applaud such a move. The critical question was: Would they be upset enough to quit the service? Disappointment did not necessarily mean members would leave. "Few anticipate any lasting shift in perception of AOL, providing that the marketing, distribution and access of the Adult service [are] exceptionally responsible," read the memo. "One exception is in schools, where AOL is now seen as safe; this changes perception."

Multiple issues had to be considered. Some members were concerned their names would be sold as part of a mailing list if they subscribed to the adult channel. Some were afraid that additional racy chat would find its way to the main service. And many were worried about kids' managing to gain access to the channel, even though it would be protected with passwords and credit card verification. To help ensure that kids weren't using the channel, Seidmon Associates suggested that AOL should consider separate billing to monitor and verify kids' usage—perhaps reflecting dates and times.

"However," the Seidmon report noted dryly, "spouses' exposure to bill could be objectionable."

Among the conclusions reached: "Content should be characterized as uncensored (much more liberal than commercial online content) yet strictly legal (responsible)." And finally, "This phase suggests a notable opportunity, especially since many men haven't successfully entered adult Web sites." In other words, AOL's channel could have strong appeal to men who wanted to access porn online but didn't know how to find it.

Based on the research findings, AOL's Rande Price wrote, "There appears to be an opportunity for the company to further explore the development of an online area for adult content."

Vic Sussman, AOL's Director of Creative Programming and formerly an editor at *U.S. News & World Report,* later took on the task of searching out porn online, to find out who was producing it and what was available. Months later, at AOL's expense, he flew to California for the annual International Conference on Prostitution, in the belief that he would be able to meet some adult content providers there.

In retrospect, researching an adult channel seems foolish, an idea that could only bring AOL more headaches. At the time, it was one of many efforts to find ways of keeping people on the service. Churn was playing havoc with AOL's members, and the company's bottom line was at stake.

Excessive churn also blew away the controversial accounting practice the company had long used to allow it to show profits. An entry on the company's balance sheets—"deferred subscriber acquisition costs"—represented marketing money that AOL was spending to attract customers via direct response advertising, but was not counting against earnings. Instead of immediately entering, as an ordinary expense, the costs of the floppy disks it was sending out, AOL had counted them as "investments" to be paid for over two years.

Professor Abraham J. Briloff of City University of New York was one of the first to note the issue. In a paper he delivered at an American Accounting Association conference, in August 1995, he called AOL's method of accounting for marketing and acquisitions "in-your-face arrogance." He never accused AOL of illegality, but he made a more salient point: without deferring certain marketing costs, AOL was not profitable.

Few had paid attention to Briloff or to AOL's neat accounting trick, done in full view of a winking Wall Street. The financial statements made it appear that the company was earning profits when, in fact, the mountain of deferred cost had grown to more than $300 million by June 30, 1996.

AOL had long noted that its accounting method was legal—the magazine industry, for example, routinely practiced it. But by the summer of 1996, debate began to surface as to whether the practice of deferring these costs was a wise accounting method or a desperate measure to keep up appearances so that investors would continue to pour needed cash into the company.

The method was certainly a calculated gamble. Spreading out the cost of acquiring a member might make sense if the subscriber agreed to stay with the service long enough for AOL to recapture its investment. But with growing costs per subscriber—some analysts claimed those costs had tripled to $150— and with churn cutting into the length of time the users were staying, the game of chance AOL was playing could quickly become more precarious.

AOL could only speculate how long users would stay. AOL officials had insisted that the average sign-up lasted 42 months. Goverman and others insisted that the correct figure was more like 15 months. Dubious analysts and company officials went back and forth—did users have to stay 30 months or 35 months, for the company to break even? Could AOL trust the estimates, when the new medium had so few historical patterns? As marketing costs ballooned—the company had to attract ever more customers to keep growing—some began to worry that AOL was digging a financial hole it could never hope to climb out of. Wall Street had not yet zeroed in on the financial implications of deferring marketing costs—that controversy would reach its crescendo in the fall. For now, it was simply flabbergasted at the prospect that AOL might stop growing.

So was AOL. "Members are canceling every day in large numbers—large enough to make a significant and material difference to the bottom line," intoned AOL vice president Katherine Borsecnik at an employee meeting.

Where were AOL's customers going?

the price is not right

Many former AOL subscribers were going to Internet service providers (ISPs), which had become more prevalent throughout the country. In the spring, AOL had hoped to stave off the threat by its many attempts to turn the Internet into an advantage. But the company watched in dismay as the growing number of ISPs grew even larger in 1996. Thousands of small operations—and a few huge ones—were jostling to sign up computer users. The competition for customers became increasingly ferocious. AOL's most loyal and lucrative members were beginning to leave in accelerating numbers.

Hadn't AOL invested hundreds of millions of dollars in Internet technology over the past two years? Hadn't the company gotten the "best-of-breed" browsers when users had demanded it? Hadn't the planners prepared well enough to thwart ISPs?

They had not. The reason became clear after Audrey Weil, whom Case had now put in charge of member experience, traveled to AOL's Jacksonville call center in the summer, to talk with the customer service representatives and learn what the customers were telling them. After a few days of interviewing the operators, she prepared a report, "A Trip to the Front Lines," in which she laid out the concerns of the members.

What was the biggest complaint of AOL users? Not the widely mocked and irritating blue bar that appeared when members downloaded information. Not the frequent unsolicited junk e-mail. Not dropped connections.

Their overwhelming gripe: the ticking clock. Users didn't want to pay by the hour anymore.

No matter what AOL provided in terms of experience, the members' increasingly loud chant for the unlimited usage now being offered by ISPs was dangerous for AOL, Weil knew. "We still could not figure out a way to do it profitably," she said.

Case agreed. "We had temporarily beaten them back on technology and by incorporating Internet content better, and now the hundreds of ISPs were hammering us with price," said Case. "This was a big problem with no easy solution."

The move to the "20/20" pricing plan was meant to assuage this problem, but customers were still nervous about hourly fees. It was difficult to have a pleasurable user experience online when you were constantly worried about going over your time limit, they complained.

Investors, wary of any price change that would have a dramatic effect on AOL's balance sheet, began to express dismay about the new 20/20 plan. Under the new pricing scheme, users could stay online for up to 20 hours each month for $19.95. After that, an hourly fee of $2.95 kicked in. For moderately heavy users, the savings were substantial—under the old plan, 20 hours of use would have cost $54.20.

The company was already exploring other ways of making money—through online transactions, selling ads on the service, and selling AOL merchandise—but the huge bulk of its revenues (more than 85 percent) still came from subscriber fees. In trying to compete price-wise with the much smaller, cheaper-to-run ISPs, was AOL cutting itself off at the knees?

Within the company, pricing strategy debates had gone on since day one. In the early years, instant reaction to moves by Prodigy and CompuServe had been vital for survival. But now AOL found itself in the position of a follower—and a slow one, at that. It had allowed the ISPs to dominate the pricing game. Some in the company advocated an immediate change to a flat rate, no matter what the consequences; others insisted that AOL's offerings were better than the no-frills products of the ISPs and therefore deserved a premium price for as long as possible.

Case decided to take the middle road, using the 20/20 plan as the first, best step. He hoped that enough light users would go to the 20/20 plan, paying $19.95 for far fewer than 20 hours a month, to make up for the revenues lost when heavy users were online for 20 hours. In that scenario, revenues would not drop significantly and users would be happy.

But consumers' desire for flat-rate pricing was unquenchable, even though the $19.95 monthly fee was often more expensive than most customers' average monthly bill of $17.

Case had heard from one AOL member who insisted that she was being cheated by AOL's hourly rate pricing. When he checked her average monthly usage, he found that she would be paying AOL more under the flat-rate price of $19.95. When Case informed the user of that fact, her reaction was immediate.

"I don't care," she told an incredulous Case. "I am being cheated by you."

Her response was representative of a troubling shift in customer attitude that became increasingly clear during the summer of 1996. When the service had been small and scrappy, in the early days when Case would chat with subscribers in the chat rooms and answer all his e-mail personally, AOL felt like a community. Now that AOL had become the Goliath of the online world, the company was losing the close-knit feeling its early users had shared.

Members' ire was further fueled by a troubling series of serious customer service missteps by AOL that began in mid-1995 and would stretch on through 1997, stumbles that quickly took the form of legal actions.

AOL's first major customer-service-related lawsuit was filed in August 1995, in California Superior Court, by an attorney named Stephen Hagen, who challenged the service's unorthodox way of rounding off the time a subscriber spent online. Any fraction of a minute was rounded off to the next minute, for every single online session. AOL also added 15 seconds to each session, to cover the time required for AOL to sign on and sign off the user, but those extra 15 seconds did not show on the screen display that told members how long they had been online.

In other words, each time an AOL subscriber was online for just 46 seconds, he or she would have a total online time of 61 seconds and would be charged for 2 minutes. The practice was especially galling because AOL was the only online provider that did it. CompuServe rounded off to the next minute for every session, but did not add 15 seconds for signing on and signing off. Prodigy was the fairest of all: sessions were tracked to the second, then rounded off to the nearest minute only at the end of the month.

Subscribers were outraged. The charges made it look as though AOL was trying to sneak money out of customers' pockets without adequately notifying them of the company's billing policies.

That issue, at least, came to a closure of sorts in late June 1996, when a preliminary settlement in the Hagen case was announced in San Francisco. AOL agreed to automatically award every member one free hour of usage (worth $2.95 at that time), and more if the member had spent over $300 on connect fees for the service. Former users were paid out of an $800,000 fund AOL had set aside. They got the equivalent of one hourly fee for every $300 they had spent on the service.

It was a Pyrrhic victory. One hour of time per user hardly seemed worth all the effort that had gone into the suit, especially when AOL was handing out many more free hours to new users nationwide, as part of its marketing effort. The real gainers were the lawyers who had pleaded the case against AOL. Their take was $2.3 million in fees, paid by AOL.

The company may have been out of cash, but under the settlement AOL was allowed to continue the practice, as long as customers were adequately alerted to the 15-second add-on.

But other legal guns were now pointed at the company. In June 1996, while the California suit was wending its way through the system, reports surfaced that AOL was also under investigation by New York's Attorney General, for more billing problems. Within weeks, fourteen more states and the Federal Trade Commission were also looking at AOL's billing practices.

First came the complaint that all of the major online services, including AOL, automatically began billing new subscribers after their free trial period had ended, without giving sufficient warning that the subscribers needed to cancel if they didn't want to pay. The issue was not the automatic billing; it was, once again, the companies' methods for letting consumers know the charges would be levied. Second to be scrutinized was AOL's practice of deducting money from subscribers' checking accounts before the company had received authorization to do so.

The negativity of the legal battles—combined with worries about pricing, churn, and the Internet—began to take a hefty toll on AOL's share price. The company's stock soon became one of those most frequently shorted, and people betting against AOL were in control of the story that Wall Street was now hearing. Their tale of woe was not helped by Case's sale, on May 21, of 275,000 shares of AOL stock (about 8 percent of his holdings) for $14 million, to help pay for his upcoming divorce settlement.

By June 6, AOL's stock was hovering at $48 a share, a 33 percent decline from its May high. It seemed, said Case, "like everyone was finally chanting all at once: 'Ding, dong, the witch is dead.'"

out of the frying pan

Could it get worse?

Perhaps so, thought Steve Case, as he watched his number-two man, Bill Razzouk at the podium at the AOL Partners Conference at the Grand Hyatt Hotel in downtown Washington on June 12.

Ted Leonsis had dreamed up a new-agey title for the conference, using a Japanese word he particularly liked: "Building a Digital Keiretsu." Leonsis had defined the word for the gathering as "a group of companies characterized by close interconnections and relationships, often with cross shareholdings." He wanted to project the idea that there was a bigger bond between AOL and its content partners than just a buyer–seller relationship.

But some of the content partners felt that another Japanese word seemed more appropriate for their state: hara-kiri, the ancient art of disemboweling oneself.

Their major grievance was over the change in pricing, scheduled to start July 1. AOL executives had decided not to tell their information providers—called IPs—anything about the 20/20 plan before they had announced it to the public in May. They had felt it was more important to ensure pricing decisions were kept secret from competitors than it was to let the IPs know about them in advance.

The partners were upset, as most of them were largely dependent on the $2.95 hourly fee for their income. The 20/20 plan meant that they would all have to begin to ratchet up advertising on their sites or face a withering of revenues.

Content providers also began to become restless over the Web issue. If they wanted to be on AOL, they had to spend the time and money required to produce their sites using AOL's proprietary "Rainman" computer language. With six million members browsing its online content, AOL believed it was worth the trouble—no matter how inconvenient—for content providers to conform to its protocols. Increasingly, though, the IPs did not agree.

All the uncertainty made the partners a nervous audience. So Steve Case tried to inject some levity into the gathering before he delivered his speech, "Why AOL Will Remain the Global Leader in Interactive Services." As he walked out, casually dressed in his trademark khakis and denim shirt, the voice of "God" boomed out over the loudspeaker, heckling Case with a series of the insistent questions that were already preying on everyone's mind.

Aren't all consumers going to the Web? Won't competition crush AOL? What will become of content partners? And, the voice demanded: What was Steve Case going to do about it?

Case's theatrics made the crowd laugh and eased some of the pressure. Then he launched into the cornerstones of the Case philosophy: AOL had to go mainstream. The focus must be on consumer experience. Competitors can be made into allies. AOL should be everywhere.

"There is still a long road ahead," said Case, noting that only 11 percent of U.S. households were online. "We're going to run and gun for the other 89 percent."

Then it was Bill Razzouk's turn to speak.

Case's speech had created a bit of good will, but it quickly dissipated as Razzouk launched stiffly into a speech titled "Delivering the Promise." His points about improving member experience at AOL were salient, but his dry, monotonous style undercut his message.

The title was ironic because, in the back of the room, Steve Case was thinking that the promise expected of Bill Razzouk had not been delivered at AOL. Though few knew it at the conference, Razzouk—lauded only a few months before as a mature leader for a maturing business—had all but lost the confidence of AOL's top echelons.

AOL executives had, in fact, debated whether to let Razzouk speak at all. They worried about his stiff manner and his discomfort with the hipper AOL style. Was it right to feature someone who might be leaving the company within weeks? But if Razzouk wasn't prominent at the conference, they knew, it might look just as bad.

aol.com

The multifaceted problem had resulted from different personal styles inside the company and fast-changing external trends that Razzouk seemed ill-equipped to handle.

Razzouk was a southern gentleman, an old-style executive from a hierarchical business environment. He was not accustomed to the looser, beer-bash-at-the-office style of a young company like AOL. The difference in style was not an automatic recipe for disaster, however. The company's joke line was that everyone at AOL wore khaki pants and modeled themselves on the laid-back image of Steve Case, but there was actually a mix of personality types at every level of the company. Len Leader, for example, was the personification of buttoned-down decorum—in direct contrast to Leonsis's caviar-and-champagne style.

But the difference was neither Leader nor Leonsis had tried to change AOL's relaxed corporate structure. The moment he came in, Razzouk issued a series of orders that rankled people in the company. No more recorded voice mail answering the phones, Razzouk decreed, because it pissed off customers and partners. No more huge staff meetings where everyone had input, because it made for disorganized thinking.

At one 7 A.M. meeting that Razzouk had called, he locked out Mike Connors, head of the AOL technology team and the man charged with keeping the entire AOL computer system running, for being late. Connors stood outside the door for a few moments, while Razzouk waited to let the lesson sink in. When he finally opened the door, he greeted the unsmiling Connors with a sarcastic, "Oh! Glad you could make it!"

Such finicky attention to minor detail was irritating in AOL's relatively unstructured—and occasionally chaotic—working environment. Razzouk knew his policies were not welcome, but he flared at any suggestion that they were inappropriate.

"The goddamn place was falling apart!" charged Razzouk. "It was time to pick it up or just lay it down. You can't just have people sauntering around, in and out, whenever they please."

To Razzouk, his attempts to instill order at AOL were a bitter pill the company resisted swallowing. He felt that his suggestions for changes at the company were met with skepticism and reluctance, if not outright dismissal. AOL was very disorganized, he thought, and that had led to a lack of information about where the company was going. Why did the churn numbers come as such a surprise? With the looming problems, AOL was going to have to grow up fast.

The more he tried to impose discipline, the more the employees rebelled. The gap widened between Razzouk and AOL's tightly-knit management group, many of whom considered him a mini-tyrant.

Rumors soon began cropping up that the flamboyant Leonsis, rubbed raw by Razzouk's style, had issued an ultimatum to Steve Case following the partners conference: Either Razzouk goes or I go.

It was not true, both men later asserted, but Case was becoming increasingly worried that Razzouk's process-oriented corporate style was not appropriate for the company's climate.

Case could see why Razzouk had been effective at FedEx; its operation was all about execution. But Case had misjudged AOL's stability. It seemed to him now that the changes rocking the online world were part of a major new paradigm. There was no luxury of time. Razzouk simply was not getting enough "traction" in the job. Razzouk had not grown up with the odd permutations of the online world. He acted like the corporate executive that AOL had hired him to be, when what was needed was another visionary.

"Something fundamental was happening in the industry," said Case, "and I needed to fully engage. I needed to roll up my sleeves and get in there. I couldn't afford to sit on the sidelines."

What were the alternatives? If Razzouk stayed, his ineffectiveness would hinder the company at a critical time. If he went, Wall Street's confidence in the company might go with him, because such a sudden departure would raise a dark cloud of questions and doubt that could drive the stock down lower than ever.

Case also knew that a power shift would cast him as a man who was afraid to cede any control in his company. He had tried to delegate, some would surmise, but couldn't.

On the long airplane trip to Japan in early May, Case and Razzouk had had a talk about the many problems Case saw emerging. Then, the two men had decided that Razzouk should stay. In late

May, as Razzouk prepared to close on the purchase of a $1.7 million house in McLean, Virginia, and was finalizing the sale of his house in Memphis, they had spoken again about the issue. Again, Case had decided Razzouk should stay on.

But by June, even Case's reluctance to bring more negative attention to the company couldn't disguise the fact that Razzouk's tenure at AOL was not working out. Finally, he placed the uncomfortable call. Case was in Aspen, schmoozing with the nation's top executives at a Kleiner, Perkins conference. Razzouk was in Memphis, packing up for the move to Virginia.

The conversation was short. While neither man would divulge the details of what was said, Case's message, according to sources, was clear: things weren't working out, and Razzouk should not uproot his family from Memphis.

When he returned from the Aspen retreat, Case called a staff meeting to announce that Razzouk would be leaving.

Almost as soon as the word was out, the whispers and conjecture began: straight-shooter Bill Razzouk had not liked what he found. He had spent four months learning the inner workings of AOL and had realized it was built on sand that was fast shifting. He was getting out while his reputation was still intact.

"It looked," said Jim Kimsey, "like he had looked under the rock and didn't like what he saw."

No suspicions were allayed by the reasons officially given for Razzouk's departure, which few believed. To make it look as though Razzouk was not being let go, the pair said the decision was mutual.

"As the school year ended and the process of uprooting my family began, we came to realize that moving from Memphis was simply not in our best interests," claimed Razzouk in an AOL press release.

It was a spin and everyone knew it. But behind the scenes, AOL tried to ensure Razzouk would not leave the company too disgruntled. Upon leaving, he received $950,000 for salary and extended benefit payments.

It rankled Razzouk, in the months to come, that AOL began to do exactly the kinds of things he said he had been egging them to do. AOL, Razzouk thought, "had a lot of barons, and a couple of princes and kings . . . at executive staff meetings, there'd be as much bullshit as in medieval times."

In his mind, instead of someone focused only on meaningless details, he was "the guy who started the conversation" on slashing content costs, moving to unlimited pricing, restructuring the company, and other drastic measures to jump-start the company's sluggish performance.

To Razzouk, "AOL was like an adolescent child; it could do brilliant stuff but then turn around and do something really stupid." Case and his company just weren't ready to grow up, and he was the one who suffered for it.

The only thing AOL had done, he believed, was kill the messenger.

don't get off the boat

In a way, Case knew that what Razzouk had been drilling their teeth about was true—AOL needed yet another entirely new direction if it was to survive.

Feeling that he had to get back in touch with what was going on at all levels of the company, Case directed the twenty-five people who had been reporting to Razzouk to now report directly to him. It was time to take control.

All through July, the AOL 3.0 launch team rushed to get the product ready for fall delivery. They were running behind, and Case knew that AOL desperately needed the kind of boost the newer, improved software would give the company. With Razzouk gone, Case took a very active role, holding long, intensive meetings once a week to push the product along.

When Case began to hold meetings in which dozens of people gave him direct input on what was happening at all levels of AOL, Ted Leonsis noted dryly to Case, "Well, we're now pretty much organized so everybody in the company reports to you."

July became a period of intensive corporate introspection for Case and the executive team. The company's vague summer sluggishness was quickly giving way to the rumblings of major change. And the more Case looked at his company, the more he was beginning to realize that nothing short of a complete overhaul would do. Over its history, AOL had periodically reorganized itself, but this would have to be different.

But, if AOL were truly to reorganize, the question was: How?

And would a major change, especially after the Razzouk debacle, further erode confidence in the company? Widely criticized—even mocked, by some—for continually changing its business model, AOL couldn't afford to put off any longer its already skittish investors and analysts. More bad news from the stock market, Case knew, and he would be in serious trouble indeed.

AOL's difficulties were further exacerbated in July. CompuServe announced declines in membership, and a spin-off of the subsidiary recently approved by Block shareholders was losing luster (and would be postponed in late August). Though a drop in CompuServe's membership might logically seem a good sign for AOL, Case found himself facing a negative investor mood toward the online business in general.

"There has been considerable confusion and speculation in recent weeks about the online services market and AOL in particular," he said. "This uncertainty was heightened this week when CompuServe announced they were experiencing a decline in membership, which led some short sellers to assert that this might be a proxy for online services in general."

It was not, he insisted. But clamor over the power of the Web and online service churn intensified.

All this might go away, Case thought, if AOL could find the right man to replace Bill Razzouk. Any perception that the business might be out of control at the world's number one online service, helmed only by a lonely-at-the-top Case, could not be allowed to intensify.

In a mop-up article about the management debacle, *The Wall Street Journal* had chosen a surprisingly prescient metaphor to describe Razzouk's inappropriateness for his job at AOL. "Recruited to impose discipline on a swaggering, MTV-style operation," the

Journal remarked, "Mr. Razzouk rankled the tightly-knit coterie of veteran AOL brass."

It was an ironic comment, because the answer in Case's mind began to point toward the swaggering cofounder of MTV, Robert Pittman.

If Steve Case was the Vanilla Man, heading up the "J.C. Penney of cyberspace" out in the cornfields of Virginia, Robert Warren Pittman was his *über*-hip antithesis. A slickly packaged media pioneer at home among the New York gliterati, Pittman, like MTV, was a testament to the power of image.

Pittman, 42, had come a long way from the sticky-hot small Mississippi towns where he grew up. The son of a Methodist minister, he learned early how to adapt to new situations and new places, as time and again his father was transferred to churches all over the state.

At the age of six, he was thrown violently from a horse at his grandfather's farm. The accident cost him his right eye. Doctors fitted him with a glass eye, a condition that might understandably have impaired the young boy's self-confidence. Who wouldn't be self-conscious about such a handicap, especially during the awkward years of adolescence?

Not Bob Pittman. In fact, he managed to twist the situation to his advantage, as a story told by his high school teacher, Thomas Sasser, in GQ Magazine showed. Pittman was in for a paddling by Sasser and dutifully assumed the position. But when Sasser whacked him on the rear end with his paddle, Pittman popped his eye out, giving the young teacher a scare he never forgot. There were many other "eye" stories, including one in which Pittman would tap his eye with a straight pin while sitting in class, hoping to unnerve his teachers.

Pittman was a scrawny, television-addicted Southern kid, but he believed he was destined for bigger things than he could find in Mississippi. He wanted to be rich and famous and wasn't afraid to tell everybody so.

Like the young Steve Case, he was drawn initially to music. After landing his first job, as a radio announcer at WCHJ in Brookhaven,

Mississippi (a job he took so he could afford flying lessons), Pittman worked his way up and began a slash-and-burn music programming career that led him from Milwaukee to Detroit to Pittsburgh to Chicago and, finally, to New York City, where he was credited as being one of the hottest programmers in the country.

Along the way, Pittman—who had taken a few college courses but had yet to finish a degree—began developing the expensive tastes and high-profile lifestyle that would become his trademark. He flew his own plane. He rode Harleys. And he was possessed of an insatiable desire for accomplishment.

He also never let an opportunity slip by. In 1978, when ratings cooled at WNBC, the radio station he was programming for in New York, Pittman seemed to have burned out the blistering comet of his radio career by the age of twenty-five.

Soon after, he was offered a job at Warner Amex Satellite Entertainment Company (WASEC), a cable-TV company, and he eagerly switched. That decision would bring him all the glamour, money, and fame he had been hoping for.

Pittman and his boss at WASEC, John Lack, founded a new station that arguably would change the face of television. It was called Music Television, or MTV. The all-music cable channel debuted on August 1, 1981, and within five years, the whole country knew the "I want my MTV!" slogan (borrowed from the "I want my Maypo" tag line). The channel became profitable, and music video releases were greeted with more attention than the albums themselves. In 1984, Pittman was voted runner-up to Peter Uebberoth as *TIME* Magazine's Man of the Year.

In August 1995, Pittman and a colleague, David Horowitz, attempted to buy MTV Networks through a leveraged buyout. The attempt failed, but it provided the ever-restless Pittman with a glimpse into a new world: dealmaking and finance.

He left MTV in late 1986 and started his own company, Quantum Media, Inc., to make media-related investments. Quantum (ironically, Pittman had chosen the same name as AOL's precursor company) was not exactly a failure, but neither was it the huge success Pittman had hoped for. It was further hurt when the stock market crash of 1987 dried up investment money. So in 1990, he took a job as CEO of Time Warner Enterprises, a business development unit of Time Warner Inc.

By this time, Pittman was a bona fide celebrity—wealthy, handsome, and invited to all the chi-chi parties. He and his picture-perfect, mountain-climbing wife, Sandy Hill Pittman, were even dubbed "Couple of the Minute" by *New York* Magazine in the summer of 1990.

But not everyone thought Pittman a star. He acquired a less lustrous reputation as a man who took more than his share of the credit. Lack and others were considered central to MTV's success, for example, but most people remembered the charismatic, photogenic, and silver-tongued Pittman as MTV's creator. "Of course, no one was taking credit for it when it struggled at first," said Pittman. "At the end of the day, I think I was the leader of a product that was created by a team of talented people."

And Pittman's aura attracted more opportunities. After Time Warner Enterprises acquired the financially ailing Six Flags theme park chain in 1991, for $600 million, Pittman also became the CEO of the Six Flags Entertainment Corporation, where his job was to gun the attendance numbers and improve earnings. Time Warner sold 51 percent of the division, in April 1995, for more than $1 billion—$200 million in cash and an assumption of its $800 million debt—to Boston Venture Partners. Pittman's piece of the deal was estimated at $40 million.

If running roller-coaster rides seemed decidedly un-hip for a guy who had spent the 1980s at the vanguard of the pop-music scene, Pittman's next choice of employer was odder yet—Century 21 Real Estate Corporation. Pittman was attracted to the job, mostly because the New Jersey-based services company that owned it— HFS Inc.—was run by Henry Silverman. Pittman had served on the HFS board. He had known Silverman for many years and admired him. There was also a lot of money involved—$1 million in salary and a $1 million bonus, as well as 8 percent of Century 21.

Nonetheless, it struck many as odd that the leading sage of the 1980s urban zeitgeist found himself in the suburbs of the 1990s.

Pittman, not one to miss a trend, had taken note when the online medium exploded into public consciousness in 1995. When he was just about to start working for Century 21, he picked up the phone and called Steve Case. He wanted to learn more about the Internet and the online world, he said. Could they meet for lunch? It was slated as a casual lunch when Case, Leonsis, and Pittman met, in July 1995, at the American Café, near AOL. But as Case and Leonsis talked to Pittman, an idea occurred to both of them. When Pittman got up to go to the bathroom, they looked at each other.

"What do you think?" asked Case.

"We should get him on the board," answered Leonsis.

All during lunch, Case had been thinking the same thing. Pittman, he thought, would be a perfect addition to the AOL board: he was media-savvy, smart, and ambitious, and his connections might give the company some flash. By August, Pittman was in.

Almost immediately, the taunting began. Case wanted to pique Pittman's interest in AOL enough to persuade him to take a position in management; he knew Pittman was more intrigued by the new medium than by fixed-rate mortgages.

So Steve Case aimed at the jugular.

"Woooo, love those yellow jackets, Bob. Very fashionable," Case would needle in a mocking tone, referring to Century 21's trademark gold jackets. "C'mon, is this really your purpose in life? To work with a real estate company?" Could this really be the future of the wunderkind of MTV?

Pittman was itchy. But he had just started with Century 21, and he had promised to stay on for at least two years. The timing was not right for him to look seriously elsewhere. Now that he was on AOL's board, he could take at least some part in the company; perhaps later he could consider joining the management.

But that didn't stop him from talking. Even before Bill Razzouk left, in the summer of 1996, Pittman and Case were in discussions about what positions might be right for the restless executive. Initially, they talked about Pittman's heading up Digital Cities, AOL's effort with the Tribune Company to create localized interactive services nationwide.

But after Razzouk departed, everything changed.

All the ideas Steve Case had been mulling over, throughout that difficult summer, were finally starting to coalesce. For a long

Above: Thirteen years after he joined a volatile company called Control Video Corp. (which later morphed into Quantum Computer Services and then finally America Online), Steve Case celebrated AOL's switch to the New York Stock Exchange from Nasdaq in the fall of 1996. To honor the company, Wall Street was temporarily renamed "WAOL Street." (courtesy AOL) *Below:* "Would you like some peanuts with your diskette, ma'am?" The 1990s were the decade of the ubiquitous AOL diskette. Hundreds of millions were distributed throughout the United States—handed out by flight attendants on American Airlines, packaged with flash-frozen Omaha Steaks, dropped onto stadium seats at football games and, of course, sent by mail. The strategy was annoying, excessive, risky— and extremely successful. (photo by Nancy Andrews)

Above: Bill Von Meister—tireless entrepreneur and inventor—was the creative spark behind the company that later became AOL. In 1982, he concocted the idea of sending video games to home computers by telephone. The plan flopped, but his vision of giving people what they wanted online endured. Von Meister died broke—and largely unrecognized for his role in helping found AOL—in 1995. (© 1985, *The Washington Post.* Reprinted with permission. Photo by Lucian Perkins.)

Chief techie Marc Seriff (right) and Tom Ralston, who was vice president of operations, in one of the early computer rooms of Quantum, the company that was later called AOL. Seriff was the programmer who got the original "Q-Link" service up and running in late 1985, a night when the tiny company toasted its first online success with cheap champagne after managing to attract 24 simultaneous users to the service. One night soon after, the system crashed when 60 users tried to log on simultaneously. (courtesy Marc Seriff)

"There must be a pony somewhere in this shit" was Jim Kimsey's graphic assessment of the mess the company was in when he got involved in the mid-1980s. A West Point graduate, Vietnam veteran, and successful restaurateur, Kimsey guided the floundering business back from financial disaster so many times, the company acquired the nickname the "online cockroach." (photo by Katherine Lambert)

Senior Vice President Audrey Weil started at Quantum when there were only 30,000 users. PC-Link, launched by the company in 1988, was the online service created to work on Tandy's DeskMate computers. With PC-Link, Q-Link, and AppleLink Personal Edition, the young company struggled to create a market niche. (photo by Nancy Andrews)

Billionaire Paul Allen, the reclusive cofounder of Microsoft, nearly bought out the ragtag AOL team before they realized what was happening in the early 1990s. Allen responded to Steve Case's pique at his takeover attempt by saying, "This is America and I should be able to invest in AOL if I want to. What is wrong with that?" (photo by Richard Brown Photography)

Bill Savoy, Paul Allen's right-hand financial man though he was still in his twenties, purchased AOL shares for Allen and clashed with Case. Before a face-to-face meeting with Allen in May of 1993, Case requested that Savoy not attend. (photo by Richard Brown Photography)

"I can buy 20 percent of you or I can buy all of you," one of the richest men in America said to Steve Case in a 1993 meeting. "Or I can go into this business myself and bury you." But, as Bill Gates found out with Microsoft Corp.'s Microsoft Network, building an online business isn't quite the same thing as building a software empire. (© 1997, *The Washington Post*. Reprinted with permission.)

When talks with AOL broke down in 1993, Bill Gates instructed Microsoft executive Russ Siegelman to create Microsoft's own online service. Siegelman threw himself into the task, battling skeptical software engineers, company indifference, and the emergence of the Web as a force in the online world before unveiling MSN in August of 1995. One poll had estimated MSN could attract up to 19 million users in its first year, but by May of 1997, the number of users was stalled at just over 2 million.
(© Carolyn Caddes, 1997)

Above: Matt Korn, an IBM veteran, joined AOL in 1993 and set to work figuring out how to scale the system for the floods of new users Steve Case had envisioned. In this Polaroid photo, taken in November of 1993, he's posing in front of AOL's plan to beat Prodigy and CompuServe—by figuring out how to increase the maximum possible number of simultaneous users beyond 8,800. (courtesy Matt Korn)

Below: Marketer Jan Brandt is the person mostly responsible for blanketing the U.S. in AOL diskettes. Her efforts were both a boon and a burden to AOL. So many new users signed up in the mid-1990s, the service suffered significant slowdowns and quickly acquired the nickname "America On Hold." (photo by Nancy Andrews)

Ted Leonsis, who joined AOL in 1994, was as effusive as Steve Case was reticent. A natural showman, Leonsis was never afraid to add a splashy spin to any situation. When Tom and Dave Gardner, the brothers behind the Motley Fool financial site on AOL, chided Leonsis about taking undeserved credit for the Fool's success, Leonsis's response was as brief as it was brazen: "Boys," he told them, "myth is reality." (photo by Nancy Andrews)

With the Microsoft Network in development and AOL still lagging behind CompuServe, late 1994 was a turning point for the company. So Ted Leonsis led a company pep rally to arouse anti-MSN fervor. At the end of an impassioned presentation, he brought out "the dinosaur," representing Microsoft, for employees to sign. Hundreds rushed forward, pen in hand, and some with tears in their eyes. (courtesy AOL)

Buttoned-down Federal Express executive Bill Razzouk was hired as AOL president in early 1996 to help it grow up. A no-nonsense, make-the-trains-run-on-time kind of manager, Razzouk quickly irritated the looser AOL ranks. His tenure at AOL lasted only four months.

The company's current headquarters sits at the corner of AOL Way and Pacific Boulevard, across the street from a Wal-Mart store. The vast building—so different from the company's original and cramped digs—acquired the nickname the "Mother Ship," while other employees, in a nod to the rolling hills of Virginia surrounding the spot, called it "Green Acres." (photo by Nancy Andrews)

Jean Villanueva, AOL's longtime communications chief, was one of the coterie of executives who shaped AOL's rise from its earliest days. Intense and extremely devoted to making the company a success, Villanueva acted as a kind of lightning rod for Steve Case. In 1996, she and Case disclosed to the AOL board that they were involved in a personal relationship.

Brothers Tom and Dave Gardner signed a deal to put their pioneering financial site on AOL in August of 1994. But their first big online splash occurred before that, on Prodigy, where information they posted as a parody about a fictitious penny stock on a fake stock market roused very real threats from angry Prodigy users. (© 1998, The Motley Fool, Inc.)

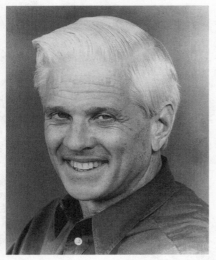

Technology head Mike Connors, also an ex-IBMer, was the one charged with figuring out how to keep the fast-growing online service from spinning out of control and how to fend off challenges from Prodigy, CompuServe, Microsoft, and the World Wide Web. The question was: Could the proprietary service keep up with all the changes and keep customers happy? (courtesy AOL)

AOL's data center is like a high-tech oasis, with its cool blue carpet, indirect lighting, and the constant, soothing hum of machinery. And it was here on the morning of August 7, 1996, that the tech crew realized they had a huge problem when the entire AOL system wouldn't come back up after a routine upgrade. The blackout would last nearly nineteen hours. (courtesy AOL)

Above: As AOL's head of investor relations, the dapper Richard Hanlon tried to calm investors worried about the tumult facing the company in late 1996. Constant speculation about the company's troubles drew Hanlon's pithy response: "If [the critics are] right, we'll just go out of business. You don't have to make a big intellectual debate about it." (photo by Nancy Andrews) *Below:* Chief Financial Officer Len Leader was AOL's key player in the dicey quest to keep the company from running out of cash. Precise, quiet, and intense, Leader was content to stay in the background while he fashioned the daring accounting techniques that won both praise and scorn from observers. (photo by Nancy Andrews)

Battling busy signals became a way of life for AOL users in late 1996 and early 1997. And mocking the company also became a staple of satirists, comics, and just about everyone else in America. (Chip Bok with permission of Akron Beacon Journal and Creators Syndicate)

Steve Case's placid exterior was severely tested during the access crisis and the series of missteps that followed. Having spent years trying to put a "human face" on the service in an effort to build an online community, Case now found that, to users, he was the personification of AOL's shortcomings and mistakes. At the height of the crisis, Case's online mailbox crashed under the weight of 17,000 e-mail messages he received in one two-day period. (courtesy AOL)

Nebraska Senator James Exon set in motion more than a congressional debate when he introduced legislation that became the Communications Decency Act. He framed the focus for one of the most troublesome disputes about cyberspace: Who is responsible for what Internet users see? And the senator's presentation of the infamous "blue book" was an object lesson in getting maximum effect out of political props. (© 1995, *The Washington Post*. Reprinted with permission.)

Lawyer Bill Burrington, originally from Elm Grove, Wisconsin, guided AOL's anti-CDA efforts with a midwestern politeness and an unpretentious demeanor. (courtesy Bill Burrington)

A goateed, hip, and extremely ambitious Bob Pittman got his start in radio, first as a DJ, then as a programmer. As one of the founders of MTV, Pittman went on to find the fame and wealth he had dreamt of during his boyhood in Mississippi. (courtesy Bob Pittman)

"Wooooo, love those yellow jackets, Bob!," Steve Case needled the restless Pittman about the trademark yellow jackets of the Century 21 real estate company, Pittman's employer when he was considering coming to AOL. In the end, Pittman couldn't resist the allure of another high-flying and uncharted industry. (courtesy Bob Pittman)

The boot-wearing, tough-talking David Colburn was dispatched to negotiate with potential partners of AOL, including discussions in 1996 with both Netscape Communications Corp. and Microsoft about which browser AOL would use on its service. The deal ultimately struck gave longtime nemesis Microsoft a boost and Netscape a definitive slap. (photo by Karl Schumaker)

"I think every antibody in the company reacted when I got here," said advertising head Myer Berlow. With his Armani suits, slicked-back hair, and urban-hip style, the self-proclaimed "Darth Vader" of AOL stuck out among the khaki-clad D.C. suburbanites peopling the company's hallways. (photo by Giorgio Palmisano)

Above: Miles Gilburne, the cerebral lawyer and longtime AOL dealmaker, helped fashion the complicated three-way deal that gave CompuServe to AOL and put the company far ahead of MSN. (photo courtesy Miles Gilburne) *Below:* "I never did mind the focus on my imminent demise," insisted Steve Case, "because the facts are on my side." It is this single-minded zeal that enabled Case to turn AOL, the "JC Penney of cyberspace," into the place millions of people want to be. It is not the fastest, flashiest, or most reliable service around, but it is indisputably the leader in cyberspace—at least for now. (© 1994, *The Washington Post.* Reprinted with permission.)

time, Case, Leonsis, and the board had considered dividing AOL into three businesses—split among the service, the network, and content.

Over the summer, AOL had hired 100 advertising employees and had also engaged Nielsen Media Research to measure members' use, in preparation for a new push into advertising sales. Pittman, with his background in cable TV, would be able to help AOL make this shift perfectly.

Almost as soon as Razzouk was gone, Case began the pursuit, phoning Pittman and trying to lure him into a job at AOL. By this time, his quarry was not an especially difficult catch. After only one month, Pittman was already "90 percent convinced," said Case.

But 90 percent was still not a deal. So Ted Leonsis was designated the closer.

Back in December, in the midst of his divorce from Sandy, Pittman had flown his private plane down to Florida to visit Leonsis at his opulent beach house. Bob Friedman, a mutual friend who had worked with Pittman at MTV and who now headed New Line Cinema Corporation's television division, was there as well. As the men lounged around the pool, sipping drink after drink, Ted began musing on one of his favorite topics, the 101 things he wanted to do before he died.

"I want to rent a yacht," he said dreamily, "call it the *Midway,* as in 'midway through life,' and take it on a fabulous cruise."

"Wanna go?" he asked Pittman and Friedman.

Sure, came the answers. Why not? Anything seemed reasonable from the vantage point of a beautiful seaside pool on a warm Florida night. The often-blustery Leonsis was probably all talk, anyway.

But he wasn't. By early August, the yacht was rented, the trip— a leisurely one-week cruise in the Mediterranean—was planned, and Pittman, Friedman, and Leonsis were ready for some upscale relaxation. The only work Leonsis had to do was to convince Pittman to join AOL's executive team.

It wasn't just a command performance for Ted. He liked Pittman and saw him as a kindred soul who could help steer AOL in yet another different direction. Leonsis had a distinct taste for glitz and glamour; his particular weak spot was Hollywood and the entertainment world. Pittman was a walking ad for that world, and Leonsis wanted him on board to help nudge AOL in that direction.

The party—consisting of Ted Leonsis and his wife Lynn, Bob Friedman and his wife Elissa, Bob Pittman and his girlfriend Veronique Choa, and another couple—flew to Nice, France. From there, they took a limousine to Monaco, boarded the 125-foot yacht, and set sail in the Mediterranean for a week of wining, dining, sunning, and schmoozing.

Over the course of the cruise, Pittman and Leonsis engaged in spirited debate about AOL. Was it a loved brand or a needed one? Would it beat back the threat of the Internet? Was the new interactive medium just a fad or a profound shift in communications?

Soon, the troupe put in at Positano, a chic port village just south of Naples, Italy. They ambled off the boat and wandered down to a little café where they settled into a table for a midday meal. There was hardly anyone around, so they struck up a conversation with the café owner.

"Where are you from?" the owner asked in accented English.

"Washington, DC," answered the ever affable Leonsis. "I work for a company called America Online. Have you ever heard of it?"

"Oh!" exclaimed the owner, "I have something for you!" He reached behind the counter, retrieved an Italian newspaper, and handed it over.

Ted Leonsis didn't know much Italian, but the headline wasn't hard to understand.

"AOL É Morte."

AOL is dead.

growing pains

where were you when the lights went out?

Just after 7 A.M. on the morning of August 7, 1996, Steve Case sat down in front of the computer in his home in northern Virginia. He waited as the modem dialed into AOL and the familiar high-pitched whine told him he was connecting.

He watched as a message reading "The system is temporarily unavailable" popped onto his screen. Case knew the tech crews took down the system between 4 A.M. and 6 A.M. on certain days, for upgrades and maintenance, so he assumed that something had briefly delayed the restart of the system. It had happened so many times before that he didn't see any reason to worry.

Case grabbed his keys and headed out to his gray Infiniti. As he pulled out of his driveway and got on the road to AOL's network operations center, in nearby Reston, Virginia, he was already thinking about what he wanted to say to Mike Connors's technology team at a meeting that had been planned for that morning.

The Reston facility housed the data center, the place through which all the masses of data about AOL usage moved, as restless members across the world trolled for information, for entertainment, for each other. When AOL executives wanted to impress visitors, they took them to the data center and showed them the

rows of gleaming machines with their pulsing lights, their soothing
hum, their miles of wires coiled beneath the raised floors.

The control room—with its low ceiling, cool blue carpet, and
indirect lighting—was the center of the ceaseless activity. Screens
constantly blinked and jumped with information: how many people were signing in; when mail was being delivered; where the system was becoming sluggish; the results of testing software that
endlessly dialed into various access numbers nationwide to determine busy-signal and connection problems.

Case knew that only early-morning activity would be going on
when he arrived for the meeting. AOL's busiest time was every
weeknight at 10:34 P.M., Eastern Standard Time, except on Thursday nights when *ER* was on the NBC television network. For
now at least, the place would be calm as much of the nation slept.

But as Case headed for the conference room that overlooked
the space where the entire AOL system was monitored, he noticed
something odd. None of the screens seemed to be moving. Connors greeted Case and told him the obvious: the system was still
down.

The problem was that no one on the operations team could figure out why.

direct hit

The answer lay somewhere in the complex system architecture
that was divided between the two data centers in northern Virginia—one in a nondescript building (unmarked, as a protection
against cyber-terrorism) in Reston; one in the original headquarters in Vienna. They shared a common network—contiguous
from Reston to Vienna—which linked together all the "pods,"
each of which handled 16,000 simultaneous users, and some shared
system resources.

AOL's technical team had long envisioned creating a parallel
network, so that the service could still run if random parts of it
were down. At many individual spots in the system, this kind of
parallelism already existed, so that, if one or more of those parts

failed, there was enough capacity to cover the problem. But AOL's fast growth, its lack of the amount of money needed to create such a system and the nagging question of whether AOL should be drastically expanding a proprietary network—all these issues had contributed to AOL's present condition. For all intents and purposes, AOL had never become fail-safe.

Matt Korn, AOL's 36-year-old operations head, still dreamed of such an overall parallel network, which would operate at a planned data center, scheduled to be built near AOL's new headquarters in Dulles.

But when Korn came to work on the morning of August 7, 1996, he was faced with a nightmare—a system outage that would last almost 19 hours and would escalate the decidedly harsh criticism already been aimed at AOL.

There had already been grumbling about AOL's technical expertise, which many industry observers felt was not adequate or reliable. Too many users had clogged the system in early 1994, slow response times and glitchy Internet access had irritated customers in 1995, and there seemed always to be some power outage, hardware failure, or software problem to deal with. Was AOL operating too close to the edge, placing too much faith in the endless tolerance of long-suffering customers?

Running the AOL system—which, in the two years between June 1994 and June 1996, had gone from 900,000 to 6.2 million members—had become a daily challenge. Besides adding new features and expanding capacity each day, Korn and his hundreds of technicians had to make sure the current system was always up and running.

"It's similar to trying to keep a space shuttle mission going indefinitely," is how Korn described the task. "At least for them, when the shuttle comes down, the mission is over and they can relax. We never can."

Korn, who grew up in Queens, attended the Bronx High School of Science and had been interested in computers as a teenager, writing programs to play games and compute the value of stocks and bonds. Although he began his college career at Yale University with the intent of becoming a doctor, soon enough, his longtime fascination with computers kicked in. He switched majors and earned a computer science undergraduate degree from Yale in 1980. On finishing college, at IBM's Thomas J. Watson Center, he was a programmer in the computing systems department, which had responsibility for operating the data centers and providing information services to all of the researchers.

After a fellowship at the University of Wisconsin, where he worked on his graduate degree, Korn returned to the Watson Center and was assigned to networking jobs, including a series of projects related to the Internet. He ultimately became senior manager of all of IBM Research's networking—an important position because, with distributed computing on the rise, networks were the heart of the data center's thrust.

But, thought Korn, he had also become a "double indirect."

"Most jobs in my field entailed running computer support for a company, like the people who keep the computers running at a hospital, bank, insurance company, or even a computer company, like IBM," said Korn. "Typically, the chief financial officer of one of these institutions will label the computer guys as 'support,' 'overhead,' or, most brutally, 'indirect.'"

Worse still, he figured the research division of IBM was already indirect with respect to the entire corporation, because it was not a sales or product development group that immediately added to the bottom line. And he was part of the computer center, an indirect in the research division.

"It didn't take me long to figure out that I was a double indirect," said Korn. "I figured that when the times got tough at IBM, as they were destined to at the end of 1992, the first place to get trimmed would be the double indirects."

So he welcomed the call, in late 1992, in which Mike Connors—whom Korn had once worked for at IBM—proposed he come to AOL.

With 230,000 members in 1992, AOL was small. Only 2,300 users could sign on at once. But the company was entering a period of hypergrowth, and the idea of scaling a system like AOL's was too tempting for Korn to resist. With a kind of nerdy pugnaciousness, he relished figuring out the system's complexities.

"We are doing something that nobody has ever done before, and that is a tremendous intellectual challenge, which we all find exciting," said Korn. "It's kind of like the scene in the *Apollo 13* movie, where the lead guy dumps a box of parts on a table at Mission Control, and tells the assembled team to figure out how to keep the astronauts alive with just the parts in the box."

Best of all, his role was direct. "At AOL, the product was the system—so we are the most 'direct' people that there can be. Without us, the system does not run and there is no product," said Korn. "There is a joy in being direct."

And a terror, especially now that Korn was in the *direct* line of fire.

houston, we've got a problem

The trouble had begun at 4 A.M., when the team had taken down the AOL system in order to replace some high-capacity switches, as part of a relatively routine upgrade. Switches function like a traffic cop: They direct information coming from all over the country to the appropriate computers throughout the AOL network center.

It took about two hours to change the switches. When they finished, AOL technicians tried to bring the system back up as usual. But the system didn't respond.

Almost immediately, the team began a process known as "backing out." Step by step, they undid what they had just finished doing. Theoretically, if they undid what they had just done, and restored the system to the state it was in before the upgrade began, it should then work.

But after painstakingly retracing their actions, the team could not get the system to respond properly. And bringing up an unstable system could have consequences far beyond the problem they were trying to find.

The clock was ticking, and the system had been down long enough to begin attracting notice. The workday was beginning on the East Coast, and if the system wasn't restored soon, members would be seriously inconvenienced. It seemed to the team that they had to be able to get it going soon. After all, how much could have gone wrong in a routine upgrade? Surely, they would isolate the problem quickly. Korn brought in teams of techies to work out all possible scenarios.

At AOL headquarters in Dulles, the mood was subdued. For many employees, their work *was* the service. Without it, content producers couldn't update pages, software programmers couldn't fix little bugs, and nobody could communicate via e-mail. The familiar clickety clack of keyboards was virtually silent; the work day was unavoidably stalled.

Lunchtime came and went, and the system was still down. By now it was becoming clear that this was no ordinary, quick-fix outage. This was a full-scale blackout with no end in sight. Not only was there concern about members, but the stock was beginning to show signs of investor worry. As the blackout stretched into its tenth hour, observers began to wonder whether there was something seriously and irreparably amiss within AOL's complex computer system.

Had the system been hacked? Minor intrusions by hackers were not that unusual on the AOL system; member profiles had been altered, internal AOL memos had been stolen and circulated online, graphics on certain sites had been electronically vandalized. Had a hacker somehow disabled the entire system? If so, AOL's problems would be much bigger than just this single blackout. The viability of the whole system would be in serious doubt for the long term, and, by extension, so would the viability of the company.

Jean Villanueva, who had first learned of the problem at a 9 A.M. staff meeting, retreated to her office on the fifth floor, where she began drafting a statement for the press. She had taken part in a conference call with Korn in the morning and felt sure that the problem would be resolved any minute. The trouble was, the minutes kept ticking by, with no solution in sight.

"You never know it's a crisis," said Villanueva later, "until you're so far into it that it's just undeniable."

By midafternoon, it was undeniable.

There was one bit of good news, though. By isolating and evaluating all the external events that could have affected the system at the time it went down, Korn and his team were able to determine that hackers had not caused the blackout. He called the executives in Vienna with the good news.

Villanueva drafted a short press release:

> Beginning at 4:00 A.M. this morning, America Online experienced a service outage as part of the Company's regularly scheduled maintenance update and software installation. The Company confirmed that a technical problem in the installation of new host software has created a delay, causing the system to be unavailable to its more than 6 million members throughout the morning.
>
> "Every possible resource is being brought to bear to restore the service," said Steve Case, chairman and CEO. "We regret any inconvenience this may have caused our customers and we will work to ensure that the problem does not reoccur."

Once the press release was out, phone calls, which had been trickling in all morning, started flooding the AOL switchboard. Camera crews from every major station were arriving, and public relations head Pam McGraw met them in the lobby of the building, dutifully giving interviews to each.

This was a public relations person's worst-case scenario. Reporters wanted information, and the only thing McGraw could tell them was: "We just don't know what's wrong yet."

"At other times, we had always had a good idea of what the problem was and how soon the service was going to be restored," McGraw said. "But there was little I could say since I didn't have answers, so reporters were just tearing their hair out about it."

The reporters' frustration was all the more understandable because AOL's press operation had not endeared itself to journalists, who generally considered it dysfunctional. It had failed to keep pace with the company's growth, in much the same way other elements of the service had. AOL executives had been shocked at the results of a poll the company commissioned not long before the outage, in which reporters vehemently expressed their displeasure with the press operation. The complaints were numerous: being forced to wait for simple answers that sometimes never came; limited access to key executives; and Steve Case's chilly style, which discouraged rapport. In the coverage of the blackout, AOL might find itself paying for its corner-cutting with the press.

It was not until the late afternoon that there was a breakthrough. ANS, AOL's network access provider subsidiary that provided AOL's data center with routing information—the "roadmap" of where information goes into the system—had identified an error in a routing table it had sent to AOL in a routine upgrade.

Ordinarily, receiving erroneous routing information wouldn't present a problem; AOL's diagnostic systems detect those types of errors. But the routing information had been sent automatically at 5 A.M., while the AOL system was down for the replacement of the switches. No one had told ANS about ongoing maintenance, and ANS had not asked.

With the diagnostic systems not operating, the tainted information was not detected. "We didn't have our force fields in place," said Mike Connors. "The result was akin to someone using a faulty map to find a location in a city—the system got itself in a series of endless loops."

When the AOL system wouldn't come back up after the switches had been replaced, the technicians assumed the problem lay in the work just done. They had spent hours looking in the wrong place entirely. And it wasn't until ANS alerted them to the error that the first part of the problem was solved.

But, after correct routing information had been inserted, the system still wouldn't come up. The incorrect routing information had created another problem in networking software provided by Cisco Systems Inc., a vendor. There was a bug in the operating system for the routers, which was exercised by the particular incorrect routing information from ANS. Once the bug was identified, a Cisco rep at the data center began the task of installing new code to correct it.

At last, the problems were solved. Korn and Connors informed Case, who had come over to Vienna to cheer the technology team on. At 10:45 P.M., the system finally came up again, nearly 19 hours after it had gone down. Korn and his team were too exhausted to cheer.

Back in Dulles, the public relations team realized the timing was incredibly fortunate: they had 15 minutes to contact all the local TV stations before the 11 P.M. newscasts. With luck, the news that the blackout was over would be broadcast. Villanueva, McGraw, and the rest of the communications staff stayed in the now-empty building on AOL Way until after 2 A.M., calling reporters, faxing out information, and explaining what had happened.

As she went home, Villanueva was tired but exhilarated. She felt that AOL—most especially, Korn's techies—had handled the crisis and had managed to get the situation settled as quickly as it could.

"I think everything's OK now," she told Case.

CHAOS@AOL.COM

But when Villanueva looked at the next morning's papers, she was in for a shock. The coverage was massive—and decidedly negative. The media stories suggested that the whole AOL system might be inherently flawed or overloaded to the edge of collapse.

"America Online Goes Offline," announced a *Washington Post* front-page headline. *The New York Times,* too, devoted considerable space to the outage, noting it on its front page and running a long article, "Data Network Suffers Biggest Blackout Ever," on the front of its "Business Day" section. The major television networks used the story as their lead.

But *The New York Post* headline, above a picture of a grinning Steve Case, summed up the outage in many people's minds: "CHAOS@AOL.COM!"

Villanueva was astonished at the media frenzy, especially considering the fact that it was not a dry news day: scientists had just reported finding possible evidence of life on Mars. "In a way, the press coverage was the highest compliment ever paid to us," she said. "It was like, 'We discovered life on Mars today,' but AOL was the lead story on CNN." Imperceptibly, over time, AOL had evolved from—as Ted Leonsis put it—"a service people liked to a service people needed."

Indeed, the heavy coverage spoke volumes. The company had become the world's largest online service provider, an international phenomenon whose influence stretched to its millions of members and far beyond; yet, most AOL insiders still saw it as a little upstart company in northern Virginia. Growth had come so fast that many of the staff seemed not to understand that public and press perception of the company had undergone a radical change. Little, scrappy David had become Goliath without realizing it.

"What's the big deal?" seemed to be the sentiment among AOL staff about the post-blackout press furor. Did the fact that AOL was down for a day really deserve these screaming front-page headlines? A massive power outage that affected millions in the western states that same day received far less coverage than AOL's blackout.

"If *The Washington Post* didn't deliver for a week because of an ice storm," said Matt Korn, "no one would suggest that the whole newspaper was about to collapse." His argument was specious: keeping a system like AOL's up and running is, needless to say, far more complex than printing and delivering a newspaper. And the implications of problems, therefore, are much farther reaching.

Case saw opportunity in the coverage: in a letter to members he tried to spin it to the company's advantage.

"Without making light of yesterday's outage, an additional interesting theme did emerge that's noteworthy," Case wrote in a letter to members. "The disruption caused by the temporary unavailability of AOL illustrates more clearly than ever before how important AOL has become in the daily lives of our members. From a high-tech gimmick, AOL has evolved over the past several years into a critical part of real people's lifestyles and it is missed when it's not available."

Even if its content was true, the letter smacked of ill-timed self-satisfaction. To frustrated members, Case's wiggling was irritating. How dare he pat himself on the back when he had just let his customers down? Steve Case—the marketing genius—seemed lamentably out of touch with his membership.

His remedy also seemed to come up a bit short, at least from a perceptual point of view. To compensate members for their lost day of service, Case announced an across-the-board one-day rebate—the equivalent (depending on a user's payment plan) of between 32 and 64 cents.

In AOL's fourth-quarter-earnings conference call, held the day after the blackout, Case tried to leaven the situation with humor.

"I'd summarize the call in three ways," he said in his trademark deadpan tone. "First, it was a great year. Second, it was a pretty good quarter. Third, it was a really bad day yesterday."

aol sucks

It was a good day, though, for those who had come to loathe AOL. The outage, combined with an even worse crisis just over the horizon, made hating AOL something of a national consumer habit in late 1996. For some, the practice would gain almost religious fervor.

The most vocal AOL-hater was a freelance writer named David Cassel. It was he who penned the classic anti-AOL screed following the blackout in August. Set to the tune of Don McLean's "American Pie," the lyrics were as caustic as they were perfectly rhymed.

I can't remember if I cried
When I realized that Steve Case had lied.
But something touched me deep inside
The day the service died.

And so it went, verse after verse, bouncing to e-mail boxes all over the Internet and becoming a cult hit. From there, the parodies kept coming: "Billing Me Softly" and "If It Seems Quite Crappy" (to the tune of "If It Makes You Happy"). Some Web sites mimicked the AOL interface, inserting fake "channels" and insulting graphics. All over the Web, people were putting hours of energy into mocking AOL.

The phenomenon had its roots in early 1994, when AOL users first got access to the Usenet newsgroups on the Internet. At first, computer users had to have a certain degree of Internet savvy to participate in the newsgroups. Not everyone knew how to navigate the arcane world of the Internet, so there was something of a natural weeding-out process. Newsgroup users were proud of their "netiquette" and protective of their environment.

Then came the invasion of the AOLiens.

Novice AOL users were used to the fast, clipped "conversation" of chat rooms, where comments scrolled by quickly and abbreviations were useful for getting a point across in as few words as possible. Let loose on the newsgroups—which are essentially message boards, without the same time constraints as live chat—AOL users quickly exasperated the regulars with their one- and two-word postings, especially the ubiquitous "Me too!" in response to other postings.

Irritated newsgroup users quickly formed a new online discussion group called alt.aol-sucks, and soon the boards were overflowing with complaints about the service and its members. Then, as the popularity of the Web grew, there was a predictable migration to creating Web sites—some very elaborate—to get the anti-AOL word out.

After the outage, all across the Web, dozens of such sites sprang up, with numerous variations on the same theme: "AOL sucks." From serious commentaries on the company's weaknesses to glibly corrosive wisecracks at its expense, the "AOL Sucks" phenomenon exploded.

There were so many Web sites that other Web home pages were devoted merely to linking to them all. "America Online Sucks!" "AOL Watch," "Why AOL Sucks," "America Outtaline"—the list grew each week. Many of the Web page creators were former AOL users, and a surprising number were high school students—14- and

15-year-olds who had a sophisticated grasp of HTML coding and unrelieved disdain for AOL, which they called the "Internet on training wheels."

Some of the sites were hilarious. "Nikki's 1996 AOL Recycled Diskette Collection" page, for example, featured full-color photographs of do-it-yourself Christmas gifts made from old AOL diskettes, including such festive fare as "Christmas Angel," "Floppy Ornament," and "Hanging Mulberry Potpourri." "Michael P. Lambert's Custom AOL Disks Page" was another attempt at disk art, with the author mangling, shredding, decorating, and otherwise defacing AOL disks into "works of art" with names such as "Unholy Triptych," "Shake-n-Bake" and "Cole Slaw."

The undisputed king of the AOL-haters' hill was Cassel. He was an early and frequent visitor to the alt.aol-sucks newsgroup, after having become an AOL user in 1993.

The more Cassel looked at the service, the more he found to criticize. "Terms of Service" guides were draconian and capricious in their enforcement of "standards" in the chat rooms. AOL was an easy target for hackers. AOL wasn't keeping "spam"— junk e-mail—out of its users' mailboxes. AOL tech support was inadequate. The list went on.

So Cassel created his own "AOL List"—an electronic newsletter chronicling AOL's transgressions and shortcomings—and began circulating it in October 1996. In his pursuit of negative information about the company, Cassel was zealous. His newsletters were packed with specific information: dates, stock information, membership figures, quotes from a variety of analysts. No rumor or fact was too small for him to investigate, as long as it was against AOL.

Cassel's persistence at ferreting out and aggregating negative information about AOL began to bring him media attention, especially as AOL's crisis state intensified in the winter of 1996. Major newspapers such as *The Washington Post, Boston Globe,* and *Los Angeles Times* began to quote him in news stories, and Cassel quickly became more than just another of the self-published AOL critics.

For fellow AOL haters, Cassel's "AOL List" newsletter and "AOL Watch" Web site were the living gospel: the honest truth about what they considered was a deceitful company. In fact, Cassel made many good points in his criticisms—especially about AOL's customer service problems over the next several months.

But he also severely diluted his message by his persistent use of anonymous "AOL employees" as sources of information and irrelevant or downright silly accusations that were scattered too often among the more relevant information and borderline-libelous assertions.

Another odd facet of Cassel's criticism was his fascination with—and seeming approval of—hackers. In newsletter after newsletter, he took AOL to task for having suffered intrusion by hackers, consistently blaming the company while saying nothing about the responsibility of the hackers themselves. In fact, in one newsletter, Cassel defended hacking as a sort of learning exercise, writing that "beyond chat room malcontents are young computer enthusiasts, finding security holes as a way of exploring, testing limits, and learning about the online world firsthand."

In the same newsletter, he called the epidemic of "password fishing"—the theft of passwords in order to get free access—"poetic justice" for the company. And Cassel furthered the efforts of hackers by publicizing Web pages they had set up to display stolen internal memos from the company.

At times, Cassel seemed simply to be grasping for something to complain about. "[A] pessimistic cloud hangs over AOL's building in Virginia," he wrote after a round of layoffs. Part of the reason, according to one of Cassel's standard anonymous sources, was that "[N]o one likes working in Dulles. The average commute time is now one hour." In another newsletter, Cassel quoted an anonymous source as saying that volunteers were "finally realizing that AOL is a for-profit company"—as if that were a great, shocking surprise.

For all his shrill commentary, Cassel was still a good source for information on things that AOL was doing wrong. In the months following the August outage, he would have no shortage of reportable material.

landing the planes

The growing ranks of AOL haters and the aftermath of the August outage had become relatively minor worries by the early fall of 1996. A number of important and complex issues were facing Case and his company, among them: a shift to the New York Stock Exchange; a grand and costly introduction of the new 3.0 software to the millions of AOL customers; a restive investor community to placate; a financial rejiggering that would alter the entire business plan of AOL; and, finally, a wholesale restructuring of the company.

"It was as if we had all these airplanes flying around overhead," said Case. "And I was the air traffic controller, trying to make sure they all landed OK." Indeed, none of the many overhauls AOL had been through had been as extensive or multifaceted as the one Case was now orchestrating.

The first goal was to raise the visibility of AOL so that the release of its new 3.0 software at the end of September would gain maximum attention. Over the next three months, the company would spend $100 million on bringing in new customers and retaining current ones. It planned a full-scale press to get to 10 million members within a year.

In mid-August, the company kicked off a thirty-city "AOL on the Move" marketing tour. Two trucks, filled with demo equipment, toured the country, bringing AOL's improved service to the general public through "interactive fairs." The most significant day of the tour would be its end date, September 16, in New York City. Steve Case planned to take a step that he hoped would stabilize his company's volatile stock, which had now dipped below $30 per share. AOL was moving from NASDAQ to the "Big Board"—the New York Stock Exchange (NYSE).

The night before the transfer, AOL executives were feted with cocktails on the Exchange floor and a dinner in a suite of formal rooms upstairs. Oil paintings of past NYSE chiefs were hung on the surrounding walls. "God, look at all these old, white, scary guys," whispered one AOL vice president to another. "They would die again if they knew *we* were here."

On September 16, the NYSE closed off Broad Street to accommodate AOL's marketing caravan, and Case got to ring the bell that opened trading. The street sign in front of the NYSE's Wall Street location had been altered for the day to read "WAOL Street." "For us, this is tremendous," said Case. "The kind of thing every entrepreneur dreams of."

AOL hosted a bigger event two weeks later, when it sponsored the Monday Night Football game on September 30 in Philadelphia. Analysts and the media were invited guests, and free software was available in a tent set up in the parking lot. As part of a stunt, Steve Case had the embarrassing task of carrying onto the field Kerri Strug, the young gymnast who had become famous for her performance in the Summer Olympics. Despite a badly hurt left ankle, she had completed her scheduled vault, helping the U.S. women's gymnastics team win the gold medal.

Some of the company's observers were worried that AOL was beginning to injure itself with this marketing blitz in the face of a declining stock and a continued negative cash flow. (AOL's financial statement for fiscal 1996 showed its total cash flow from operations as −$66.7 million.)

AOL had always been a "leap-of-faith" stock for its investors, many of whom expected that, after Case had built a huge subscriber base, the company would eventually throw off money from other revenue streams, such as advertising and commerce. Instead, the new, and costly, marketing and advertising program indicated that AOL would keep building at investors' expense and the AOL executives would make a bundle. Constant shifts in strategy had been needed to get AOL to its market position; now Wall Street had begun to agitate for a firm plan that would yield profits on a reliable basis.

During the football game, analyst Mary Meeker—who had been bullish on AOL for a long time—turned to Ted Leonsis and asked a question that was in many minds.

"When are you going to stop spending and start making some *real* money?"

the big turd

Investors' desire for returns presented a sticky problem for AOL. Wall Street wanted cash flow immediately and profits soon after, but AOL members wanted unlimited access to the service for a flat fee. The $19.95 all-you-can-eat access plan had become the standard for ISPs, and AOL was finding it harder and harder to explain why its service was worth $2.95 per hour when users could have the whole of the Internet for a single flat rate.

If AOL adopted a flat rate, the loss of revenue could be devastating, thanks to AOL's bigger overhead and a lack of any real historical knowledge about how users might behave. AOL's heavy users, many of whom spent upward of $300 a month on chat rooms and games, were a significant part of the company's income. Offering a flat rate could have the double-edged effect of increasing usage while decreasing revenues.

A flat rate might also awaken the members that AOL insiders referred to as "sleeping dogs"—people who never used the service but kept paying for it month after month.

Compounding the problem was the fact that, as with everything else in this industry, there was no precedent that might give guidance. Theoretically, AOL could diversify its revenue stream—through advertising, merchandising and the like—to adequately offset the loss of subscribers' fees. But no one knew whether it could be done successfully, or how quickly. Ad sales were up from 1995's $6 million, but the increase was not enough to guarantee financial health.

Through the fall, AOL executives debated the pricing issue. Some felt an increase was not needed because the new 3.0 software and the 20/20 plan would jump-start growth. Others thought a flat rate was the only path to take. Case was certain of one fact. With AOL's millions of customers and well-known name, shifting to a flat rate "would be like dropping a nuclear bomb on the industry."

For AOL, the move would be more like jumping off a cliff and hoping that an invisible current of air would keep the company aloft.

In the end, though, AOL didn't jump. It was pushed.

On October 10, MSN announced a revamping of its service, including a move to unlimited access at a $19.95 flat fee. Though the pricing move had been rumored for several weeks, the announcement had the effect of a gauntlet thrown at AOL's feet. AOL stock soon fell to $24, its lowest point of the past year.

After the MSN announcement, the Motley Fool boards were filled with pessimistic posts about AOL's ability to go to flat-rate pricing. "ISPs are in a competitive market and $20 is their price," wrote one AOL user. "How can AOL, with huge content, marketing and personnel costs charge the same amount? I graduated from Yale with an MA in Econ and I can't figure out how AOL is going to make any profit."

Unbeknownst to those posting on the message boards, Steve Case was perusing the postings, trying to get a sense of customer mood. A week after the MSN announcement, he decided it was time to respond.

He posted a message assuring jittery investors that he was "listening and watching to get a handle on what we could [do] to make existing members even happier." The bulk of his message contained vague marketingspeak: "key indicators," "qualitative feedback," and "value proposition." Near the end, though, Case dropped a cryptic hint of the overhaul that was coming.

"Soon," he wrote, "the fog will lift, and a reinvigorated AOL will move into center stage. Then, you won't have to wonder what we/I have been up to!"

Fog was an apt metaphor, considering the position Case was in.

Price was not the only change under consideration. After months of internal discussions, suggestions, and debate, Case had decided to split the company into three parts. AOL had undergone a number of restructurings in its history—it was a company joke that an annual rejiggering of its divisions was a tradition at AOL. But this plan was different and much more drastic. It had become clear that there were completely different mandates for the various sections of the company, and leading them all under one catch-all aegis was making less and less sense as the company grew larger.

So Case decided that AOL would consist of three separate operating divisions: (1) ANS Communications, which would handle the access infrastructure under the helm of Bruce Bond; (2) AOL Studios, which would develop content under the leadership of Ted Leonsis; and (3) AOL Networks, the flagship online service, to be headed by Bob Pittman.

The lure of the new medium had proved irresistible to Pittman, and, provided he could satisfactorily negotiate his departure from Century 21's parent company, HFS, he was ready to join up. Case aimed to be able to announce the restructuring and the addition of Pittman at the same time.

And that wasn't all. Case had finally decided to eliminate one of the sticking points that had seriously undermined the company's credibility among investors: the practice of deferring the cost of acquiring new subscribers.

AOL had long employed the controversial practice of spreading its payment of direct marketing costs over a two-year period rather than paying them as they were incurred. The company had always argued that members stuck around for more than two years, on average, so the cost of acquiring them could be considered an "investment," to be paid out over a similar period.

The practice wasn't illegal, but it allowed AOL to show profits when in reality there were none. And if AOL's bet that members would stay at least two years proved to be wrong, the mounting pile of deferred costs—already more than $300 million—could smother the company. Kimsey had taken to calling the accounting practice "the big turd," since it "sat in the middle of the company and smelled up the place."

There would be a personnel change too. Jean Villanueva would soon make public her decision to take a leave of absence from AOL, the company to which she had been devoted for a decade.

The demands of her job, her pending divorce, her two young children's need for more attention at a difficult time and the growing pressures within the company, because of her relationship with Case, proved too much.

And, finally, the price shift was also on the table. With no cash flow, no profits and no guarantee of stable alternate revenue sources, how in the world could AOL afford to move to flat-rate pricing? Could the company quickly begin to capitalize on where it had come from?

When MSN jumped into the flat-fee pool, AOL really didn't have a choice. The company could not realistically begin a new pricing scheme by late October, which was shaping up to be the likely time for the other announcements, but it could announce concrete plans to move to flat-fee pricing.

"The elements were coming into place, and all that remained now was to put the whole plan in motion," said Case. "We had been playing defense too long and now it was time to play offense."

It was time, in other words, to jump off the cliff.

busy signals

selling water in a flood

"I've seen this movie before," announced Bob Pittman in his first public utterance as the new president of AOL Networks.

The date was October 29, 1996. Pittman, Steve Case, Ted Leonsis, and other AOL executives were gathered in a New York hotel room. There, they were holding a conference call with journalists and the financial community to announce the company's restructuring, new pricing plan, deferred subscriber acquisition costs write-off and the addition of Pittman to the AOL executive team.

Though he was a relative outsider in the online business world, Pittman was anxious to show he knew what was going on in the medium.

"I was in the cable network business, oversaw the launch of six cable networks," he said in his trademark Mississippi drawl, quickly employing his legendary status as one of the founders of the MTV. "And this looks an awful lot like that period, when you see the mass market embracing a new product."

"In the early 1980s," he continued, "people looked at MTV and said, 'Oh, your subscriber fees are most of your revenue. Advertising is not very material.' What they missed was that the growth rate of subscriber revenue would not keep up with the growth rate of the advertising revenue, and again, I see the same thing here. If you ask where do I envision America Online being in the future, other revenues are going to be the significant profit contributor, not subscriber revenues—though I think we'll continue to grow subscriber revenues."

Pittman went on. "I have not seen the excitement, the opportunity, the sort of high-class problems like AOL faces, since the early days of MTV," he declared in yet another flat-out attempt to link his past glories to his new job. "This is clearly a company that is sitting astride the new mass market."

And did he mention MTV? joked Ted Leonsis to the others in the room, as he munched on a burger and fries nearby.

In fact, it was a perfect performance from Pittman. This was a man, as they say in his part of the country, who could sell you water in a flood.

AOL needed that charisma. The faithful were losing faith, and its main evangelist, Steve Case, seemed to be losing his touch.

For years, AOL had been the true definition of a "concept" stock. After all, no one had any idea where the Internet phenomenon was headed. But with every new iteration of the company, Steve Case had claimed that AOL had solved whatever problems were currently dogging it; that things were going to be different; that the company was on top of the situation. As long as Case could keep them believing in his vision for AOL, the company could continue its sprint for market share, fueled by the hundreds of millions of dollars in wishful investor money. Nobody knew where the industry was going, but Case had proved remarkably adept at stepping in the right direction at the right time.

And he was trying to do it yet again. With the announcements, Case was hoping to send out a new sermon to the market and the industry. With its pricing change, AOL was reasserting itself as the value leader—it gave premium offerings for generic prices. With the restructuring, it was playing the role of the aggressive number one brand. With the write-off, it was responding to Wall Street's concerns. The bottom-line message: AOL was once again on the attack.

If Case's powers of persuasion were to falter, however, the investors might disappear, leaving the whole enterprise to collapse. And in October 1996, AOL was mired in the worst investor doubt it had faced since its earliest days. The share price of its stock had plunged, in less than six months, from more than $70 to a low of $22⅜.

AOL investors were indeed tiring of the fly-by-the-seat-of-his-khakis style that Case had perfected for running AOL. They wanted to see stability and consistency. "Case had been on this crusade and it was beginning to wear us out," said one major investor. "And he did not seem to feel as if he had to reconcile what he said today with what he had just said yesterday, even though it was totally different."

Even some on Case's board had begun to feel itchy. They worried that the company was drifting into a dangerous decline and Case was running out of remedies. "Sooner or later, a fox runs through all its tricks," said one board member. "And that's when the dogs take over." Not surprisingly, rumors of a takeover by major telecommunications and media companies, such as AT&T and Disney, began to surface once again.

The situation was ripe for the bears to attack. And there were suddenly a lot of them, armed with heavy ammo, much of it provided by the company itself. Short sellers—investors who make their money by betting that overpriced shares of stock will fall—now firmly controlled the AOL story, declaring that AOL would never be really profitable.

Even AOL's thick-skinned bulls were beginning to question the company's perennial insistence that it had a viable business model, beyond its determination to grow huge. Many listeners had finally grown tired of the same old spiel. Sure, AOL was a good product and it had done a remarkable job in attracting customers and building an industry. But *now* what? Could AOL leverage its position, its subscribers, and its ubiquitous brand into anything meaningful? The demand in the financial community was becoming increasingly direct; its catchphrase was borrowed from a recent Tom Cruise movie, *Jerry Maguire*.

Show me the money.

paper profits

What AOL showed on October 29 was that there wasn't any money and there hadn't ever been any.

There was only an ugly number: $353.7 million.

That was how much money AOL had lost in the first quarter of its 1997 fiscal year, due to the write-off of "deferred subscriber acquisition costs." The company would now account for all ongoing marketing expenses as they were incurred; it had cleaned up its books and removed what had become a growing worry for Wall Street. The new accounting, said financial officer Len Leader, was "gold–standard."

More like lead, said some wags, as AOL's former paper profits dropped to the bottom of the deepest sea. Figuring in the write-off, AOL had a staggering $3.80 loss per share. In comparison, if AOL had chosen not to abandon the controversial accounting practice, the company would have reported quarterly earnings per share of 17 cents.

Profitability seemed a distant dream. As investor and longtime AOL critic David Simons put it, "AOL should hold its next shareholders' meeting at an *Annie* revival: 'Tomorrow! Tomorrow! I give ya profits, tomorrow! You're only a quarter away!'"

AOL executives were defiant, especially Leader. "We take strong exception to any notion that we are playing games," he told *The Wall Street Journal.* "This company has been very forthright. We should be commended for acknowledging our mistakes and reaching out."

Leader, a punctilious, careful man, was not usually given to such strong declarations. Quiet and somewhat remote, he was a close adviser to Case, who trusted him implicitly. Leader had come to AOL in late 1989 after a five-year stint at Legent Corporation, a groundbreaking software firm also located in the Washington area. He had previously worked as an audit manager for the accounting firm of Price Waterhouse.

He had come to AOL because of the challenge of taking a small company public, and, as AOL's most precise and conservative corporate officer, he had provided a lot of its stability. But Leader had also designed the series of edgy accounting techniques that had allowed AOL to stay afloat and prosper. And now that the financing and accounting had become increasingly controversial, it was Leader who had to defend it.

Regarding the short sellers, he told another interviewer: "Any company that is (a) in new territory and (b) carries a level of controversy is ripe for short sellers. They make their money on misfortune, and by sowing fear and doubt."

To critics, however, Leader's shift of AOL's accounting methods was the needed proof that AOL had basically been a big smoke-and-mirrors show. The $354 million loss represented costs AOL had endured over time but had never charged against earnings. Now, effectively, all the cumulative profit the company had ever made was wiped out. Financially, AOL had been a bust.

A message on the Motley Fool board spoofed the situation: "The Emperor hath no Pants, AOL hath no Profits! AOL is a perfect case to make me scratch my head and wonder how companies can dupe shareholders and still be seen with a sparkle."

Columnist Allan Sloan was equally colorful in his analysis. "By deferring those costs, AOL over the year reported profits $385 million greater than they would otherwise have been—which would have been far enough below zero to make the Arctic seem tropical," he wrote. "I'm intrigued by AOL's ever-changing accounting and by the way it manages to keep telling Wall Street whatever it wants to hear."

But no one was more thrilled than a combative investor named David Rocker, for whom AOL represented the soft-headed thinking now prevalent on Wall Street. To him, AOL's bulls had never seemed to care about the bottom line—a situation that made him incredulous and supremely piqued about AOL's continued success.

"Keep those plates going, Steve!" barked Rocker, in a succinct summation of how Steve Case had kept investors in the AOL fold. "They just kept changing the numbers. It's like: 'Look at my right hand; now, look at my left hand; now at my left foot; just don't watch the numbers!'"

Rocker, the son of an accountant, was one of the most vocal critics of AOL on Wall Street, and with good reason. As a short seller of the stock, he made money when the company's stock price went down. It was to his advantage to keep investors aware of AOL's weaknesses, so he wasn't shy about enumerating, whenever possible and in the most colorful terms, the company's shortcomings.

To Rocker, AOL's readjustment of its accounting method was finally an admission by the company of exactly what he had long been preaching.

"This company has consistently and continually painted itself as other than it is, in order to meet voracious cash flow needs," argued Rocker. "It has been a marriage of convenience between AOL and Wall Street: See no evil, hear no evil, speak no evil. . . . They are morally bankrupt! For them, every revenue is ordinary and every expense is extraordinary."

And now, with the switch to flat-rate pricing, Rocker felt that AOL was moving toward an even less financially viable model. "It's great marketing plus a good product, but they haven't been able to price it to make a return," he said. "And now they turn around and make it cheaper? It's like inviting a busload of fat people to an all-you-can-eat buffet."

In AOL's view, the company was merely guilty of ignoring profits and focusing on something deemed more important: market share. Richard Hanlon, AOL's vice president of investor relations, insisted that the whole question of whether AOL was turning a profit was moot.

Hanlon, who had come to AOL in 1995 after stints as an independent consultant and as head of corporate communications at Legent, now had to take Leader's new numbers and make them work for Wall Street.

His tack was that investors would just have to trust AOL management's ability to read the "tea leaves." "Wall Street has never placed the greatest value on whether the company makes money or not," argued Hanlon, a dapper Brit whose reserved and genteel manner directly contrasted with David Rocker's New York-style bombast. "Usually it's an overall belief in where the company is headed."

Because he worked in investor relations, Hanlon was taking much of the flack about AOL's changes. Typical of the comments directed his way was one irate stockholder's accusation, "You put out another strategy du jour and expect us to applaud."

Hanlon knew it was frustrating for investors, but he also knew that AOL's permutations were necessary for survival. "If we didn't change, we wouldn't be around long enough to be criticized. We have become the biggest for a damn good reason," he said, his usually placid features growing suddenly animated. Didn't all these naysayers appreciate what AOL had accomplished? "You'd think the supporters and investors would thump on the table and say, 'MY GOD, PEOPLE!' "

The October shifts now taking place were going to end AOL's long summer torpor. AOL was *not*—as Rocker was insisting—reinventing itself to save its skin. "Isn't it the case that, in a business like this, what you are really doing is you're finding your way," said Hanlon. "And, if Rocker's right, we'll just go out of business. You don't have to make a big intellectual debate about it."

dis-content

Still, investors were restless. And while some members may have been pacified—at least temporarily—by AOL's move to unlimited access, plenty of others were not.

A number of AOL's content providers were also upset—not only about the pricing change, but about the fact that AOL had not given them any warning that it was coming. Some content providers learned of the change when they logged on the service on October 29, the day of the announcement. This was the second time in a year that AOL had done this, and content providers were angry at their shabby treatment by the company.

Steve Case's reason for not alerting the content providers was simple: he didn't want news of the price change to get out early.

Telling AOL's hundreds of content providers in advance would have practically guaranteed a leak, and the momentum Case was so earnestly seeking would have been lost. Still, being the last to know was frustrating.

The etiquette breach was not all that shook them up. The pricing switch could mean a severe curtailing of their revenue—or worse, the dumping of their sites by the company. Most content providers would have to focus immediately on generating revenue through advertising and transactions, because AOL hourly fees were not going to be there much longer.

The content field was about to undergo a kind of Darwinian selection. Some of the more savvy content providers, such as the Motley Fool, had understood the change would come and were already working on developing alternative revenues. But others were caught flat-footed. The services worth most to AOL were those—like Motley Fool or Hecklers Online—that differentiated the service from its competitors. But hundreds of other sites that were interesting but not particularly unique would likely be abandoned.

Another group that was perturbed at the pricing change was the cadre of loyal volunteers working for AOL. The company had long offered free online time in exchange for labor-intensive tasks such as monitoring chat rooms, a barter exchange worth more than $300 per month for some volunteers. But with the advent of unlimited access, there was no money to be saved by having AOL pay for online time, since the maximum cost of service in a month was $19.95. Not only did AOL not make a move to compensate volunteers for the loss, it actually began charging them for the service—$3.95 per month. AOL appeared to be effectively saying that all the volunteers' hours were worthless.

Controlling costs would now be a major issue. In the immediate, the restructuring meant AOL would lay off 300 workers, nearly 20 percent of whom were GNN employees, who were losing their jobs thanks to AOL's decision to shut down that service. The decision to excise GNN made sense—it was, after all, meant to be the Internet access arm of AOL, a need that had been effectively obviated by Web access and unlimited pricing on the flagship service.

But the company's shift to unlimited access—a move expected to better members' perceptions of the service—started off with a terrible misstep that eroded much of the goodwill it could have engendered.

Believing that the overwhelming majority of customers wanted unlimited access, no matter what their current usage, AOL management settled on what seemed the least complicated way to make the switch: all AOL users would automatically be billed $19.95 for unlimited access, starting on their December billing date, unless they specifically asked for another of the available pricing plans.

Switching customers automatically to a higher rate, without their active consent, was asking for trouble. And AOL got it, in the form of formal complaints from states' attorneys general all over the country. Washington State Attorney General Christine Gregoire led the way, thanks to her state's "negative option" law, which makes it illegal for companies to charge customers for goods or services that they have not ordered.

Negative publicity and a protracted investigation were not what AOL needed as their new pricing debuted. How should the executives handle the problem?

"Well, let's just get on a plane and go out there," said Bob Pittman.

So Pittman and AOL Assistant General Counsel Randall Boe flew out to Washington. In an agreement signed on November 22, AOL agreed to provide a pop-up screen asking members to proactively choose which pricing plan they wanted. As is usual in such cases, AOL declared in the letter that its practices were "fair, reasonable and legal," and that it had only signed the agreement "to alleviate the Attorney General's concerns."

There would be a lot more to be concerned about soon enough.

drinking from a fire hose

In an executive meeting before the pricing change, Matt Korn had jokingly brought up what could happen to user demand when flat-rate pricing kicked in on December 1, 1996.

"It could be like drinking from a fire hose," he quipped.

The Wall Street Journal's Walt Mossberg pondered the same thing in his November 14 column. "AOL seems to be entering one of its periodic, major service slowdowns," wrote Mossberg. "This is because membership growth has picked up again, and new flat rates taking effect next month should attract even more new members. As a result, the service expects to be straining to keep up all winter, before enough new capacity is available to meet demand."

AOL executives themselves were always aware that the service might have trouble keeping up with demand. The issue was debated all summer. And as November drew to a close, the company sent out mailings to members warning that the "sudden increase in use" could "create some temporary 'traffic congestion' especially during our peak periods, which are typically 8 P.M. to midnight."

In anticipation of the move to unlimited access, AOL had struck a new deal with BBN Corporation, a Cambridge, Massachusetts-based Internet access provider, in mid-October. Under the agreement, BBN was to build out AOL's TCP/IP dial-up network, AOLNet, to ensure that the company could handle the expected growth in usage.

The numbers were impressive. Under a four-year, $340 million contract, BBN would add at least 70,000 modems per year to AOLNet, which at the time of the agreement had slightly more than 170,000 modems. In the first year, in other words, BBN would increase AOL's user capacity by more than 40 percent.

Internal AOL testing before the price change had indicated that AOL should expect about a 50 percent jump in usage. The network would be behind, but only slightly. Theoretically, that is. One other sticking point was that the BBN expansion wouldn't take place all at once; by December 1, not all the new modems would be ready.

The question remained: was AOL ready?

On December 1, the day AOL went to unlimited access, a preview of the answer was already apparent.

More than 2.5 million hours of member sessions were logged, an enormous increase over the 1.6 million hours on an average day in October. And already with this increase, the service experienced some slowdowns.

The next day, AOL announced it would spend—in addition to the BBN deal—another $250 million by the end of the fiscal year to expand the dial-up system.

The race to keep up with customer demand was on.

Despite fears of network slowdown, many analysts liked what they saw. The buzz around AOL was hot again, and new members were rushing into the service after a painfully slow summer. In the month of October, AOL added 275,000 new members—only 125,000 fewer than it had added in the entire previous quarter. And November was shaping up to be even better. The stock responded. On December 2, AOL shares leapt more than 13 percent, closing at more than $40 a share.

As December ticked away toward the holidays, the frenzy at AOL grew. The changeover was structured so that members' pricing plans changed on their billing date—not on the first of the month for everyone. As December went by, more and more members' accounts went to unlimited access.

More free time over the holidays, people receiving new computers and signing up for AOL, ever-chillier weather keeping people indoors—all these things added up to more people on line for longer hours. And the more time people spent online, the greater was the likelihood that they would find something of interest and would want to spend more hours online.

At AOL headquarters, the mood was a potent blend of excitement and stress. As the New Year passed, the membership number was storming toward eight million. The service had added an extraordinary half-million customers in December alone.

And now that AOL had matched the price of the ISPs, what was to stop the company from attracting millions more new members? After all, AOL was the "Internet on training wheels"—much easier to use than ISPs, and therefore more likely to attract the "newbies," or new users who had never been online. At this rate, 1997 would surely be the most triumphant yet for the company.

Steve Case echoed that view in his January 3, 1997, online letter to members: "We pledge to you that in the year to come," he wrote, "whether you're a charter member or brand-new to the online world, there will be no place online—or anywhere else, for that matter, like AOL."

How true that statement turned out to be. But not at all for the reasons Case envisioned.

are you busy tonight?

All across America, as 1997 began, a certain sequence repeated itself over and over again.

Dial up. Modem noise. Busy signal. Disconnect.

In December, AOL officials were joyous at the surge in sign-ups. But by January, there was a problem. Mail had doubled from 12 million to 24 million pieces a day. Users were logging on 4.5 million hours a day, up from 1.5 million. And hundreds of thousands of new members were pouring in the door.

And jamming the entrance. Nationwide, more and more angry and frustrated people sat at their computers, attempting to dial into AOL. Once, twice, three times, using different access numbers and chanting good luck rhymes, AOL members tried to get online to check their mail, their stocks, or their chat rooms. And repeatedly, they heard busy signals. Once they got on, they made a bad situation worse by hanging online longer than usual, so as not to lose their connection.

Even AOL executives—who used the system constantly—were locked out and not able to use a costly 800-line (that they used for free), because the line was flooded with members willing to pay extra connect fees to get online.

Once they were able to sign on, furious members used the service to flame Steve Case and complain in newsgroups. In offices and bars and at bus stops, AOL was becoming a hugely popular topic of conversation. Even people who had never been online, and some who had never used computers, now associated AOL with poor service. Everyone, from hairdressers to cabbies, seemed to have an opinion on what AOL had done wrong.

Something had to be done—and very, very quickly. When Steve Case responded, he shot himself in the foot yet again.

On January 16, AOL announced it was investing $100 million more in its network, on top of the $250 million pledged earlier. At the same time, it was suspending its television ads and adding more customer service reps to deal with agitated members.

These moves all made perfect sense. More money meant more modems, which meant fewer busy signals. And members were glad to see marketing curtailed—how could AOL accept new members, after all, when it couldn't serve the ones it had?

That same day, Steve Case committed arguably the worst blunder imaginable. He asked the customers now paying for unlimited access to limit their use.

In his online letter to members, Case first described AOL's efforts to alleviate the access crunch. Then, toward the end of the letter, he wrote:

> There's also something you can do to help, and that is to moderate your own use of AOL a bit during our peak evening periods. Although we of course want you to enjoy all that AOL has to offer and benefit from unlimited use, during this transitional period it would be helpful if you were sensitive to the needs and frustrations of your fellow members. Some people have told us that because it is difficult to get online, once they are online, they never want to sign off—even when they aren't using it. . . . Just as you would be sensitive about using a public phone booth if others were waiting in line to use it (although you are entitled to use it as long as you want, most people are considerate of the people waiting to get a turn), it would be helpful if you could be considerate of the needs of other members of the AOL community. Use AOL as much as you want during the day, but try to show some restraint at night during the next few months when we're in this transitional mode.

What in the world was this? Was AOL unlimited or wasn't it? Members were irate. Who was Steve Case to take $19.95 per member for unlimited use and then ask them not to use the service so much?

This was simply going too far, and thousands of members wrote to Case directly to let him know it. Seventeen thousand messages arrived in a two-day period, causing Case's mailbox to crash from all the traffic.

As bad as the access problems were, AOL suffered more from the perception that it was out of touch with and insensitive to the members' concerns. No longer was this cast as consumers receiving an inadequate product. People were taking this almost personally.

But, however enraged they were, there was not a whole lot the members could do. Some quit the service, some signed petitions circulated via e-mail, some even undertook the task of suing the company themselves.

What really got AOL to rethink its transgressions, though, was the further involvement of states' attorneys general in its business.

The AOL access disaster was a dream issue for the states to take on. First, it had an extremely high profile, which made it a big draw for a publicly elected official—such as a state attorney general—to become involved in. Second, the charge was relatively straightforward: the company had collected a fee, promised a service, and then failed to deliver it. Third, the issue truly resonated with voters; AOL users seemed to feel personally affronted at the way they were being treated. Steve Case had wronged them, and they wanted satisfaction.

Having just dealt with the company in the previous November, during the automatic-price-hike flap, the attorneys general were ready to charge in, fix the problem, and bask in the favorable headlines.

On January 23, representatives for twenty attorneys general met with AOL representatives in Chicago. About half the participants were actually present at the meeting; the other half "attended" by phone. Though the meeting was generally cordial, the talk turned tough quickly.

New York State's combative attorney general, Dennis Vacco, appearing on CNBC on the evening of the meeting, declared of AOL: "The bottom line is they're not making the service available

and people are paying money for a service they aren't receiving."
So Vacco took the step that immediately propelled his office into
the headlines. He threatened to sue the company.

In a letter dated January 27, but faxed to AOL several days beforehand as a "heads-up," Assistant Attorney General Eric Wenger
informed the company that the New York Attorney General intended to sue AOL for:

1. Repeatedly and persistently engaging in deceptive acts and
   practices in connection with the sale of online service and
   the servicing of the resulting orders;
2. Repeatedly and persistently engaging in false advertising in
   relation to the business referred to in paragraph 1 above;
3. Engaging in repeated and persistent fraud.

AOL, by law, had five days to respond to the letter before the
attorney general would sue. There was compelling reason for the
company to try to make a deal and avoid a suit. It was one thing to
be associated with poor service, but quite another to have your
company tarnished with the word "fraud." Already, the mention
of AOL among wired Americans was drawing sneers and scorn
from members and nonmembers alike. How much damage could a
fraud lawsuit do?

Or would it be seen, on the other hand, as simply grandstand-
ing by the government? The attorneys general, after all, were
always on the lookout for a hot issue that would define their reputations. When Dennis Vacco thrust himself into the lime-
light over the AOL debacle, it seemed he had found his pet
issue: "Vacco's Tobacco" was the mocking nickname one AOL
executive gave the New York Attorney General's crusade.
But how would that crusade affect the members' perceptions
of AOL?

It turned out to be a moot point. Any ideas Steve Case may
have had about protecting his faltering reputation and that of his
company were all but shattered on January 24, when a blistering
column appeared in *The Wall Street Journal*.

The "Front Lines" column, written by Thomas Petzinger, went beyond the usual criticism of sloppy management, busy signals, and overzealous marketing by AOL. It effectively branded Steve Case as unethical.

"The service breakdown at AOL is an ethical issue," wrote Petzinger. "Today's topsy-turvy business world does not excuse a company from offering a product it knows it cannot reliably deliver."

But the big slap in the face was at the end of the column: "We need to send a message to everyone claiming that new technologies demand new business rules. A lot has changed, yes—but not the role of trust. Don't recruit customers if you harbor the slightest doubt about your ability to serve them, because they have customers of their own. And if you do, we'll take our business elsewhere." An italicized note at the end of the column added: "To that end, please note my new e-mail address, tompetz@msn.com."

Steve Case was livid when he read the column, and it affected him deeply. "It's fair to criticize anyone for anything, but to attack someone's character without knowing the facts is terribly unfair," he said. "[The column] said I was immoral, and I'm not. We went to unlimited, and we had problems. The motive was to do the right thing for members and our profits even took a hit."

This was Case's theme again and again. The members wanted unlimited, so AOL gave it to them. It wouldn't have worked, Case believed, to promise members unlimited and then ask them to wait several months while AOL built up its modem base to accommodate the demand. He was certain they would prefer to get unlimited sooner rather than later, and deal with the consequences as they came up.

Case had considered, at first, putting the choice to a vote among AOL members. If the members themselves had chosen to go ahead with unlimited, come what may, they would have had no one to blame but themselves. And Steve Case wouldn't have found his ethics being impugned in one of the most influential newspapers in the country.

But it was too late for that. All Steve Case could do was weather the battering he was taking. And it wasn't over yet.

no comment

On Sunday, January 26, an audience of tens of millions of Americans watched their televisions go blank. Then, against the backdrop of the empty screen, they heard the sound of a modem making repeated attempts to log on. Finally, after a moment's silence, a message appeared on the screen: CompuServe's logo, with the tagline, "Looking for dependable Internet access? CompuServe. Get on with it." The number to call: 1-888-NOTBUSY.

It was Superbowl Sunday, and CompuServe had just mocked AOL in front of one of the largest television audiences of the year. After weeks of relative silence about AOL's troubles, CompuServe had suddenly decided to go on the offensive. The move was surprising, considering that the service had recently announced a decision to focus on business customers, but it was effective.

If AOL's reaction to members' criticisms was patient and contrite, its reaction to the CompuServe slap was swift and curt. "It's like people saying that they should come to our restaurant because it's empty," scoffed Steve Case to *Newsweek*.

But nearly two months after the unlimited access had gone into effect, AOL still seemed months away from being able to keep up with demand and was risking being permanently associated with ineptitude and indifference.

Still, Case did not want to admit guilt, nor did he want to offer blanket compensation to his suffering members.

Case had said as much in interviews, when he was asked about possible refunds. As late as January 27, AOL spokespersons were saying that the company was "not considering" blanket refunds for members—although some members who contacted the company specifically to ask for refunds were being compensated. But after AOL received the letter from Attorney General Dennis Vacco, Case realized the company would be better off settling the matter and moving on. Within days, an agreement was reached.

AOL would offer several different forms of compensation. First, all customers could get a free month of service if they requested it—no questions asked. They did, however, have to send a "snail mail" letter to a post office box in Ogden, Utah, to get it.

Alternatively, members could request financial compensation in differing amounts, depending on how much time they had spent on AOL during the months of December and January. The longer members had been able to stay online, the less compensation they were entitled to. For example, a customer who had used the service two cumulative hours or less in December was entitled to a full $19.95 refund. A customer who had spent between eight and fifteen hours a month, in contrast, was eligible for $4.99 in compensation. Those who had spent more than fifteen hours a month were not eligible for a refund—but they could still get the free month of service, no questions asked.

The agreement also stipulated that AOL would make its cancellation procedure easier, by "any reasonable notice," including phone, fax, and mail. And finally, AOL had to stop its marketing juggernaut entirely, by canceling its "Jetsons" TV ad campaign, its cable TV ads, and its new mailings—including diskettes.

And because he was the embodiment of service, Case was also urged by his executives to film a message to customers, telling them that AOL was trying its best and was sorry for the trouble it had caused them. In the tape, Case—clad in his trademark khakis and a bluejean shirt—walked stiffly through offices, explaining AOL's efforts to end the crisis, while employees scurried in the background. Internally, the commercial, which aired widely on television, became known as the "grovelmercial."

Just before the refund deal was to be made public, Case was doing an interview in downtown Washington, DC. Part of the agreement with the New York Attorney General had been not to discuss any details before the agreement was public. But what Case didn't know—and was about to find out, rudely—was that the news was already out.

Case stepped outside the building and found himself facing cameramen and aggressive questions about the agreement. Startled by the ambush, he turned to hurry away, mumbling "No comment" to the assembled news crews.

"I could only say 'No comment,' as anything else would have been breaking the agreement," said Case later. But when a New York television station ran footage of Steve hustling off to his car, saying only "No comment, no comment," Case looked, if not like a criminal on the lam, then certainly like a man with something to hide.

Case was at a nadir. "There were a lot of very cynical, negative questions, but I could deal with that," he said. "But sometimes it's hard to get beat up day in and day out."

The long, frustrating winter had tainted the service, perhaps irreparably. From Wall Street to Main Street, both AOL and Case would have a major struggle ahead to reclaim their reputations.

"It's weird," he said. "But it felt like AOL had finally come of age."

And so—quite painfully—had Steve Case.

truth, justice, and a little bit of sex chat

courting trouble

The steps outside the Supreme Court, in Washington, DC, were slick with frozen, slushy rain, even though it was already late March of 1997—a time when cherry blossoms and spring temperatures usually brighten the nation's capital. From a wall of television cameras hastily set up under the gloomy, gray sky, the glare of spotlights illuminated the face of Bill Burrington, AOL's assistant general counsel, who stood before the crowd of soaked reporters and spectators like a man in a daze.

The Court had just heard the case that could make or break AOL, and the frantic months of preparation showed on Burrington's wan face. The single biggest threat to freedom of speech on the Internet—the Communications Decency Act (CDA) signed by President Bill Clinton a year before—had undergone its final challenge in a session that began at 10 A.M. on March 19, 1997. The day had finally come, the arguments were finished, and now Burrington had to make it through the final press conferences before taking a much-needed rest.

Reporters milled about, listening and taking notes as software makers, lawyers, antiporn activists, high schoolers, and anyone else with an opinion argued vigorously in tight little knots of people.

Off to one side, a group of teenagers organized by a local antiporn group stood chanting, "Children don't need this stuff! Enough is enough!" while carrying picket signs that read: "Child molesters are looking for victims on the Internet."

And in front of the biggest gaggle of television cameras and reporters, representatives of both sides of the argument were making their arguments to be shown on the six o'clock news nationwide.

One by one, supporters of the CDA stood before the phalanx of media to have their say. Donna Rice Hughes—already ensconced in history as Democratic Senator Gary Hart's love interest in the sex scandal that brought down his 1988 presidential bid—spoke of the need to protect children from smut, her conservative dress, sensible brunette hairdo, and serious demeanor in stark contrast to her former reputation as a party girl. Cathy Cleaver—a striking blonde attorney wearing wire-frame glasses and a bright red coat—spoke on behalf of the conservative Family Research Council. She praised the CDA for safeguarding children from the seamy side of the Internet.

Then it was Bill Burrington's turn to defend the online industry and AOL. With his boy-next-door good looks and unfailing politeness, he exuded the same clean-cut image as his opponents. His soft-spoken gentility carried over into an aw-shucks manner, making Burrington a great Washington anomaly: a lawyer who seemed like a guy you wouldn't mind knowing. A transplanted Midwesterner, Burrington, at age 35, seemed not a bit jaded by the cynicism that pervades the nation's capital. Arriving at the Supreme Court that morning, he had even felt a lump in his throat when he looked around and considered the historic decisions that had been made in the courtroom.

Today, history was once again being made, and he was right in the middle of it.

But at that moment, no enthusiasm showed on Burrington's face as he stood wearily by the side of Bruce Ennis, the experienced First Amendment attorney who had just argued the case against the CDA before the nine Justices. It had been a grueling year leading up to the Supreme Court arguments, and as the impromptu press conference continued under the sleet and rain, Burrington increasingly looked like a man at the end of his tether.

8

From the tightly packed huddle of onlookers came a shouted question. "AOL, can you protect children with your service?"

Burrington stepped to the microphones. "We have had parental control tools on AOL for over two years now," he began, stooping slightly under an umbrella, reciting one of AOL's main defenses against the CDA. "We can block access to. . . . "

"No you can't! You can't!" shouted a woman suddenly, as she pushed her way in front of the cameras. Shaking her finger at Burrington, the woman ignored reporters' irritated pleadings to pipe down, and launched into an angry attack on the world's largest on-line service.

"It doesn't work," she yelled, drowning out Burrington's attempt to respond. "I know it won't work! I've used it!"

"Get out of the way!" shouted back an annoyed cameraman, while the gathering began to buzz. Reporters, including Nina Totenberg of National Public Radio, waited, hands on hips, for the woman to finish.

But Jodi Hoffman, representing a group called Restore America's Moral Pride, had come all the way from Florida for this argument, and she was not done yet. She impatiently pushed a strand of her long blonde hair out of her face and continued.

"You all keep saying there's no problem," she charged, finger wagging in accusation at Burrington. "Well, if there's no problem, then why was this law passed?"

Up in front of the microphones, Burrington paused. Ironically, this woman could not have said it any better.

Why, indeed?

As serious as AOL's access and pricing troubles were as 1996 ended and 1997 began, another, perhaps more dangerous, issue had been brewing since early February 1995, and indeed long before that—a problem that could do potentially irreparable harm not only to AOL but to the entire Internet industry.

It had begun when Democratic Senator Jim Exon, a veteran lawmaker from the heartland state of Nebraska, had become troubled by some of the racier content available over the Internet, and had decided that something needed to be done.

18

But the bill that Exon ultimately introduced, on February 1, 1995, set in motion angry accusations that his actions would kill the Internet, by severely chilling the free speech that had been its hallmark. The introduction of his Communications Decency Act marked the beginning of the greatest legal test for the new online industry, and perhaps most especially for its largest player—AOL.

In its final form, the CDA would criminalize "the transmission of any comment, request, suggestion, proposal, image or other communication which is obscene or indecent, knowing that the recipient of the communication is under 18 years of age."

In addition, it sought to penalize "whoever . . . uses interactive computer services to display in a manner available to a person under 18, any comment, request, suggestion, proposal, image or other communications that, in context, depicts or describes, in terms patently offensive as measured by contemporary community standards, sexual or excretory activities or organs."

The penalty: a fine of up to $250,000 and up to two years in prison.

The thorny First Amendment conflicts caused by the controversial law were obvious. But, for a company like AOL, the law's vague language had implications that were perhaps even more troublesome from operational and financial standpoints.

How would AOL—with its thousands of chat rooms and millions of postings on its message boards, in addition to offering users access to the sprawling World Wide Web—ever be able to monitor its service to ensure that no users under 18 could see anything indecent? And what exactly qualified as indecent, anyway? Did "contemporary community standards" mean that traditionally conservative communities such as Memphis, Tennessee, or Biloxi, Mississippi, could determine that materials posted on the Web from, say, New York or San Francisco were offensive?

And AOL had even actively explored opening its own porn connection. Though virtually no one outside the company knew it, during much of the long debate over the CDA, AOL was researching how it could make money off online porn. The company had never progressed beyond the research stage for the premium "adult content" channel, but if even that news got out, AOL's stance as a family-friendly service would be severely damaged. And so would its ability to effectively fight legislation like the CDA.

For AOL, bigger issues than revenues were at stake. The CDA aimed at the very heart of the industry AOL had helped build. From the moment the bill was introduced, it would be fiercely debated by a sprawling cast of characters. They included the Christian Coalition's Ralph Reed, the American Civil Liberties Union, Donna Rice Hughes, Newt Gingrich, the Center for Democracy and Technology, and a collection of representatives from the online industry, including AOL's Bill Burrington.

From an idea in the head of a politician, through the tortuous byways of the U.S. Congress and onto the desk of President Clinton, the CDA would be challenged all the way to the Supreme Court. At the end of the process, the online industry would never look at itself in quite the same way again.

your chat room or mine?

In December 1991, in AOL's then-minuscule customer relations department at 8619 Westwood Center Drive, in Vienna, Virginia, historic Supreme Court battles were far from anyone's mind.

Though she ran the marketing department, Jean Villanueva also oversaw the company's relationship with its small number of users. Customer complaints, for the most part, were about billing snafus and glitchy software. The company, which had not yet gone public, had only about 150,000 subscribers and offered a service that only worked for Apple II, Macintosh, and DOS computer users. AOL was a minor company in a still-insignificant industry.

While working late one evening, Villanueva was jolted by a call from a reporter at KRON, the NBC affiliate in San Francisco. "I just wanted to give you a heads-up," he told her. "We're running a story about child pornography on AOL tonight."

Having never seen such a topic listed on the complaint sheets before, Villanueva was dumbfounded. "Let me call you back in 15 minutes," she told the reporter. She bolted out of her office to consult with the customer service representatives who sat right outside her door.

This was definitely a "flash item" in the department. All telephones were turned off, and everyone gathered around Villanueva, who stood atop a folding chair she had dragged into the middle of the room.

"Have we had any calls from customers about child pornography?" she asked the reps.

"No," they all answered, they had not. There had been complaints of members' sending unsolicited mail, using sexually explicit language in chat rooms, and trading adult porn. In those cases, members were in trouble if they violated the company's "Terms of Service" (TOS), which prohibit members from impersonating others, harassing other members, and "facilitating the distribution of sexually explicit or other content which is deemed by AOL Inc. to be offensive." Members who were caught breaking the rules would be "TOS'd," in chat-room slang: tossed out of the chat room and allowed one more warning. If their actions were particularly offensive, they were kicked off of AOL.

But there was no record of any complaint about child pornography.

Baffled, Villanueva called the reporter back, and managed to learn that an AOL member had contacted the television station directly.

By now, it was getting late. Resolving to meet the problem head on, she got the member's name. She then asked the service reps if that particular member had ever called in about child porn—the answer was still no.

So Villanueva telephoned him that night.

The member told her that he had initially complained to the police, but they had done nothing. Frustrated by their inaction, he had decided to go to the press, even before contacting AOL. Villanueva asked the customer to e-mail her the offensive material (which he said had been sent to him by other AOL members). So he did.

Villanueva downloaded the files with a feeling of dread. Would it really be as bad as she feared?

It was.

She and other AOL officials—including Steve Case and chief technologist Marc Seriff—stared for a moment at the pictures of what Villanueva called "obviously really extreme child porn." Villanueva shuddered. On the screen were photographs of young children having sex with other young children, with adults, and in large groups. It was horrifying to see—and even more so because it was coursing through the electronic veins of AOL.

Her shock had an element of willful naïveté. AOL, much like Prodigy and CompuServe, had become mini-cities in cyberspace, and now the seamy side of the community had inevitably surfaced. Villanueva, Case, and Seriff—the small coterie of executives who ran the company at that time—knew their next moves were critical.

The San Francisco television station had used the term "child porn ring" in its report on AOL; for an industry very much in its infancy, such words were poison. They might form consumers' first and most lasting ideas about the online world. Because AOL's big selling point was its "community" environment—a pleasant place to communicate electronically—AOL could not allow this depraved image to take hold. In addition, AOL was preparing to go public in the spring of 1992, and this kind of publicity would not play well on Wall Street.

But there were also questions of law; child porn is illegal in all fifty states. The pictures that had been sent to Villanueva needed to be reported to the proper authorities immediately, now that AOL knew about them. That same night, Villanueva called the Federal Bureau of Investigation.

Because the pictures had been sent to her and were now her property, Villanueva could turn over the offending e-mail without violating any member's privacy. But the FBI would surely want more from AOL—member files, account information, the ability to trail people's movements through the system.

This was a problem.

"We can't panic," Villanueva thought, knowing AOL would have to negotiate the tricky Scylla and Charybdis of this crisis— finding a way to stop the transmission of these vile pictures while also protecting the privacy of its members. In addition, as a small company with limited financial and human resources, how much could AOL do to find smut in the huge flow of information cascading through the growing service?

Villanueva, Case, Seriff, and others met all weekend with lawyers from their outside counsel, pondering what to do and trying to create a workable policy. They decided to cooperate with authorities, but only those with proper court orders demanding information or action. They decided to investigate strong technological solutions that were not too invasive to members. And they wrote a letter to the AOL community warning about the problem.

the house that sex chat built

But the problem could not easily be fixed.

The company, in an effort to provide a unique service for its members, had created an almost perfect environment for such fetid fare to flourish. With its anonymous screen names, easy attachment of graphical files, and many unmonitored chat rooms—which were already developing into one of AOL's biggest draws—AOL was especially well suited to the needs of porn traders. They could slip anonymously in and out of the ether, seeking out fellow porn lovers without a trace.

This architecture was designed into the entire AOL system, which encouraged multiple screen names without requiring that users identify themselves. This unique setup differentiated AOL from competitors and created a more unrestrained place to visit.

Anonymity made things interesting in the AOL chat rooms, which had three separate categories. First, there are the AOL-designed rooms, sponsored by the company, with thematic names like "the breakfast club," "fiber and needle art," "thirtysomething," and "born-again onliners." Any member could browse the list of rooms and join chat in progress.

Second, there were public member-created rooms. Any AOL member could create his or her own topic for a chat room, which then could accommodate up to 23 users at a time. The member-created chat rooms—with names like "married and flirting," "submissive men," "firemen m4m," and "crossdressers2,"—were also listed for all members to browse through and freely enter.

Third, there were private member-created chat rooms, which AOL members could create for themselves and their friends—or anyone they chose to invite. These private chat rooms were unique in several ways. Unlike the public rooms, which were all listed by name so that any AOL member could decide to "enter" one and chat, the private rooms were not listed. A member had to already know the name of the room in order to find it—a perfect way to keep out unwanted guests.

In one other, more important way, the private chat rooms were different. Whereas the public rooms were patrolled by AOL's volunteer "guides," who acted as chaperones of sorts, to ensure that members behave, the private chat rooms had no guides and, therefore, virtually anything was fair game. What was to stop a group of men from forming a private AOL chat room specifically to trade pornographic pictures—or worse, child pornography? The answer: Nothing. The only way a private chat room could be checked out or shut down was if someone made a complaint—and when the only people who are in a chat room have been specifically invited there, the chances of a complaint are pretty slim.

Not surprisingly, AOL's private chat room service—a service with no equivalent on either CompuServe or Prodigy—was a popular place to trade porn of all kinds. The company had pledged to cooperate with authorities when criminal activity was discovered (it could trace its users if need be), but many felt that AOL's efforts were reactive rather than proactive. Because it refused to police its private chat rooms, the company gained a reputation of being "soft" on pornographers and pedophiles.

The online service had made that decision quite intentionally. AOL, the executives decided, would not restrict the privileges of the many because of the transgressions of a few. A judgment was made: Privacy meant privacy, even if people were going to use the service for unsavory purposes.

"A lot of people thought we gave a wink and a nod to that kind of behavior," said Villanueva. "But we never did. We just made a decision that the members' privacy was the most important thing."

In meeting after meeting—for the debate never seemed to end at AOL—company officials used the same reasoning. AOL was like a common communications carrier, not directly responsible for what was being carried if they did not know what it was. People use the telephone to plot criminal acts all the time, the AOL mantra went, but that doesn't mean all telephone calls should be screened.

Steve Case had compared the problem to that of another high-flying company. "Federal Express knows that things are going out in their packages that they don't like—drugs, or laundered money, for example," he said. But that doesn't mean they stop sending packages, or insist on inspecting every single one. Privacy issues—and cost—prohibit that approach.

But that argument is oversimplified. Online services represent an entirely new medium, unlike any other. Telephones, for example, are largely made up of specific point-to-point conversations. Although there are occasionally random prank or harassing phone calls, a child placing a telephone call is in no danger of having a pedophile break into a conversation to make a lewd proposition.

In a chat room or with e-mail, a person is much more exposed. It is much easier to become a target—especially when the person doing the harassing can stay anonymous. In chat rooms, one wanders randomly and meet hundreds of people. Online chat room conversations are less like telephone conversations than they are like hotel lobbies—a word AOL uses for its chat anterooms—but with a key difference. In an actual hotel lobby, a visitor can *see* a creep who's lurking around. And most people know better than to talk to strangers.

On AOL, with its homey graphics and wholesome community image, it was easy to be lulled into a false sense of security that the service was protecting against undesirables. And the TOS staff, however well intentioned, was frequently inadequate for the task at hand.

The controversy came down to a simple question: Was it commendable or irresponsible to protect users' privacy to such a degree?

The only real alternative to the problem was to shut down the unmonitored rooms, ramp up guides in the public rooms, and perhaps even screen e-mail. And these were not options, since they were at the sweet spot of AOL's business in terms of attracting members and garnering hourly fees. Chat, for example, represented one-quarter of all member hours online throughout much of AOL's history.

It's difficult to gauge exactly how much of AOL's early revenues came from sex chat and the downloading of porn photos. An October 1996 article in *Rolling Stone* estimated that, assuming half of all AOL's chat was sexually oriented, by spring of 1996 the company was raking in up to $7 million every month from sex chat alone. Steve Case, in the same article, estimated that less than half of all chat was sex-related.

Before the shift to flat-rate pricing in the fall of 1996, AOL was realizing substantial revenues from users who would spend upward of 100 hours a month online, usually in the chat rooms. The hourly fees added up quickly; some users regularly paid bills of more than $300 per month.

Clearly, chilling chat room speech and spending more on monitoring would mean chilling revenues.

And perhaps more importantly for a small company like AOL, the bawdy chat rooms drew members. AOL's privacy policy in the chat rooms, according to some industry observers, was one of the main reasons the company was able to steamroller Prodigy.

"That's why AOL has eight million members and Prodigy had faded to a shadow of its former self," said a high-ranking executive at Prodigy, who watched in fascination and dismay through the early 1990s as AOL began its climb.

Prodigy, the number two online service in 1991, had so far stayed out of the chat phenomenon altogether. In an effort to keep adult-oriented material away from its younger members, Prodigy created the so-called "Frank Discussions" message boards for adult topics, complete with a "wall" designed to keep underage users out via credit card checks.

Within just two months, however, the idea of having adult-oriented message boards was deemed too racy by Prodigy's straitlaced corporate parents, IBM and Sears. In its efforts to remain "family-friendly," the company junked "Frank Discussions" and continued to resist setting up chat rooms on its service—a decision that locked it out of the lucrative per-hour chat income that was beginning to fill AOL's coffers and increase its member base.

Prodigy execs even ordered that every single message received from members for posting on the service's message boards had to be checked first for any inappropriate content. This unwieldy, time-consuming policy frustrated Prodigy's customers and inhibited the service's growth. Across the electronic divide, AOL's message boards were a virtual free-for-all.

In the midst of one of its many controversies over its practice of meddling in its users' activities, Prodigy communications director Geoffrey Moore made no apologies for attempting to bar "uninhibited, titillating conversations" from the service.

"We make no apology for pursuing a value system that reflects the culture of millions of American families we aspire to serve," he wrote in a *New York Times* column. "Some people confuse private messages with public editorial features . . . editorial discretion . . . does not limit speech in any Constitutional sense."

Moore even suggested that those interested in such fare could use other services. The obvious choice was AOL, which soon became known in online circles and in the media as "The House that Sex Chat Built."

As AOL grew, through 1992 and 1993, racy publicity—which would, at first glance, seem to be a public relations nightmare—didn't always hurt the company. AOL was finally in the news, and it was seen as a hot, hip place to be. That was no small advantage for a tiny company intent on establishing its brand name. Whatever the context, AOL was being mentioned alongside industry heavyweights CompuServe and Prodigy.

The hype was heating up but, for the huge majority of Americans, the Internet sex debate was still the province of the technological elite. In the early 1990s, very few Americans were online; it was mostly tech-heads and journalists debating a rather abstract issue. Average America might find the issue titillating, but it had nothing to fear from online perversion.

Then, in May 1993, a tousle-haired ten-year-old boy named George ("Junior") Burdynski, Jr. was reported missing from his home in suburban Maryland. The disappearance of this average kid in an average suburb caused ripples of alarm in the local press. Then, while investigating Junior's disappearance, police detectives made a discovery linking the case to the world of cyberporn.

During the search for the boy, they happened upon a man in nearby Hyattsville named James Kowalski, who was never implicated in the crime. When they learned that Junior had been coming over to Kowalski's house to play with his computer in the weeks before the disappearance, detectives searched Kowalski's home and computer files in the hope of finding some clue to Junior's fate.

What they found instead were nude and obscene photos of kids, as well as writings by Kowalski—who was an AOL member—bragging about his sexual exploits with children.

The blend of child porn, kidnapping, and computers was incendiary. Sexual perversion had reached out an electronic hand to grab Middle America by the throat.

Although neither Kowalski nor another man arrested, Stephen Leak, was successfully linked to the disappearance of Junior Burdynski, both were convicted and jailed on charges of child abuse and pornography. Junior has never been found.

Now, the mainstream media were hooked. The online world was trumpeted in story after story as a frightening, lawless place—a happy harbor for digital deviants. In chat rooms and message boards, wherever one looked, naughty, raunchy, or downright disgusting behavior was going on—at least that's what the news stories argued. Proponents of the Internet began to fear that the hype surrounding sex online was drowning out the positive aspects of the industry.

Throughout 1993 and 1994, reporters eagerly rooted out examples of the worst antisocial behavior online. And not only was child porn an issue, but stalking, harassment, and murder were as well. "Online" and "Internet"—and, by extension, AOL—began to connote a haven for perverts and stalkers rather than a promising virtual world of discovery.

indecent proposal

In this atmosphere in the fall of 1994, Senator Jim Exon first began floating his ideas about Internet "decency" in the 103rd Congress. The Exon legend holds that the senator was watching his grandchildren playing games on the computer one day and decided then and there that he needed to find a way to protect them from online smut. But the senator claims that no one thing inspired him to propose the bill. He had simply heard and read enough, and decided something needed to be done.

Exon was proud of the fact that he had been around and active in the earlier days of the Internet, when it was used as a government tool for the transfer of military information.

"I knew all about the information superhighway," said Exon. "It's the most important tool for the dissemination of information since the printing press. I've been a very big supporter of it."

Yet many saw Exon as a Luddite meddling in an area he knew nothing about. He was held in disregard by many in the online world, who were unconvinced of his technological knowledge of and concern for the new industry. The bill was, some thought, a reactionary slap at the new medium for the purpose of garnering headlines—besides being a poorly drafted piece of legislation.

"It had all the right ingredients—porn, children, cyberspace—all the issues that make for great debates," said one AOL official, echoing a common opinion at the time. "And all this coming from Exon, this old hayseed from the Great Plains."

The first legislation Exon proposed never made it to the floor of Congress, dying quietly when the session expired. But the signal had gone out that the online industry had a problem that was bigger and more concrete than mere public perception.

Robert Butler, outside counsel for Prodigy, was the first to act. When he got wind of the proposed legislation, he recognized quickly the potential danger for the online industry. Representatives of AOL, Prodigy, CompuServe, and MSN were invited to a meeting at Butler's office at the powerful communications law firm of Wiley, Rein & Fielding, in downtown Washington, in late 1994.

One of those in attendance was William W. Burrington, a young lawyer for a Washington-based trade group, the Interactive Services Association.

Bill Burrington had come a long way from his roots in Elm Grove, Wisconsin, a wealthy suburb of Milwaukee. The son of a father who was a printing industry executive and a mother who set aside her high school teaching career to raise her two children, Burrington had lived the kind of all-American life typically immortalized in *Reader's Digest* anecdotes.

Growing up in Elm Grove, young Bill had been imbued with the Republicanism that was common in hard-working, middle-class America. He was a quintessential overachiever, the kind of kid who is golden from the moment he steps onto the Pee-wee league football field or dons a Boy Scout neckerchief. The unflagging idealism that Burrington would later bring to the CDA debates, he guessed, had its genesis in the happy, settled childhood he was privileged to enjoy.

His idealistic urges were particularly stoked by an event that Burrington still recalls without a trace of self-consciousness. When Burrington was about 13, President Gerald Ford came to town. As the youngest Eagle Scout in the history of Wisconsin, Burrington had been chosen to make a presentation to the president. In preparation for the big event, he decided to write President Ford a personal letter.

"Dear Mr. President," the letter began. "You and I have a lot in common. We're both left-handed, we both played center on our football teams, we're both Eagle Scouts." Burrington slipped the letter to the President during his formal presentation, excited to have a chance to communicate personally with such an important man.

Two months later, Burrington's father came in from the mailbox, calling for Bill. There was an envelope from the White House; inside were a picture and a handwritten note from the President. The note praised Burrington for his achievements as a scout, and encouraged him to get into public service.

He was hooked. Before he even finished high school, Burrington would go to work on a congressional campaign—the unsuccessful 1978 bid of Republican Sue Shannon.

Burrington's Republican leanings changed over the years. Toward the end of his college years at Lawrence University, in Appleton,

Wisconsin, his rock-solid conservative beliefs began to shift in response to the liberalism that is common on American college campuses. But his devotion to the political process itself never flagged. He earned a law degree at Marquette University, volunteered and worked for a number of political campaigns, and finally accepted a position, in July 1989, as general counsel for Representative Jim Moody (Democrat, Wisconsin).

He moved to Washington, intending to get some Hill experience and then return to Wisconsin to run for Moody's seat himself. But after a few years of working on the Hill, he began to see the life of a congressional representative in a different light. The endless rounds of fundraising and schmoozing seemed to him a thankless, joyless job.

When his work for Moody ended, Burrington instead turned to communications law, taking a position at Miller & Holbrooke, a Washington-based boutique law firm. He stayed only two years, then worked as executive director at the National Association for Interactive Services (NAIS), the trade group of the 800- and 900-telephone number industries. After that, he opened his own law firm, taking on clients such as the Interactive Services Association.

At NAIS, Burrington saw firsthand how the actions of a few—in this case, the "dial-a-porn" 900-number telephone services—could ruin an industry for the many.

"What do you think of when you hear the words, '900 number'?" said Burrington. "You think of sex lines . . . there were a whole range of other services offered, but sex is all anyone thinks about." An entire industry had been tainted because an issue had been allowed to get out of hand.

Exon's idea for a CDA brought Burrington a dizzying sense of "Here we go again." He knew that porn often drives new media, because the porn industry is always looking for new methods of distribution. And, true to form, it was one of the first problem issues to surface in the online world. Burrington knew that the industry needed to learn some lessons fast.

"If the industry did not take it seriously up front," Burrington said, "they would start to become defined by it." So, at the meeting in Butler's office, he recounted his experience with the 900-number industry, and warned the group to be aware of how quickly public perception could shift.

Everyone gathered knew the Exon bill would be back. And because other political forces were at work in 1994, its return would bring worse trouble than they had expected.

In the late fall, Washington's political zeitgeist took a massive shift to the right. In the November elections, both Houses of Congress were captured from the Democrats by the Republican Party. Newt Gingrich became Speaker of the House, "family values" became the watchword of the land, and the "Republican Revolution" was unleashed.

It was a good time to be against the licentious excesses of the Internet.

During that fall, Bill Burrington began interviewing for a position on AOL's legal team. For months, Burrington, hoping to get some free-lance work from AOL, had tried to schedule a meeting with Ellen Kirsh, AOL's general counsel. But she and her legal team—made up, incredibly enough, of only her and two other lawyers—were always swamped.

When they finally met for lunch at the American Café near AOL headquarters, Kirsh quickly proposed another idea—Burrington should come on board to help AOL in the legislative arena. Despite the obvious importance to the company of emerging legislation, the overextended AOL legal team had no one working full-time on it.

A quick series of meetings was arranged. Burrington was interviewed by Steve Case, Ted Leonsis, Len Leader, and Jean Villanueva, and was soon hired as AOL's point man on the Hill. AOL needed help there—fast.

On January 31, 1995, the day before his official start date at AOL's Vienna offices, Burrington joined a meeting of online industry representatives from all the major providers—AOL, CompuServe, Prodigy, and the about-to-be-launched Microsoft Network—as well as representatives from the fledgling Center for Democracy and Technology (CDT), a First Amendment group.

He had not officially started his new position at AOL, and nothing concrete had been proposed in the Senate, but Burrington knew that a conflict was unavoidable.

"We'd better get ready for a storm," he told the group.

Within hours, during Bill Burrington's first day on the job at AOL, Senator Exon reintroduced the CDA, this time to a more receptive audience: the Republican-controlled 104th Congress.

Although not a computer expert, Exon felt passionately about curbing pornography online. The headlines brought him a degree of fame (some would say, notoriety), but participants on both sides of the debate believed he genuinely wanted to tailor a bill that would protect children without infringing too much on freedom of speech.

He wanted—implausibly—to placate those on both sides of the debate—from the American Civil Liberties Union to the Christian Coalition. He also did not want to pass a law that later would be struck down. "I was not interested in an exercise in futility," the senator would say later. "I wanted to pass a law that would stand up under constitutional scrutiny."

Over the next couple of months, as they fine-tuned the bill, the senator and his staff took suggestions from a range of sources. Burrington waded right in, despite a split opinion on tactics in the anti-CDA camp.

Some civil rights purists, such as the Electronic Frontier Foundation (EFF) and the CDT, believed that even negotiating with Exon's side was a bad tactic. Why fight to make the bill as fair and unrestrictive as possible? Let them pass a blatantly unconstitutional, anti-free-speech bill, went the reasoning; it will then be overturned by the courts later.

For Burrington, that tack was impossible; AOL didn't have the luxury of assuming a bad bill wouldn't stand up. In his more progressive bones, he believed the CDA was the wrong approach, but his effort to shape the bill was part of his trying to protect his company, not a question of theory or ideology. If the CDA were to become law, AOL might have to restructure major parts of its business; Burrington had no choice but to sit down with the drafters of the bill and try to influence the language as best he could.

Some argued that AOL's willingness to negotiate with Exon gave the CDA a legitimacy it might not otherwise have had. CDT head Jerry Berman described a disheartening meeting he and his colleague, Daniel Weitzner, had with Exon's counsel and the key drafter of the CDA, Chris McLean, one afternoon in February. Berman had made the trip to Capitol Hill to present McLean with a letter signed by dozens of organizations and companies opposed to the CDA. Standing in Exon's office, McLean opened the letter with a flourish and quickly scanned down to the signatories to see who claimed to be against the bill.

Then, pen in hand, he began ticking off the names of companies that had already sent someone to begin negotiations on the bill's language. He put neat check marks next to AOL, Prodigy, CompuServe, and on down the list, until only the civil liberties organizations were left.

"These are the people who have come by to work with us already," he told Berman, indicating the check marks.

The message was clear: Why withdraw the bill when so much of the opposition was ready to sit at the table and negotiate the language?

It was a classic divide-and-conquer strategy. Berman left Exon's office that day feeling that knives had been unsheathed in the battle over the CDA.

Considering the threat to AOL if the CDA were to become law, Burrington, the newly minted director of public policy, was granted an astonishing amount of leeway to decide AOL's tactics. AOL's top brass were aware of the CDA and the problems it presented, but there was so much else to worry about in the still-struggling company that Burrington was basically left to deal with the issue as he saw fit.

He negotiated with the Senate staffers, dealt with the press, and networked with attorneys for the other online services. He sent regular memos and updates to AOL's executives, but he rarely received guidance—or any response at all. For all intents and purposes, AOL was entrusting its legislative affairs entirely to Burrington.

"People [inside the company] were very much aware," said Burrington. "But, to my surprise, I was able to work this thing in a manner that I thought was best."

The industry had long put its bet on parental control software, which blocks material containing key words—such as "sex" and "breast"—as the solution to protecting kids using the Internet.

All the major online services—including AOL—provided parental control software to all members, free of charge. Though the software was often buggy—blocking sites with words such as "Sussex" and "Essex" when asked to block the word "sex," for example—the industry still maintained that such software was a far more reasonable way to keep objectionable material away from kids. If parents were given the power to control what their children saw online, went the industry's argument, then the CDA would simply be unnecessary.

In the meantime, the CDA was moving through legislative channels, forcing some troublesome issues.

Could online services realistically keep under-18 users from seeing anything deemed indecent?

And a thornier question: Should they even have to?

How was "indecency" defined in the online world anyway? Was it like the world of broadcasting, where even certain curse-words are off-limits during daylight hours? Or should the Internet be regulated more like the print world, with its almost-anything-goes latitude? Was online like print or like broadcast?

The problem was, it was neither. It was a completely new medium, about which the vast majority of Americans knew little, and for which new rules would have to be written.

In March 1995, after spending nearly two months negotiating with civil liberties groups and representatives of the online industry, Exon submitted a reworded version of the bill. Antiporn activists were aghast: the new bill had added defenses that would remove all liability from online service providers. Under the new wording, companies like AOL wouldn't be held responsible for content they didn't produce themselves.

Exon had, in the opinion of longtime antiporn activist Bruce Taylor, been "hoodwinked." And the antiporn forces were determined to do something about it.

► chapter.twelve

supreme courting

enough is too much

A trio of conservative activists quickly set to work on the increasingly controversial bill: Bruce Taylor, head of the National Law Center for Children and Families; Cathy Cleaver, of the Family Research Council; and Donna Rice Hughes, director of communications for Enough Is Enough, an antipornography organization.

Taylor, Cleaver, and Hughes were poles apart in their levels of experience in dealing with the issue. Taylor, a straight-talking, sardonic attorney, had worked on antiporn issues since 1973, when he was a law student. His entire career had been devoted to fighting pornographers, and he had taken on some of the most notorious. In his Fairfax, Virginia, office, Taylor displays a framed courtroom sketch of himself arguing in front of the U.S. Supreme Court. The case: *Hustler* pornmeister Larry Flynt versus the State of Ohio.

Cleaver, too, was a veteran in the antiporn wars, having worked for the National Law Center before moving to the right-wing Family Research Council. A sharp-tongued lawyer, Cleaver was a natural in front of the camera, and she was a favorite among news reporters looking for colorful quotes.

Hughes, on the other hand, had first gained fame in a more un-conventional way: She was the love interest of then-presidential hopeful Gary Hart in 1988, when she was still known as Donna Rice. After taunting the media with a challenge to find evidence of his philandering, Hart had been caught with the South Carolina-born model, thereby propelling his candidacy into oblivion and Rice into the history books.

America had gotten its first glimpse of Donna Rice in the now-infamous photo showing the blonde ex-cheerleader sitting primly on Hart's lap next to the "Monkey Business" pleasure boat. That photo, which was invariably coupled with newspaper accounts play-ing up the "bimbo angle," had led most Americans to believe that Rice—who had graduated Phi Beta Kappa in biology at the Uni-versity of South Carolina—was a lightweight. Stung by the charges in the press, she dropped out of the public eye after what she now refers to as "the scandal," and reassessed where her life was leading.

Aside from a final foray into modeling—including her photo shoot for "No Excuses" jeans—no one heard much from Donna Rice in the next several years. In her own words, "When the scan-dal happened, I realized how far I had gotten away from my be-liefs. I came back to my faith, and sort of said, 'OK, God, use this for your glory.'"

In 1994, she was invited to come on board a northern Virginia-based antipornography group, Enough Is Enough. She enthusiasti-cally accepted and, soon after, began to research the issue of online pornography. In May 1994, she married business executive Jack Hughes, and took his name.

Donna Rice Hughes's transformation was complete.

By most accounts, the efforts by Taylor, Cleaver, and Hughes were geared toward crafting a workable bill, even if that meant angering some allies of the bill, such as the more conservative Christian Coalition and the American Family Association. The latter wanted no concessions to what it called "the red-light dis-trict of the information superhighway." The more restrictive the bill, the better.

But Taylor, who characterized his role as "explain[ing] what effect certain language would have" rather than lobbying, said he "didn't think the language needed to go that far. I wanted to give the industry a chance to do what it said it wanted to do"—protect children from pornography.

Yet Taylor didn't disguise how he felt about the industry. To him, AOL and other Internet service providers were "a new breed of pornographers."

In the old days, he felt, pornographers knew they were pornographers. "They operated on the fringes. Their attitude was, 'I don't care if you like me,'" he said. "Now they operate like accepted society."

The online services, said Taylor, would "sabotage the whole stupid Internet to protect a few dirty pictures. . . . I don't mind arguing about law and philosophy, but I don't want kids to suffer in the meantime."

With the influence of the trio, the bill moved back toward its more restrictive roots.

On the other side of the issue, the anti–CDA forces scrambled to organize. While the CDT corralled civil liberties groups, Burrington helped rally the other players in the industry, organizing weekly strategy meetings in law firms up and down Washington's K Street. Besides trying to influence the CDA language as it developed, the group took another tack— trying to initiate counterlegislation.

Their champion in the Senate was Patrick Leahy (Democrat, Vermont), one of the few senators who actually used the Internet regularly. He was sufficiently alarmed by the proposed CDA to take action of his own, and on April 7, 1995, he proposed a bill that would mandate a study by the Department of Justice on how to empower users to screen out unwanted material. "We must find ways to do this," said the senator when introducing the bill, "that do not invite invasions of privacy, lead to censorship of private online communications, and undercut important constitutional protections."

But the bill, like so many others, faded before making it to a vote.

The CDA had better chances, partly because it would be attached to the enormous steamroller of the 1996 telecommunications reform bill, and partly because the U.S. Congress has always loved to pass antipornography laws. Political slam dunks in terms of positive press back home, most antiporn initiatives pass by over-whelmingly lopsided votes. So even before it came up for a vote in June, the CDA looked like a sure thing.

But a few things about the CDA gave its supporters cause to worry about its prospects for easy passage.

First, the fact that a computer user must proactively seek out such material was a powerful argument against the bill. If someone doesn't want to see dirty pictures, went the reasoning, he or she doesn't have to go to them.

Second, because child pornography was already illegal in every state and obscene material could not legally be transported across state lines, the online industry argued that these types of crimes, when committed online, were already covered under existing laws. AOL had already complied with existing antiobscenity laws when obscenity was discovered on the service, so why was another law necessary? And the new language—especially the word "inde-cent"—was vague, and prone to dangerous interpretation.

Perhaps more important, Burrington knew that the Senate was about to take the first slippery-slope step in restricting many other forms of communication online. Not only would photographs of sexual perversity be affected by the bill, he argued, but a wide range of other so-called "indecency" as well. That included conversations about sexual behavior, the use of the "seven dirty words"—even, theoretically, safe-sex information, photos of classical nude paint-ings, and the texts of books like *Ulysses* and *Lady Chatterley's Lover*.

Bruce Taylor and Donna Rice Hughes argued vehemently that the "indecency" standard didn't include these things. But the prob-lem was, nobody could agree on just what "indecency" did include. And left to individual jurisdictions in states and counties across America, it was anyone's guess what a particular judge might rule.

Burrington knew that one overzealous prosecutor in some juris-diction was enough to make trouble. "And who are they gonna go after?" he insisted. "The highest visibility, biggest media bang for the buck"—AOL.

Burrington and others in the industry obviously preferred hav-ing no CDA at all. But if there was going to be a bill, they believed a preferable, less restrictive standard could be used in the language.

Instead of banning "indecent" material online, they preferred the looser "harmful to minors" standard. Although Bruce Taylor and some others who supported the CDA argued that "harmful to minors" is no less restrictive than "indecency," Burrington and Berman felt strongly otherwise.

"'Indecency' is naughty words, the things your mother tells you not to say. Whether it has any redeeming social value is not considered," said Berman. "To ban 'indecency' is an extremely restrictive standard. 'Harmful to minors,' on the other hand, is soft-core porn on up, the kind of thing you put a brown-paper wrapper over in a convenience store."

If there had to be a CDA, argued Burrington, it should restrict only porn, not simple curse words and sexual innuendo.

These were some of the many points that Burrington hammered on as he knocked on doors of the Senate and buttonholed politicians, in an effort to scuttle the bill. Why was there a need to saddle the fledgling online industry with burdensome regulations that could kill it in its crib? It was a persuasive argument to make before Republicans, who were touting less government intervention in business.

The debate grew heated as the Senate vote neared. With both sides feeling as though the other side "just didn't get it," one participant in the debate—Donna Rice Hughes—had an idea.

With the help of Deen Kaplan, a computer-savvy fellow anti-porn activist, Hughes sought out the vilest examples of sexual deviancy and obscenity she could find online. She then downloaded lists of photo titles—with wording like "Sexy redhead eats shit like candy!" and "Schoolgirl fucks her sister's tiny shaved twat with a dildo!"—and bulletins from a BBS listing titles such as "Rape, torture, pussy nailed to a table!" Without including any pictures, she printed the lists and put them in a manila folder, to which she then attached a bright red "Warning" label.

Hughes made dozens of the folders, all with the red warning label. Then, on July 6, 1995, she made a phone call that would set in motion one of the more sensational events of the CDA debate.

She called Chris McLean, Exon's legislative assistant and the key aide in crafting the bill. Enough Is Enough had planned a luncheon presentation on Capitol Hill the next day, and Exon, along with fellow senators Bob Dole and Charles Grassley, was scheduled to speak.

"Make sure you're there on time to see my presentation tomorrow," Hughes told McLean. "There's something important that you need to see."

The next day, at the luncheon, Hughes gave a cue during her speech, and scores of well-dressed men and women seated at tables laden with coffee cups and half-finished lunches tore open the envelopes. A shocked silence fell over the room as the luncheon guests flipped numbly through pages filled with the foulest smut. In one swoop, Donna Rice Hughes had transformed the debate, for the luncheon guests, from the realm of the abstract to the very tangible. She wanted Senator Exon to do the same on the floor of the Senate.

"Until you show this to members of the Senate, they're not going to get it," Hughes said to McLean. "As long as people think we're talking about the kind of airbrush nudity you find in *Playboy,* they aren't going to respond."

Immediately after the luncheon, Deen Kaplan and Exon's staff went back to the senator's office to get online. Kaplan, apologizing beforehand for what he was about to do, showed the group some of the raunchiest photographs he could find online, including some of women having sex with a range of different animals.

The staffers were appalled, but they also realized that Hughes' idea was brilliant. This was the tool they needed to spur the Senate to action.

Just as Hughes had done earlier, the staffers downloaded the material, but this time they included pictures. Then one of them grabbed an ordinary blue binder to put the presentation in.

The infamous "blue book" was born. One week later, Exon would use all of its powerful shock value in the televised Senate debate.

Only a few days were remaining before the Senate vote in June. Burrington, Bob Butler, and others representing the industry continued to meet with Taylor, Cleaver, and the Senate staffers in an effort to once again reshape the CDA's language in their favor before the vote.

Despite their bitterly opposing viewpoints, the participants later recalled their meetings as having had a generally respectful tone. Burrington, whose company had perhaps the most to lose from passage of a strict CDA, was invariably described by participants as polite, even cordial. Until just before the Senate vote, during a meeting at Exon's office.

The meeting was going badly for Burrington, who felt that the pro-CDA side wasn't giving any leeway on changing the language. Even after hours of discussions, there was no budging, and the months of wrangling were coming to a head. Tempers were wearing thin as both sides tried to push their language into the bill.

Then Exon's chief of staff, George Pallas, decided to bring in the Senate chaplain, Lloyd John Ogilvie, to sit in on the meeting. Chaplain Ogilvie entered the room, said a prayer, then took a seat to listen to the proceedings.

For Burrington, this was too much. He flipped.

"I mean, I'm sitting in this conference room, and all around me is so much Nebraska football memorabilia, I feel like I'm sitting in a coach's office. Then they bring in the chaplain. It was so bizarre!," said Burrington. "He was brought in to remind us to 'Do the right thing.' . . . So much for separation of church and state."

According to Bruce Taylor, the chaplain's appearance at the meeting cast a "funny feeling" around the room. And that was no surprise, argued Taylor. "Why shouldn't they feel funny about having a chaplain watch them as they fight to keep porn free and available in cyberspace?"

Everybody clammed up, said Taylor, and the anti-CDA forces felt inhibited about how they talked in front of the chaplain. In his eyes, "That should have been a sign that something's wrong with your argument, if you have to change your language in front of a chaplain—or a nun, or a mother or whoever."

And Chaplain Ogilvie's role in the debate wasn't through. On June 12, two days before the vote on the CDA, he offered an unusual prayer in the Senate.

"Almighty God, Lord of all life," he began, "We praise you for the advancements in computerized communications that we enjoy in our time. Sadly, however, there are those who are littering this information superhighway with obscene, indecent and destructive pornography."

The prayer continued in that vein, before shifting to a plea for God's guidance: "Give us wisdom to create regulations that will protect the innocent."

Two days later, Exon opened debate on the Senate floor.

Exon, wanting to ensure that no one had missed the message of Ogilvie's prayer, opened his remarks by quoting the prayer in its entirety. He then invited his colleagues to have a look at the contents of the blue book. The senators flocked by Exon's desk and into the cloakroom, where a copy of the book had also been put, to stare gape-mouthed at the photos.

To Leahy, the CDA's fiercest opponent, the whole exercise was farcical. Ninety percent of the members were not even aware of what the Internet was, he believed, "but when there were obscene and objectionable photographs, they seemed to go into the cloakroom over and over again."

The blue book was a powerful prop. "Of course, it was effective," Burrington said. "They just dug into the Net for the worst stuff, to give the Senators a backbone."

Instead, he thought, why not put together another binder of stuff that was neither obscene nor child porn, but that might be considered indecent under the CDA—things like safe-sex Web sites, or breast cancer awareness material? Perhaps that would educate the Senators to the real issue in the CDA debate.

But the blue book was simple, shocking, and effective. In his high-handed political masterstroke, Exon had reduced the complicated issues to one statement: A vote for the CDA is a vote against sexual perversion. A vote against it is a tacit concession to pornographers.

The CDA passed the Senate overwhelmingly, 86–14. Leahy was crestfallen, especially at the reasoning given by a number of his colleagues for their pro-CDA votes. "Let the courts sort it out," they told him. "Why should we stick our necks out?"

"Even when it passed, several of the senators knew it was unconstitutional, but they told me, 'How can you vote against this?'" recalled Leahy. "It became an issue, they said, of standing up for America."

Bill Burrington expected as much; he had been hearing the same thing from the politicians he had spoken to. He spent June 14 at work, as usual, not tuning into C-SPAN to watch the debate, and not waiting on the edge of his seat for the news of how the vote went.

"It was a joke," he said. "I knew how they were going to vote. Nothing at all would have changed the outcome as long as we were dealing with this issue and this set of facts."

Burrington, like Leahy, felt the senators were just passing the buck to the courts, an odd sort of Washington tango. "It was an example of one branch telling another branch: 'Look, we know this trashes the First Amendment, but we want to go home,'" said Burrington. "You guys clean it up."

That argument was bolstered by the existence of a special provision in the CDA that allowed challenges to the law to bypass the usual channels and go directly to a three-judge federal panel. None of the usual legal wrangling was necessary: the senators provided a direct path to the courts, apparently in the hope that someone else could settle the debate.

Although the CDA had passed its first legislative hurdle, all was not disaster for AOL and the online industry. Just a week after the CDA had passed the Senate, House Speaker Newt Gingrich, the central figure in the Republican Revolution, came down very publicly on the industry's side.

"It is clearly a violation of free speech and it's a violation of the right of adults to communicate with each other," he said of the CDA. "I don't think it is a serious way to discuss a serious issue, which is, how do you maintain the right of free speech for adults while also protecting children in a medium which is available to both?"

For Burrington and his allies, it was an unexpected godsend from an unlikely place. Perhaps due in part to Gingrich's expressed disdain for the Senate's version of the CDA, the version the House would pass two months later, in August 1995, was much more industry-friendly.

porn again

But before then, both the industry and AOL endured a few more blows to their images.

In late June, just weeks after the Senate vote, *TIME* magazine ran an explosive cover story titled "On a Screen Near You: Cyberporn," which featured cover art of a bug-eyed child, bathed in an eerie light, looking in horror at a computer screen.

Written by Philip Elmer-DeWitt, the story quoted extensively from a soon-to-be-published study of online porn undertaken by a team of researchers led by Carnegie Mellon University undergraduate Marty Rimm. The study, which had had virtually no peer review, made a number of alarming—and, later, hotly disputed—claims. Rimm defended his methodology and decried the criticism.

The study's flaws would not be revealed until the cover story had hit the newsstands and the panic had already been unleashed. Thanks to exclusivity agreements with *TIME* and the *Georgetown Law Journal,* which had agreed to publish the study's findings, there had been no chance for potential critics to review the Rimm study in advance.

Nonetheless, *TIME* went ahead with a remarkably one-sided story, granting unprecedented legitimacy to what would ultimately be judged a seriously flawed study.

Among the statistics that stirred anxiety was this statistic quoted by the team: 83.5 percent of the pictures in the Internet's "Usenet" newsgroups with digitized images were found to be pornographic.

Unfortunately, too many people involved in the serious debates about online regulation had absolutely no idea what that meant. Republican Senator Charles Grassley of Iowa, for example, seemed to have no conception of what "Usenet" meant, when he commented on the study in remarks on the Senate floor on June 26:

> The university surveyed 900,000 computer images. Of these 900,000 images, 83.5 percent of all computerized photographs available on the Internet are pornographic. Mr. President, I want to repeat that: 83.5 percent of the 900,000 images reviewed—

these are all on the Internet—are pornographic, according to the Carnegie Mellon study.

The specter of 83.5 percent of all photographs on the Internet being pornographic would be enough to make all but the staunchest free-speech advocates blanch. But Usenet is not the Internet, of course. It is a collection of message boards that can be accessed through the Internet, but it is only a small part of it.

Grassley's statement was akin to his looking at a collection of *Playboy* magazines and declaring that, based on extensive research, all magazines in America are filled with pictures of naked women.

Despite his demonstrated lack of understanding of the medium, Grassley then decided to propose his own bill to regulate cyberspace. His bill would penalize "computer system operators [who] knowingly transmit indecent material to a child . . . [and] 'willfully' permit their system to be used as a conduit for indecent communications intended for children."

Once again, AOL and the industry found themselves facing a serious legislative threat. Burrington considered the *TIME* cover story one of the most irresponsible pieces of journalism he had ever read, but the damage was already done and the article provided more fuel for what was turning out to be an online roasting.

"When enough of that kind of attention builds, it doesn't matter whether it's true or not," he said. "People who have never been on a computer before will say, 'Oh yeah, the Internet. That's all about sex.'"

That was the general mood on July 24, after the CDA had already passed the Senate, when parties from all sides of the debate met in a conference room on Capitol Hill for the first-ever hearing on the cyberporn issue.

Burrington was there to testify, by invitation, on behalf of AOL. His goal was to make clear why, from AOL's standpoint, it would be virtually impossible to police e-mail and message board postings. But how could Burrington accurately convey that situation to people who might never even have been online?

He couldn't, as he soon found out.

Grassley leaned into his microphone and announced to the hearing room that they would now hear from "William Burrington, legal counsel to American Airlines." Ripples of laughter flowed through the stuffy room. Burrington smiled to himself and shook his head. To him, the gaffe neatly summed up the attendees' attitudes and lack of self-education about the issues.

Also testifying at the hearing was Barry Crimmins, a standup political satirist from New York, and onetime writer for the *Dennis Miller Show*. Crimmins, a progressive who had frequently skewered the very politicians who now were inviting him to testify on behalf of their cause, was a caustic, excitable performer. He had found success in his adult life, even opening shows for standup comic Steven Wright and singer Jackson Browne, among others, but beneath his comic exterior, he was a haunted man. As a child, he had been sexually abused.

Crimmins was well-known to AOL; he had exchanged correspondence with several of its employees, warning that pedophiles were lurking in the chat rooms. He had trolled through AOL's chat rooms for hours, posing as a 12-year-old boy, and he had a scary story to tell—to America and to America Online.

"I am here to tell the American people that not only are their children unsafe *on* America Online," he testified at the hearing, "they are unsafe *because* of it."

Crimmins's coining of a catchy phrase was most damaging to AOL's public image. Describing the service's chat rooms as a place where "the pedophiles come after you like they're flies and you're rancid meat," Crimmins also stated that "computers and modems have created an anonymous 'pedophile superstore.'"

It was a perfect soundbite, and reporters dutifully included it in stories published all over the United States.

The irony was that, although Crimmins's testimony did much to fuel the fires of fear over the Internet's seamy side, he was vehemently opposed to the CDA. In characteristically colorful style, Crimmins declared that passing the CDA to combat smut online would be like "outlawing altar candles because they might be used by an arsonist to burn down a church."

But though he agreed with AOL on the CDA issue, Crimmins was otherwise disgusted by what he called the company's taste for what he dubbed "blood money."

"They're scummier than the mentally ill people out there that make child porn," he said, "because they claim they're not doing anything wrong."

AOL stuck to the policy that it didn't want to restrict privacy for its members because of the transgressions of a small percentage of users. At charges that AOL turned a blind eye to child pornographers, Bill Burrington bristled with anger. "It's an absurd and ridiculous thing to think that our executives just say, 'Well, gee, we can just ignore this, we're making money on it,'" he said. "You don't build a mainstream mass communication medium by doing that kind of thing."

Steve Case agreed. "We were worried about the abuses," he said. "But we still felt that, on balance, it's better to err on the side of providing tools, volunteer monitors, and education."

The hearings made headlines across the country, but Grassley's proposal ultimately went nowhere. The CDA, on the other hand, was continuing its path to passage.

One month after the cyberporn hearing, to the relief of the industry, the House overwhelmingly passed a much more lenient legislation proposed by Representatives Chris Cox (Republican, California) and Ron Wyden (Democrat, Oregon). It focused on filtering software rather than on removal of offending material from areas accessible to people under eighteen years—which, the industry argued—is basically the entire Internet.

All that remained now was for the House and Senate bills to be reconciled into final legislation. Wrangling between opposing sides continued well into the fall, and the pressure was on for everyone to get their opinions on record before the final language was voted on.

dreaming of ralph

In the early morning hours of September 13, a nasty shock was in store for certain AOL users all across America. FBI agents in 20 different cities began knocking on doors. After presenting search warrants, the agents entered the homes and began seizing computers and disks, searching for child pornography. The operation, code-named "Innocent Images," had begun in the wake of Junior Burdynski's disappearance more than two years before. By the time of the September raids, which were the largest to date in the Burdynski investigation, 80 people had been arrested, pornographic photos of children as young as two years had been found, and more arrests were on the way.

Although the FBI had chosen to focus on AOL for the crackdown, the company itself was not accused of any wrongdoing. According to the company's executives and the FBI, AOL was chosen simply because it was the largest online service. AOL had been apprised of the operation and had cooperated with the FBI along the way.

The day of the crackdown, Bill Burrington gave 17 television interviews, always stressing the same point. The crackdown was "not about the medium. Child pornographers are always looking for ways to distribute their wares. It's about the crime, not the way it was carried out."

To some opponents of the CDA, the crackdown was ample evidence that the CDA was unnecessary. David Sobel, of the Electronic Privacy Information Center, wrote: "Existing federal law gives law enforcement agencies all the authority they need to crack down on alleged online pornography. There's no need for new laws. Period."

For the CDA's proponents, however, the arrests were simply more evidence of the growing perversity online.

On Capitol Hill, negotiations on the CDA language continued. One night in December, just before the final vote on the language, Bill Burrington had stayed late in his office, poring over e-mail and reading through the current CDA text. He grew frustrated that the controversy had been blown so out of proportion by all sides, and pondered what to do about refocusing the debate on the real issues.

He went home and slept fitfully. Half-awake, he had a "fantasy dream" that kept playing out in his head—a secret rendezvous with Ralph Reed, leader of the right-wing Christian Coalition and one of the online industry's more vociferous critics. Reed's organization had made cleaning up the Internet one of its 10 goals in its "Contract with America."

Burrington would tell no one: It would be a stealth mission, taking the form of a private, heart-to-heart lunch at Reed's Virginia headquarters. Burrington would take his laptop over and show Reed what the Internet was really all about—not dirty pictures, but a source of great things.

Burrington truly believed, deep down, that if he could just present Ralph Reed with the real facts of the Internet and parental control software, Reed might change his mind and decide to partner with the industry.

Burrington actually called Reed, but the meeting never took place. The unlikely pair played phone tag back and forth until the time ran out.

"I guess I was a little delusional," said Burrington later.

On December 5, 1995, Leahy made a last-ditch argument on the Senate floor: "One wonders if, in the future, recipes for Chicken Cacciatore sent online will only call for dark meat to avoid using the dreaded 'B' word."

Contrasted with the seriousness of the child porn cases, his remark seemed almost glib, yet it was the kind of statement that sent tremors through the industry. Could even the word "breast" be considered indecent online? Who was to judge? Would this bill be the beginning of the end of the Internet's promise?

The next day, December 6, the House and Senate conferees met to vote on the final wording, as part of a megameeting to reconcile the language of the massive telecommunications reform act that was moving through Congress. The gathering place, a large conference room in the Capitol, was swarming with pols, their staffers, and lobbyists—all eager to influence the final outcome of their small part of the legislation.

Burrington was present, and he expected to be there the whole day because the CDA was only a small section of the comprehensive telecom bill. Representative Rick White (Democrat, Washington) was the anti-CDA side's point man that day, and, earlier than Burrington had expected, White brought his compromise to the table.

When the 33 members of the committee went into caucus, Burrington waited nervously in the conference room.

After what seemed like an eternity, the representatives emerged, their faces solemn. There was good news and bad news for the industry. The committee had accepted White's compromise, which included the more lenient "harmful to minors" language in exchange for keeping in some of the criminal penalties of the Senate bill.

But at the last moment, Representative Bob Goodlatte (Republican, Virginia) suddenly proposed another amendment, the sole purpose of which was to substitute the word "indecency" for "harmful to minors." Like the senators, months before, the representatives were now faced with a challenge to "do the right thing for the children." And so, by the thinnest of margins—17 to 16—the committee members had voted the indecency standard back in.

How could things have gone so wrong at the last second? Later, Burrington was shocked to find that even diehard Democratic liberals, Representatives Pat Schroeder (Colorado) and John Conyers (Michigan) had abandoned ship and voted for the stricter standard. The fight was over, and the industry had been shot down by friendly fire.

"We knew when push came to shove, the politicians thought it would be a lot easier to go home and tell their constituents that they voted for children and against porn," said Burrington.

Dejected and drained, Burrington drove west from the Capitol to AOL's office in Vienna. Few of the people bustling around the headquarters—AOL was experiencing huge growth at this time, and new hires filled the corridors—knew how profoundly the decisions made only ten miles away might impact the company.

"There was so much on everyone's plate," sighed Burrington. "Anyway, from day one, I figured this would go to the courts and we would have our day."

courting trouble

Indeed, AOL would need the courts badly, for now the bill was virtually certain to become law. On February 1, 1996, the CDA, using the "indecency" standard, was voted in as part of the telecommunications reform package.

Ralph Reed of the Christian Coalition called it "one of the most important pieces of legislation in our lifetime."

A week later, President Bill Clinton signed the bill into law. During the entire progress of the CDA through the legislative system, detractors wondered where the famously pro-Internet White Houses forces were. Where was technocrat Al Gore? Why wasn't Clinton speaking out against online censorship? The White House was conspicuously absent on the issue—more evidence, to Clinton's critics, that he was pandering to conservatives after the drubbing his party had taken in the midterm congressional elections.

For Burrington, the past year had been something of a trial by fire. The CDA had been introduced by Exon on his first day at AOL, and he had thrown himself headlong into his work. Now, despite all his efforts, a law had been passed that posed a major threat to his company.

But for all the battles the CDA had weathered to become law, things were only beginning in the judicial arena.

It was time to regroup. In early February, just after the CDA became law, Burrington had breakfast at Washington's Old Ebbitt Grill with Jerry Berman of the Center for Democracy and Technology.

"What do we do now?" asked Burrington. What was the best way to challenge the law? Who would be the industry's choice for counsel? How should the second phase of the CDA battle begin?

By raising money, and lots of it, was the ready answer, because this case was headed all the way to the Supreme Court. By the time it was over, the CDA's opponents would spend more than $1.3 million, with AOL picking up about 10 percent of the tab.

Other anti-CDA forces were already heading to the court. Almost immediately after the President signed the CDA into law, a coalition led by the American Civil Liberties Union (ACLU) filed suit in U.S. District Court in Philadelphia, challenging the CDA as unconstitutional.

The online industry was not eager to join with the ACLU. Among other reasons, the ACLU's argument focused too narrowly on the First Amendment. To attract a broad coalition of major industry players, Burrington and Berman knew that an appeal had to focus on the fact that the CDA, as written, did not protect children.

"To get major corporations to join us, you must know that most don't like the sound of a case that is 'trying to protect indecency,'" said Burrington. "This was all about defining the online world completely and showing we were responsible. And it was a wrong message to say that the First Amendment was the only important thing—because it was all important."

A new organization, with AOL and the CDT at the lead, was formed. The Citizens' Internet Empowerment Coalition (CIEC, pronounced "seek") would file another suit. As before, Berman was in charge of organizing the civil liberties and public interest groups, while Burrington went after the industry.

They also searched for the best lawyer possible for their case. Bruce Ennis, a noted First Amendment lawyer from the Washington firm of Jenner & Block, was finally chosen.

But before the CIEC even had time to get a suit together, U.S. District Court Judge Ronald L. Buckwalter issued an order temporarily blocking enforcement of the CDA. Writing that the law "would leave reasonable people perplexed," Buckwalter effectively gave the Internet community a little breathing room before the Philadelphia case's March court date.

In late February, the CIEC—which included AOL, Apple, CompuServe, Microsoft, Netcom, and Prodigy among its members—filed suit in Philadelphia, after determining that a favorable hearing was most likely in that district.

The suits from the ACLU and CIEC were combined, and a three-judge panel—composed of Judge Buckwalter, Judge Stewart Dalzell, and Chief Justice Dolores Sloviter—convened on March 21 to hear the case.

Burrington was called as a witness on Monday morning, April 1, the third and final day for the CIEC/ACLU argument of the case, to provide information on parental blocking tools and the impact of the CDA on online companies.

Using an aquatic metaphor, Burrington compared AOL to "a resort with a large swimming pool, and our pool has gotten much bigger very fast; it's a private, closed resort and there are some lane guidance and some lifeguards, and we check the water temperature. Then there's a little channel that leads directly into the ocean, and that would be the Internet."

The idea was to give the judges a sense of the vastness and interconnectedness of the medium, to underscore that "effective protection of children from exposure to inappropriate material can only occur at the level of individual users."

He testified that AOL might have to stop providing bulletin board and chat services altogether, to ensure that minors weren't seeing any potentially indecent content. There simply was no technologically feasible and financially viable way to keep minors out of those areas.

"We can't create this absolutely perfect vacuum, and so there is some common sense required there," said Burrington.

He also testified that the "indecency" restrictions under the CDA would result in the censorship of constitutionally protected speech for adults, turning AOL into a place where the only speech that would occur would be discourse appropriate for children. A fear of criminal liability would likely cause AOL management to play it safe rather than sorry—removing information about health, for example, from the service.

One question from Justice Department attorney Anthony Coppolino inadvertently struck the point home.

"If another magazine such as, for example, *Smithsonian,* contained depictions of remote tribes, for example, with little or no clothing, would this also be the type of material that you believe subject—," asked Coppolino, "might subject America Online to liability under the Communications Decency Act?"

"Absolutely," declared Bill Burrington.

Burrington's mood lightened considerably in the Philadelphia court sessions, as it became clear, through their questions, that the judges had done a prodigious amount of homework on the subject.

Whereas the congressional legislators had seemed not to know or care exactly what the Internet was all about, the judges in Philadelphia wired the courtroom with a T-1 circuit and small local area network for fast demonstrations of Internet technology. It was the first time a federal court had been wired to the Internet for purposes of a trial.

The moment that may have been the turning point came on April 12, when government witness Howard Schmidt was being questioned by Judge Dalzell. Presented with the famous *Vanity Fair* cover photograph of Demi Moore, naked and pregnant, Schmidt was asked whether it would be considered indecent under the CDA.

In a rambling response, Schmidt replied that because it was not an "educational" image, it could be considered indecent according to certain community standards. The photo had been displayed on magazine racks all over America, yet a Web site owner who wanted to show it was supposed to have "a user ID or a pass code or something along those lines," testified Schmidt.

Although supporters of the CDA would later argue that there was no way the photograph could be judged "indecent" by the standards defined in the law, the damage was done. "That was the one defining moment that blew apart the government's case," remembered Brian Ek of Prodigy. "It became clear how vague and undefinable the law really was."

The judges in Philadelphia agreed and, in June, announced their unanimous decision. The CDA as written was unconstitutional.

The CIEC organizers waited in Jenner & Block's Washington offices for the news to come to them—appropriately enough—via e-mail from the court, which was sending the entire 175-page opinion online. The winners' celebration was joyfully chaotic. The news media deluged them with calls, and they began to digest the victory the court had handed them.

Industry leaders hailed the decision in grandiose terms. CIEC attorney Bruce Ennis called the ruling "a truly landmark decision." Microsoft's Bill Gates declared it "a victory for anyone who cares about freedom of expression or the future of the Internet."

It was one of the "craziest days" of Burrington's young life. The group members tried to speed-read the lengthy decision aloud as it came over the computer. When they had had a chance to digest all 175 pages, Burrington realized with excitement that the judges couldn't have written a more favorable opinion.

For Burrington, three sentences of the decision captured perfectly his own feelings about the new medium.

"Cutting through the acronyms and argot that littered the hearing testimony, the Internet may be fairly regarded as a never-ending worldwide conversation," wrote Judge Stewart Dalzell. "The Government may not, through the CDA, interrupt that conversation. As the most participatory form of mass speech yet developed, the Internet deserves the highest protection from governmental intrusion."

Dalzell went on to address AOL's concerns: "It is also a tricky question whether an America Online chat room devoted to, say, women's reproductive health, is or is not speech of the service itself, since America Online, at least to some extent, 'creates the content of the communication' simply by making the room available and assigning it a topic. Even if America Online has no liability under this example, the service might legitimately choose not to provide fora that led to the prosecution of its subscribers."

Not everyone was exhilarated by the court's eloquent words. Cathy Cleaver, the Family Research Council attorney who had worked so hard on refining the CDA's language, compared leaving the Internet unregulated to "leaving a loaded gun in a playground." Advocates of the CDA had expected a tough battle in Philadelphia, but they weren't ready to give up the war.

a supreme challenge

The next step was the U.S. Supreme Court. On July 1, the Department of Justice appealed the Philadelphia decision to the highest court in the nation.

If the industry had lost sleep over the CDA legislative battle, the coming battle would make those months seem almost leisurely. The Supreme Court agreed, in December 1996, to hear the case in March 1997.

Good news; but one sticky issue caused tensions to erupt among the anti-CDA forces. The task of arguing the case in Philadelphia had been split by the ACLU and the CIEC lawyers, but, under Supreme Court rules, only one lawyer per side could argue any case before the Court. The lawyers' request to allow them to split the argument time was quickly denied, so the question was: Who should wage the final battle in one of the hottest cases of the decade—the ACLU's Chris Hansen or the CIEC's Bruce Ennis? Who deserved this historic responsibility?

With egos flaring and unease growing, Hansen suggested an odd solution: Let's flip a coin.

A coin? Burrington was incredulous. "Whoa, whoa, whoa," he said, raising his hands and shaking his head in disbelief. "Guys, don't you think we should take this a little more seriously?"

With so much riding on the case for his company, a toss of the legal tender was not a bet that Burrington wanted to make. He liked Hansen and admired him, but Ennis had experience in more than 250 Supreme Court cases. After a discussion, it was decided that the winner of a moot court competition would get the case.

Ennis won the moot court arguments in late February. With the Supreme Court date a mere three weeks away, the CIEC and the ACLU swung into action, frantically preparing their man for the test ahead.

The day of the Supreme Court arguments, March 19, dawned gray and bitterly cold. From very early in the morning, a kind of sleety snow had been falling off and on, snarling traffic into Washington and tying up commuters from all over the metro area.

Burrington was tired, wired, and irritated as he tried to make it across town in a cab to the Supreme Court building. He and Berman had hired line-sitters to wait all morning so they would be sure to have seats and could witness the historic case they had both worked so hard on.

But the icy rain and snow were coming down hard, and Burrington got there too late to meet the line-sitter and collect his ticket into the high court.

After all this time and all the work he had done, he would have to settle for a seat in the attorneys' lounge, where the arguments would be piped in. Burrington was crushed. Of all days, why did a freak spring snow flurry have to come on this day? He spoke to a marshal, explained his plight, and then gloomily went to the coatroom to check his coat.

A few moments later, the marshal tapped him on the shoulder. "Come with me," he said. Burrington, to his delight and relief, was in.

Donna Rice Hughes, in comparison, had her seats in hand well before the arguments. The active and vocal CDA supporter, whose Enough Is Enough had filed an amicus brief in the suit, and two other CDA supporters had received tickets courtesy of the office of a sitting Supreme Court Justice: Clarence Thomas.

The courtroom was packed. Finally, the justices filed in and the court came into session. In a move that underscored the importance of the case, Chief Justice William Rehnquist declared that each side would have 35 minutes—as opposed to the usual 30—for argument.

"The Internet is a revolutionary advance in information technology. It also provides a revolutionary means for displaying patently offensive, sexually explicit material to children in the privacy of their homes," began Seth Waxman, the government lawyer chosen to argue the Department of Justice's case in favor of the CDA.

"All of the laws regulating the display of indecent materials in theaters and bookstores, on radio, TV, cable, and telephone—all of these approach insignificance when the Internet threatens to give every child with access to a connected computer a free pass into the equivalent of every adult bookstore and video store in the country."

Questions from the judges came fast. One of the most provocative queries was from Justice Stephen Breyer: "Suppose a group of high school students decide to communicate across the Internet, and they want to tell each other about their sexual experiences, whether those are real or imagined. They're all—every high school student who would do this, then, is guilty of a Federal crime, and subject to two years in prison?"

Waxman seemed a bit flustered, but responded that yes, the students would be in violation of the law.

The idea of imprisoning a 17-year-old high school student for chatting online with friends about sex was absurd. And yet, the CDA as written would do just that.

Waxman argued his case under a continuing peppering of questions by the Justices. He seemed to be put off-balance at times by the constant interruptions, and he never really established enough momentum to make his point.

Bruce Ennis, on the other hand, opened his remarks by stating—luckily for him, uninterrupted—four reasons why the injunction against the CDA should be upheld, effectively nullifying the law: "The CDA bans legal speech. It will not be effective. There are less restrictive alternatives that would be much more effective. And the combination of an imprecise standard, coupled with the threat of severe criminal sanctions, will chill much speech that would not be indecent."

Ennis, in the first 20 minutes or so of his argument, was subjected to somewhat less skeptical questioning. He argued that it was impossible to screen all Usenet groups, Web sites, chat rooms, and the like, and that it was economically prohibitive for most Web site owners to screen for age. In response to a question by the acerbic Justice Antonin Scalia, Ennis told the Court that "all of the 12 million Americans who subscribe to the Internet through the major online service providers get, at no additional cost, the parental control options . . . ."

"So, there will be no cost involved in any part of this alternative to the parents?" asked Scalia.

"Not if the listener uses those software programs," responded Ennis.

Ennis also got off what looked to be a powerful point, in response to Justice Ruth Bader Ginsburg's question: "Do other nations regulate cyberspace?"

"China attempts to regulate speech that's critical of the Chinese government," responded Ennis, savoring the implied rebuke to those who would take the United States down the same moral road as a repressive communist regime. "This law sends the wrong signal: that governments have to regulate speech."

But Justice Scalia brought Ennis back down to earth quickly with his observation: "It's a weak argument that the U.S. can't lead the way in this endeavor."

By 11:30 A.M., the arguments were finished. Lawyers, reporters, activists, and observers spilled out onto the steps in front of the Court to continue the argument under a canopy of gray skies.

When the press conferences and media frenzy finally died down, Burrington, Ennis, Berman, and others were drained. They piled into cabs and went to the Barrister, a cozy eatery near the CDT's offices, to have lunch and relax.

Burrington, ever the well-mannered Midwesterner, was not one to drink during a workday. But this day, he ordered a Sam Adams beer and stood to express his respect and admiration for the group he had worked so closely with over the past two years.

With glass raised, he toasted first Bruce Ennis, then the team effort that had brought their case to the Supreme Court.

His next toast, no one but Burrington would have thought to offer, especially given the length, intensity, and cost of the fight that the industry had been through. He raised his glass again and offered a toast in honor of Senator Exon, who had set in motion the CDA.

Despite the threat to his company and to free speech on the Internet, Burrington believed that Exon, in many ways, had done the industry a favor by making it face the problems of protecting children. He had made the industry grow up.

And now the long battle over the CDA was hurtling toward its decisive moment: the Supreme Court's decision in June.

wishing and hoping

The interim months were no less hectic for Bill Burrington. Although the CDA was his highest-profile issue, there was no shortage of other major public policy debates facing AOL: encryption, privacy, online taxes, copyright, consumer protection, and the question of whether to allow gambling online.

He had plenty of work to occupy his time, but in the back of his mind, there was always an anxious awareness that the nine Justices would deliver their decision soon, and it could be disastrous for AOL. While many were predicting that the online side would win, Burrington refused to declare victory prematurely.

The Justices had to deliver all their decisions for the term before the end of June. As the weather grew hotter and the first few weeks of the month ticked away, Burrington began scheduling his appointments around Monday, Wednesday, and Thursday mornings, the days the Court was most likely to announce the CDA decision. The CIEC team had a plan in place for the day of the decision: they would convene at the offices of Jenner & Block for a 1 P.M. press conference—which would give them enough time, they hoped, to read the opinion and formulate a response.

On the designated mornings, someone from CIEC was on hand at the Court, in case the decision was announced. And each time, the word would spread via an informal phone tree: No decision yet. Maybe next time.

On the morning of Thursday, June 26, Bill Burrington was at his office in downtown Washington, preparing for a business trip to Europe the next day. Though he was anxious not to miss the day of the decision, this trip—which would include Internet policy meetings in Brussels, Paris, and Bonn—had been planned for weeks. Today was the last possible day, after months of waiting, that he could be in town to take part in the planned CIEC press conference.

Burrington was online, reading an e-mail message, when he heard the voice of AOL public relations man David Eisner.

"The decision is in!" shouted Eisner, at the precise moment when an AOL Instant Message popped up on Burrington's computer screen from David Phillips, general counsel of AOL's European joint venture, who was in London.

Burrington looked in amazement at his screen. "Congratulations!" read the message—they had won. But it was not the victory that had Burrington in a thrall. It was the fact that a single electronically transmitted word from London was alerting him to a momentous event that had taken place mere blocks from where he sat. The moment perfectly encapsulated the astonishing power of the online medium.

The news was better than Burrington could have dared to hope. The Justices had ruled, 9–0, that the CDA was unconstitutional, declaring that the provision criminalizing "patently offensive display" was in violation of free speech.

"[T]he CDA effectively suppresses a large amount of speech that adults have the constitutional right to receive and to address to one another," wrote Justice John Paul Stevens in the majority opinion. "That burden on adult speech is unacceptable if less restrictive alternatives would be at least as effective in achieving the legitimate purpose that the statute was enacted to serve."

Another part of the decision, however, was not unanimous. The Court struck down the provision penalizing those who knowingly send indecent material to a minor, but by a 7–2 vote, with Justice Sandra Day O'Connor and Chief Justice William Rehnquist dissenting.

"I write separately to explain why I view the Communications Decency Act of 1996 as little more than an attempt by Congress to create 'adult zones' on the Internet," wrote Justice O'Connor in the dissenting opinion. "Our precedent indicates that the creation of such zones can be constitutionally sound."

Although the CDA was dead, as Justice O'Connor's words made clear, the spirit of it was far from gone. Within days, new legislation was being discussed, and the debate on what governments should do about the Internet was renewed again.

The reaction was spurred, perhaps, because the full texts of the opinions were available all over the world almost instantly, thanks to a special arrangement that CIEC's John Morris, an attorney with Jenner & Block, had made with the Clerk of the Supreme Court.

Morris and the CDT's Jonah Seiger had waited at the Supreme Court that day, in the hope that the decision would be handed down. Immediately after the decision was announced, they raced to the Court's lobby, where a staff member from the Clerk's office met them with a copy of the entire decision on a single computer disk.

Immediately, Morris and Seiger were on the front steps of the Court, booting up the laptops they had brought. Morris put the disk into his computer to convert the decision—which had been saved by the Justices in WordPerfect 5.1—to an ASCII text file.

Then he saved it on another disk he had brought with him, so as not to risk corrupting the original.

Morris handed the second disk to Seiger, who popped it into his drive, dialed an Internet connection with a Ricochet wireless modem and hurriedly uploaded the text of the decision to the CDT's Web site. The site had already been linked to others worldwide, so the decision was available simultaneously on more than 12,000 Web sites.

All of this was completed within eight minutes of the Court's announcement.

Later, at the offices of Jenner & Block, where Bill Burrington and other CIEC members were gathering for a press conference, a final irony was revealed.

The disk Seiger had used to convey the decision worldwide was no ordinary one. When he ejected it from his computer, Seiger had to laugh when he saw the label.

It was an old AOL disk, repurposed for a new task.

During a search in his home office, John Morris had been unable to find a blank disk. But he had "about 40 of these AOL disks lying around," he said, as did many other average Americans targeted by AOL's relentless marketing machine. And, like so many others, he did the logical thing: he erased the AOL software.

Voilà! Morris had an empty disk, ready to record the results of the first great legal battle for cyberspace.

When he was told about it later, Bill Burrington grinned. At least one of the 250 million disks AOL had sent out had not gone to waste.

Not at all.

après le déluge, bob

the pitchman cometh

In a darkened conference room in New York City's Grand Hyatt Hotel, Bob Pittman strode to the podium and stood beneath a glowing screen where the AOL logo was displayed.

The date was February 11, 1997. AOL was in the thick of the worst press slamming of the access crisis. Its users were irate. The company was the butt of nationwide derision, from jokes by Jay Leno to lawsuits and angry op-ed articles, and it had just booked a $155 million loss for its second quarter. AOL was a company in chaos once again.

Pittman had been at AOL for slightly more than three months. He was cool and composed as he prepared to address the Goldman Sachs Technology Investment Symposium. Some of the most influential people in the Internet world were gathered here for presentations and debate on the future of the medium.

In the audience, short-seller David Rocker hissed across the aisle in a loud stage whisper, "You know what Pittman's nickname is? They call him Robert *Pitchman!*" Rocker guffawed loudly at this pun and then turned his attention back to the podium, where the man he was spoofing was just beginning his pitch.

"TV viewing is declining," declared Pittman, his Mississippi accent giving a cadence to his speech. "This is something that has never happened in my lifetime. And personal computer ownership is going up. Before, people bought PCs because they needed them, and then they considered whether to go online. Now, people are buying PCs specifically so they *can* go online."

As he warmed up, Pittman's demeanor became folksier and more amiable. His dark suit and red tie bespoke luxury and taste, but his manner was pure down-home. Executives who preceded him at the podium had flashed endless slides of graphs and charts and had recited the dull patois of conference presentations. But, Pittman waxed on about his upbringing in a small town where the local grocer was eased out of business when mega-supermarkets showed up. And why was that?

Because of people like Bob's mom, Lanita, said Pittman, who began to make important buying decisions based mostly on brand names. "We became a nation of brand buyers," he said. "And brands will always win in the end."

But that wasn't enough. "Convenience is king," he added, sounding more and more like a Southern preacher than an executive of a billion-dollar company. "It's kind of like boating. Remember how popular that used to be? Well, if you want to go boating, you've got to load the boat up, take it down to the river, then it takes you three hours to get it in the water. You sail for an hour and then it takes you three hours to get it out again."

He continued, resting his arm across the lectern in a way that conveyed a just-us air of intimacy to the nondescript room. "Now these days we've got all these boating magazines saying 'Boatin's coming back!' But I'll tell you something," said Pittman, pausing for effect. "It ain't never comin' back. Because nobody wants to spend that kind of time. People want convenience."

The message he was delivering: AOL was branded convenience or—as he labeled it—"convenience in a box."

To hear Pittman tell it, everything was just that simple. Forget about the busy signals, the cash flow problems, and the scarcity of profits for a company already in its second decade of existence. Members were angry, for sure, but they were not leaving

because, as Pittman correctly noted, no serious replacement
option was in sight. The Internet was still too confusing; online competitors were not as good; new technologies were too
premature.

AOL would win because it was simple, convenient, and well
known, and these traits were enough to keep attracting users.
And, as it further developed into the great consolidator and navigational guide it was destined to be, everything else would
come—advertising dollars, transactional revenues, millions upon
millions of "eyeballs"—the unfortunate descriptor for the size of
the online audience.

Pittman's smooth, confident, uninterrupted delivery made it
seem almost possible that the audience of investors could believe
what he was saying. But the tougher questions—about cash flow,
losses, and expenses out of control—would doubtless come in the
"breakout session" that immediately followed all the presentations.
Investors would then ask questions in a more intimate setting,
away from the prying eyes of the press.

Later, Pittman led a group into a smaller conference room,
where he took a seat facing them at a long table, as if holding court.
The windowless room became jammed with people, and it quickly
grew stuffy. It was time to get down to serious business.

But the investors, many of whom had lost a lot of money over
the past year by betting on AOL, were still caught in the thrall that
Pittman's address had created. The questions were puffballs lobbed
at Pittman. Why was the nasty press so focused on AOL's problems?
Was 20-to-1 a decent ratio of modems to users? How was the development of new software progressing?

One questioner ventured a harder question: "Perhaps it's not
the right time to ask this, but what's the timetable for AOL to raise
prices, such as for premium channels?"

Pittman breezily swatted the query aside. "You're right. It's
not the right time to ask that question," he quipped. Laughter
undulated through the room. No matter how grave the issue,
Pittman was sweet-talking his way through. Others who had seen
Pittman in action had noted how listeners got "sucked into the
charm zone."

But not everyone was so bewitched. David Rocker was beside himself that no one was asking Pittman the questions that Rocker considered pertinent. As the easy queries continued and his own frustration grew, Rocker spoke up and took aim at the center of the charm zone. "Your working capital has declined by $140 million," he announced loudly. "Isn't this a problem?"

"Well," answered Pittman, chuckling and shifting slightly in his chair, "I didn't finish college, so don't ask me a question like that. I'm a marketing guy." Laughter filled the room again, even though the head of a major division of AOL could be expected to know quite a lot about the bottom line. Pittman did know but preferred not to acknowledge reports that AOL might be bleeding to death cashwise.

"I'll pass that question to Richard Hanlon," he murmured.

Hanlon, the dapper and soft-spoken Brit who served as AOL's vice president for investor relations, then deferred the question to CFO Len Leader. But Leader, as Hanlon noted dryly, was not in attendance, so the question would unfortunately—for the time being, at least—go unanswered.

But Rocker wasn't through. "Are you going to run out of money?" he prodded. "You have a $600 million marketing cost annually."

The annual outlay was, in fact, a penetrating issue for AOL, and the question that was well worth asking if one was an investor. But, Pittman only delivered a vague answer about achieving certain marketing levels, and told the group that AOL's balance sheet was a "in transition," and then guided the discussion to safer ground. Soon, Rocker sat impassively in his chair, well aware that control of the show was back in Pittman's hands.

"God, I don't believe that performance," grumbled Rocker, as he left the room not long afterward. "What a piece of work Pittman is."

A piece of work, indeed. And with AOL experiencing a nadir in public opinion, he was just the piece it needed. Bob Pittman was definitely not Steve Case—a fact that, as 1996 ended and 1997 began stormily—would prove increasingly important and perhaps even a bit troublesome for AOL.

bob, bob, bobbing along

AOL was in enough trouble already—a situation that everyone in the United States seemed to be aware of.

Driving down 13th Street in northwest Washington that winter, for example, AOL lawyer Bill Burrington pulled his Del Sol convertible into an Amoco gas station. As he prepared to fill up the tank, a homeless woman walked slowly over to his car and peered down at Burrington's personalized license plate, which he had just received that day and had proudly attached to his car. "Do A . . . O . . . L," she read aloud, slowly drawing out the letters of a company that, Burrington assumed, she probably knew little about. But she puzzled over the plate for only a moment before her face suddenly brightened in recognition.

"Hey!" she declared. "Isn't that the one that's got all the busy signals?"

It was a funny line from an unlikely source. But it was not the image that any consumer service company wanted to project. And it was directly opposite from the expectations of Case and his team, in the summer of 1996, as they made plans to change AOL dramatically to meet the new challenges posed by the growth of the Web.

The jarring changes included a shift to unlimited pricing, a dicey strategy that many feared would decimate the bottom line; another new interface called "Casablanca," which offered elaborate capabilities and other multimedia bells and whistles; new deals with Hollywood and other big players, such as famed programmer Brandon Tartikoff, to further strengthen the AOL brand; fast-paced international expansion to bring AOL to the rest of the world; a shift toward new business models, stressing unproved strategies that relied heavily on advertising and transactional revenues; a huge and expensive marketing and advertising campaign to raise AOL's visibility; the creation of new companies, such as a business-oriented service; and increased efforts to expand online city information services.

Most importantly, Case had split the original company into three distinct parts—AOL Networks, AOL Studios, and its ANS

Communications networking subsidiary—as part of a signal that AOL had moved into high gear and was gaining maturity as a media company. To analysts being briefed on the changes before they were made in the fall of 1996, Case had announced succinctly: "It's a new day . . . this is AOL on the attack."

And the walking personification of that new day appeared to be Robert Warren Pittman—a proven executive with star quality who had been brought on board to juice up the company and lend it the sheen of experienced management. Even his quote, in the online profile of the AOL service, spoke of racy aggression: "In life you either make dust or eat dust."

Kicking up dust didn't come cheap. Pittman was already earning $1 million a year and had pocketed a $1 million bonus, along with generous stock options and a hefty stake in Century 21. Earlier, his exit package at Time Warner, which included a $20 million payment for his equity in Six Flags, was reportedly worth more than $40 million.

For his services during the first eight months at AOL, the company paid him about $500,000 in salary and bonuses, plus a range of typical executive perks: $800 per flight-hour for the plane he piloted, and $250 per hour for a copilot; $5,000 in monthly rent for two years, in the Washington area; a promise to buy Pittman's house in rural Connecticut if he decided to sell it; and $80,000 in moving expenses. The total package was less than he was making before, but the real meat of his compensation lay in generous stock options that would make Pittman a rich man if he were able to improve AOL's share price substantially. When he signed on, Pittman got stock options for 400,000 shares he could buy at $24.63 and another 100,000 at $70—worth close to $40 million only 18 months later.

To AOL, the price was right. "He is exactly what we had in mind," said Case over and over, as he briefed reporters at a suite in the Essex House in New York City, on the day of the Pittman announcement in late October 1996. Sitting next to each other in the hotel room, the pair seemed perfectly matched—Pittman playing the genial, outgoing gladhander in contrast to Case's thoughtful, cerebral type.

Some AOL board members had been seeking a change in management for a long while. Most of the board admired Case,but others—especially the thorny Jim Kimsey, who was particularly disturbed when the stock price fell to the low $20s late in 1996—had wanted new blood in the company for a long time. Some major investors were equally restless and had begun to agitate for change. Case was considered a genuine strategic thinker, but there was a growing feeling that he might not be up to leading the company to the next level without some high-class help. Case himself, weary after the tumultuous summer, wanted some respite from being the chief decision maker, especially because day-to-day management had never been his strong suit.

"Steve recognized that we were in a new chapter for AOL . . . and knew that we needed someone to manage things well, and that's what attracted him to Bob," said Ken Novack, AOL's influential outside counsel, whom some in the company had nicknamed "the *consigliere*." "We all wanted someone who could be the hands-on, disciplined one to run the P&L, as opposed to the visionary."

Novack had called the hiring of the former MTV star the "Pittman adventure."

Case's choice of such a strongly formed executive would be seen as a mature move, too. He had become sensitive to the many comparisons of AOL's culture to that of Apple Computer: insular, not open to change and resistant to the shifts that were shaping the online world. Unlike some arrogant "founder" personalities, who resisted giving up the reins of the companies they had nurtured, Case was bringing in a powerful personality and handing over the keys to the most crucial part of the company—the massive AOL service.

At the November 14, 1996, employee meeting, Case put Pittman—along with Ted Leonsis, the new head of AOL Studios, and ANS chief Bruce Bond—at the front and center of the AOL troops. It was a perfect idea, thought Case, who did not relish the extraordinary public attention that being at the top of AOL attracted. "Outside of the industry conferences, where I was much more comfortable," said Case, "I did not particularly like the rock star aspect of it."

The same could not be said of Pittman, nearly 43, who dripped glamour with his wide circle of famous friends, from *Rolling Stone* publisher Jann Wenner to John F. Kennedy Jr. "We're the right place to be . . . the wind is at our back," enthused Pittman as he prowled the stage with the kind of energy that stirred up the audience. "Anyone saying 'AOL is over' is not looking at our demand."

Newspaper articles on the appointment quickly touted the Pittman difference and hailed him as the savior AOL had long needed. "Turnaround Task at AOL" said *The Washington Post.* Could Bob Pittman "pull off a rescue of AOL?" asked the *New York Post.* "Can Bob Pittman upgrade AOL?" was the query from another story.

The spin was good for AOL stock, which immediately began to rise on news of Pittman's appointment. Wall Street liked Pittman already. He was a known quantity and the new turnaround at AOL was a good "story" for investors ready to believe again.

But inside AOL, nervous longtime employees knew that Pittman represented a lot more than just another hire. Until then, all the executives at AOL had been clearly under Case's sway and had accepted being subordinate to his singular leader status. Leonsis, while creative and powerful, was always second banana to Case. And the Razzouk hire had been seen as strengthening day-to-day operations, but not diminishing Case's front-and-center position at AOL.

Pittman was different. He was a board member. He didn't need the money. He was charismatic. He was compelling. He was a legendary figure in his own right and had brought a pioneering mind to the media industry. Given the turmoil that had shaken AOL over the summer and early fall, AOL probably needed Pittman more than Pittman needed AOL.

Most of all, Pittman was an executive and a strong leader. Some observers could envision him as being able to replace Case.

After the Razzouk debacle, there was little wiggle room for Case. He had to make the relationship with Pittman work, or AOL's ability to grow far from its start-up roots would be doubted.

"This is just another executive-suite revolving door for Bob to walk through, and he could walk out just as easily, without a lot of damage to his reputation, if things did not work out," fretted one

AOL executive at the time. "But, for Steve, AOL is everything and that makes him vulnerable."

More than a few shivers went through the AOL ranks. Would Pittman begin firing the old-timers and replacing them with his own favorites? Would a dangerous rivalry develop between Case and Pittman? Why were all the newspapers saying that Pittman was going to "save" AOL? Did AOL really need saving or was that a manipulation by Pittman's longtime friend and high-powered personal public relations guru, Ken Lerer, to make Pittman look great?

"If Pittman improved the company and the stock rose, he'd look like a genius," said another executive. "And if not, people would say it was an impossible situation and he'd still look great."

That need for spin control took hold quickly. As soon as Pittman arrived, Lerer's team, from New York-based Robinson Lerer & Montgomery, also landed and quickly took over the public relations of the AOL message. Case, now that Villanueva's departure had left a gaping power vacuum in AOL's communications department, had hired a group of advisers from the Washington office of a competing firm, Fleishman-Hillard Inc., to look after his interests. Dueling PR firms were now inside the same company, with the internal communications department severely weakened.

"It was like New York sharks coming in and eating up the lesser fish from Virginia," said one top-ranking employee. "The joke was: When a rebellion starts in a third-world country, where is the first place the revolutionaries take over? The radio station, of course." Some decided that when Steve Case's famed monthly letter to the millions of AOL users was signed "Bob," the coup d'état would be over.

Pittman had no apologies for bringing in Lerer's aggressive and sometime prickly team, some of whom were soon hired by AOL. "I knew Kenny and he knew me, and there was no time to figure out who was good and who was not with all that was going on," he said later. "I had to hit the ground running, and I trusted Kenny to tell me what I needed to hear."

The uneasiness caused by Lerer's presence was not helped by the intense drubbing Case began to suffer in the media as the access crisis worsened during the winter. He became the walking personification of AOL's poor image and was the butt of many jokes in newspaper columns and cartoons. Pittman, on the other hand, remained seemingly untouched by the furor.

"Should CEO Steve Case go or stay?" asked one of the sassier Internet polls. "Go: Case should quit before he gets the ax, and return to his job modeling for the Gap. Or Stay: Steve Case is a marketing genius who will overcome AOL's troubles and the technology will soon catch up." A whopping 58 percent decided Steve should get the heave-ho.

The high-profile Technology, Education, and Design conference was held in California that winter. Its audience was packed full of the leading lights of the digital age. Legendary organizer Richard Saul Wurman had the crowd in stitches when he played the sound of a telephone busy signal as Case made his way to the stage for a speech. "Thank you for my kind introduction," said Case, taking the jest in good humor.

But it was a winter of nonstop mocking. The irreverent *Mad* Magazine dubbed him "Steve Nutcase" in one of its spoofs of the service. Nutcase offered consumers "double" unlimited hours. For $39.95, they gained access to his "information one-lane dirt road with a toll booth every 200 yards."

"No offense, Steve, but I hope you have a bodyguard with all the enemies you make," joked the interviewer in the satire. In fact, some members of the AOL board had considered, several years before, putting bulletproof glass in Case's office. They also had urged him to take a defensive driving course.

The ribbing was only irksome, compared to Wall Street's growing unhappiness, especially after AOL showed the $155 million second-quarter loss. Among its expenses were $74 million for general business reorganization, and $26 million for the company's settlement with the states' attorneys general. The widespread displeasure was made clear when AOL's biggest Wall Street cheerleader, Morgan Stanley's Mary Meeker, came down much harder than ever on AOL in a February 7 report titled "¿Cuando llegará el mañana?"— "When Will Tomorrow Come?" She too had grown weary of AOL's empty promises and, after the massive charge in the fall, Wall

Street had been expecting some real profits to show up at AOL. Meeker was disappointed.

"AOL is a company with a split personality—it always does good stuff and bad stuff. . . . The good news: AOL has lots of subscribers and high usage levels, or in short, too much demand. The bad news: AOL will lose money again in the March quarter," wrote Meeker. "The good news: our instinct tells us AOL is on the cusp of breaking out (after years of building) and that the stock price (after a lapse or two) should climb. The bad news: the numbers tell us we are wrong."

As the access crisis reached epic proportions, Case and Pittman tangled several times over the pace of the slowdown that agreements with state governments required. Pittman had signed on to grow the service, and he was hamstrung. Case thought that AOL had to appear to be doing everything it could to control its growth, in the face of members' unhappiness.

"It got very testy since the spring was supposed to be the breakout time," said another executive who witnessed one unpleasant exchange over the pace of marketing, where Case ultimately prevailed. "Bob did not expect to be up to his eyeballs in a modem crisis, and it bothered him that it delayed his plans."

Pittman went to Coca-Cola headquarters in Atlanta, on a meet-and-greet visit, to attempt to sell the giant soft drink company on advertising on AOL, part of a new focus on attracting mainstream advertisers to the service. Pittman had known the Coca-Cola executives from his days at more traditional media companies, and hoped that the earlier relationships would allow him some leverage. He wanted them to think about AOL in a more serious way.

But instead of an ad contract, he got a lot of teasing from a group of people who probably knew, more than most, exactly what Pittman was feeling.

"We thought New Coke was bad," joked Coca-Cola's Steve Koonin about AOL's image in the midst of the access crisis. Pittman knew Koonin was making the point that big brands could survive a misstep. The question was: had AOL reached that level of strength?

Indeed, the AOL brand, which Pittman felt was the company's key strength, was under siege. Had it been "baked" hard enough by Case over the years to withstand the pressure it was now getting?

If not, thought Pittman, the story of AOL might be over. "It was a test, for sure," said Pittman. "But I felt it was a big brand and would hold up."

grand brand?

Because to Pittman, brand was everything for AOL.

The company had spent hundreds of millions over the past decade on a single idea initiated by Case: Make AOL a household name. Everything—from AOL's surviving the current crisis, to its ability to generate critical new revenue streams—depended on brand leadership.

"There are few real brands in this world, and it is very, very hard to build one," said Pittman. "And I swore I'd never ever try again to build one from scratch." Would the AOL brand have to be reconstructed from a crumbling heap?

Perhaps not, he thought, as usage of AOL grew through the winter of 1996–1997. Instead of a cutback, AOL usage had skyrocketed from 46 million hours in September to 102 million hours in December (when the flat-rate fees kicked in) and then to 125 million in February. People complained but, surprisingly, they still stayed with the service. They were unhappy with how they were being treated, but members, by and large, didn't want to switch to another service. They just wanted AOL to work the way it was supposed to. A Nielsen poll commissioned by AOL showed that users watched television less, as they used the service more.

To Pittman, even in the midst of a terrible crisis, this was all promising news.

"Long lines are endemic at Disney World. Folks hate them. But offer Six Flags as an alternative, and they look at you like you are crazy. They don't think anything is a substitute for Disney," he said.

"Coke? Complain about prices. Someone can say, 'Drink RC, it's cheaper.' Consumer reaction? 'No, thanks.'"

"It's the brand, stupid," he told AOL employees. "We have to know how to use our brand to perpetuate the lead we have." Despite the fact that the AOL name was being pummeled daily, it was time to harvest the asset into which they and their investors had poured so much money.

But could they actually do it? Pittman had doubts initially. "I think there was a sense that the company was Steve and a lot of assistants," said Pittman. "People were fearful of any changing of the guard, especially because Steve had become such an icon to everyone."

Pittman, though considered a legend, was an odd bird to AOL employees, especially compared to Case. With his glamorous friends, jet-set lifestyle and big plans for change, he was at first feared. Even his office was different. Pittman had it decorated expensively with white shag rugs, huge oddly shaped lamps and green apples in a bowl as a design touch. Staff members gawked at it when he was not in town. This decor was not the AOL way.

The old way had to change, thought Pittman. A key problem, he felt, was that everyone, from the top executives on down, felt they could—and actually needed to—go to Case for every decision. Indeed, after Bill Razzouk had left, Case had taken a definitive hands-on approach to decision making at the company. Now, all major moves seemed funneled through him. "I did not feel it was my job to make decisions for a lot of managers on every level of the corporate structure," said Pittman. "The goal was to turn Steve's vision into an operating plan by defining and developing a growth strategy with all senior managers. Then we could turn that strategy into an operating plan and work on building a corporate culture that perpetuates the strategy."

At the same time, under the go-go energy of Leonsis and in the rush for growth, anything went at AOL. Employees were hard at work on an infinite array of activities, some of which made no sense to Pittman.

"Wall Street was demanding that we develop new revenue sources right away, and did not think we had demonstrated enough of an interest in shareholder value," he said. "While it was critical that AOL did everything it could to make itself the leader, it was time to stop dreaming we could do it all." Among the ideas that were being looked into: selling books and reselling long-distance services—areas in which, Pittman felt, AOL had no particular expertise.

Instead, why not help those who were already in those businesses and, in the process, get them to pay AOL for that aid? After years of building the AOL brand and attracting millions of customers, it was time to leverage the asset—or "harvest" it. (The term soon became widespread at AOL.)

The decision was a 180-degree turn from AOL's strategy only a few years before. In 1993, AOL had bragged to its customers that it had a no-ad policy. Such bravado was not possible after the hourly usage fees were removed.

Earlier, the company had begun, in earnest, to develop "alternative revenues"—mostly from advertising fees and transactions—but the results were negligible ($6 million for all of 1995). The figure had jumped to $100.2 million in 1996, but that still was not the level of revenues that AOL needed after replacing hourly rates with a flat fee.

Big-time advertisers—Coke, Pepsi, Procter & Gamble—were still sitting on the sidelines in late 1996. Advertisers (mostly technology companies) had spent only $55 million for online ads in 1995. Even the $301 million spent in 1996 compared poorly to the $37 billion spent on newspaper ads and the $34 billion on television commercials. Various research groups were making startling predictions of billions of online ad dollars in the years ahead. But would the income surge come in time to lift AOL, whose huge costs put it at the greatest risk?

Before Pittman arrived, the move toward alternative revenues lay in the hands of another unusual New Yorker—Myer Berlow—who hit AOL like a visitor from another planet in the spring of 1995. He had arrived with the title of vice president of national accounts and he developed programming and business models for AOL's large partners—Time-Warner, ABC, and Viacom.

Berlow, who had grown up on a farm in the Midwest, had logged a twenty-five-year career in advertising in New York, Los Angeles, and Mexico City. His resume was relatively traditional; he brought to AOL no particular experience that gave him an edge in the new world of interactive advertising.

In reality, Berlow was a harbinger of things to come at AOL and, therefore, stuck out like a very sore thumb at the company. With slicked-back hair and silky black suits, he seemed, to the old guard, a combination of a New Yorker cartoon with a mobster fashion style—an image that Berlow often joked about himself.

"I think every antibody in the company reacted when I got here," said Berlow, who dubbed himself the Darth Vader of AOL. "The idea of selling the service to advertisers had not been something very ingrained in the company ethos."

Nor was it ingrained in the ethos of deep-pocketed advertisers, although getting them to sign on was precisely what Berlow was charged with doing.

"Traditional advertisers were ambivalent, if not openly hostile to the idea," he said. "So a lot of time had to be spent educating people, often without any deal at the end of the effort."

Advertisers' complaints were many. Ways of gleaning accurate information about usage were still primitive; demographics were unclear; unlike people who watched a network television show, users were fragmented all over the system rather than focused on one place. Perhaps most problematic of all, this was a brand new medium. There was no history, only the undetermined future.

Most advertisers wanted to test online advertising in a very small way, relying on "banner" ads that sat like billboards on the AOL service. A user had to click on the banner ad to see the page of the advertiser.

Berlow, frustrated, called this kind of ad the "plankton" of the business. "No one is going to click on it forever, and it only makes advertisers think this medium is not very effective," he said. What he was *not* saying was perhaps more important: The giant whale of AOL could not live on plankton alone.

landing the big fish

AOL needed some tastier morsels. In the new interactive medium, traditional advertising would not be enough. People did not sit still, as they did when watching television; instead, they moved about. Why not use that movement rather than be disadvantaged by it? With AOL's ability to immediately serve consumers just what they wanted, the best way to advertise was to combine ads with commerce and transactions, creating what could possibly become an end-to-end selling solution.

This was not a new idea, but AOL, unlike most Web sites, had users' credit card numbers stored in its system and could therefore bill them more easily. And AOL executives knew the market statistics: advertising, $125 billion; catalog sales, $75 billion; direct mail, $120 billion; and telemarketing, $100 billion. Perhaps on-screen ads were less important to AOL than to broadcasters. Then why wait for the brand ads, which would eventually come? AOL was a replacement for other media the brand-name companies had long depended on. AOL had more definable benefits in competing with printed catalogs, direct mail and telemarketing.

"We will add Coke and P&G, but they will not be the 800-pound gorillas in this medium that they are in television," Pittman told his troops. "So we'll have to do something different."

And, he thought, AOL was the only service big enough to do anything different. It was time to take advantage of its size by publicizing its usage in more detail, something it had avoided doing before. In the second quarter of 1997, AOL had 153 million page views a day in content, 136 million in People Connection, 131 million in e-mail, and 62 million on the Internet. People were spending more than a half-hour a day on the service. There was growing proof, at least in a poll commissioned by AOL, that television usage was being affected by online activities of consumers.

The audience was ripe for the picking, and harvesting began on February 25, 1997, when Pittman announced a deal with an unknown long-distance reseller, Tel-Save Holdings Inc., of New Hope, Pennsylvania. For the privilege of being able to market discount long-distance services to AOL users, Tel-Save would pay $100 million to AOL as an advance on future commissions, along with a percentage of profits, and warrants to buy shares of the company. Until then, Tel-Save had about 500,000 business customers but wanted to break into the consumer business. With competitors such as MCI and AT&T, Tel-Save found it prohibitively expensive to garner customers via traditional advertising. AOL was cheaper, and Tel-Save could avoid additional costs by billing its AOL customers online.

A series of deals soon followed. On March 4, AOL opened to advertisers its 14,000 chat rooms, which logged one million hours daily; on June 10, CUC International, based in Connecticut, agreed to pay AOL $50 million over three years, to market its portfolio of discount retail services; on July 7, a popular Web-based bookseller, Amazon.com, inked a deal to pay AOL $19 million over three years, to be the featured book retailer on aol.com, AOL's Web site. Soon after, Barnes & Noble made a similar deal (the tab was later raised to $40 million) to be the bookseller on the proprietary service. And 1-800-FLOWERS agreed to pay AOL $25 million over four years, to sell on the service.

In the summer of 1997, AOL decided to begin charging "rents" of $250,000 or more to retailers for their spots on AOL. In the past, the company had relied solely on receiving a large cut of sales. After years of lackluster results, AOL found that retailers had no risk and little incentive in their online efforts if they had too-low costs. Now, AOL's role would be much like a shopping mall—a deliverer of customers rather than an outright partner—as part of Pittman's theme of letting everyone do what they did best. The change was important because AOL was guaranteed revenues and no longer had to rely on variable commissions.

"It's location, location, location," said Pittman, espousing one of the oldest tenets of retailing and real estate.

As part of a wholesale trend toward fudging the lines between editorial content and commerce all over the Web, AOL was redefining its relationship with its content partners. The signal event was a deal AOL struck in July. CBS SportsLine agreed to pay AOL a fee to be a primary tenant on AOL's sports channel. Under this kind of arrangement, content providers became "anchor partners."

The agreement was part of a larger effort within AOL to slim down and begin to shift the relationship it had had with companies that provided it with information for customers. Under the hourly plan, content providers were paid a percentage of fees, based on the time users spent on their sites. When the flat fee went into effect, AOL had no incentive to pay, especially when many of the providers began to port to their own Web sites the same content they posted on AOL. With the advantage of being on AOL so diminished, why should AOL pay for content it could point to for free? In addition, why should AOL make its service more crowded and confusing by having too many providers whom few people were visiting? With increasing control over distribution, why shouldn't getting content become a source of profit rather than an expense with no return? And didn't those content providers compete with AOL for ad dollars?

"It would make me the number one candidate for the moron hall of fame, if we kept paying people for so little," said Pittman. "So I thought perhaps we should stop paying for nothing."

The wholesale redesign of the service came under the control of Barry Schuler, the president of creative development for AOL Networks. Schuler had come to AOL when it had bought his interactive multimedia company—Medior—in 1995. At AOL, Schuler was in charge of programming, product, and production. The new features that would be on the service in its new 4.0 version—called Casablanca—were left to David Gang, senior vice president of new products.

Schuler's redefining of AOL was an extension of Pittman's idea. AOL now provided the whole package: access, navigation, communications, content, Web surfing, and some broadcast.

A round-faced computer enthusiast who styled himself as a new kind of television network kahuna, Schuler was convinced that this was the only attractive offering to the average consumer, despite the complaints of the Web elite.

"The Web is disaggregated, and that's not what consumers want," said Schuler. "So with the largest concentration of consumers in cyberspace . . . it makes sense that we should only pay for exclusive content, exchanging exclusivity for our members."

Working in AOL's favor was the end of the "gold rush to the Internet," which was yielding only fool's gold. "There are all these great sites," said Schuler. "But none can make any money since they can't get enough audience there."

To Schuler, it was not an issue of what was right or wrong. "This is simply becoming a consumer play, and AOL has the consumers," he said. "The industry has never liked the idea of a powerful company like AOL . . . but in a lot of ways, [having] open standards was wishful thinking."

If AOL could bring exclusive or special value content to its users, it would attract even more audience. Soon, AOL was getting big providers like *The New York Times, Business Week,* ABC, and others to design special events and offerings for AOL customers. But just as quickly, out went a series of content partners who either did not want to accept AOL's new carriage demands or did not have enough traffic to stay on the service. The changes left disgruntled partners across cyberspace.

Among the most controversial departures were the games offered on AOL. The games area was targeted for "premium" pricing—content that users would be willing to pay extra for. To clear the way for AOL Studios to create a pay-for-play games service called WorldPlay, a series of popular games sites was jettisoned. AOL customers who thought that the flat rate bought them unlimited access to all content sent angry online protests. Under the new plan (the type initiated later by MSN), subscribers would pay $1.99 an hour for WorldPlay, in addition to the $19.95 monthly rate. To some members, no matter how much extra value they got from improved games, the replacement was a classic case of bait-and-switch. Many AOL users contacted government regulators and organized boycotts.

Typical was the experience of MetaCreations, a longtime games site on AOL. Its contract was canceled in August 1997.

"AOL demands that we begin to pay excessive fees, when [no fees] were previously charged," said MetaCreations chief executive Mark Zimmer at the time. "This is simply no way to treat the companies and customers who have helped to build your business."

a charge too far

The changes at AOL were perhaps inevitable, and definitely permanent. Because under Pittman, AOL had a new and important constituency—its longtime investors and Wall Street, who had finally demanded that AOL grow up financially.

But had AOL gone a bit too far down this road? In June 1997, longtime AOL critic David Cassel revealed that AOL was preparing to hand out its members' telephone numbers to telemarketers who were in partnerships with AOL, and that AOL had tried to sneak in the practice by making an unpublicized change in its "Terms of Service" rules. The new TOS rules read, in part, that AOL "may make the list with telephone numbers available to companies with which AOL has contractual marketing and online relationships for the purpose of permitting such companies to offer products and services over the telephone." Under the TOS, AOL already had claimed the right to rent out subscribers' names and addresses, but had previously said it would not give out phone numbers.

At first, an AOL spokesperson said numbers were being given only to partners, such as CUC and Tel-Save (the practice was touted without irony as a "member benefit"), and noted that users could opt out by changing their preferences. Privacy groups were outraged. How dare AOL hand out user's telephone numbers without explicit permission or adequate disclosure?

AOL had planned to do just that, right before the practice got underway in late July. But, when it was decided that the practice should be tested first, to get members' reaction, a staffer in marketing and a lawyer for AOL had made the TOS changes without telling higher-ups. They thought that, by making the TOS changes, they would protect AOL from criticism; the practice would at least be mentioned in the AOL rules. Instead, AOL looked deceitful, ready to sell out its members to anyone. The ensuing controversy forced AOL to backpedal furiously.

"It was a low-level screwup that made us look like idiots," said Pittman. "It was an idea we knew would be controversial."

Too controversial for AOL, it seemed. In a letter to members on July 24, 1997, Steve Case admitted that AOL had planned to become a telemarketer and to allow a limited number of partners to join in the venture. About the lack of notice, he stated, "Obviously, by not being proactive, we've generated a lot of confusion and concern." He then announced that AOL had changed its mind and would not give out phone numbers to partners. But he also reserved the right for AOL to call users—a move that AOL's pricing change nemesis, New York State Attorney General Dennis Vacco, promised he would monitor closely.

But the damage—yet another self-inflicted wound—was done and AOL looked sneaky. So, Case was even more contrite in his August 1997 letter to users. "AOL has always sought to keep you informed about what we are doing that affects you and why we are doing it," he wrote. "But when it came to last month's telemarketing issues, we messed up, plain and simple."

Case had made a similar admission in October 1994, regarding a decision to rent AOL's list of customers' addresses. "In retrospect, I think we made some mistakes," he wrote then. "The first, and in my opinion by far the most important one, was that we did not proactively and directly notify our existing members about this new program—before initiating the program. . . . As a result, some of you first learned of our list rental program by reading an article in a newspaper—and felt, quite understandably, somewhat betrayed."

In 1997, AOL was so large that its every move got nationwide notice—a situation that AOL would have to learn to live with. Some employees grumbled that AOL was being held to unfair standards. That was the price for being number one. When an AOL lawyer was arrested that summer for allegedly sexually assaulting a boy he met on AOL, the charges got tons of negative attention. The closing of AOL's experimental enterprise unit, which specialized in developing AOL services aimed at businesses, was noted widely. Every poll that indicated weakness was touted in the media, and every screwup was magnified to extremes. And when controversial Web gossip columnist Matt Drudge—whose column also had begun to appear on AOL—was sued in August by White House aide

Sidney Blumenthal for defamation (Drudge had alleged spousal abuse), AOL was also named in the $30 million libel suit.

Even when it finally announced its fourth-quarter results on August 7, 1997, there was controversy despite solid indications that AOL had begun the serious task of controlling costs. Its 42 percent increase, bringing its sales to $476 million, included a tripling of alternative revenue streams.

"The shell game continues at America Online Inc.," noted *PC Week Online,* about the results, since they also included a restatement of third-quarter earnings and an unexpected shift of a charge from the second quarter to the fourth that were requested by the SEC. So the profits reported for the two quarters were turned into losses.

For the quarter ending in March, the SEC had specifically questioned the way AOL had booked revenues from its deal with Tel-Save. AOL agreed to add $5 million in revenues, rather than $12 million, and to account for the rest over a longer period of time. The third-quarter profit of $2.6 million quickly became a loss of $4.7 million. The SEC also directed that a $25 million charge for renegotiation of content partner contracts had to be moved from the quarter ending in December to the quarter ending in June.

The changes clouded what were to be AOL's bright summer results and prolonged its reputation for using too-aggressive accounting practices. Had the original financial entries survived, AOL would have posted a $10.9 million profit—well above Wall Street's expectations.

"It definitely didn't look good, and was even a bit disturbing," said Mary Meeker of Morgan Stanley, "even though everything else was pointing upward."

When analysts began to sort out the numbers and noted huge increases in usage in spite of all the bad press, the stock began climbing again in late summer. When AOL announced it had reached nine million members on September 2, its share price hit close to $69.

"If you still harbor a grudge, I have advice for you: *Get over it*— AOL is proving it has the right stuff—particularly by comparison. Consider its performance [versus] that of Prodigy or the Microsoft Network. Even its closest rival, CompuServe, continues to cast about for a new strategy, while its financial losses mount," wrote Patrick Houston on the Ziff-Davis online news site, in the fall of 1997. "AOL stands with Coca-Cola, Procter & Gamble and Nike as one of the premier brand-names marketers (and companies) of our time. It's a sales game, folks, and AOL does it well."

Such sentiments were exactly what Pittman and Case had long wanted to hear. But selling AOL well was only part of the elaborate contest for domination of the online world. Within a week, they would show just how well AOL could play the buying game too.

▶ chapter.fourteen

the enemy is us

a chance meeting

At the Kennedy Center Honors—a glamorous annual gala at which the nation's outstanding artists are celebrated by Washington's power elite—in December 1995, Steve Case saw his past and his future at the very same time.

Among the crowd in the enormous red-carpeted entrance hall of the Kennedy Center, Case saw Henry Bloch, legendary chairman of H&R Block—the corporate owner of AOL's longtime rival, CompuServe. Bloch had been part of an attempt to buy AOL early in 1991. His serious bid of $50 million would have surely wiped AOL off the online landscape, had a deal been consummated.

Instead, AOL had survived and prospered by attracting millions of customers, and CompuServe's strength had dwindled. With the Microsoft challenge threatening to kill them both, Case had approached CompuServe again in early 1995 to discuss the possibility of some sort of merger but had been rebuffed. CompuServe's officials had decided that the market was still wide open.

Now, CompuServe had become weak. It would soon show two quarters of unheard-of losses and would make a costly decision to delay its spin-off as a subsidiary of H&R Block. The Block directors would also later decide to junk a much-touted and expensive experiment: a family-oriented service with the silly name of "WOW!" The noises out of Block's Kansas City headquarters, regarding the shriveling asset located near Columbus, Ohio, were becoming more painful as time progressed.

Case knew that Block had begun a discreet search for buyers, a kind of silent auction in the online world, to unload CompuServe. AOL was an obvious choice as a potential buyer. As owner of a service and a network, it was in the same businesses as CompuServe.

Besides vaulting AOL to the undisputed leadership in the online industry, and taking out its chief competitor, the prospect of buying CompuServe was breathtaking for Case and others who had been at AOL for a long time. They had never had much respect for Prodigy or, as it turned out, Microsoft's MSN, but CompuServe was another story. Although too slow and too steady, CompuServe represented *quality* to Case. It was the highly respected granddaddy of the online world, and had survived for nearly three decades. The fact that the upstart AOL might acquire CompuServe was heavy with symbolism about the past and the future of the online industry.

And the timing might finally be right. Case knew that the staid company's patience with the online business was running out. So he meandered over to Bloch in the gala crowd.

"We should talk," said Steve Case.

a chipping of the old block

CompuServe—once the undisputed leader of the online world—had indeed fallen on difficult times. Growing financial losses, a brain drain from upper management, and declining membership were taking a serious toll. H&R Block, the conservative tax-preparation giant that owned CompuServe, had sat back on its heels while the company had quietly dominated in the early years of the online phenomenon. Now, the folly of that strategy was growing increasingly apparent.

As AOL had gained ground and surpassed it in 1995 and 1996, CompuServe had tried to innovate. It introduced a new service called WOW! in March 1996, which was aimed at the family market. Designed with bold colors and easy-to-use graphics, it was an attractive offering that *The Wall Street Journal*'s Walt Mossberg had hailed as a possible challenger to AOL as the favored choice of average consumers.

But WOW! was too late. AOL had already captured those users, and the service failed to take off. Company executives announced in late November 1996 that on January 31, 1997—only ten months after it had debuted—WOW! would be shut down. The cost of developing and marketing the failed experiment (only 100,000 customers had purchased it) had been steep: reportedly, $70 million.

"WOW! was a big decision that did not turn out to be attractive to the consumer market," said Frank Salizzoni, president and chief executive of H&R Block. "And it ended up contributing to the problems at a tough time."

Indeed, CompuServe could ill afford the costly experiment, considering the mood of the online industry in 1996. CompuServe and AOL had both experienced serious rumblings of trouble that summer; churn had viciously increased. In August 1996 (the month when AOL suffered its paralyzing nineteen-hour blackout), CompuServe reported a first-quarter loss of $29.6 million. In the same quarter a year before, the company had had a net income of $26.8 million. The fiscal health of the service, which had a long record of profit, seemed to be faltering.

Even as it cited investments in WOW! and expenditures to improve its infrastructure as the key reasons for the poor showing, CompuServe acknowledged that declining subscriber growth was damaging its bottom line. CompuServe wasn't having trouble bringing in customers—during the quarter, nearly 900,000 new subscribers were added—but it simply couldn't keep them. The company suffered a net loss of subscribers overall in the quarter; more customers left the service than joined it.

The outlook for the next quarter was also not encouraging. CompuServe president and chief executive Robert Massey anticipated that the company would show a second-quarter loss as well.

In the meantime, CompuServe executives would try to staunch the hemorrhaging of money. A series of "cost reduction measures" was planned: sell the Spry corporate computer software group; consolidate some offices; write off some software costs; and lay off 150 employees, or 4 percent of the workforce.

In contrast, despite all AOL's problems, its membership was at least still growing. There was room for optimism, if Steve Case's exhortations to push toward critical mass—where advertising leverage could then rescue the balance sheet—were to be trusted. Where cash was absent, momentum could pay the bills, at least for a time.

CompuServe was not only losing money; it had lost momentum—to AOL. And its owners were ill disposed to spend the kind of bets that Case put on the table in order to win. In the high-stakes gambling that was taking place, Block was not a risk-taking player and AOL was.

The Block board members were already wary of the rapidly changing high-tech market. A spin-off of CompuServe was part of the impetus plans they had formally approved in July 1996. While CompuServe was a quiet, smoothly humming market leader, all had been well. But when the company needed some attention and vision at the helm, Block decided to opt out— an easy decision because Block still held 80 percent of CompuServe's outstanding shares.

But the service's deteriorating situation hindered Block's plans to exit the market. Few buyers wanted to take the shares off Block's hands at the price the company felt it needed to get. After the weak first-quarter results were announced in August, the Block directors postponed the spin-off plans, hoping things would get better. Their hope proved to be no more than wishful thinking; the second-quarter results were shaping up to be even worse than Massey had predicted.

In October, when the company issued warnings that the results would be poorer than expected, CompuServe's stock fell 12 percent, to only $9.25 a share. It was a long way from its initial public offering price of $30, in April.

When the second-quarter losses of $58 million—including a series of one-time charges—were announced in November, compared to a $14 million profit the year before, tensions rose. Executives had a lame excuse: there had been a delay in sending out the service's new software. Without the new, glitzy software to rouse and maintain interest in the service, the officials said, the customer drain had continued.

It was time, CompuServe declared, to get "back to basics." No more would the service try to compete with AOL for casual users. According to Bob Massey, "We're going to refocus on our existing leadership among business, professional and technical users, as well as our traditional base of consumer subscribers." And he flat-out called the consumer market a "bloodbath."

"We made the judgment that we had to stop the spending and go back to our knitting," said Salizzoni.

Though its value had dropped off a cliff, CompuServe stock still was receiving "buy" recommendations from some analysts. Merrill Lynch titled a December report on the company "The Clouds Are Lifting"; Salomon Brothers and Goldman Sachs also recommended purchasing the stock in December. After all, the service still had around three million members, not including the nearly 1.7 million users of "NIFTYServe," a Japanese licensee of CompuServe technology. And CompuServe's network services division, which provided data network services to corporations (Visa International's billions of worldwide credit card transactions, for example, were carried over the CompuServe network), was robust. There was obvious value there, and perhaps things would soon calm down a bit.

They didn't, partly because of CompuServe's stubbornness at not offering flat rates to its users. In February, just before announcing a third-quarter loss of $14.2 million, Massey suddenly stepped down. A 20-year veteran of CompuServe, he had been integral to building its important and profitable networking division, and had been promoted to president and chief executive in June 1995. When Massey had taken over the helm, AOL and CompuServe were virtually neck-and-neck in the race for subscribers, the popularity of the Web was about to explode, and the future of the online services market was yet to be determined.

Only 18 months later, AOL was enjoying net gains of hundreds of thousands of customers a quarter, and CompuServe was shrinking. The unsurprising result: Massey was out. Salizzoni, who had taken over at Block that fall, stepped in at CompuServe until a successor could be found.

Massey resigned on a Monday. On Thursday of that week, the poor third-quarter results were announced. The loss was less dire than Wall Street had predicted, thanks in part to more cost cutting. The company had, for example, sheared $15 million from its marketing budget—a move that certainly helped the numbers in the short term. But how wise was it to gut marketing when the service was bleeding away members? The company brass seemed to have given up on the long term for the sake of bulking up its quarterly reports.

At the company's headquarters in Upper Arlington, Ohio, just outside of Columbus, the mood was dark. Over the previous nine months, management had shaved 500 jobs from the company—or 14 percent of the workforce. The downsizing had been kept quiet during the course of the year, but on February 24, a short item detailing the cuts appeared in *The Wall Street Journal*.

One could have been forgiven for reading right over the downsizing story, which was only four paragraphs long. But on page B3, CompuServe appeared again—this time, in an unlikely full-page ad that was as much a direct slap at AOL as it was an appeal for customers.

In the top center of the ad was a gray box—representing a computer pop-up message—containing these words: "The number you have dialed is not answering. Please try again later." Below that was a square "OK" button and a cursor arrow. Then came the ad text: "No, it's not okay. Your computer screen tells you one thing. You're feeling another. After all, what could be more maddening than being told you can't get your e-mail, stock quotes, or other mission critical information?" As with the television ads it had sponsored during the Superbowl in January, CompuServe was making a direct and aggressive bid for disgruntled AOL users.

Though it made sense for competitors to take full marketing advantage of AOL's troubles, CompuServe's ad campaign was an odd choice. Only months before, CompuServe's management had said that the service would focus on business customers and in-tranets. Why now was it making a play for home users—especially those who, by the very fact that they would be defecting from AOL, would be showing themselves as high churn risks?

But these were desperate days for CompuServe. And, in Virginia, Steve Case was sure that CompuServe's confused moves were signaling that it was time to pounce on an incredible opportunity, one that would send shock waves throughout the industry. Rather than being offended by the Superbowl and newspaper ads, he thought they displayed a rare sassiness from a company that had long been thought of as moribund—a promising sign that it was not dead yet.

"I thought it was clever and showed that CompuServe had some spunk," said Case. "And it gave me the sense that it was a company in need of vision and passion."

So perhaps the offhand suggestion he had made to Henry Bloch at the Kennedy Center the year before wasn't so crazy after all.

talk, talk, talk

In the meantime, AOL was enduring its own winter of crises: connectivity problems, public relations missteps, investigations by attorneys general, lawsuits, quarterly losses, and a growing impression that Steve Case and his company were corrupt, crass, and callous.

In fact, the entire online world seemed to be flirting with collapse. Prodigy had faded to a weak shadow. CompuServe was withering fast. AOL was suffering from a bad image due to the access crisis. Were the days of the proprietary online business over?

But as the winter gave way, AOL began to regain its footing, thanks in part to Bob Pittman's charisma infusion, and rumors took to the air. On April Fools' Day, shares of both AOL and CompuServe enjoyed a healthy spike—AOL rose $3.25 to $45.75, and CompuServe jumped $1.14 to $11. The reason: a technology report called Wall Street Strategies had reported that AOL would "make a play" for CompuServe. According to press

accounts, AOL was considering ponying up around $1.2 bil-
lion—which the cash-strapped company would provide via stock
or equity—for its rival. At that price, AOL would need to issue
26 million new shares to do the deal.

The purchase could be worth it, despite the stock dilution.
With AOL at eight million members and growing, and Compu-
Serve at around three million members (that figure didn't include
the nearly 1.7 million members of NIFTYServe), a deal would
make AOL five times the size of its nearest competitor, MSN. A
merger would also bolster AOL's struggling network by adding
CompuServe's 80,000 modems to AOL's 275,000—an increase
of nearly 30 percent.

Talks had been progressing throughout the late winter and early
spring, between the two companies and their investment bankers.
AOL was being advised again by Lazard Freres, and CompuServe
by Salomon Brothers.

"We had finally decided that our motivations were different
and that CompuServe had become too much of a capital-intensive
business," said Salizzoni. "So we started talking to buyers over the
winter—some of whom were interested in the network, some in
the service, and a few in the whole thing—which made it a long
and tedious process."

At CompuServe, there was not any question that Block had put
the company on the block. "If they could not spin it, they were
going to sell it," said Dennis Matteucci, who had been brought in
on an interim basis to help run CompuServe after Massey's departure. "I think the mindset had been never to lose money, and so
the mindset to make investments was just not there. Block simply
could not stomach the expenditure needed."

In fact, said company sources, CompuServe executives had
been chastised by Block officials for the cost of the lively Superbowl ads, which Steve Case had grudgingly admired.

"They told us we had wasted money," said one disgruntled
CompuServe executive, "when it felt like it was one of the first
times in a long time that we had shown a little fighting spirit."

When officials from AOL came to Columbus in the late winter
of 1997 to do due diligence on the company, they were greeted

with more welcome arms than they had expected. After enduring cuts and disdain from Block officials as they slowly bled to death, CompuServe employees wanted some changes—fast.

"The AOL folks understood us in a way Block just did not," said one executive. "We all thought: the enemy is us."

Miles Gilburne, AOL's senior vice president of corporate development, grasped the mood at CompuServe well. "They were faced with a daunting challenge of finding someone who could manage both businesses," he said. "So it was a good fit with us because there were not many companies around that had such synergies."

Finding synergies was Gilburne's job. He was in charge of looking at acquisitions for all the divisions of AOL, and then getting the managers to buy into them.

A laugh line around AOL was that the bearded Gilburne—with his cerebral and professorial air—only had a body as a vehicle to carry his brain around. Indeed, like Case, Gilburne was often thinking of the big picture, the kind of moves that would bring AOL to complete dominance.

Gilburne had come to AOL in 1995 with David Cole, with whom he had worked in building NaviSoft, the Internet software company bought by AOL in late 1994. Earlier, Gilburne had had a long career in an early-stage venture capital funding firm; before that, he was the founding partner in the Silicon Valley office of the law firm of Weil, Gotshal and Manges. Gilburne got his law degree from Harvard and his undergraduate degree from Princeton.

"When I joined AOL, it was a no-brainer, because it was clear that the market was poised to take off," said Gilburne. "The opportunity at AOL was a monster."

Now, he would be part of making AOL into a Godzilla, if he could get the deal with CompuServe done.

The appeal of the deal, according to Gilburne and Case, was the powerful CompuServe network. A purchase would eliminate the problems the strained AOL network was undergoing, and would push the ANS networking subsidiary into the big leagues. AOL had bought ANS in 1995 for only $35 million—$20 million in cash and $15 million in stock. But although ANS had been an important player in the networking business, its principal client was still AOL.

ANS had created an important competitive advantage for the AOL online service over the years, by allowing it to control network costs, to grow at a healthy pace, also to strike better deals with other network vendors who provided connectivity.

"Since ANS was ours, it would jump when we said 'Jump,' and that really had helped us recover from the access crisis," said Gilburne. "It was comfortable and so there was a rationale for holding on to it."

But networking—building vast data systems that linked up people and businesses—had become a large-scale global business. Competitors were the fast-growing WorldCom Inc. (which, in 1996, had acquired MFS Communications Inc., which had bought Fairfax-based UUNet earlier) and the major telephone companies.

"The network business was a strong one, and compelling," said Gilburne. "But only if you were willing to get bigger. If not, you had to get bought."

Also attractive to AOL were CompuServe's international online services, which had remained strong even as the U.S. service had suffered. AOL, under the management of Jack Davies, had made aggressive incursions into Europe and Japan since 1995, but buying CompuServe would give it a huge leg up as it competed with government-owned services and others run by Microsoft. An AOL–CompuServe combination would put AOL at the forefront of the market and give it footholds in other parts of the world where CompuServe had already set up business.

But there were also serious reservations regarding such a huge transaction. Reports from AOL technologists told Gilburne that the network, while robust, was getting antiquated, and integration with AOL's systems would take a lot of investment. Other AOL officials were more disturbed by the weaknesses and morale problems at CompuServe in the wake of Block's neglect.

Many observers wondered whether the two companies' cultures were compatible enough—it was "like the guys at Animal House were thinking of taking over the Honors Society," opined Daniel McGinn in *Newsweek*. Another issue: Would the Justice Department's antitrust division frown on the online monolith (10-million-plus customers) that would result?

But the first and foremost quandary was the perception, on Wall Street and in the media, that AOL was itself too troubled to be even thinking of taking on such a momentous addition. Its own users were still disturbed by the access problems. AOL's profitability and ability to generate new revenue streams were questionable. AOL's management was spread dangerously thin. Was buying CompuServe right now a good idea?

"We had been in a crisis mode at AOL, and so it felt a bit like it was not an ideal time," said Case. "There was the risk of taking our eye off the ball and how that could be perceived."

It might be seen, said Gilburne more flatly, "as a frolic and a detour."

Internally, some powerful players agreed. Bob Pittman and Ted Leonsis were firmly against the move. Both thought the attention, energy, and financing that such a transaction would entail would be better focused at their divisions.

"The more I looked at it, there was no plus there. We'd be doubling down in ANS where there was no traction for us, and it would take resources from somewhere else," said Pittman. "CompuServe was on such a pedestal for a lot of people here, so buying it was irresistible. But I could certainly resist."

Mike Connors, Matt Korn, and the technology staff had been under intense strain for months, dealing with the access crisis. "There was so much already on our technology plate," said Gilburne. "So we were not sure that so much mindshare should go out at a time when things were so troubled."

But there were outside time pressures. Block wanted to move the deal along before Congress closed a tax loophole known as the Morris Trust. The ruling would allow Block to separate itself from CompuServe and combine it with AOL on a tax-free basis, thus negating a hefty $150 million tax bill for Block. But the Morris Trust, said Gilburne, also made it hard to think about other kinds of deals, including those with multiple parties.

Rumors in the press and among investment bankers suggested that others were very interested in CompuServe. One particularly disturbing possibility was that Microsoft would beat out AOL for the purchase, more than doubling MSN's member numbers and,

more importantly, denying AOL the chance to become the undisputed numbers king of the online world. Matt Drudge, the Internet
gossip monger, declared in his April 8 column that Microsoft
lawyers had been "spotted around the CompuServe compound
over the weekend," and were possibly "offering double . . . any
AOL package." Indeed, MSN had been considering purchasing
CompuServe in a joint deal with GTE Corporation and UUNet.

"There was a lot of pressure on the deal, and the feeling that
our hand was being forced was unnerving," said Case.

Was MSN interested or was Block just trying to get AOL to
complete the deal? There was a risk to not acting. If MSN bought
CompuServe, said Case, "There would be a strong perception and
a sense they were winning, and it would be World War III."

During the next week, as he talked to his rattled executives and
as the two companies continued to trade proposals back and forth,
Case became more jittery about the deal.

By April 18, the day the AOL board gathered to meet on the
subject, *The Washington Post* reported that AOL had "cooled to
outright purchase" of its rival, though it was still considering purchasing parts of the company.

In fact, Case had become lukewarm to the whole idea. He
started off the meeting by expressing growing reservations—discussing the benefits but also listing the many risks. "I think if I had
pounded the table it might have been done, but I was not pound-
ing the table," said Case.

Gilburne said Case's being on the fence slowed momentum considerably, even before news came, at noon, that legislation to close
the Morris Trust loophole had just been introduced on Capitol Hill.
That bulletin created a complete interruption of the debate, and the
AOL board decided to table the idea, though most agreed that the
drive toward a purchase had been lost.

The Block board, which had been waiting in Kansas City for an
offer from Case, was furious at AOL.

"There was tremendous hostility from Block, who decided
Case had dragged out the negotiations to get a lower price or even
kill the business," said one source close to the deal. "There was bad
blood and a lot of mistrust."

Gilburne was not surprised. "Block had been pushing for sale for so long, and then the likeliest deal came to a grinding halt," he said. "So, in their mind, we left them at the altar."

Case also understood their pique. "I can see why it was frustrating and embarrassing to them," he said. "Ending up selling to us was hard enough."

try, try again

As spring edged toward summer, the picture became more and more muddled. CompuServe continued to suffer setbacks from a variety of sources. In late April, shareholders filed suit against the company, complaining that management hadn't warned investors about unfavorable trends in the online market when CompuServe was taken public. Since the public offering, CompuServe stock had lost half its value, and shareholders felt they had been misled.

An April incident in the company's German unit jolted nerves throughout the online industry. A CompuServe official was arrested by German authorities for facilitating the distribution of pornography and of Nazi propaganda. All U.S. online services faced difficulties in other countries, where laws with regard to free speech were more stringent. Would CompuServe's growing European presence now be hampered by the threat of arrest of its employees? Could the company convince the German authorities it should not be held liable for material that was viewed through its service?

The chances of that outcome seemed slim, especially after reports circulated that German investigators had entered CompuServe's offices and begun searching through filing cabinets and desk drawers for porn. No clearer sign was needed that they did not understand the difference between providing porn and providing access to the Internet, on which there happened to be porn.

At the same time, there was an announcement that promised to alter the balance of power in the data networking business and make everyone take another look at all available companies, including CompuServe.

GTE Corporation, the massive telephone company based in Stamford, Connecticut, announced a deal to purchase BBN Corporation, one of the top Internet data carriers, for $616 million—well above its $450 million market value. The purchase instantly turned GTE into a major player in the Internet networking arena. "We're getting ready for the twenty-first century," GTE chairman Charles R. Lee told *The Wall Street Journal*. In one swoop, the company had gained a valuable position against its rival, AT&T. And BBN, though currently unprofitable, had an impressive pedigree; it had helped build the Internet. A BBN engineer had pioneered the use of the ubiquitous @ symbol in e-mail. (AOL was, in fact, a BBN customer.)

The purchase took MSN out of the picture. MSN had contemplated buying CompuServe with GTE. And now, it seemed, Microsoft would counterattack. Microsoft may not have been interested in CompuServe, but it was obviously interested in its members. In mid-May, MSN began sending out trial diskettes specifically to CompuServe users. Two weeks later, CompuServe launched its own carpet-bombing marketing campaign: 2.5 million pieces of direct mail were posted in an attempt to lure new members. In addition, 1.5 million pieces were sent out to retain current subscribers.

Discussions with AOL were seemingly derailed. CompuServe sought ways of bolstering its service's flagging performance, even as Block continued to look for a buyer. CompuServe had already announced a redesign of the service (its popular forums would be rearranged to make them easier to find) and launched a new ad campaign. These moves that were interpreted as a sign that the chances of an AOL buyout had completely dimmed.

They had not. They had only moved to a time Gilburne had christened "Phase II."

Now that an all-stock deal was not required, as it had been under the Morris Trust, AOL had a lot more flexibility to bring in partners. More importantly, its stock was rising, which made it cheaper to do a deal; internal troubles had calmed down; and no competing offers seemed pending at CompuServe. The AOL team could relax a bit and consider what it really wanted.

the enemy is us

One early idea had been to involve its international partners, Mitsui and Bertelsmann, in a joint venture, but those talks went nowhere. Another all-stock offer had been made by AOL during the summer—valuing CompuServe at $10 a share, or about $1 billion. But that figure was not enough for Block, and no counteroffer came because Block suddenly had a prospect in the New York-based investment firm of Welsh, Carson, Anderson & Stowe. Welsh Carson specialized in acquiring and building established business in two fields: health care and information services. In most cases, the firm bought divisions or subsidiaries of larger companies—especially those that were no longer compatible with the goals or capabilities of their parent companies. Using money provided by investors, Welsh Carson bought out companies under the direction of a small core of partners and staff.

Welsh Carson also had history with CompuServe—it had sold it the Source many years before. And, in an ironic twist, the Source had been founded by none other than Bill Von Meister—the man who introduced Steve Case to the online world.

While the Welsh Carson talks were continuing, AOL moved in a number of ways. First, Bertelsmann's Tom Middelhof, who was an AOL board member, began to talk with Salizzoni about the possible deals that could be done—either one involving just Bertelsmann, or one that brought in Bertelsmann and AOL. Middelhof, unlike Case, was someone Salizzoni seemed to be willing to work with.

In parallel talks, Middelhof and Case were meeting with John Sidgmore of UUNet, the subsidiary of the Jackson, Mississippi, telecommunications giant, WorldCom. Sidgmore and Case knew each other well from the days when AOL considered buying UUNet. They began to conduct a series of meetings, at breakfasts and at AOL's outside law firm.

An idea began to be hatched: Link the three companies in some deal that could benefit all. An early notion was to somehow combine ANS, UUNet, and CompuServe, and share the companies.

"But there was no easy way to figure out who would run what and who would own what," said Sidgmore. "Steve did not want to sell ANS outright, because I don't think Steve has ever sold anything."

Indeed, the idea of exiting the network "backbone" business completely was a difficult option. "The question was: Should we bulk up with some sort of UUNet relationship or should we try to do it ourselves?" said Gilburne. "There was definitely no easy way for us to maintain a major share if UUNet stepped in."

AOL continued to form other bids ("The scary part was that perhaps we would actually win," said Gilburne) even as it kept up talks with Sidgmore.

"We did think that, whoever won—be it UUNet or Welsh Carson—we would at least have a shot at getting the online service, because we were the obvious one for them to offer it to," said Case. "Though it was a scary idea not to get the network business and then be left with ANS at a size that was too small to compete."

The idea of getting the CompuServe online brand, which would give AOL a better entry into the business market, was still compelling. The three sides—UUNet, AOL, and Bertelsmann—struggled for weeks over the variety of options available. When Sidgmore finally agreed to give AOL attractive terms for a long-term networking contract—which would allow AOL the comfort of controlled costs for connectivity and drop its costs—Case decided that he should let go of the network business altogether and "double down" (Pittman's term) in the online services business. Better still, under such a deal, Pittman was firmly on board, along with Leonsis.

But was it too late? On September 4, *The Wall Street Journal* reported that H&R Block was "nearing a deal" with Welsh Carson. Quoting "executives familiar with the situation," the article reported that "Welsh Carson wants to purchase a controlling stake from Block, while Block would retain a minority interest. . . . [A] deal could be announced as early as this week."

It was. But the victorious suitor was not Welsh Carson.

Because on Friday, John Sidgmore was in the Block boardroom, describing to the directors the idea that he, Case, and Middelhof had hatched.

"They were going to make the deal with one of us, and I was not leaving until they knew our story," said Sidgmore, who had decided to wait until Block made a decision.

Their tale was compelling. WorldCom would buy CompuServe for $1.2 billion, paid for by a stock swap. It would then turn around and trade CompuServe's online services division, plus $175 million in cash, to AOL, in exchange for AOL's ANS communications subsidiary. With a $75 million payment to AOL, Bertelsmann got a more lucrative stake in the combined AOL/CompuServe European service. Finally, AOL would sign an attractive five-year deal making WorldCom its largest network service provider and guaranteeing AOL's costs.

Everyone would get what was really wanted. H&R Block finally rid itself of CompuServe and received fast-rising WorldCom shares (at a rate of 0.40625 WorldCom share per share of CompuServe) in return. By jettisoning ANS, AOL could focus more on content and the service itself, rather than on technical "plumbing." AOL also received CompuServe's 2.6 million members, an instantly enhanced international presence, and a seat on WorldCom's board. And WorldCom received, along with ANS, CompuServe's successful network services division.

After Salizzoni told Sidgmore of the decision by Block to sell to him, the pair worked out some of the finer points of the deal that Block had wanted changed and then shook hands.

Sidgmore immediately called Case, who in his typical taciturn style did not immediately ask Sidgmore the outcome.

"So?" asked Case finally.

"So, it's ours," replied Sidgmore.

"Good," said Case simply.

For Gilburne, the end was almost anticlimactic compared to the long struggle to get the deal done. "I was happy to close it," he sighed.

AOL executives were gleeful; they had pulled off the once-unthinkable coup of the digital decade. An air of jubilation permeated AOL headquarters, from the cubicles right up to the plush corner offices on the fifth floor of the Dulles headquarters that had been dubbed "Green Acres." Just six months before, AOL had been the laughingstock of the online world. Now it was the conqueror.

At the partners' conference a week later, Tom Rielly of Planet-Out gave all the AOL senior executives T-shirts that probably signaled one of the main reasons for the favorable outcome. "75263.8688@aol.com," the lettering on the shirts read, making fun of CompuServe's complex numbered e-mail addresses. At AOL, the same address was simply: "planetout@aol.com."

On September 8, the day the deal was announced, AOL's "Buzzsaw" humor columnist Bill Shein couldn't resist a jibe at CompuServe. In his column, he wrote:

ATTENTION COMPUSERVE USERS: RESISTANCE IS FUTILE. YOU WILL BE ASSIMILATED.—In a complex deal that still must be approved by antitrust regulators, America Online has acquired the consumer online business of CompuServe, AOL's chief rival. Bob Stevenson, the only remaining online service user on Earth who is not using AOL, said in a statement that he plans "to hold out for as long as possible, but I must say, that Buddy List feature is quite appealing."

Block had a swipe of its own to make; its anger at AOL lingered. In the negotiations, for example, Block executives preferred to work with Sidgmore, with no one from AOL present. And in H&R Block's official press release announcing the deal, there was not a single mention of AOL. Technically, that was perhaps appropriate enough; the WorldCom–AOL part of the deal did not directly involve H&R Block. But it was indisputable that no sale would have happened if AOL had not been a major part of the negotiations and the deal. What's more, millions of CompuServe users were about to be handed over to AOL.

Block's press release considered those facts not important enough to merit comment. The only reference to CompuServe's online users was this statement by Salizzoni: "This is a strategic transaction that provides significant value to both H&R Block and CompuServe shareholders and places CompuServe's assets in excellent hands for the benefit of its networking and online customers."

The message: Block had finally been able to dispose of its Compu-Serve albatross; whatever happened next was not its business. Salizzoni had no apologies. "My deal was with WorldCom and I thought of it as two separate transactions," he said. "But AOL got a fantastic deal . . . getting [CompuServe's online service] and some cash for giving up their network business."

As to the notion that Block was perhaps sore about how it had all turned out—losing the race so definitely to AOL—Salizzoni was brief. "I'm just not going to comment on that," he said.

But as long as everybody was taking jabs at everybody else, why shouldn't MSN get into the act as well? In a letter to users, posted on the service, MSN vice president Laura Jennings wrote: "We view this announcement as an opportunity, as millions of consumers reexamine their online service options. Over the years, CompuServe provided its members with a quality online service. At MSN, we're also focused on providing our members with a valuable and secure online experience. Like CompuServe, we appreciate our members' desire for privacy, nonintrusive third-party offers, and reliable access."

MSN hoped that disappointed CompuServe users would defect before allowing themselves to be passed on to AOL. Even though AOL was promising to maintain CompuServe as a separate service, MSN wanted to appeal to those who looked down on AOL as unsophisticated, uninteresting, and unworthy of being number one. It was no stretch to assume that CompuServe users, who tended to be computer-savvy, business-oriented customers, would loathe becoming part of the AOL juggernaut.

Many assumed that also would be the reaction of CompuServe's employees. Having been rivals of AOL for so long, and now having been so roundly trounced by the "training wheels of the Internet," how would they react to being owned by their former foe?

Quite well, actually. Salizzoni had come, on the day of the deal announcement, to give a goodbye speech (he did not mention AOL at all). The next day, Steve Case and Bob Pittman took a trip out to CompuServe's headquarters to say hello. And although the prospect of being owned by AOL might have left a bitter taste in some employees' mouths, anything was better than languishing under the aegis of foot-dragging, indecisive H&R Block.

"I think everyone was fed up and wanted a decision to be made," said Dennis Matteucci, who led Case and Pittman in a series of meetings with their new employees, held in the gym of CompuServe's fitness center.

Case was dressed in his typical khaki ensemble. Pittman cut a fancier figure in a suit. "I'm a Southern boy and my Momma told me to wear a suit when you meet new folks," drawled Pittman charmingly.

The shy Case was even more endearing. When Matteucci handed him and Pittman CompuServe T-shirts, Pittman quickly put his on over his suit. But Case began stripping off his own shirt to display his stomach to the crowd as he changed into his new T-shirt.

"Close your eyes," he joked to them.

When the audience kept looking on, he jested, "I am serious. Close your eyes."

They didn't; they clapped and whooped instead. These guys were definitely not at all like the stiffs of H&R Block. "They made a very good impression," said Matteucci.

The jolly scene was recounted a week later, when TIME magazine hit the newsstands. On the cover, Steve Case, posing in his standard khakis-and-denim-shirt combo, stood with his hands on his hips like a monarch surveying his empire. Wires snaked out of his body. "AOL's Big Coup," read the headline. "The Web was going to kill it. Microsoft was going to bury it. But by grabbing CompuServe, America Online keeps on growing."

"Bury" was precisely the word Bill Gates had spoken to Case only four years before. The TIME story was an upbeat account of complete victory for AOL.

The majority of the press coverage was similarly positive, but there were some naysayers' voices in the mix. Despite all the crises the company had survived in the past few years, and with no acknowledgement of its continually tested ability to realign and refocus itself, AOL was delivered a familiar charge, and a more familiar metaphor, in a negative essay, on September 15, on the editorial page of The Wall Street Journal.

The essay, by Stefanie Syman, executive editor of an online magazine called *Feed,* ran under the headline "Is America Online a Leviathan Or a Dinosaur?" Three years after *Wired* magazine's use of the same metaphor had inspired Ted Leonsis's anti-MSN pep rally, which galvanized the company for the battles ahead, Syman was recycling the idea. Her thesis: AOL had pulled off quite a coup with the CompuServe acquisition, but, in the long run, AOL was a company on the way down.

"[I]t's true that AOL will not die a quick and sudden death," Syman wrote. "But it may well fade out, lumbering in the background as the service of choice for the least savvy users. It might, like Sears, Roebuck & Co., survive by serving a respectable portion of American consumers, but have only a waning influence over their habits or the retail marketplace. It might, in other words, persist. But just going on is not nearly as sexy, or as profitable, as dominating."

How unusual that in the weeks after the deal, in the wake of being on the cover of *TIME* and receiving general acclaim for AOL as its stock started soaring upward, Steve Case did not entirely disagree with Syman.

Too jubilant a mood had bothered him in the past; the current high was almost too much. "Now the view of AOL is that it is unstoppable, even though everyone was saying we were out of business just months ago," he said, looking out the window of his Dulles office. Less had changed than people thought. "I don't like the 'sky is falling' perspective, but it's equally silly to say the war has been fought and won by us."

For Steve Case, it seemed, the ride was never over.

back to the future

If you look at Steve Case long enough, you realize finally that he looks like a bit of a blank slate. Perhaps it is because his face is a such a placid one. It is not often that you will see a strong emotion cross it—not anger, not joy, not sadness.

So what you see there, in the end, is whatever you want.

And if you listen to Steve Case long enough, you realize that what he is saying is always a variation of exactly the same theme. Perhaps it is because his voice remains modulated and calm—almost robotic like an animatronic dummy at Disneyland. His points come out in full paragraphs, often sounding dry or even a bit dull. Over and over, he describes the same vision of a vast online community.

So what you hear, in the end, is whatever you want.

You recall a flip and thoughtless comment by an editor who once told you he did not like AOL because it was so middle-of-the-road, so bland, so vanilla.

And it finally hits you—that is why AOL has managed, over the years, to survive vicious cycles of trouble; to keep standing, where others have fallen; to prosper, when those thought to be knowledgeable about such things had predicted its demise.

Because Steve Case—and, by extension, AOL—is so middle-of-the-road, so bland, so vanilla. AOL's sites might not win design awards, but they are clean and easy to navigate; the conversations in its chat rooms may seem nearly mind–numbing to some digerati, but they are probably a lot closer to the mundane lives of most Americans; its technology might not be the fastest or coolest or hottest, but, for the most part, it is pretty easy to work and eventually catches up (though recent e-mail lapses are becoming almost inexcusable).

As politicians will tell you, being average is not a bad way to be.

But AOL has also won—until now, at least—because something else sits behind the pacific face of Steve Case. In this carefully controlled world he has created, flashes of complete and definite craziness form a secret countenance found in every entrepreneur, every visionary who latches onto an idea and never lets go.

Critics of AOL would label it reckless and, to some degree, they would be correct. Aggressive accounting and use of its high–flying stock as currency has placed investors' funds at risk at times— though those same investors were pretty pleased when the stock inevitably rose. Its proclivity for playing close to the edge on customer service, and its lapses in giving its users what they paid for have been thickheaded, even though it tries hard to fix it. To get where it is, AOL has employed a heedless style, full of rash decisions, audacious moves, and impetuous shifts.

Was it an online games company? Yes, until that business died. Or a private-label service for computer manufacturers? Certainly, but that didn't quite work out. Perhaps it preferred to go head-to-head with rich, well-known competitors rather than taking an offer to get out? OK, though that seems kind of stupid. It offered a proprietary online service just when the open Internet was growing fast. Dumb. It cut prices and then pissed off all its customers because they couldn't get online. Dumber.

So, he's not just kidding when Steve Case suggests that the theme for AOL might be: "We're not dead *yet.*"

Indeed, AOL did everything to survive, living up to its long-ago moniker as the cockroach of the online world. It managed to continue to evolve into whatever shapes were needed. It is not an overstatement to say that, over the past year, AOL has become an entirely different company. It has had to change quite dramatically to stay out front in the online world. And it will doubtless have to change again, just to be able to stick around longer.

A key question can still be asked: Will AOL someday become a has-been in cyberspace history, or will it keep growing into one of the biggest media companies in the world? Speculation ranges from (a) a complete breakdown and the bankruptcy of AOL to (b) a buyout by a bigger media fish or (c) its emergence as the most important business in cyberspace.

But whether AOL makes it or breaks it, its journey will continue to be the thing.

Perhaps it is best to review some of the challenges and possible scenarios ahead, before coming to judgment.

the return of the beast of redmond

Trouble aplenty can be expected to come from Microsoft. It has regrouped and relaunched MSN and has vowed to spend billions of dollars to win the war for cyberspace. But, as many know, Bill Gates has expressed disdain for MSN in numerous off-the-record comments to the media and to analysts, and rumors of its sale or shutdown are everywhere. Questions about Microsoft's true commitment to the industry are valid; its software business is its core focus. AOL, a competitor to MSN, makes a much better customer for Microsoft's technology.

But, Microsoft's commerce-oriented Web sites—such as Expedia and CarPoint—are promising, and it is clearly aiming to be a big player in the race to bring the PC and television together to provide a range of interactive services. Microsoft is a company that keeps coming back and chipping away at competitors.

And Microsoft's recent investments in cable and also in efforts to turn the television into an online device, such as its $425 million purchase of WebTV, are troubling trends for AOL. While it has been attempting to figure out what to do to deal with the inevitability of broadband access in the next decade, AOL has been slow to make the kind of aggressive moves that Microsoft has made in this arena. Some might argue that this is smart given the uncertainty about how these technologies will play out eventually. But it is clear that the era of linking to an online service over a telephone using only a computer is coming to an end. How AOL fits into the new scenario is still unclear. And since Microsoft is likely to have a strong voice in the entire scheme, AOL must carefully think about how it must deal with Microsoft going forward.

"We're certainly still afraid of Microsoft," said Case. "We'd be stupid if we were not."

yoohoo, it's yahoo!

Perhaps a more potent threat, many suggest, will come from Internet search and directory companies like the Santa Clara, California-based Yahoo! Inc. These companies have been turning themselves into "portals" for the Internet. An easier way to describe them might be: they want to become the AOL of the Web. But so does AOL, which has lately been trying to goose its own Web site to give users access to the service from Internet connections at work or anywhere.

Several years ago, in fact AOL tried to buy Yahoo! for $2 million, said company founder Jerry Yang. "And we probably would have taken it if the offer was just a little bit higher" he noted. Now, Yang is worth hundreds of times that amount. Valuations for Yahoo! stock have become stratospheric, in anticipation of the company's rise.

A raft of efforts like Yahoo! are out there—Excite; C/Net's "Snap" interface for Internet service providers; @home, a cable modem-based service that could take off if cable modems ever do (so far, that has been a very big *if*). Microsoft will also make a play in this game with a new megasite called "Start."

All of these companies have been adding a range of features to their sites, in a breathless series of recent acquisitions and deals: chat, stock quotes, Web page publishing, personalized home pages, free e-mail, bulletin boards, easy navigation, horoscopes, and just about everything else.

This expansion is all part of a bid to establish solid ties with users and thereby generate enough steady and regular traffic to garner more ad revenues. Once they "capture" the users, it is thought, they can harvest the flock.

Sound familiar?

A lot of the frenetic activity is part of an attempt to avoid what most experts expect is inevitable: a shakeout of the Web. Too many sites are sitting all by their lonesome in cyberspace, chasing the same eyeballs. Some have learned that content is not king unless it is accompanied by distribution.

And, who has that distribution, having already captured users and gained the right to charge monthly debits against their credit cards? AOL, of course. With its solid relationship with customers— few other alternatives are as easy to use—AOL does not have to struggle as much to sign up loyal users.

The downside? The Web is a more vibrant and exciting place than the proprietary AOL service can ever be. The upside? AOL can point out to the Web, connecting to all that content for free. Even if AOL is a slower route, most users do not seem to be annoyed enough by the Web wait to quit in droves.

And, even using these portals, the Web is still much too confusing for the average person who just wants to e-mail family, get flight information, and perhaps download a dirty picture or two. The digerati can scream their fool heads off about how simplistic AOL's interface is, but complexity is not a good selling point.

Will there be a challenge from the Internet service providers? They had better worry about big networking providers like World-Com eating their lunch. And the less said about the sorry track record of the telephone companies, the better. They have thus far blown off their obvious advantages in this arena to companies like WorldCom and AOL, and their bureaucratic ways are likely to mean they will keep doing so.

The failure of the telephone companies is perhaps the hidden story in the rise of AOL, which over time has been as much helped by the incompetence of their competitors as the genius of their approach. After a series of disastrous attempts to conquer the online world, for example, AT&T continues to plod on with yet another service that has failed to catch on with any fire. No surprise then that AT&T, like many telecommunications and media companies, has made discreet inquiries in recent years about buying AOL and finally admitting its inability to create such a service itself.

But why—at least—at this point should AOL consider selling as its stock price rises and its prospects brighten? A linkage with a massive company, despite the advantages of adding even more distribution and marketing clout, would only serve to slow down AOL right now. But such a sale in the future, especially if growth begins to stall again, is not unthinkable. In fact, it may be probable.

spam jams and other slams

Various other threats to AOL are born of internal lethargy and external threats.

One of the thornier problems the company will face is unsolicited junk e-mail, or "spam." The problem is epidemic among AOL users; their likely inexperience with computers makes them easier to abuse. By company estimates, nearly one-third of all incoming e-mail is spam. Some AOL users, especially those who spend time in the chat rooms (where marketers can copy down their screen names), receive dozens of unwanted e-mail messages every day. Spam is AOL users' number one complaint to the service. The company has undertaken several initiatives to blunt the problem—suing spammers; providing online tools to help weed out unwanted mail—but a sure solution is nowhere in sight. Besides, AOL is not in the best position to argue against spam on any high moral grounds. The company adopted the process of essentially spamming its own members by subjecting them to unwanted pop-up screens whenever they log on. Members can opt not to receive the pop-up screens, but that fact is not exactly promoted on the service, and it's difficult for many members to figure out how it's done.

Hackers will continue to present a potential problem for AOL—and for the entire online and Internet world. Hackers' skills include "phishing" to obtain passwords; altering graphics; and intruding

into "secure" environments on the service. They constantly become more and more sophisticated, and no service can totally protect itself against them. AOL has been lucky so far, in that hacker
activity has tended more toward taunting the service and stealing
the equivalent of monthly fees from members, rather than anything more sinister and far-reaching.

In this same vein is the continued weakness of the AOL network. Repeated mail outages, busy signals, and slow connections to
the Web are among the many problems that AOL foists upon its
customers in a way that could have a negative effect as the Web becomes easier to use. Too often, AOL comes in dead last in surveys in
these important benchmarks of customer service. Though customers appear to be tolerant thus far, in ways that make many Web
rivals shake their heads in disbelief, AOL hands its competitors an
effective weapon that it need not. As free e-mail, easy chat, better
navigation appears on the Web—as it will without any doubt—the
ease of use differences will narrow and disgruntled customers could
flee. While everyone in the online world suffers from a range of snafus, as the top dog, AOL will bear the brunt of displeasure.

The specter of federal regulation—on copyright and encryption
issues especially—hangs over the service and the entire industry.
The CDA was killed by the Supreme Court, but similar bills have
been introduced. A variety of child porn stings on AOL have made
it clear that, although the service does not welcome this activity, it
is hard to combat and policing is still too lax. At the center of all
these issues, there is one question: Can and should online services
be held responsible for what their viewers look at? It is still not clear
how Congress and the courts will ultimately spin on this issue.

One other, very sticky point is keeping the industry and its
users on edge. With the increase in all kinds of personal information on the Web, and with hackers milling about and credit card
numbers floating around, people are growing more and more
concerned with ensuring that their privacy is respected. AOL
took a particular beating on this issue early in 1998, when an
AOL member services representative confirmed to U.S. Navy
authorities that a sailor, Timothy R. McVeigh, was the owner of
a certain screen name. McVeigh's member profile implied that he

was gay; the Navy took the information it had gleaned from the AOL representative and brought proceedings against the sailor. For privacy advocates—and everyone else—it was a chilling reminder that nothing on the Web or on online services can really be assumed to be secret or protected. As more and more people undertake tasks on the Internet, this issue will only grow in importance.

and now for something completely different

By the end of 1997, things had finally begun to cook at AOL. It had added 2.9 million new customers for the year, its brand awareness levels were more than quadruple the nearest competitor, it was seeing its commerce and ad revenues improve as costs declined and Pittman's firm management style was creating a unified executive team that was arguably the best in the industry. Even its longtime bears were becoming docile and forecasting sunny weather for the perpetually storm-tossed company. "We believe that the company has now reached a point where its success, if not completely assured, is highly probable," wrote UBS Securities analyst Jon Cohen—who had been one of AOL's toughest critics over the years—on December 4. Now he predicted a $100 price target.

It was a leap for the careful Cohen, but one that proved too conservative. By March of 1998, euphoria over AOL had pushed its stock well above $120. Even Case had seemed to loosen up with observers describing him as relaxed, in command and even a bit joyful.

Which is precisely why, because it was AOL, it was time for more change.

After watching usage continue to climb and ad revenues not growing fast enough, on February 9, the company announced a $2 price hike in monthly fees that would goose its revenues. The move caused the stock to leap upward, but caused a bit of worry for some who felt that a rise in price could mean that subscriber growth would slow and that AOL confidence in its ad strategy was waning a bit. In fact, AOL had considered a wider range of options, including a limit on hours and even a higher fee for access to special gated sections of AOL. All were deemed too complex in the end compared to a simpler price increase.

In addition that day, the company also announced another dramatic change—the folding of the AOL Studios division run by Ted Leonsis back into the main company. The 1996 plan for three companies within a company that had so occupied Case was now completely reversed. With ANS gone, Case felt that one unified and powerful AOL was the best course of action.

In the new configuration, Leonsis would report to Pittman—the new president and chief operating officer of the company—and his troops would be disbanded. Layoffs at the studio division numbered about 100 and it seemed to the outside world like a demotion for the high flying Leonsis, who had been integral to bringing on Pittman in the first place.

Indeed, the move came as a disappointment for Leonsis, who had long dreamed of creating the first major online studio that would churn out hit properties. He had spent the last year trying to raise money for the venture and staff it up, launching several expensive sites and even contemplating the possibility of a public offering. By early 1998, he had had a deal in place for AOL and two outside investors—Bertelsmann and Madison Dearborn Partners—to funnel $250 million into the money-losing studio.

But, an increasing feeling that outside investments were unnecessary as AOL's stock surged combined with a series of accounting problems, caused Case to call Leonsis and nix the deal. "He said it was time to put on my corporate hat and come back home," said Leonsis. "At first, I went through personal shock, then denial and a desire to undo the decision, a day of anger and then mourning. Now I am in the acceptance and renewal phase."

Still, Leonsis—who would now run the development of new properties for the AOL mothership—was not leaving as some had thought he would. "This is the biggest stage," he noted. "And, no matter how many times we change, I still have the best seat in the house."

Pittman too was beginning to feel that way. When he first arrived at AOL, he had never thought he would stay long. AOL was

Steve's show, not his. Now, with the restructuring, he had to agree not to make AOL just another corporate revolving door he would spin through.

"I had to make an unspoken agreement to the company that I would make more of a commitment that I had thought I was going to at first," said Pittman.

Wall Street certainly seemed thrilled with that idea, especially when Pittman delivered AOL's first clean profits the very next day on February 10. For the second quarter ended December 31, 1997, AOL earned $20.8 million on revenues of $592 million.

some final words from chairman case

As AOL hit its 11-million-member mark early in 1998 (the figure did not include the millions of expected CompuServe additions) and polls were showing that AOL was the number one Web site accessed from home, Steve Case still remained restless. Even the fortune of close to $400 million he had accumulated had not pacified Case.

There are all the new devices to consider—network computers, handheld units, televisions that talk back. There are the constant questions regarding AOL's role when broadband access becomes widely accessible to consumers ("AOL-TV!," noted Pittman). There are worries that home usage has its limits, although the popularity of cheaper PCs during the 1997 Christmas season was a plus for AOL. There is an annoying need to be an industry spokesperson—a role being thrust on Case and carved out by AOL's new general counsel, George Vradenburg.

Case has been amused to hear that the mood of Silicon Valley—which was altogether snide about AOL only six months before—has become admiring. But he continues to show frustration because people want to celebrate now.

Case does not, throwing out a series of clichés to describe where the company is at this point in time. There's still many more innings to play—we're perhaps at the bottom of the second or the third, he said. This is a marathon, not a sprint, he noted. It takes 10 to 20 years to build a mass market, he insisted, it doesn't just happen overnight.

But, he added, his internal anchor is consistent, as it has always been.

"When people ask me why or how I did it, it's like asking a basketball player, 'Why do you play basketball?,'" said Case, who would doubtless prefer to keep such thoughts of personal motivation mostly to himself. "Probably because you want to be the best."

He was simply curious about the online world, he finally volunteered, and wanted to play a defining role in making it become a real mass medium.

"So I never did mind the focus on my imminent demise, because the facts are on my side," said Case. "And the fact is that the dust settled and I am still standing, and that pretty much says it all."

But Case also said he fears everyone and still remains the most paranoid person at AOL. "I learn a lot from history, because no one thought much of AOL and here we are," he said. "So I exaggerate the risks and diminish our advantages."

And for the future? "We'll see, won't we?" said Case in a terse and enigmatic way that leaves listeners wondering whether he has some insight of what tomorrow will bring.

Because although Steve Case is not telling you this, deep down you suspect he probably has a notion of what the truth is.

And the truth is: Nobody knows.

revenge of the anti-nerds

he's got the whole (wired) world in his hands

Maybe Steve Case *did* know.

It certainly seemed that way as 1998 drew to a close. Suddenly, Case was being hailed by the media, the digerati of Silicon Valley, and Wall Street as the smartest businessman in cyberspace and the new medium's undisputed king.

It was a delicious bit of irony. Less than two years before, he had been widely derided by these same people as a fool, a loser, and a bit of an odd bird—a man whose quiet, aloof ways and clunky proprietary online service were obviously out of step with the lightning-fast entrepreneurs of the Internet.

Case had not changed one iota—he was still the chary cipher he had always been—but so much else was different now. The cockroach had actually won. His victory culminated in an astonishing announcement made in the early morning of Tuesday, November 24, 1998.

America Online would buy Netscape Communications—at one time, the high-flying icon of the Internet age—in a stock deal valued at $4.2 billion, a price that would top $10 billion when it was finally culminated. The complex purchase would include an important and lucrative multibillion-dollar side partnership with Sun Microsystems Inc. AOL would land squarely in the power center of Silicon Valley.

It was an unusual scenario for Case, for AOL, and, perhaps most especially, for Netscape. With the media now trumpeting AOL's genius at consumer marketing and with AOL's stock hurtling skyward, the purchase of Netscape was a landmark event up and down the thin peninsula just south of San Francisco. Despite its near dominance of the online industry, AOL had long been regarded by Silicon Valley as being too simplistic, too cheesy, too corny.

The technocrats had, in turn, celebrated Netscape—the legendary company that had played the pioneering role in commercializing browser software for the Web—as the most dashing symbol of the digital age. After going public in a stunning debut in 1995, the company had taken off spectacularly, attracting scads of talented employees and glowing media headlines.

Netscape's popularity gave it many choices—too many, perhaps. Over the years, it had snubbed a variety of overtures from AOL that would have brought the two companies closer. AOL's frustrations led finally to a controversial deal with Netscape's archenemy, Microsoft. By offering AOL a coveted and impossible-to-refuse place on the desktop of the dominant Windows operating system in the spring of 1996, the deal effectively soured any AOL–Netscape relationship for years.

Microsoft had instead taken deliberate aim at Netscape, and the intense attack had hurt Netscape badly. And, as it turned out, the strategic lapse that allowed the defection of AOL to Microsoft was a definitive blunder in Netscape's pitched war against the software giant, because Netscape did not anticipate one of the key battles that it could ill afford to lose. Helped by the millions of AOL customers who began using its browser, called the Internet Explorer, Microsoft continued to make important gains in market share over the next several years. Its tactics in that fight finally came under investigation by the Justice Department, but Microsoft had forced Netscape to dramatically change its strategy. To begin, Netscape decided to make its Navigator browser free and to give away its source code.

And, faced with a dwindling business, Netscape finally paid heed to Steve Case's longtime urging to make Netcenter, its highly trafficked Web site, into a major hub on the Internet. Netscape executives hoped this "portal" strategy would allow them to restore the company to its former glory by adding e-mail, commerce, content, and other services—creating what could only be described as an AOL of the Web.

But now AOL was buying Netscape instead. How could such a thing have happened?

how such a thing happened

When Margie Mader arrived at her Netscape office on the very last day of 1997, she was looking forward to an easy eight hours. With many of her colleagues off on holiday vacations, the intensity of working at one of the world's hottest technology companies was dialed way down. Mader scribbled a languid to-do list: Have a long lunch, organize files, call some friends and gossip, get on the Web and look for information about a new car that she had been dreaming of buying. She had decided on an Infiniti and wondered how early she could slip out of work to shop around for one.

But before she could do anything, her phone rang, and Mader was plunged into what she would later dub "The Lost Month." On the line was Netscape chief administrative officer Peter Currie, who told her to come see him immediately. Mader had been in charge of hiring new employees since she arrived in 1996. That day, she saw her job's unfortunate flip side. She would be coordinating the first-ever mass firing of Netscapers.

What a difference a year had made. Not long before, Netscape had been receiving between 5,000 and 7,500 resumes a month, from people who desperately wanted to work at the world-changing company. Netscapers chased a digital dream with intensity akin to members of a religious cult. Since its founding in 1994, Netscape had attrition rates in the low single figures, an unusual record in the highly competitive job market of Silicon Valley. Recruiters in its human resources department had mostly acted like admissions officers in elite Ivy League colleges. Their task was simply to pick the best and the brightest.

Now, hundreds of these elite employees—up to 20 percent of the workforce—would have to go. Most would be cut from sales and marketing, Currie guessed, because Netscape was quickly losing ground in those areas. The fourth-quarter numbers had just been calculated, and Netscape had finally "hit the wall." Deals the company had expected to close had not come through. Without them, the quickly declining revenues from Netscape's browser could not buck the increasing competition from Microsoft's free Internet Explorer. Netscape was about to report its first loss since going public—$88.3 million—Currie told an incredulous Mader. It was time to recalibrate, which, in simple terms, meant laying off 500 people toiling in businesses the company was abandoning. The drastic restructuring of its operations would focus on greener and more lucrative pastures.

Mader, an ebullient woman whose jovial manner recalled talk-show host Rosie O'Donnell, had once looked forward to every new day at Netscape. On her business card, instead of a traditional title, she had inscribed: "Director of Bringing in Cool People!"

"I thought perhaps I should change my business card to better reflect what I was doing," she said. "So instead of hiring cool people, I had turned into 'Director of Firing Cool People.'"

Indeed, she soon would have to begin communicating with managers scattered through the company's dozen ice-blue buildings on its campus in Mountain View, California; creating a company newsletter and an information center to keep employees updated; managing the expected shock, anger, and grief of those leaving *and* those staying; and assuring employees that there was no master secret "list" of the doomed.

It would turn out to be a bruising experience for her, even though most Netscapers gave her high marks for her deft handling of layoffs. "What a terrible core competency to have," she said. "And because the aura of Netscape was so incredible—it had been nothing but *up* here for everyone for so long—it made it all the worse."

This was exactly the response that public relations head Rosanne Siino expected from the outside world when she prepared to release Netscape's preannouncement of the bad news on January 5, several weeks before official earnings were to be reported.

Siino was not wrong; on that one day, the company was flooded with more than 300 calls from the press. For Siino, a small woman with an intense but cheery demeanor who had come to Netscape in its earliest days after working for legendary cofounder Jim Clark of Silicon Graphics Inc., this was the sharper side of the two-edged sword of technology fame and fortune.

When Siino had arrived at Netscape in 1994 as employee #19, she was in public relations heaven. "Everything written about us was so positive that it simply was a case of how fast you could answer the phone to talk to another reporter about another great article they wanted to write," she recalled. Now, though, the calls had a single and disquieting theme: Was Netscape dead?

Siino even found herself shooing away the television news crews that soon appeared in the Netscape parking lot like rubberneckers at a grisly accident and tried to interview employees about the "tragedy."

"I guess they wanted to get a good shot of the body lying on the street," she quipped. "So we did not have a lot of high hopes."

Neither did investor relations director Quincy Smith, a dark-haired whirlwind who had come to Netscape from a career in investment banking at Morgan Stanley. His frenetic energy and fast-talking style would soon be put to good use. While Siino interfaced with the press, Smith had to deal with Netscape's other extremely important audience—Wall Street. His main job: "Feed the Street." But its enormous maw was never satisfied.

"The message had to be a simple one: 'We continue to believe that Netscape's market opportunity is very large,'" said Smith. "Of course, the big question, for everyone, was whether we could regain our momentum through the transition or would the bad media buzz and investor psychology cause the company to fail."

The whole world was watching. "We were in a fishbowl," he added. "And there was no way to pretend we were not."

The layoffs were only the start. Netscape's real challenge, for much of 1998, was a traumatic and dramatic rejiggering of its operations to better face critical challenges. Among the problems: the continuing withering attack from giant Microsoft, which aimed directly at Netscape's heart with its own free browser offering; a slow-moving response to that challenge, including a stubborn refusal to give away the Netscape browser; a jarring series of business shifts that some wags in the Valley took to calling "Netscape's strategy *du jour*"; a growing reputation for arrogance, even among some of its strongest supporters; and—perhaps most troublesome, considering technology's stock-options-crazy culture—a weariness with the whole saga among Wall Streeters, which sent Netscape's high-flying stock to the basement.

As the company began to sketch out its future direction, one issue was clear: Because the Internet industry was changing so rapidly, whatever choices it made, Netscape could ill afford to trip up.

"Getting through this tough time will be all about execution," said Netscape board member John Doerr. "For Netscape, it is as simple as that."

Doerr, a slight and bespectacled man who wielded great power as one of Silicon Valley's most powerful venture capitalists, made this declaration in June, at a Netscape strategy day for analysts, investors, and others. "Flashpoint: The Net Economy" was the theme of the meeting, held at the former Army base at Presidio, with stunning views of the Golden Gate Bridge and San Francisco Bay as a backdrop. Netscape's top executives had mustered themselves to explain to the expectant crowd what the company planned to do to revive itself.

Netscape management had already begun a mad scramble to keep the company together and to move forward. The broad array of actions ranged from restructuring its management and pushing aggressively into the competitive arena to become a central destination point on the Web to repricing its employee stock options. There were also a few tricks: Pumping up the surviving troops with pep rallies and parties, staging pugnacious public presentations to declare victory before the battles had even started, and giving away the valuable browser source code. Executives even used wordplay—euphemisms like "blip" and "foot fault"—to describe the dicey situation the company was facing.

Wording was important, as it has always been at Netscape. Part of the whirlwind company tone had been set by a popular management book—Geoffrey Moore's *Inside the Tornado*—that instructed many at Netscape in how to cope with intense hypergrowth. Now, with the forward momentum seemingly ended, Netscape turned to the transition management work of William Bridges, who posited that companies in crisis could best redirect and motivate employees from inert shock to one of their periods of highest motivation.

The problem was: With the overcast gloom of the financial results and the layoffs, employees were beginning to wonder exactly what their once-hot company had turned into. Perhaps a loser?

Tom Paquin, who was employee #7 at Netscape, got pummeled about the situation repeatedly. As one of the earliest staffers, the stocky and forthright Paquin—whose job title was "Netscape Fellow"—considered himself an informal conduit between top executives and the rank and file.

He had been there in the very early days when workers at the small startup had been crowded shoulder-to-shoulder in the cramped original headquarters in downtown Mountain View; he had been there when the Navigator browser had its first debut and set the Internet world on fire; and he had been there at the golden moment on August 9, 1995, when Netscape went public and they had all become instantly rich beyond their wildest dreams.

Suddenly, what he was hearing was troubling him. People began to approach him with doubt in their voices. What was the buzz and how could they get a fix about what was coursing through the underground currents of the company?

"All of a sudden, people were telling me that the sense of changing the world here was gone and that we had become just another software company in the Valley, like any other," he recalled. "People had come to Netscape for something more—to be part of a movement that was about more than products." He believed that Netscape needed to get back some of that "religion."

A silver bullet was indeed needed, and it came first in the form of Netscape's popular browser, whose market share and revenue had been declining in the face of Microsoft's controversial on-slaught. With the luster of the flagship browser fading, morale had inevitably begun to drop.

Spirits were especially low in the divisions dedicated to the browser's development. Once the heroes of the company, they now had a potential dog on their hands. Costs were high and revenues were declining. "Winner to loser in a flash," said one programmer.

This climate was bad, since the Navigator browser was more than just another piece of software. As one of the key products that jumpstarted the commercial development of the Internet, it was the principal reason so many knew the name *Netscape*. It had always been a point of Netscape pride. Could it become that once again?

In a series of meetings, employees and executives talked about the inevitability of giving the browser away, to match Microsoft. The proposed move was probably one of the biggest open secrets in the industry. Would it end up further underscoring Netscape's loss of momentum?

As a group in the client products division met one day in January, an even bolder move that had been suggested the year before by chief technology officer Eric Hahn was put forth once again. Why not give away the source code for the browser?

Many Netscapers immediately recoiled at the idea. The source code—most basically, the digital recipe that programmers create when making software—is considered the most valuable property a technology company possesses. Giving it away was a big risk. It would allow anyone to develop and proliferate Netscape's pro-gramming, taking much of the control out of the company's hands. But such an act could also reinstate Netscape as an innova-tor—the whole world would potentially be developing for the company an image that was as important internally as externally.

"We would immediately be at the forefront of what was hap-pening on the Internet, something that had once united Netscape as a company, a galvanizing idea, born of the spirit of the young hackers who had founded this place," said general manager Bob Lisbonne. "We thought this could be a time to introduce a whole new future to people, to say, 'Here is how we will be different.'"

On March 31, the day the source code was released, Netscape chief executive officer James Barksdale led an impromptu rally of employees in the Planet Moz cafeteria—named after the "Mozilla" free source code project. Thanking the teams who had quickly prepared the code for public release, he declared simply, to the cheers of employees: "We can still change the world."

With his honeyed Mississippi twang and an engaging personality that oozed charm—the twin nicknames he had acquired over the year, "Jimmy Love" and "Bark," seemed particularly apt—Barksdale was famous at Netscape for rousing employee meetings that were designed to inspire the troops.

Since he had arrived at Netscape, trailing a sterling reputation in top jobs at FedEx and Craig McCaw's cellular empire, his tenure had been marked by a Teflon manner that extended outside of Netscape as well. Barksdale had long been a kind of rock star of the Valley; he was mentioned almost universally as one of the most respected figures in the business. In her essay on companies in crisis, cyberguru Esther Dyson noted that "charisma is key" for survival, and pointed to Barksdale as a master.

But Barksdale knew charm was prone to fade; it would not carry the company forward into its next difficult phase. When it became clear in January that Netscape's fast ride was over, he said he felt a "new chill" seep into the company, clinging to Netscape like the clammy fog that drifts nightly along the northern California coast.

"I guess what has happened has been both a curse and a blessing, because we had to take stock of ourselves in ways we never had before, and take an important step in the maturity process," said Barksdale. "Everyone goes through it."

What he wanted most to avoid were comparisons to another Silicon Valley shooting star, Apple Computer, the legendary personal computer company that was widely believed to have blown its chance to dominate the market by remaining insular and refusing to send its technology far and wide.

"Everyone knows no tree grows to heaven, so a lot more realism was a good thing," said Barksdale. "That said, people want to be on a winning team and if they think a team is losing, they can become quickly disenchanted . . . there is only *do* and *not do,* there is no *try.*"

After the browser announcement, a series of software deals with big companies such as Citibank happened quickly. More importantly, Barksdale had decided on a wholesale restructuring of Netscape that would cleave the company into two key parts: the Internet networking software business aimed at enterprises, and a Web division that took advantage of the site that was the default for Netscape's browser. Here, millions of users would meet to trade electronic mail, view content, check stock quotes, and, it was hoped, provide advertisers with an attractive demographic to yield Netscape ever-stronger revenues.

Netscape had let that business slip away for years. It had been notoriously slow in taking advantage of the browser traffic that automatically passed through its site, even as other companies like Yahoo grew and thrived. Yahoo had, in fact, gotten most of its early users from free placement for its directory service on Netscape's site. Netscape had even once given its young student founders free office space—a particularly stinging irony since Yahoo's founders had become billionaires and were now considered the new visionaries of the Internet.

Put in charge of righting that wrong was longtime Netscaper Mike Homer, a fireplug of a man with a hard-charging reputation both inside and outside the company. After stints at a number of Silicon Valley companies—including Apple—he had come to Netscape at its apogee. He had previously been head of the sales and marketing operation, but now felt that success in the "portal" business was crucial to the future of Netscape.

Insiders also hoped that leveraging the browser traffic that passed through Netcenter would boost the languishing stock price to the sky-high levels being enjoyed by other Internet companies.

"We were not being valued in the same way the others, like Yahoo or Excite, were, because we had always been seen only as a browser company," said Homer. "But that was about the past and not the future, so we suffered."

Improving the stock price was indeed an important aim. Netscape employees, like those at most Silicon Valley companies, were motivated by the value of their stock options. As Netscape's share price declined, many Netscapers found those options "under water" (more expensive to purchase at their "strike" price than at the current stock price). This was a major problem as Netscape shares fell from an $85 high in late 1995 to a low of $16 at the beginning of 1998.

Netscape cofounder Marc Andreessen understood such worries. The baby-faced techie had at one time been called "the next Bill Gates," but he saw his own wealth decline precipitiously in 1998. At age 27, he understood all too well the mood at a company where the average age was only 32 years. The troubles of 1998 were a shock; it was the first time most of the staff had experienced anything but spectacular upward momentum. And the growth had definitely stalled at the same time that the realization of the bone-wearying work that lay ahead had begun to sink in.

"We were on a rocket ship and it only got bigger and better, so . . . we seemed as if we were running out of gas all of a sudden," said Andreessen, who had had practically no seasoning in Silicon Valley's world of swift starts and abrupt stops.

He filed to sell 25 percent of his own shares in March 1998, at prices that were near an all-time low—a move that made people inside and outside the company wonder what was up. In his typically breathless patter, sometimes punctuated with wild gesticulations, Andreessen defended his stock sale decisions.

"It's my fucking money, so I should be able to do whatever I want with it," he said flatly, admitting that he understood that such a move by a high-profile Netscape executive did have its repercussions. "Everyone was nervous . . . I mean, they were like, '*Whoa, whoa, whoa, what now?!?*'"

To combat this kind of sentiment, Netscape repriced its options to a lower strike price. And to further underscore the idea that the stock price was important, Barksdale gave back 300,000 shares of his own options to allow for distribution to employees. With the raft of changes, results improved. The company broke even in the second quarter and eked out a small profit in the third quarter.

But despite the company's best efforts and the important changes being made, a pall still hung over Netscape as the summer progressed. Attrition rates—which had reached a high of 25 percent in the spring—declined, but not substantially enough. Netscape staffers were actually beginning to return the near-constant calls from headhunters whom they had once ignored. And the stock remained sluggish, a vexing problem in a region where young, seductive companies rose up daily to offer wealth, power, and cachet to the most talented.

Was the stark poster plastered all over the walls of Netscape's buildings in the fall of 1998 a sign of the times? The placard made a generous offer of $1,000 to any employee who brought in a new prospect to be hired—something Netscape had never needed to do before. "Building a great company requires three things," read the poster. "People, people, and people."

And, perhaps, a fourth factor that would soon prove to be much more significant: An AOL takeover.

the aoliens have landed

Life in Dulles, Virginia—3,000 miles east of Silicon Valley—throughout 1998 seemed an exact opposite of Netscape's turmoil. After the purchase of CompuServe in the fall of 1997, AOL had taken off and never looked back as it made a series of critical deals and expanded its membership base quickly.

The success came from a variety of directions. The iconic General Colin Powell joined its board, giving a huge boost to the company's reputation; the roster of AOL subscribers passed the golden 10 million mark; lucrative deals were struck with a wide variety of companies, from Time Warner to Web music retailer Music Boulevard; its new 4.0 software was testing well and was likely to be a hit; Steve Case was named to the prestigious Board of the New York Stock Exchange, another indication that AOL had arrived; quarterly results continued to improve, and ad and commerce revenue boomed; and, most importantly, the stock price blasted upward, causing most analysts on Wall Street—including even the most virulent critics from the past—to become AOL's biggest cheerleaders.

So it was with an expansive viewpoint that Steve Case and AOL president Bob Pittman heard Netscape's Jim Barksdale recount the changes being made at Netscape during the first six months of 1998. The three were attending the annual May gathering in Aspen, Colorado, hosted by a powerful Silicon Valley venture firm, Kleiner Perkins Caufield & Byers, for the leaders of the companies they invested in.

Case—who had long wanted to be closer to Netscape—thought that what Barksdale was saying made a lot of sense. Relations between the two companies had been improving over the past year, helped by a series of small deals between them—one for instant messaging, another for local content distribution. The renewed contact had begun to sooth the residual angry feelings and had reintroduced to the pair their many commonalities.

"They had repositioned the company and it became really much more interesting for us," said Case, who thought Netscape had been unfairly given up for dead. "There was always a lot of joking back and forth, but I felt there might be a much better opportunity than ever for a much more significant relationship."

Indeed, with AOL's relationships with commerce partners growing and with its pending acquisition of ICQ—literally, "I Seek You," an Israel-based Web chat service for which AOL forked over $287 million in June 1998—which would give AOL more of a Web presence, Netscape might be the perfect fit.

One of the key motivations for AOL was a growing concern regarding the explosion of Web-based "portals" such as Yahoo, which had attracted tens of millions of regular users by expanding offerings of e-mail, commerce, and other services, to create on the Internet a central destination spot similar to AOL's proprietary service. AOL dominated the user base in the home; Yahoo, with a strong brand name, was the leader in the business market.

Netscape was also strong among business users, so closer ties between the pair could help AOL. In addition, Pittman had long been interested in owning a stable of well-known brand names on the Internet, to combat Yahoo and others like it. A combination of AOL and Netscape would bring together two of the best-known names in cyberspace.

Case was also intrigued by Netscape's moves in the software sector. He was particularly struck by one development in which Netscape seemed to be taking a page out of rival Microsoft's playbook: using its dominant software to benefit another business. Through a new series of critical hookups between its Netcenter site and its popular Navigator browser, Netscape was heading toward an integration. New buttons on the browser led directly to Netcenter services such as e-mail, "smart" browsing, software updating, and greater personalization. The browser-and-site unit now looked more like a computer desktop. AOL did not own a browser, but the ability to leverage one by linking it seamlessly to a Web site had the potential for great differentiation over competitors.

If AOL owned Netscape, it would also own a very important piece of real estate on the desktop, an idea that later intrigued AOL dealmaker Miles Gilburne, who dubbed the idea "the persistent client." Because its aggressive window took over a computer, AOL was a definite persistent client, as was the AOL-owned ICQ service. If the browser could be added, "We could possibly have a 24-hour relationship with the user," said Gilburne. "And that is a big thing to think about."

The most persistent client of all, of course, was Microsoft's Windows—the world's dominant operating system. AOL had in fact, made its fortune riding on the back of the company Netscape's Andreessen had called "the beast of Redmond." The question was whether AOL could actually take some of that power itself, as the interactive world changed the entire technology landscape.

Microsoft had indeed been an important partner, but it was also AOL's most obvious foe going forward. The 1996 agreement with Microsoft stipulated that AOL had the right to terminate the relationship on January 1, 1999. Perhaps it was time for AOL to begin to consider its options, especially since its influence had grown and its relationship with Microsoft was shifting again. Renewed efforts by Microsoft to reconfigure its MSN online service were a sign that it was once again becoming more of a competitor. And its continuing integration of Internet services into the operating system would surely minimize the advantages of being on the desktop, from which AOL was getting fewer and fewer new customers. Had AOL's brand name grown enough to allow it to find other ways of attracting an audience?

Finally, AOL's relationship with Microsoft had been further poisoned by the recent antitrust trial, in which one of AOL's top executives had testified as a witness for the government. The trial centered on the race to distribute Internet navigational software. The Justice Department had accused Microsoft of illegally gaining market share at Netscape's expense by leveraging the power it had with Windows. The government had specifically alleged that Netscape's browser market share declined dramatically because of illegal practices by Microsoft, such as when AOL decided to embed Internet Explorer into its service in early 1996 rather than using Netscape's technology. At the time, AOL said it had chosen Microsoft because it had better—and free—technology, and, as an important part of the agreement, Microsoft gave the AOL service prominent placement in a folder on the Windows desktop.

Senior vice president David Colburn—who had struck that deal—testified that AOL only made the initial deal with Microsoft because of the desktop placement, and, as part of the deal, Microsoft required that AOL minimize any efforts to give customers access to the Netscape browser. His written testimony, dated October 27, 1998, was a direct shot over the bow of Microsoft's flagship:

> AOL would not have been willing to negotiate a browser license with Microsoft had Microsoft not indicated a willingness to bundle and to promote the AOL client software in some form with Windows. Distribution and promotion on the Windows desktop was one of AOL's goals—indeed, the most significant one—negotiating a browser agreement with Microsoft.
>
> It was AOL's objective to have both Navigator and Internet Explorer available to its members, allowing them to choose which browser to use. Microsoft, on the other hand, attempted to secure exclusive distribution and promotion for Internet Explorer, with no or few exceptions for distribution or promotion of a competitive browser. . . . In the end, the deal struck with Microsoft was a trade-off: AOL obtained a form of bundling with the Windows 95 operating system and promotion on the Windows 95 desktop, and

Microsoft obtain virtual exclusivity for its browser on AOL, preventing AOL from providing any significant promotion or distribution of Netscape's Navigator browser.

AOL was willing to agree to virtual exclusivity with Microsoft—something to which AOL would not otherwise have agreed—because AOL believed that inclusion in the Windows operating system and on the desktop was essential to mitigate, at least partially, the adverse competitive effects of Microsoft's bundling of MSN with its operating system, and because such inclusion had very significant distributional advantages that could not be obtained in any other way.

AOL would not have been willing to negotiate a browser license with Microsoft had Microsoft not been willing to bundle and promote AOL in its Windows operating system and on its desktop. And AOL would not have been prepared to accept the restrictions on its distribution and promotion of Netscape Navigator had Microsoft not insisted on those restrictions as an element of the licensing agreement.

AOL must and does strictly limit its distribution, promotion and advertising of Netscape Navigator. Microsoft has sought to strictly enforce these restrictions, and has carefully monitored references to Navigator or Netscape on the AOL service.

Colburn then described the "Promotional Services Agreement" signed on October 28, 1996, in which "Microsoft agreed to pay AOL $.25 per member for each member that AOL successfully converted to Internet Explorer from another browser. In addition, Microsoft agreed to pay AOL $600,000 if AOL succeeded in converting a substantial portion of its installed base to Internet Explorer by a certain date."

Colburn characterized Microsoft's Windows desktop offer as one that AOL could not refuse. After illustrating how important the desktop position was to AOL—more than 10 percent of AOL signups, almost a million, came from the Windows folder in fiscal 1998—he was clear: "At the end of the day, the telltale part of it was the other value we're getting on the desktop."

By 1998, though, maybe AOL did not need that piece of real estate quite so much. At the very time that Colburn was dissing Microsoft in a courtroom, in Washington, D.C., AOL executives were deep into secret discussions with Netscape about buying the company.

the art of the deal

Netscape executives were thinking along lines similar to AOL as they looked toward the future. Early in 1998, they had drawn up a three-year plan. One of its most attractive options was to have the struggling company acquired by a larger firm. The company had already had talks with other Silicon Valley powerhouses such as Sun, Oracle Corporation, and International Business Machines Corporation.

But, as 1998 progressed, Netscape officials began to favor a plan that Mike Homer dubbed the "Fox network strategy"—the building of a viable fourth power that could compete successfully, even if on the fringes, with a trio of bigger Internet players. Microsoft, Yahoo, and AOL were predicted to be that trio.

To gain that fourth spot, Netscape would have to get bigger by uniting with another small player. One name suggested was Excite Inc. In April 1998, the scrappy Redwood City, California, Internet search and directory company had edged out competitors and struck a two-year deal to provide search and other services for Netscape's Netcenter, an arrangement that had brought the two companies closer together.

Excite's chief executive, George Bell, was also thinking hard about how to survive in a universe of giants. Excite had done as much as it could until then. A series of aggressive deals to buy smaller firms and link with powerful partners had gained it a decent position. But Excite still lagged well behind Yahoo, which was not an ideal situation.

"We both needed to do something, since we were not going to break out on our own," said Bell, who proposed his idea to Peter Currie, Netscape's chief administrative officer. The ensuing talks centered on merging the two companies as equals, allowing Excite to run the media side while Netscape ran the software business. Still, the proposed deal needed an endorser of the strategy—a "validator" that would give it heft via a major investment or alliance.

To the planners, who knew that the Netscape browser might need a lift, AOL was the natural candidate since it could soon be free to use Navigator more prominently again. And, because AOL held a 10 percent stake in Excite and had improved its relations with Netscape, maybe it was a good fit.

After a series of talks between Excite's George Bell and AOL's David Colburn, the companies agreed to hold a meeting in July in Reston, Virginia, near AOL headquarters. In a cramped hotel room on a humid summer day, Bell sketched out the idea further with Netscape's Barksdale and AOL's Pittman.

Afterward, Barksdale continued talking to Bell during a private plane ride that delivered Bell to his summer home in Maine. According to Bell, Barksdale seemed positive and said to him: "I am enthusiastic."

But, by early August, the deal had not moved forward in any discernible way. The two sides argued over various problems with the potential arrangement, including who might have control over the combined Web sites. "It felt a lot like herding cats," said Bell. "And, since it was moving sideways, there is trouble when a deal loses momentum."

Actually, the deal hadn't lost momentum, although it was about to lose Excite. AOL's top dealmakers had come up with a better idea, being cooked up by Miles Gilburne, who had been the major force behind AOL's acquisition of CompuServe the year before.

Gilburne had been intrigued by the "persistent client" notion. His thoughts then settled on Netscape, with which AOL had long wanted a significant link. As he watched the changes at Netscape, he started to envision the development of more significant synergies.

He had several big ideas. He loved the browser—or "the client," as it is called in technology circles—in a way that few companies could. The browser's declining market share, the focus of so much negative attention, could be reversed if a company saw it as more than simply a way to navigate the Web with a piece of software. It was, instead, an important tool in linking together a wide range of services, technologies, and devices.

"I think it was a shock to Netscape that someone saw the client as an asset rather than a liability," said Gilburne. "But who else could love the client, except a company who had their own client—which is just what the AOL service was in essence."

Gilburne was also intrigued by how Netscape's demographics and "psychographics" differed from AOL's. Netscape aimed heavily at the workplace rather than the home, and was focused on more experienced users. By being almost the complete opposite of AOL, Netscape minimized overlap. And Netscape's experienced team of Web programmers filled a giant hole in AOL's staff, which was largely dedicated to its proprietary service.

Finally, as AOL had increased its advertising relationships over the years, it had found that many clients needed a larger end-to-end solution to become true retailers on the Web. AOL could serve their ads and get them distribution but could do little to help them get up and running.

Gilburne remembered how AOL had once been in the data network business and there were not enough networks to carry the load of traffic at the reasonable prices that AOL needed. AOL had bought a data network and later sold it when enough capacity was available at good prices. And, much further back in its history, before computers were widespread, hadn't AOL's antecedent built modem-like devices that allowed users to download video games over the telephone? So shouldn't AOL be in the business of driving standards in this new burgeoning e-commerce arena?

"It was in our interests to accelerate electronic commerce," said Gilburne. "So I thought, how could I get some of these businesses to jump the fence any better than offering them a way to do it?"

He had proposed such an idea to IBM, but had had no success. At that time, looking for a way to mitigate the risk on such a major deal, he had thought about splitting Netscape in two. Now, Gilburne had decided that he wanted to keep the software business. He thought about completing the electronic commerce picture by pulling in a big partner to help proliferate the technology.

The obvious choice was Sun, the hardware and software maker that concentrated on large corporate computing. Sun wanted to get into the electronic commerce market on a level where it could compete with rivals like IBM, so gaining access to Netscape technology made a lot of sense. In addition, Sun had long wanted to be more of a presence in the Internet service provider market, of which AOL was the leader. And, best of all, Sun and AOL had already been talking for months about a range of ways to bring the two companies closer.

Netscape also needed a "transformational" event, said Peter Currie. When Gilburne arrived in Mountain View, California, right after Labor Day, with "no papers, no people, just his hands in his pockets," Currie was intrigued. The Excite deal seemed promising; Currie assumed Gilburne had come to talk about it.

Instead, in what Currie described as a "strategic mindmeld," Gilburne laid out his ideas to Currie, as well to Homer, Smith, and, later, Barksdale. "Suppose we buy you?" asked Gilburne finally.

The Netscape team was taken aback. Was AOL serious? At what price? Were they ready to handle the expected wrath from Microsoft, which was still an important AOL partner? And what about the software business—would AOL handle it or bungle it?

As Gilburne began to explain, Currie was still worried. Was this just a flight of fancy by the cerebral Gilburne? AOL was famous for floating, often all at once, a wide range of options to companies it sought as allies. Was this one of those times, especially since the earlier talks with AOL had centered around an investment in an Excite–Netscape deal?

"We're serious," assured Gilburne.

When Excite's George Bell tried to reignite his deal two weeks later, Currie cut off the expected talks by telling Bell that Netscape was moving in a "different direction."

A different direction, but one that was more than a bit twisted.

After more "circling and sniffing," AOL retreated behind its curtains for a month—a move that unnerved Netscape. "We though, what's up?" said Currie. "Are they just jerking us around? Because we had been jerked around by these guys before, with the browser deal."

But Case soon met briefly with Barksdale in a private New Jersey airpark to vouch for AOL's good intentions, and Gilburne met

Currie in the San Francisco airport to promise him that AOL was still very interested. Netscape executives then traveled to Dulles, Virginia, in late October, and, on November 10, Case and Pittman made a secret jaunt to meet with them at a Sheraton hotel in Silicon Valley.

But there was still no firm offer. With trepidation, the Netscape team arrived at the San Francisco offices of AOL's investment bankers, Goldman Sachs, in the early evening of November 17, to talk about formalizing the deal. They needn't have worried. The companies dickered over price a bit, but they had a basic agreement to buy Netscape by the end of the night. Nicknames, all with a Greek origin, were given to the companies as the deal was prepared: Apollo for AOL, Zeus for Sun, and—borrowing from the all-time classic story about weary people who desperately needed to get home—Odyssey for Netscape.

One surprise was the lack of leaks to the media or to rival firms, but the very next day, a story in *The Wall Street Journal* suggested that the pair were talking. The article focused on a possible browser deal and an investment, but it did not suggest the huge deal that was brewing. Nonetheless, as news of the talks spread, Netscape stock began to rise significantly for the first time in a long time.

AOL lawyers descended on Netscape to work out details. On Friday, November 20, the Netscape board met and approved the deal with few objections after their bankers, Morgan Stanley, explained the all-stock offer that valued Netscape at upward of $4 billion.

The last part of the deal was the complex Sun agreement. William Reduchel, Sun's chief of strategy, said it took the rest of the weekend to complete, because it included seven interlocking contracts. As part of the deal, AOL was in a position to net $1.25 billion over three years by licensing Netscape software to Sun. The guarantees from Sun were: $975 million in sales royalties, and $10 million a year in cooperative marketing fees.

For its part, AOL agreed to purchase $500 million in hardware and services from Sun, and to pay Sun a $5 million monthly licensing fee for its Java software and $1 million monthly for technical support.

The agreement had the potential to mold a formidable combination, a worthy competitor to challenge Microsoft's emerging plans to create, on the Internet, huge host computers to manage a plethora of information, software, and personalized services for a monthly fee.

"Now that AOL and Sun were combining forces, with Netscape as the mixer, Microsoft had a much more potent competitor," said Lise Buyer, who had become an analyst with Credit Suisse First Boston, "It's no longer David versus Goliath, but Goliath versus Goliath."

Indeed, by Sunday, November 22, when word of the deal started to emerge on the Web sites of *Newsweek* and *The Wall Street Journal,* the reaction was intense. Since the Sun deal was not yet done, Netscape could say nothing. But the frenzy became so intense that, by Monday, AOL and Netscape had issued statements that they had been in talks.

It was no surprise that almost as soon as the deal was revealed on Tuesday, Microsoft reacted with indignation, loudly pointing to it as proof that the software giant faced intense competition and that the government trial was unnecessary. Microsoft chairman Bill Gates privately seethed about AOL's dominance of the consumer market, which he had been unable to break—in part, because he had sacrificed his own online service, MSN, when he put AOL on the Windows desktop. At the time, it had been more important to best Netscape, which was considered a larger threat by Microsoft. As it turned out, Netscape had provided the perfect shield for AOL to grow powerful.

A more poignant irony, given that Gates had become the personification of a monopolist at the end of the twentieth century and whose company was on trial for antitrust violations: He also had been critical of the federal government for failing to intervene in AOL's previous acquisitions of CompuServe and ICQ.

Case deflected the complaints, noting that he did not want to, and could not, compete against Microsoft in the operating system market. His protest was a bit calculated, in truth. While the operating system market was still very important, changes being introduced by the Internet were likely to make it less so over time.

Would that mean AOL could be called the Microsoft of the Internet? "We're not even close," said Case, returning to an old lyric he loved to sing. "This is still early innings of this game."

But, though he would not publically admit it, Case knew AOL was way ahead of everyone.

i can't believe i ate the next big thing

Swallowing Netscape was a huge and immediate task. Less than a week after the deal was closed, Case and Pittman traveled across the country to visit Netscape officially. The premise was simple—to meet and greet their new employees at an "all-hands" meeting—but the purpose was not. The excitement of striking what was arguably the most important deal in the online industry's short history was fading. For Case and Pittman, the most critical part of the job was just beginning.

At a jovial meeting, Sun's chief executive, Scott McNealy, delivered a funny top-ten list of reasons why Netscape should have bought AOL instead. Case was a bit more serious and on his best behavior. He accepted a Netscape jacket and hat, and gave one of his patented "just folks" speeches. He presented himself as a very nonthreatening conqueror.

With the purchase of Netscape now official, AOL had the vexing task of keeping valued customers and talented employees from jumping ship. Departures were endemic to all acquisitions. "These are the most sensitive aspects of any merger," said Shaun Andrikopoulos, an analyst with BT Alex. Brown Inc. "And it is the most intangible part of a transaction."

With regard to customers, AOL had to tread carefully and present itself as a benevolent force in technology. "This deal forces AOL to walk the same tightrope that Microsoft has been walking for the last couple of years," said Mark Mooradian, analyst at Jupiter Communications, a New York City new-media research concern. "It creates various conflicts of interest."

Microsoft, in fact, had faced such conflicts when it strayed from its software roots and expanded into a host of publishing roles. Its Sidewalk line of Web sites, for instance, competed with local newspapers—even as Microsoft wanted to supply lucrative back-end technology to them. AOL, with its tremendous interests in content and in supplying consumers with Internet access, had to figure out how to reassure competitors in those areas who also used Netscape products.

Some of these customers were already agitated. Sky Dayton, chief executive officer of Earthlink Network Inc., of Pasadena, California, said that, when the deal was announced, the major Internet service provider immediately considered not distributing Netscape's Navigator browser as aggressively as in the past. That was a problem. Earthlink sent out about five million units of sign-up software with the Navigator, and the same amount was loaded with Microsoft's Internet Explorer each quarter.

"Since being promoted on the Windows desktop usually brings us a lot more referrals than from Netscape's efforts, it's probably a good time to look at the value we get," said Dayton. "We distributed them equally in the interests of fairness, but since AOL is a major competitor, I am not sure how much I want to help them."

But Alex. Brown's Andrikopoulos noted that Microsoft might not be the most appealing alternative to many. "Microsoft's true colors often show not only a competitor, but a predator to many companies," he says. "AOL has a better record of being a cooperative partner and a lot more to bring to the table now."

Some were likely to not choose between the two. Web sites that programmed content to accommodate both browsers said little would change with the deal; they wanted to attract as many users as possible to their portals, no matter what technology was being used. "We're browser-agnostic," said Jerry Yang, the co-founder of Yahoo, the largest of the central destination sites on the Web. "We want traffic of any kind to come use Yahoo."

Employees were a bigger worry. After a grueling year of turmoil, the concerns among the employees of Netscape, for example, ran the gamut—from fear of possible layoffs to worries that consumer-oriented AOL would not properly support Netscape's enterprise software business, and to the prospect of cultural clashes between the elite Silicon Valley programmers and their new owners, who operated their giant online service far away in Virginia. Netscape's relations with Sun had also been rocky in the past.

"This is the last thing I ever thought would happen," said one worried engineer, echoing a typical sentiment at Netscape. "I mean, AOL buying Netscape? It's unreal to a lot of us."

In the first electronic mail sent to Netscape workers immediately after the purchase was announced, Case welcomed his new charges into the "worldwide AOL family" and quickly complimented them and sought to reassure them that the acquisition would not rock their world.

"All of us at America Online share a tremendous admiration for Netscape and your enormous contributions to the Internet and enterprise software industry," he wrote to the Netscape team. "We want you to know that continuity of operations is important to us. We are committed to maintaining Netscape's headquarters in Mountain View and we're even more committed to maintaining the kind of culture that has made Netscape such a successful operation."

Netscape executive Mike Homer was encouraged and noted that a lot of Netscapers had newfound respect for AOL. "A lot of us were wrong about AOL and there is a valuable lesson in knowing that," he said. "We know now that there is a lot we can learn from them." Homer said that, internally, the feelings about the acquisition ranged from "wildly to cautiously optimistic."

Others noted that a log of disgruntled employees were already gone in the wake of troubles during the past year as the company reconfigured itself. Eric Hahn, Netscape's former chief technology officer, who left earlier in 1998 to focus on helping early-stage startups, said that those who stayed at Netscape were troupers.

"Those in the online business at Netscape are thrilled, but it's probably scarier for the enterprise software people, since AOL is not a software company, so it may seem like a fish riding a bicycle to them," he said. "But I think Netscape has outgrown the purists . . . for a lot of people, there has been a lot of battle fatigue and this could be a great fresh start."

Keith Benjamin, an analyst with BancAmerica Robertson Stephens, agreed. "There are going to be some rough edges, and AOL should figure in some room for errors," he said. "But

Netscape employees should probably be grateful to AOL, since they were floating on a life raft and certainly needed the help."

AOL executives knew that completing the takeover swiftly was important, given the intense competition for top talent in Silicon Valley. Executives at other technology companies had quickly begun making lists of Netscape employees whom they would like to hire away by playing on the possibility that some of those workers were chagrined by having to work for AOL. (At the same time, AOL was also planning to make some layoffs of redundant jobs.)

"It's the $62-billion question," said one Silicon Valley player. "Do the real cool guys at Netscape want to work for AOL?"

It was hoped that the hiring of Marc Andreessen—the fair-haired, barefoot *TIME* magazine cover boy who had co-founded Netscape—as chief technology officer would mitigate such problems.

Hiring him could been seen as a definite coup. Andreessen had once predicted that AOL would fail and had been one of its greatest detractors. His brash demeanor and early success had made him a walking icon for legions of young Internet programmers. He had debated Case and Microsoft's Brad Silverberg in late 1996, and had scoffed at AOL's future. The AOL business model was a dead end, with no profits possible, he had said, and Netscape's model was superior.

"The battle for subscriber retention in Steve's industry will become so bitter that you will see marketing wars the likes of which you've never seen before," he had declared in an online forum moderated by *The Wall Street Journal*'s Walt Mossberg.

In an even more biting interview reported in AOL's hometown newspaper—*The Washington Post*—only months later, Andreessen had poked further fun at the company and its financial problems at the time. "If you can't make money with eight million customers, how many customers do you need?" he asked.

Andreessen was dead wrong. By 1998, he was ready to admit it and blamed his ideas on the insularity of the Valley, where it was "hard not to be influenced by what everyone else was thinking." As he began to look at the facts, he realized that AOL had been the only company able to make the kind of shifts needed to survive.

AOL's much-criticized subscription model, for example, gave it the ability to establish closer relationships with customers than were possible with portals such as Netcenter. "They were the only company to make a serious run at the broad audience," he said. "This was no small thing."

When the idea of an AOL takeover became more serious, Andreessen said he was not disturbed. He had even started to use AOL again and liked what he saw a lot more.

"I always put my two cents in, and right away I thought the idea of bringing together the two companies was intriguing," he said. "While a lot of people might think I would be against such a thing, I think I had come around to seeing that the traditional Valley way does not always work."

If Silicon Valley had created sushi, he noted, "It would call it raw fish."

Going forward, a key factor was AOL's ability to tap into that consumer marketing mentality while still improving its technology. "I think AOL probably understands that it has got to become more of a technology company, but in the way that the makers of *Titanic* are technologists," he said. "More technology is probably needed to make things simpler—but, like electricity, technology will eventually fade into the background."

But not Andreessen nor Netscape. "While I do wish we could have made it as a stand-alone company, it's also nice to be part of a company at the dead center of the market that will surely be one of its consolidators," he said. "This is like being at NBC in the 1940s at the dawn of television, so I could not be more excited."

After a long and harsh journey, Odysseus seemed to have found his home. "All of us lost sight of some important thing that AOL never [forgot]," said Andreessen, "That the customer is always right."

And the raw fish is *always* sushi.

the past is prologue

tiptoe through the tulipmania

Somewhere, Bill Von Meister must be smiling.

At the end of the millenium, AOL has straddled the online world like a colossus.

Even though it was a company that had its origins in the fast-money dreams of the failed entrepreneur.

Even though it had lurched from being an electronic distributor of video games to becoming a maker of private-label data services and then an also-ran online business that most observers thought would end up in bankruptcy court.

Even though it had pulled off a series of dicey financial tricks that saved it from certain doom innumerable times.

Even though it had become famous for busy signals and customer service shenanigans.

Even though it had come back from death more times than Elvis.

After all that, it was now widely considered the Internet's most stable, most promising, most important "blue-chip" company.

And, all those superlatives were true.

AOL's stock had leaped nearly 600 percent in 1998 alone, and its average compound annual total return since 1993 was 143 percent.

That meant $10,000 invested in AOL at the end of 1993 was worth $848,560 only five years later. AOL's $80 billion market cap—which was heading quickly toward $100 billion and beyond—was worth more than most major media companies, such as the Walt Disney Company, which had once laughed AOL off.

One major reason for all the heat: AOL had grown a massive membership base—from just over 500,000 members in 1993 to a worldwide service with more than 15 million members at the end of 1998—and was still growing fast. And all those members spent an increasing amount of time on AOL—an average of 246 minutes a month as 1998 ended.

That meant more robust revenues and profits, especially in the high-margin advertising sector. For its most recent full fiscal year, ended June 30, 1998, AOL reported net profit of $91.8 million, or 35 cents a share, on $2.6 billion in revenue. AOL's fiscal 1999 earnings were expected to double, causing many analysts to predict that its stock would continue to surge.

At the end of 1998, a major Hollywood movie even featured AOL as a main plot point. In *You've Got Mail*, Tom Hanks and Meg Ryan played characters who meet and court on AOL. The film was named after AOL's famous online greeting—now as well known as any company slogan in history.

All these events added up to a company full of very happy and wealthy people. Steve Case had become a billionaire and was surrounded by executives who had accumulated hundreds of millions of dollars. AOL executive Ted Leonsis laughed out loud at how well AOL had done. "We all looked at each other the other day and had to do a gut check," said Leonsis, who named his recently purchased yacht "Fully Vested." "When all your dreams come true, what dreams do you dream now?"

The company that never got any high-tech respect was now poised to swallow up Netscape, and was on the hunt for more Silicon Valley properties (eBay? Intuit? Who else?) to increase its arsenal in the online wars. The irony was not lost on AOL's top executives. Most had experienced scads of scorn from the digerati; AOL bashing was de rigueur as the company struggled through a series of problems—many of them self-inflicted.

Barry Schuler, who headed the transition team to merge Netscape into AOL, remembered his colleagues' ridicule when he traded Medior, his multimedia development company, to AOL in 1995 for $31 million worth of stock. Few thought the company would make it. To make matters worse, Schuler had quickly lost employees to Netscape and other hot Internet startups.

"We got poached like crazy, because companies like Netscape represented where it was at," recalled Schuler. "AOL was definitely considered the last wave." Schuler—who also headed AOL's powerful main proprietary service and whose AOL stock holdings are reportedly worth close to a billion dollars—found himself running into a lot of people who left Medior for Netscape.

"It's a little ironic," he said. "I'm not sure it turned out quite the way a lot of people thought it would."

Schuler, who commuted between AOL's Northern Virginia headquarters to a house he still owned in Half Moon Bay, California, says the Valley's disrespect lay in an obsessive, narrow focus on delivering technology to the workplace in ways that weren't always user-friendly. "AOL's consumer focus was something Silicon Valley could not ever wrap its head around," he said. "The Valley wanted to say AOL was going to go away eventually because it was too simple, and that was always one of its biggest miscalculations."

AOL's tenacious survival seemed to have changed the minds of former detractors, who once promulgated its reputations as "the K mart of the Internet." "After not dying so many times . . . even the most arrogant of Silicon Valley mandarins cannot fail to have respect for the company," said Paul Saffo, director of the Institute of the Future, a California think tank, who had previously been an AOL critic. "Silicon Valley only slowly began to realize that, without AOL, there would be a lot less people in cyberspace, and a lot of people in cyberspace is the basis of a lot of these businesses."

AOL board member Frank Caufield said it had helped that AOL had also matured as a company in those years. "It's gone from being a standard children's crusade to a company that knows it can really affect things," he said.

So much so that Internet pundit Robert Seidman, whose popular online newsletter had long championed AOL, thought the company could even afford to make Silicon Valley pay a bit for its disdain. "The more AOL won, the worse the bias got," he said. "If I were them, I would say, 'Screw you' to the Valley, stick my fists in the air, do a dance and declare victory over the techies."

Yes, indeed. Even *Wired,* the slick technology magazine that had predicted AOL's demise so many times, had become a shadow of its former self. Its print and digital units were split up and sold off in parts in 1998.

It had been a bit of a surprise to many, noted Steve Case, that AOL had become the equivalent of a "social operating system" of the online world. Had it finally won?

The poker-faced Case—ever a careful plodder and taciturn strategist—would not go that far. And he was also not doing any gloating on a visit to Silicon Valley in early 1999. He was there to visit some local newspapers, to meet with various technology kahunas, and perhaps to show the AOL flag a little more than usual.

"There have been many theories postulated—none of which have come true—that, every year, AOL was going to go belly up," he said. "I guess we have been shadowboxing with that for a while."

And the fight, for Steve Case at least, was not even close to being over. There were always more competitors coming, ready to attack AOL with full force. The question was: Where to aim first?

At the big long-distance giant, which had already performed poorly in its nascent online efforts, but was coming back for more, armed with a big cable asset and other riches?

At the scrappy Internet company that dominated the Web and was loaded up with cash and sky-high stock?

At a bunch of traditional media companies—which had made more errors than it was polite to point out—that were still plugging away with new schemes of cyberspace domination?

And, of course, there is the software behemoth that AOL has bested, partnered with, beat some more, testified against, and then mooned by buying its archrival. Yes, Microsoft was definitely going to be setting its sights on AOL.

Thus, a scorecard of the players—all of whom are dedicated to taking AOL's place at the top of the online heap—is needed.

"the number you have reached has been disconnected"

Disconnection from its millions of users is the biggest threat AOL is facing. Within a gathering storm in New Jersey, AT&T has been plotting its strategies of interactive victory. After AOL snubbed its efforts to merge or make a major investment several times, AT&T bought itself a cable company—a very big cable company: Tele-Communications Inc. With that acquisition, AT&T moved closer to realizing its dream of owning the famed "last mile" into the homes of consumers. In the deal, AT&T also got control of At Home Corporation, which is building a high-speed cable access business to rival AOL's narrowband, dial-up service. To help it along with programming and content, At Home bought Excite Inc., an AOL competitor (and, in the convoluted world of cyberspace, once an AOL investment that has since been sold off).

The thinking on this challenge is simple. If cable television companies get their act together and roll out their "broadband" services to consumers, they could bypass AOL completely. With AT&T's backing; with the exclusive right, through 2002, to provide high-speed Internet access to 60 million households served by its many cable partners; with its own network and Excite's personalization technology; with "always-on" capabilities; and with CEO Tom Jermoluk, who is a mouthy leader, At Home could pose AOL's most potent threat in the future.

It's all a big *if*, of course. Cable television has never distinguished itself in customer service or lightning-fast execution. And, broadband is likely to roll out a lot slower than Wall Street thinks. At the beginning of 1999, At Home claimed about 331,000 subscribers to its high-speed Internet access service, or 2.5 percent of the 13.2 million homes served by upgraded cable systems.

And AOL and other competitors are lobbying heavily in federal, state, and city regulatory bodies to force cable operators to open their networks. AOL is also exploring alliances with other cable providers.

"We want to make this medium as ubiquitous as television," said George Vradenburg, AOL's head of public policy, who has been charged by Case to loose the hounds on cable companies. "They are going to lose this battle; it's just a matter of when."

AT&T disagrees, of course, and has been mounting a lobbying effort of its own aimed at AOL's heart.

Morgan Stanley analyst Mary Meeker—a longtime AOL fan—thinks that as long as AOL makes sure it has a plan in place to deal with broadband access within the next three years, all will be okay.

"They can't stay out of this arena and they know it," she said. "But AOL has been through this mania for a new technology before and knows that just because everyone is all hot and bothered about it, does not mean consumers want it as quickly."

yoohoo, it's still yahoo

Just a little upstart in 1994, Yahoo zoomed past all the big guys, built a stellar brand name in cyberspace that is second only to AOL's, and now has a valuation that surpasses many longtime media giants.

Moving quickly beyond its Internet directory roots, Yahoo has been expanding its business, adding e-mail, commerce, content, and a wide range of services to hold users onto its sites or, as it is distastefully called, increasing "stickiness." It recently anted up more than $3 billion in stock to buy GeoCities Inc., a provider of free Web pages, and nearly double that for Web broadcaster Broadcast.com Inc. Buying things has been made easier because of Yahoo's soaring stock price—an Internet leader—which has made its executives famous and rich. As one of the few independent Internet companies left, Yahoo is widely respected by Wall Street, consumers, and AOL. Its management team, headed by cofounder Jerry Yang, is savvy and well liked.

But the list of what Yahoo does *not* have is long—for example, no major distribution or access deal—at a time when the industry shows every sign of converging into major power points that offer an integrated package of interactivity under one roof. Some think Internet companies cannot live by *brand* alone. So if traffic slows, Yahoo could be in trouble.

In addition, if its high-priced stock loses steam, Yahoo may need to make an alliance with a big partner *fast.* Yahoo's shares are regarded as more stable than most Internet stocks, but consider these words of wisdom from pundit Allan Sloan, who was one of the first to correctly predict AOL's troubles years ago: "You know this Internet mania is going to come to a bad end; you just don't know how."

it's a competitive world after all

The major media companies—from Disney to Time Warner to Viacom—have all watched in horror as AOL, Yahoo, and others have blasted past them. It's not for lack of trying. Time Warner created Pathfinder, one of the pioneering Web sites, though too few surfers seem to have found their way there.

But the media moguls have trudged along, making a wide range of online bets and hoping the prices of Internet companies will drop so they can make some acquisitions. More likely, those cyberspace upstarts would buy *them,* if their growth wasn't so sluggish.

The most aggressive and able of the media companies has been Disney, which does not seem to be Mickey-Mousing around in cyberspace. It has made investments in Web sites that leverage its media properties, such as ABC.com and ESPN.com, and it bought a chunk of a portal player, Infoseek Corporation, to create an on-line competitor called the Go Network.

But, so far, Go is widely considered a lackluster performer by Web observers. It has also left the other Disney properties floating with no real cohesion.

AOL executives even compare companies like Disney to the British Empire. "They are losing tiny bits of market share every year and don't notice they are dying," said one AOL executive. Ouch.

Another interesting challenge might come from former television network player Barry Diller, who has been compiling a wide-ranging group of online properties that all center on electronic commerce. A recent bid for another portal, Lycos Inc., is an attempt to pull it all together with Diller's television assets. Lycos had itself been on an acquisition spree of Internet properties, but still lacks the critical buzz necessary to jump it to the top.

the beast is back

And what is there to say about Microsoft? It is big. It is powerful. It is aggressive. It has oodles of cash. It has a stable of respectable Web properties. It has one of the bigger Web audiences. It has a dominant operating system.

And, perhaps worst of all, it has a chip on its shoulder the size of Mars about not winning in the online arena.

A warlike comparison is not a bad one; Microsoft is the company that AOL is most likely to tangle with in the future. The billion-dollar question for the industry to answer is: What will Microsoft do in this market? It seems to have missed out on much of the thunder because of (1) an unwillingness to pay big bucks for Internet companies, (2) an unwillingness of some companies to be sold to Microsoft because of Justice Department concerns, and (3) its inability to roll out, with the necessary speed, the services in this fast-changing market.

Its MSN has been unveiling a series of small acquisitions to improve its service, but the company is likely to continue to build the bulk of the service rather than make a big buy of a company like, say, Yahoo.

One plus is renewed attention from the top. Hard-charging Microsoft president Steve Ballmer has been watching over its online assets since former interactive head Pete Higgins stepped down in the fall of 1998. And Ballmer likes to win. It's clear that Microsoft intends to use the strength of its existing business as it moves forward, tying interactive services closely to the company's robust word processing, financial, and Web browsing software.

But the company seems to have an even bigger goal. Microsoft's famed chairman Bill Gates has disturbingly dubbed that strategy a "megaserver"—a network-centric service that delivers all sorts of information to anyone, on any device.

So it is no surprise that Steve Case continues to return to Microsoft when asked about the companies he is most worried about as AOL moves forward. "They are determined to get this right," he said flatly. "And, if history is a guide, they will."

How odd, then, that Gates was being more pessimistic about his company's odds going forward. In an interview at the beginning of 1999, he compared Microsoft to a can of sugared soda water.

"Twenty years from now . . . one of the most popular soft drinks in the world, you can say with great certainty, is going to be Coca-Cola. Twenty years from now, what will the most popular operating system be?" said Gates. "It will be so much different than anything anybody thinks today . . . and there is [only a slim] chance that Microsoft can reinvent itself three or four times to be there."

Was Gates actually scared? Did the interactive future—led by companies like AOL, Netscape, and Sun, and new operating systems like Linux and Palm Computing—mean the process had started that would inevitably scratch away at Microsoft's dominance? Looking out on the vast competitive scene, one in which Steve Case loomed larger than ever before, Gates added that one of his most important jobs was to "fear everything."

That left an obvious and starkly simple question for the richest man in the world, who sat atop one of the most powerful companies in history. It was, in fact, the very same question that Case had asked himself on May 11, 1993, as he sat in a tiny windowless conference room in Redmond, Washington, and listened to Gates casually predicting that Microsoft would probably "bury" AOL.

Was it over?

Index

index

index

index